Cooperative Learning

A Guide to Research

Samuel Totten
Toni Sills
Annette Digby
Pamela Russ

GARLAND PUBLISHING, INC. • NEW YORK & LONDON
1991

Library of Congress Cataloging-in-Publication Data

Cooperative learning : an annotated bibliography and guide to research.
/ Samuel Totten . . . [et al.]
    p. cm. — (Garland bibliographies in contemporary
education ; 12) (Garland reference library of social science ; vol.
674)
    Includes index.
    ISBN 0–8240–7222–7 (alk. paper)
    1. Team learning approach to education—Bibliography. 2. Group
work in education—Bibliography. 3. Interdisciplinary approach in
education—Bibliography. 4. Learning, Psychology of—Bibliography.
I. Totten, Samuel. II. Series: Garland bibliographies in
contemporary education ; v. 12. III. Series: Garland reference
library of social science ; v. 674.
Z5814.G84C66   1991
[LB1032]
016.3713'95—dc20   90–28902
                                                                CIP

Printed on acid-free, 250-year-life paper
Manufactured in the United States of America

To:

My parents, Harold and Donna Totten, who each in their own way taught me about the crucial need for cooperation in the world.

S.T.

My grandmother, Isabelle Brown, and my aunt, Mary Alford.

T.S.

My husband, Gary Digby, who provided encouragement and support; to my children, Jeremy and Christy, for their patience and understanding; to my parents, O. C. and Elsie Dulaney, for stressing the importance of education.

A.D.

My sons, Ralph and Theodore Glaster, for their patience and support.

P.R.

Author Biographies

Samuel Totten is assistant professor of curriculum and instruction at the University of Arkansas at Fayetteville. His main research interests are in the areas of curriculum theory, instructional strategies, and the incorporation of social issues across the curriculum.

Toni Sills is visiting assistant professor of secondary education at Tulane University in New Orleans. Her main research interests are in the areas of secondary/middle school instructional strategies and teacher attitudes toward and interactions with academically at-risk students.

Annette Digby is assistant professor of curriculum and instruction at the University of Arkansas at Fayetteville. Her main research interests are in the areas of instructional strategies, early field experiences for pre-service teachers, and adolescent literature.

Pamela Russ is assistant professor of elementary education at Tulane University in New Orleans. Her main research interests are in the areas of multi-ethnic literature, academically at-risk minority populations, and the integration of reading and writing in computer-based programs.

CONTENTS

CONTENTS

Cooperative Learning

Introduction

1. OVERVIEW OF COOPERATIVE LEARNING

by Samuel Totten

Over the past decade or so, cooperative learning has become increasingly popular in many schools throughout the United States, Canada, Israel, Australia, New Zealand, parts of Europe and Africa, and elsewhere. While there are many different types of cooperative learning strategies, they "all share an interest in finding an alternative to 'frontal teaching' -- the teacher instructing the whole class at once -- or to individual seatwork by students" (Newmann and Thompson, 1987, p. 1). Stated another way, cooperative learning moves students from a passive form of learning to an active form. Concomitantly, the most effective cooperative learning strategies are predicated on the notion that having students work together is a powerful method for inducing learning and that every student is responsible for both his or her own learning as well as that of his or her other group members . Thus, the use of cooperative learning moves away from the negative and often devastating effects of competition and aims at increasing the number of "winners" in a class by bringing about success for the greatest number possible. Equally significant is that true cooperative learning strategies focus on *both* the cognitive and affective concerns of education. Such strategies aim at increasing the academic achievement as well as the cooperative or social skills and interaction of students. Finally, "there is wide agreement among reviewers of the cooperative learning literature that cooperative methods can and usually do have a positive effect on student achievement" (Slavin, 1989/1990, p. 52).

Too often cooperative teaching is misconstrued by the uninformed as simply a new name for students working in small groups or sharing materials, or helping one another. It should be clearly understood -- and this cannot be emphasized too strongly --that cooperative learning is *not* simply students working in groups, sharing materials, or merely helping one another (e.g., peer tutoring). While cooperative learning does involve students working in small groups and sharing materials, it is much more than that. It involves face-to-face interaction by all students, heterogeneous teams, structured goal interdependence (including a group goal and group recognition), individual accountability, and an emphasis on practicing social skills.

1

The use of cooperation in classrooms is not a recent innovation. Such noted educators as John Dewey and William Kilpatrick in the early part of this century and Alice Miel in the middle part of the century emphasized small group work and or cooperative tasks in classrooms. (For example, see Kilpatrick's article on the Project Method in Volume 19 [1918] of Columbia University's *Teachers College Record*, and Miel's *Cooperative Learning Procedures in Learning*. New York: Teachers College Press, 1952). Over the years teachers (elementary through graduate school) have used cooperative learning-like methods such as group projects, laboratory partners, and research teams.

Furthermore, researchers have conducted social psychological studies into various aspects of group dynamics and cooperation since the 1920s (Slavin, 1990, p. 2). Certainly a key figure among this group is Morton Deutsch, a professor at Columbia University's Teachers College, whose primary focus for many years was theory and research on cooperation. David W. Johnson, a noted researcher and advocate of cooperative learning, was one of Deutsch's doctoral students and he is noted for extending "the theoretical structures provided by Deutsch and took both theory and research on competition and cooperation into the classroom" (Pepitone, 1987, p. 8).

While cooperation has been used in varied forms in schools throughout much of this century, it was not until the early 1970s that "research on specific applications of cooperative learning to the classroom" (Slavin, 1990, p. 2) began to take place. Due to the efforts of such individuals as Elliot Aronson, David DeVries, David W. Johnson, Roger T. Johnson, Spencer Kagan, Nancy Madden, Shlomo Sharan, Robert Slavin, Noreen Webb, and others, a multitude of new cooperative learning strategies has been developed, field tested, and researched. Among these strategies are: Co-op Co-op, Cooperative Integrated Teaching and Composition (CIRC), Group Investigation, Jigsaw I, Jigsaw II, Learning Together, Structured Controversy, Student-Teams Achievement Divisions (STAD), Team Assisted Individualization (TAI), and Teams-Games-Tournaments (TGT).

Particularly noteworthy is the fact "cooperative learning is one of the most thoroughly researched of all instructional strategies" (Slavin, 1989/1990, p. 52). Topics that have been studied and researched include: impact of cooperative learning on interethnic relations, quality of student talk in cooperative learning vs. whole group instruction, integration of handicapped children into mainstreamed classes, effects of combining cooperative learning and individualized instruction, stimulation of cognitive development through cooperative task performance, effects of cooperative learning award structures on student achievement, and influence of cooperative learning on teacher practices. That is but a mere sampling of the plethora of topics/issues that have been researched over the past two decades, and does not even address the wide range of studies that have been done in regard to various curricular areas (e.g., mathematics, writing, second language learning, art, reading, geography) or specific cooperative learning strategies (e.g., Jigsaw, STAD, TGT).

While real progress has been made in the area of establishing a solid empirical base, numerous areas and concerns still need to be studied in much more depth. A classic example concerns the effectiveness of cooperative learning in grades 10-12. While ample research concludes that cooperative learning is effective in grades 2-9, there is a dearth of studies in regard to grades 10-12 (Newman and Thompson, 1987; Slavin, 1989/1990). Other key areas in need of additional study are: the extent to which the use of cooperative learning lends itself to higher order learning, the mediating effects of student talk in cooperative groups on student achievement, its effectiveness vis-a-vis long term retention, and the composition of groups on student achievement.

As Slavin (1988) points out, the need for sound research on cooperative learning (both "why and how cooperative learning produces its various effects") is vitally significant because "without a solid basis in research and evaluation, cooperative learning is no different from any of the fads that go in and out of education...Right now, the pendulum is swinging away from the 'back to basics' emphasis of recent years, and cooperative learning is a major beneficiary of this. However, without a widely recognized empirical basis, cooperative learning will swing out of fashion just as surely as it is swinging in today" (p. 3).

That said, there is a consensus among researchers on cooperative learning that if significantly positive student achievement is to be gained through the use of cooperative learning, then it is crucial that such strategies include the critical components of *individual accountability* and *group goals* (Davidson, 1985, p. 224; Newmann and Thompson, 1987, pp. 11-12; and Slavin, 1989, p. 151). Individual accountability simply means that the success of the group is contingent on every student learning the information/concepts taught. The establishment of group goals means that the team members are assisting one another to be successful and that they are working together in order to reap the stated rewards, grades, or other signs of recognition. Additionally, Slavin (1990) offers this significant caveat: "[I]t is critical that cooperative methods [continue to] be assessed in actual classrooms over realistic time periods to determine if they have an impact on measures of school achievement" (p. 17).

When designed and used correctly, cooperative learning also leads to positive effects in such areas as student self-esteem, cooperativeness, feelings about class and school, and acceptance of others (e.g., those of other races, mainstreamed academically handicapped students). Again, there is a need for additional research into many of these areas in order to assess the strengths and weaknesses of various cooperative learning components in regard to these concerns as well as to assess whether and/or how these behaviors are carried over into relations outside of the classroom or school and over various periods of time.

Commenting on key research findings, Joyce, Showers, and Rolheiser-Bennet (1987) reported that:

> Research on cooperative learning is overwhelmingly positive, and the cooperative approaches are appropriate for all curriculum areas.
>
> The more complex the outcomes (higher- order processing of information, problem solving, social skills and attitudes), the greater are the effects. The cooperative environments engendered by these models have substantial effects on the cooperative behavior of the students, increasing feelings of empathy for others, reducing intergroup tensions and aggressive and antisocial behavior, improving moral judgment, and building positive feelings toward others, including those of other ethnic groups...We would not expect that the implementation of cooperative learning strategies on a wide scale would be as thorough as in the intensive treatments reported in research literature, but solid effects should occur in schools where adequate and well-designed staff development is provided (p. 17).

The way individual teachers implement cooperative learning into their classrooms is a major factor vis-a-vis the success rate of cooperative learning. Careful consideration must be given as to how, when, and why teachers use cooperative learning in their classroom. If they implement it in a perfunctory manner, then it is highly likely that the desired effects will not accrue. Slavin (1988) notes that

> As far as achievement outcomes are concerned, for example, it is important to realize that many forms of cooperative learning have repeatedly been found to be *no* more effective than conventional whole-class methods. Practitioners who are using cooperative learning to increase student achievement must know this so that in modifying or adapting cooperative learning methods they are careful to end up with effective forms. For the Student Team Learning methods we developed at Johns Hopkins, for example, we know that team scores based on the individual learning of all team members is essential for achievement gains. It would

be easy for teachers to abandon scoring on the basis that it is
too much work or goes against their personal philosophies;
yet we have a great deal of evidence that this would diminish
the instructional effectiveness of the programs (p. 3;
emphasis added).

Despite cooperative learning's ever-increasing popularity (e.g., some
estimate that hundreds of thousands of teachers use some form of it in their
classrooms), cooperative learning has a long way to go before it will be a
common practice in most of our nation's schools. Speaking to this very point
in his highly acclaimed *A Place Called School*, Goodlad (1984) stated the
following:

No matter how we approach the classroom in an
effort to describe and understand what goes on, the teacher
comes through as a coach, quarterback, referee, and even
rule-maker. But there the analogy must stop because there is
no team. There is, instead, a loosely knit group. Each
student/player plays the same position, with varying degrees
of skill. There is no inherent opportunity or reason to
admire performances in other positions and how each
contributes to effective team accomplishment. There is little
or nothing about classroom life as it is conducted, so far as I
am able to determine, that suggests the existence of or need
for norms of group cohesion and cooperation for
achievement of a shared purpose.
    The most successful classrooms may be those in
which teachers succeed in creating commonly shared goals
and individuals cooperate in ensuring each persons success in
achieving them. The ultimate criterion becomes group
accomplishment of individual progress. But this would be
countervailing to prevailing practice, at least as revealed by
our data (p. 108).

Certainly in the six years since Goodlad wrote his book, more and more
teachers have been introduced to and have incorporated cooperative learning
into their repertoire of teaching strategies. Furthermore, the ongoing research
into cooperative learning along with the development of new strategies and the
refinement of current strategies should be salutary in their effects. A
"cooperative revolution" may indeed already be taking hold in our nation's
schools.

Davidson, N. (1985). Small-group learning and teaching in mathematics: A selective review of the research. In R. E. Slavin, S. Sharan, S. Kagan, R. Hertz-Lazarowitz, C. Webb, & R. Schmuck (Eds.), *Learning to Cooperate, Cooperating to Learn*. New York: Plenum.

Goodlad, J. I. (1984). *A Place Called School: Prospects for the Future*. New York: McGraw-Hill Book Company.

Joyce, B., Showers, B., & Rolheiser-Bennet, C. (1987). Staff development and student learning: A Synthesis of Research on Models of Teaching. *Educational Leadership, 45*(2), 11-23.

Newmann, F. M. & Thompson, J. A. (1987). *Effects of Cooperative Learning on Achievement in Secondary Schools: A Summary of Research*. Madison, WI: University of Wisconsin-Madison, National Center on Effective Secondary Schools.

Pepitone, E. A. (1987). Chains of influence on cooperative learning: From Berlin to Ann Arbor and Beyond... *The International Association for the Study of Cooperation in Education Newsletter, 8*(1, 2).

Slavin, R. E. (1989). Cooperative learning and student achievement. In R. E. Slavin (Ed.), *School and Classroom Organization*. Hillsdale, NJ: Erlbaum.

Slavin, R. E. (1990). *Cooperative Learning: Theory, Research, and Practice*. Englewood Cliffs, NJ: Prentice Hall.

Slavin, R. E. (1989/1990). Research on Cooperative Learning: Consensus and Controversy. *Educational Leadership, 47*(4).

Slavin, R. E. (1988, September). Research on cooperative learning: Why does it matter? *The International Association for The Study of Cooperation in Education Newsletter, 9*(3, 4).

2. STRUCTURE OF THE BIBLIOGRAPHY

Subject and Scope

This annotated bilbiography focuses on the research and practical applications of all aspects of the various teaching strategies that come under the rubric "cooperative learning." To a lesser extent, it also includes key research on the issue of cooperation vs. competition in the classroom and society. The actual development of cooperative learning strategies (strategies that include the components of face-to-face interaction, group goal(s), group accountability, individual accountability, and the stress on the importance of practicing and monitoring social skills) were initiated in the late 1960s and have skyrocketed in the 1980s and 1990s. Over the past fifteen years, a multitude of new cooperative learning strategies have been developed: Learning Together, Jigsaw I, Jigsaw II, Student Teams-Achievement Divisions (STAD), Co-op Co-op, Team Assisted Individualization (TAI), Group Investigation, Cooperative Integrated Reading and Composition (CIRC), Teams-Games-Tournament (TGT), etc. Research on cooperative learning has examined the various strategies used in every core subject area (e.g., math, reading, social studies, and science) to such courses as theology, golf, and computer simulations. Research has also focused on such topics/concerns as student achievement, non-handicapped students' attitudes toward handicapped students, self-esteem, learning environment, attitudes toward school, verbal interaction, cross-race relationships, cross-gender relationships, cross-socioeconomic relationships, etc.

This bibliography was developed for the express purpose of providing a comprehensive, up-to-date reference tool for researchers and educators interested in various facets of cooperative learning. To accomplish that, we have included works (articles, essays, monographs, reports, dissertations, papers presented at conferences, book reviews, and books, etc.) both researchers and practitioners at the elementary, secondary, and university levels should find of interest. Included herein are both the best and weakest works as well as those that fall in between the two extremes. Those works that are weak in some way are duly noted as are the weaknesses. We have also noted, when applicable, the extant debates between certain researchers over certain research finding/claims/methodologies. While most of the works cited are by researchers in the United States, we have also included pieces by researchers and practitioners in Israel, England, and Canada.

7

While ample research on cooperation can be found in journals and books dating back to the turn of the century, the development of specific cooperative learning strategies and the research into various concerns vis-a-vis those strategies, as previously mentioned, began to appear in the late 1960s. Since the thrust of this bibliography is on cooperative learning, per se, and not simply cooperation, the vast majority of the annotations deal with the works that have appeared since the late 1960s.

Sources of References

Numerous standard references were consulted in compiling this annotated bilbiography. Those that were consulted most frequently were the *Current Index to Journals in Education, Dissertation Abstracts, Education Index, The ERIC Sources in Education,* and the *Library of Congress Subject Catalog.* A number of data bases were also used in our search, including CARL (Colorado Alliance of Research Libraries), ERIC (Educational Resources Information Center), OCLC (Online Computer Library Center), and SCORPIO (Subject Content Oriented Retriever for Processing Information On-Line).

The major sources of items included in the bibliography are scholarly and professional journals in the field of education. Most of these only included single articles on the topic of cooperative learning. To a lesser, but still significant extent, sources were located in journals dealing with psychology.

3. OVERVIEW OF BIBLIOGRAPHIC TOPICS

Cooperative Learning Strategies

Since the mid-1970s, several types of cooperative learning strategies, including Cooperative Integrated Reading and Composition (CIRC), Structured Controversy, Co-op Co-op, Group Investigation, Jigsaw, Student Teams Achievement Division (STAD), Team Assisted Instruction (TAI), and Teams-Games-Tournament (TGT), have evolved. Beginning with references to general cooperative learning strategies, this section presents only an overview of each widely used strategy. It should be noted that because articles dealing with specific subject areas are cited elsewhere in the bibliography, many of the following divisions contain a limited number of entries.

General Strategies (Overview). This section is an overview of cooperative learning. Included are articles containing general suggestions about implementing cooperative learning at all academic levels and in all subject areas. A review of the literature, including articles by Slavin and Kagan, suggests that the use of cooperative learning has a positive impact upon academic achievement, student attitudes toward school, self-esteem, intergroup relations, race relations, and refinement of social skills.

Cooperative Integrated Reading and Composition (CIRC). The positive effects produced by Cooperative Integrated Reading and Composition (CIRC), a cooperative learning strategy designed to teach reading and writing skills to upper elementary students, are the focus of articles in this section.

Co-op Co-op. The fact that this section contains a limited number of articles appears to illustrate the need for additional research, both empirical and theoretical, involving Co-op Co-op, a project-oriented cooperative learning strategy that stresses resolution of conflicts. The comprehensive essay by Kagan, the developer of the strategy, includes the philosophy, components, and effects of the strategy. Wyatt's article describes practical application of an adapted version that focuses on group, not individual, presentations.

Structured Controversy. The focus of articles included here is the promotion of higher level thinking skills. Teachers no longer expect students simply to recite material; their goal is to include critical thinking skills represented by the upper levels of Bloom's Taxonomy. Research suggests that a cooperative learning technique called structured controversy is an effective means of achieving this goal. As Johnson and Johnson state, the purpose of structured controversy is to engage students in academic conflicts, thus resulting in critical thinking and problem solving situations. As has been the

9

case with other aspects of cooperative learning, more research needs to be conducted in this area before definite conclusions can be drawn about the effectiveness of structured controversy at all levels and in all subjects. The findings to date, however, are positive and provide a significant base for future research.

Group Investigation. Group Investigation is a cooperative learning strategy that requires groups of students to select topics from a content unit being studied by the entire class, to break the topics into individual tasks, and to carry out the activities necessary to prepare and present group reports. Essential components of Group Investigation are cooperative inquiry, group discussion, and cooperative planning. This section contains articles that present an overview of the strategy and a discussion of effective implementation procedures. Once again, the limited number of articles indicates a need for future research involving Group Investigation.

Jigsaw. To accommodate the needs of various learners, two versions of Jigsaw have been developed. Students participating in Jigsaw I become members of two heterogeneous groups, home and expert. They first meet in their home groups to receive academic material divided into sections. Responsible for only their assigned sections, the students then meet in their expert groups to discuss in depth the material and to devise an effective strategy for teaching the section. After they have had sufficient time to plan, students return to their home groups to teach the assigned material, using the strategies developed by the expert groups. Even though the components of Jigsaw II are basically the same as those of Jigsaw I, the participants are all given a common body of material. Each student then receives a topic on which to become an expert.

The authors address a wide range of topics. Especially noteworthy is the essay by Aronson and Goode that presents the history of the Jigsaw, steps involved in proper implementation of the strategy, construction of curricular materials, and effective teacher training techniques. Other articles address the use of Jigsaw strategies in a variety of settings, including seminary classes and elementary classrooms. A review of the literature reveals the generalizability of both Jigsaw I and Jigsaw II.

Student-Teams-Achievement-Division (STAD). Most appropriate for material with single right answers, STAD begins with the presentation of material by the teacher. Students then work in heterogeneous teams to master the material. Research findings indicate that STAD has been used effectively in every subject area and in grades two through college. Especially noteworthy in this section is an essay by Slavin, the originator of STAD, that offers practical guidelines for initial implementation of STAD. Most the research on STAD focuses on specific subject areas and is, therefore, discussed under the appropriate content area heading as indicated by the cross-references.

Team-Assisted Instruction (TAI). Also known as Team-Accelerated Instruction and Team-Assisted Individualization, TAI combines cooperative learning with individualized instruction and is designed specifically to teach mathematics to elementary students. Participants pursue an individualized unit of study based upon their scores on a placement test. Assigned to heterogeneous groups, team members check each other's work and assist each other with problems. Included in this section are several articles by Slavin, the developer of TAI, who concludes that the strategy has positive effects upon academic achievement, self-esteem, attitude toward mathematics, race relations, and acceptance of mainstreamed classmates.

Teams-Games-Tournaments (TGT). After participating in a teacher-taught lesson and in team study, students then engage in tournaments in which they compete with members of other teams. A key concept of TGT is that all students have equal opportunities for success in that they compete against other students with similar past academic records. This section contains articles, including several by DeVries and Wodarski, that present the positive effects of TGT upon student satisfaction, classroom climate, academic achievement, and race relations. The wide variety of articles support the generalizability of the strategy to various subject areas, including high school biology, elementary reading, high school social studies, college economics, drug education, and nutrition.

Subject Areas

Because no attempt was made to limit the search to pre-determined content areas, a wide variety of articles is included. To facilitate use of this section, the articles are categorized under the following content area headings: arts, computer science, language arts, mathematics, science, social studies, and special education. Because of the large number of entries in the language arts category, that section is divided into the following sub-sections: reading and composition, spelling, English as a second language, and general language arts skills.

Computers. Including both theoretical and empirical research, articles in this section present a variety of conclusions. Johnson, Johnson, and Stanne conclude that cooperative learning structures have significant positive effects upon academic achievement, student interaction, attitudes toward subject matter, and problem solving skills. Emphasizing the area of problem solving, MacGregor concurs with these findings as does Wilcox, who found that college students produced better work in cooperative situations than in individualistic ones. Oh, on the other hand, found no significant difference in the academic performance of students enrolled in a college programming class. In addition to research-oriented articles, this section contains articles that

present practical applications for using cooperative learning activities in a
computer science classroom.

　　Most of the authors conclude that cooperative learning has positive
effects upon students' social skills and attitudes toward school. The effects
upon academic achievement, however, appear to be inconclusive. For that
reason more research, especially studies involving college students, needs to be
conducted.

Language Arts

　　Reading and Composition. Included are practical applications of
cooperative learning activities to teach the writing process to students at all
levels, ranging from elementary through college. Stated positive outcomes of
using cooperative learning are increased individual accountability, positive
group interdependence, and better attitudes towards school. One of the required
elements of cooperative learning is instruction in social skills. The article by
Dansereau presents an innovative method for using video tapes of the
cooperative groups to discuss social skills. Even though some of the articles
included here report results of empirical findings, the majority of them offer
practical applications for classroom implementation of cooperative learning
programs that language arts teachers at all levels will find beneficial.

　　Spelling. Because of the specialized nature of this category, the
number of articles is limited. The consensus of the authors is that cooperative
learning does produce positive outcomes in spelling achievement, especially
when group rewards are presented. It is apparent, however, that more research
needs to be conducted in this area before educators can make valid conclusions
about the effects of cooperative learning upon achievement in spelling.

　　English as a Second Language. The theme of the articles included
here is that cooperative learning has a positive effect upon both the academic
achievement and socialization of students enrolled in these programs. Because
of the relatively recent interest in English as a Second Language and bilingual
instruction, more studies need to be done in these two areas.

　　General Language Arts Skills. As the heading indicates, the content
of the articles included in this section is varied. Presented are the following
topics and their relationship to cooperative learning groups: oral
communication skills, study of literature, roles of students, and classroom
teachers' personal experiences. It is also noteworthy that few studies testing
the effects of cooperative learning upon the mastery of literary content exist
and that much remains to be done in this area.

　　Mathematics. With the majority based upon studies conducted in
elementary and secondary schools, most of the articles conclude that
cooperative learning strategies have positive effects upon mathematics

students. Slavin found that most students who engage in cooperative learning activities exhibit positive self-esteem, good attitudes toward mathematics, and increased acceptance of classmates. Sherman found that secondary mathematics students experienced higher levels of academic achievement in cooperative learning groups than in individualized instruction. Novices in the area of cooperative learning will find the article by Good, Reys, Growus, and Mulryan especially interesting. To present an objective viewpoint concerning cooperative learning in the field of mathematics, the authors included both strengths and weaknesses of cooperative learning strategies. Listed among the strengths are active learning by the participants, interesting activities, increased social interaction, and increased use of critical thinking exercises. Weaknesses include lack of group dependency, lack of clarity in role assignments, student passivity, and lack of student accountability.

Even though extensive research on cooperative learning has been conducted in the area of mathematics, a review of literature suggests that much more remains to be done. The articles by Brophy, Davidson, Noddings, and Slavin and Karweit present recommendations for future research, including studies that test the long-term effects of cooperative learning upon academic achievement, the role of the teacher, the effectiveness of the grading procedures, and homogeneous vs. heterogeneous grouping.

Science. Many of the authors represented in this section express the need for educational systems to adapt to American ever-changing society. As Cromwell pointed out, cooperative learning helps to meet the needs of modern society. Discussing the role of cooperative learning in science classrooms, Johnson and Johnson answer the following questions: (1) Does cooperative learning positively affect science students? (2) What is cooperative learning? and (3) How should science teachers set up cooperative groups? Lazarowitz, Hertz, Baird, and Bowldern while acknowledging that cooperative learning produces positive outcomes in the areas of time-on-task, attitudes toward science, and absenteeism, conclude that the effects upon academic achievement are not so clearly defined. Their recommendation is that more empirical research targeting scientific achievement should be conducted before valid generalizations about the effectiveness of cooperative learning in the field of science can be made.

Social Studies. A majority of articles in this section present applications for using the Jigsaw strategy in social studies classrooms. Included are lessons plans for providing instruction in modernization in Japan, the America electoral system, and values education. Once again, recommendations for future research are outlined. Leming suggests that more studies testing the long-term effects of cooperative learning should be conducted and that future studies should include greater involvement of high-level students. Because most of the researchers represented in this section used the Jigsaw as the experimental treatment, studies that test the effects of other cooperative learning strategies upon social studies students should be done.

Students with Special Needs. Because special education attempts to meet the needs of diverse populations of students, this section includes articles on a variety of topics. Included are articles that discuss the effects of cooperative learning strategies upon the following groups of students: (1) behaviorally disordered, (2) gifted, (3) mildly mentally retarded, (4) severely handicapped, and (5) visually handicapped. Almost without exception, the authors conclude that cooperative learning has significant positive effects upon the social skills of students, their acceptance by classmates, and their self-esteem. They also agree that for cooperative learning to be effective in mainstream classes, teachers must clearly define their expectations for all students and must present appropriate group rewards. Inconclusive, however, are the results on academic achievement. As Lloyd, Crowley, Kohler, and Strain state, more research needs to be done in many areas, including situations involving mainstreamed high-incidence handicapped students, socialization, long-term consequences, and comparison/contrast with other teaching/learning strategies.

Vocational Education. This section includes articles that offer suggestions for appropriate application and implementation of cooperative learning structures in vocational education classrooms and laboratories. Illustrating the adaptability of cooperative learning techniques, positive outcomes upon student achievement and attitudes have been recorded in the following areas: home economics, agriculture, industrial arts, printing, and business education.

General

Classroom Climate and Social Needs of Students. As society has changed, so have educational systems. To meet the needs of students in an ever-changing society, educators recognize the need to incorporate social instruction within the school setting. A consensus of the authors represented in this section is that classroom climates must promote social development of students. Most of the articles conclude that cooperative learning is an effective means of establishing appropriate learning climates and of meeting the social needs of students, thus preparing them for "life in the real world." Included are articles indicating that cooperative learning promotes positive social development in the following areas: respect for others, increased self-esteem, better attitudes toward school and society, greater trust of other people, more effective communication with others, increased commitment to achieving common goals, quality of performance, improved attendance, number of friendships, and interracial relationships.

Another common conclusion throughout this section is that for cooperative learning to be highly effective in the development of social skills, teachers must recognize the importance of using group rewards and of promoting positive interdependence. Studies in which either or both of these components were downplayed reveal that cooperative learning has a less significant effect upon social development of students.

Evidenced by the number of entries in this section, much research has been done in the area of classroom climate and social development. A review of the literature suggests, however, that additional studies need to be conducted to test the long-term effects of cooperative learning upon social skills and to measure the transference of social skills from academic settings to non-academic settings. Additional studies also need to be done that target specific age groups, especially older students. Even though classroom climate and social development appear to be two areas in which most researchers agree that cooperative learning does produce positive effects, more longitudinal studies need to be done to verify the apparent conclusions.

Comparisons of Learning Conditions (Cooperative, Competitive, and Individualistic). The purpose of studies described in this section is to compare and contrast the effects that various conditions have upon academic achievement and social development of students. No significant differences were found between competitive and individualistic conditions. When comparing cooperative conditions with competitive and individualistic structures, significance positive effects were revealed in the following areas: increased cognitive skills, group cohesiveness, peer acceptance, greater communication skills, peer support, higher level thinking skills, greater overall achievement, positive attitudes towards school, and positive interdependence.

Supporting the findings of the studies described in the classroom climate section, a review of the literature supports the hypothesis that cooperative structures have greater positive influences upon student development than do competitive and individualistic ones. Additional research needs to be done in the area of achievement before positive generalizations can be made.

Cultural and Ethnic Differences. One of the goals of modern educational systems is teach respect for and acceptance of other cultures, as well as for one's own culture. According to many of the researchers represented in this section, cooperative learning has a positive effect upon decreasing prejudice and increasing acceptance. Many researchers agrees with Johnson and Johnson and that cooperative learning groups should be used in mixed-culture classrooms to promote positive perceptions. Conrad, however, points out that not all researchers are in agreement with the significant positive findings of many studies. Because inconsistencies in beliefs apparently exist, future studies need to be done, especially in the areas of long-term effects and in academic versus nonacademic settings.

Also included in this section are articles that compare and contrast the competitive natures of various cultures, including Cuban American, Anglo-Saxons, and Afro-Americans. These articles are especially useful for readers who desire to gain more knowledge about the customs and expectations of various cultures.

Teacher Education/Staff Development. Before teachers and administrators can effectively implement any new strategy in the school setting, they must be thoroughly familiar with all aspects of that strategy. The need for proper instruction in the use of cooperative learning strategies is especially important, mainly because of the number of available strategies and varied appropriate applications of each strategy. This section contains articles that describe successful teacher education programs and staff development sessions that provide instruction in the use of cooperative learning. An obvious deficient in cooperative learning instruction occurs at the university level in that pre-service teachers generally receive little or no training in the proper implementation of cooperative learning. To overcome some of the deficiencies of teacher education programs, school districts have successfully implemented staff development and in-service programs. Many of the articles in this section outline those programs and offer valuable suggestions for adapting them to meet the needs of any school district desiring to train teachers to use cooperative learning.

This section contains a good balance of theory and research. The article by Bohlmeyer and Burke is a key reference in that it presents a comprehensive survey of nine cooperative learning strategies, including their strengths, weaknesses, and appropriate applications. Teachers desirous of increasing their repertoire of teaching strategies will find the articles and texts in this section both enlightening and beneficial.

Achievement. Much of the research on cooperative learning targets academic achievement in specific content areas. Those references are listed under the appropriate headings elsewhere in the bibliography. Entries in this section describe the effects that general cooperative learning structures have upon the overall achievement of students. Findings relating to student achievement are varied. For that reason additional empirical studies should be done to test the long-range effects of cooperative learning upon overall achievement and to replicate many existing studies to ensure that all components, such as group and individual accountability, of cooperative learning are included. As Slavin indicates, if one of the components has been omitted, the results may not be valid.

Cooperation and Cooperative Learning: General Information. As the title indicates, works dealing with general aspects of cooperative learning are included in this section. Topics addressed include parental perception, general guidelines and overviews, issues involved in implementing cooperative learning activities, and bibliographies. Also included are Deutsch's landmark studies on cooperation. Used in conjunction with the section on overviews of general cooperative learning strategies, these references will provide both educators and laypeople adequate background knowledge of cooperation and cooperative learning in general.

Research on Cooperation and Cooperative Learning

This section presents findings of empirical studies and meta-analyses. Because of the large number of studies that have been done to test the effects of cooperative learning, a wide variety of findings and conclusions are outlined in the articles and books included here. Researchers will also find suggestions for future studies.

Book Reviews
Because of the large number of books in print on cooperative learning, readers need to have a basis for selecting resources to meet their needs. To assist people with selection of books, a section of book reviews is included in this bibliography. Even though the section is not exhaustive, it does offer objective reviews of key works on cooperative learning.

Film/Videos

This brief section offers a selection of audio-visual aides. Of particular note is the 1990 series of tapes by Slavin and the Johnsons.

Games

Significant in the development of cooperative learning strategies, cooperatively structured games were the forerunners of Teams-Games-Tournament and Student Teams Achievement Division. The articles in this section present the positive outcomes of such games, including increased use of peer tutoring, increased mutual concern of students, increased achievement in selected areas, and enhanced psychosocial development of students. The articles by Graves and Orlick also point out that students who participate in cooperatively structured games at school exhibit increased cooperative behavior in non-academic settings. Also included are books containing both academic and non-academic games that all teachers will find useful.

Newsletters

Educators interested in receiving periodic literature on cooperative learning will find this section especially helpful. Among the newsletters described are *Cooperation Unlimited Newsletter, Cooperative Learning: The Magazine for Cooperation in Education*, and *Our Link: Cooperative Learning Newsletter*, all of which provide teachers and administrators with practical tips on implementation of various strategies, staff development, lists of resources, and sample cooperative learning lessons.

Organizations

Anyone interested in cooperation learning research, workshops, and general resources will find this section beneficial. Included are the addresses and emphases of key organizations, including Center for Social Organization of Schools, Cooperation Unlimited, Cooperative Learning Center, and International Association for the Study of Cooperation in Education.

Additional Listings

Readers are encouraged to look under the topic "Additional Listings" to find a selection of cooperative learning materials published in the latter half of 1990. "Additional Listings" entries are cross-referenced in the subject index.

Strategies

I. STRATEGIES

A. GENERAL STRATEGIES (OVERVIEWS)

001. Brandt, R. (1989/1990). On cooperative learning: A conversation with Spencer Kagan. *Educational Leadership, 47*(4), 4-7.

Discusses Kagan's "structural approach" to cooperative learning and its effect on competitive behavior and racial relations as well as how it differs from other cooperative methods. Also describes "Numbered Heads Together" strategy.

002. Clarke, J., Wideman, R., & Eadie, S. (1990). *Together We Learn.* Scarborough, Ontario, Canada: Prentice-Hall Canada, Inc. 216 pp.

Developed by a team of Canadian educators, this volume is designed as "a practical 'how-to' handbook to help teachers implement cooperative learning strategies in all subject areas and at all grade levels across [Canada]." It addresses a host of interesting and valuable topics, including but not limited to: designing beginning group activities, five kinds of groups (informal, base, combined, reconstituted, representative), teaching cooperative skills, and evaluation of group work.

003. Davidson, N., & O'Leary, P. W. (February 1990). How cooperative learning can enhance mastery teaching. *Educational Leadership, 47*(5): 30-3.

Discusses how the blending of cooperative learning with mastery teaching (variously referred to as the U.C.L.A. model, the Hunter model, PET or Program for Effective Teaching, ITIP or Instructional Theory into Practice) makes for a richer classroom instruction and learning environment. Delineates the basics of mastery teaching, principles of cooperative learning, and ways to enhance lesson design and strengthen the learning principles.

004.   Graves, T. (1988). Review: Cooper, J., and Sherman, L.
         Cooperative Learning at the University Level. *The International
         Association for the Study of Cooperation in Education, 9*(3 and
         4), 20-21.

         The authors' study used five learning methods, including
         competitive, Slavin's STAD model, and the Sharans' Group
         Investigation model. There were no differences in achievement,
         though the students who had participated in the various CL
         models reported a much more positive experience. The author
         notes that this may be due to 75% of the students in each section
         being females, who are more willing to participate in cooperative
         structures. The grade distribution (though all received similar
         grades on a final comprehensive exam) shows that A's were
         earned more frequently by students in the cooperative classrooms.
         Another section notes that a majority of surveyed college
         "students believed that the CL approach was more effective than
         traditional lectures or lecture discussion classes that they had
         previously taken in college."

005.   Gunter, M. A., Estes, T. H., & Schwab, J. H. (1990). *Instruction:
         A Models Approach*. Needham Heights, MA: Allyn & Bacon.
         352 pp.

         Chapter 11 in this textbook for use in elementary and
         secondary education courses is entitled "Cooperative Learning
         Models: Improving Student Achievement Using Small Groups."
         The various topics addressed are as follows: "The Cooperative
         Revolution," "Preparing the Students for Group Work," "Steps
         in the Jigsaw II Model," "Steps in the Teams-Games-
         Tournaments (TGT) Model," and "Steps in the Student Team-
         Achievement Division (STAD) Model.

006.   Hollifield, J. H. (1984, May). Student team learning. *Middle
         School Journal, 15*, 6-7.

         Argues that the implementation of student team learning
         strategies can capitalize on social interaction and peer influence
         amongst middle level students so that the interaction and peer
         influence can contribute to, rather than hinder, academic learning.
         Discusses the following: Team learning in the class; three
         different strategies of team learning (Teams-Games-Tournaments,

Student Teams - Achievement Divisions, and Jigsaw), and a very brief comment on research about the effectiveness of student team learning.

007.   Johnson, D. W. (1970). Cooperation, competition, and conflict resolution. In D.W. Johnson, *The Social Psychology of Education* (pp. 153-179). New York: Holt, Rinehart and Winston, Inc.

Discusses the general nature of conflict and types of conflict occurring in the classroom. Explains that conflicts can occur both in cooperative and competitive learning contexts. Cites research, Deutsch in particular, in arguments that cooperative learning is a more facilitative environment for conflict resolution. In a cooperative classroom, more communication between members is likely to take place and disagreements and conflicting interests are more likely to be viewed as mutual problems requiring cooperative solutions.

008.   Johnson, D. W. & Johnson, R. T. (1987). The high achieving student in cooperative learning groups. In R.T. Johnson, D.W. Johnson, & E.J. Holubec (Eds.), *Structuring Cooperative Learning: Lesson Plans for Teachers 1987* (pp. 3-11). Edina, MN: Interaction Book Company, 1987.

Gives several practical suggestions for encouraging high ability students to work cooperatively in groups. Cites research showing improved grades, higher-level reasoning strategies, higher creativity, development of friendships and social skills.

009.   Johnson, D. W., Johnson, R. T., & Holubec, E. J. (1986). *Circles of Learning: Cooperation in the Classroom [Revised]*. Edina, Minn.: Interaction Book Company. 124 pp.

Presents a general overview of cooperative learning, including a comprehensive definition of cooperative learning and an explanation of goal structures, learning processes, and instructional outcomes. The teacher's role, how to create positive interdependence, how to teach students cooperative skills, and generate cooperation among teachers are subjects of other chapters. This easy-to-read book ends with a chapter on misinformation about cooperative learning and reflections on the nature and future of cooperative learning. Classroom teachers will find *Circles of Learning* provides a solid introduction to cooperative learning.

010.   Johnson, R. T., Johnson, D. W., & Holubec, E. J. (Eds.). (1987). *Structuring Cooperative Learning: Lesson Plans for Teachers 1987.* Edina, Minnesota: Interaction Book Company. 339 pp.

Features cooperative learning lesson plans by teachers who have used cooperative learning in their classrooms; also provides sample lessons for grade levels K-12 and various subject areas, including reading, language arts, mathematics, science, and social studies. Materials in the book (except those for which reprint permission must be obtained from the primary sources) may be freely reproduced for education/training activities with the addition of an acknowledgement on all reproductions. Fifth in a series of compilations of original lessons from educators dedicated to implementing cooperative learning strategies.

The book is divided into seven sections. Section I gives an overview of cooperative learning. Section II offers ten lesson plans for use in primary school. Section III's lesson plans for intermediate students range from correcting contraction and punctuation errors to planning a city park. Six lesson plans are provided for junior high school, including such topics as cooperative poetry to geometry polygons to identifying skeletons. Section V includes seven plans for senior high: control theory in the cooperative English class to cooperative typing. Section VI, "Bonus Time," offers a cooperative plan for losing weight and a game that allows for the development within a group of either cooperation or competition called the "subsistence game." Articles on the high achieving student and effectively monitoring groups finish the section. A final chapter recommends other materials and gives a guide for creating cooperative lesson plans.

Editors comment that with minor modifications, the lessons can be taught at a range of age levels and taken from one subject and used in another. Each lesson plan consists of a one-page overview followed by two to four pages of detailed instructions and in many cases materials and illustrations of teaching and learning aides.

Contains Items 008, 471, 472, 474, 512, and 616.

*   Joyner, R. (1988). Cooperative learning: Just another pretty fad?
         Focus [a publication of the Teacher Education Division of the
         School of Education & Psychology, Missouri Southern State
         College], 2 (1), 1, 3. (Cited below as Item 618.)

011.   Kagan, S. (1989). *Cooperative Learning: Resources for Teachers.*
         San Juan Capistrano, CA: Resources for Teachers. 294 pp.

         A general manual containing a wide variety of materials for
         implementing Jigsaw, detailed steps for introducing Coop Coop,
         a streamlined version of Group Investigation, and a synthesis of
         Jigsaw and Coop Coop. Includes forms, examples, and step-by-
         step instructions. A highly practical and helpful resource for
         teachers.

012.   Kagan, S. (1989/1990). The structural approach to cooperative
         learning. *Educational Leadership, 47*(4), 12-15.

         Discusses the structural approach, which is based on the
         "creation, analysis, and systematic application of structures, or
         content-free ways of organizing social interaction in the
         classroom....An important corner stone of the approach is the
         distinction between 'structures' and 'activities.'" Discusses
         competitive vs. cooperative structures, and ways for schools to
         effectively handle the structural approach. Includes an overview
         of selected structures.

013.   Lehr, F. (1984). ERIC/RCS: Cooperative learning. *Journal of
         Reading, 27,* 458-461.

         After a brief review of relevant research, the author describes
         the key components of several cooperative learning techniques:
         STAD, TGT, Jigsaw II, and Group Investigation.

014.   Michaelson, L. K., Watson, W. E., Cragin, J. P., & Fink, L. D.
         (1982). Team learning: A potential solution to the problem of
         large classes. *Exchange: The Organizational Behavior Teaching
         Journal, 7*(1), 13-22.

         Presents Team Learning as an alternative to large-group
         instruction. Included are descriptions of team learning formats
         and group instructional activities, strategies for establishing

group cohesiveness, and evaluation procedures. Also included is a helpful section dealing with potential problems and appropriate solutions. Concludes that the Team Learning process effectively accomplishes a variety of learning objectives in a large class setting.

015.   Popp, J. A. (1987). If you see John Dewey, tell him we did it. *Educational Theory*, *37*, 145-152.

Begins with a description of the traditional teacher-centered classroom and moves into an overview of classroom team structures made popular by Robert E. Slavin and his colleagues at Johns Hopkins University. Lists the four basic components of cooperative team learning: exposition, practice, evaluation, and publication of results. "A cooperative spirit develops within the teams, and no one feels alone as is often the case in classrooms based upon interpersonal competition or individualized instruction. Research suggests that it is the team recognition that is a central factor in the success of the method. Discusses the three social dimensions of classrooms:" competitive, individual, and cooperative. Presents some potential problems and appropriate solutions involved in using cooperative learning. Relates the philosophy of cooperative team learning to the beliefs of John Dewey. Summarizes that "the team study approach allows each student a much better chance to experience success in school."

*   Slavin, R. E. (1983). *Cooperative Learning*. NY: Longman. 147 pp. (Cited below as Item 659.)

016.   Slavin, R. E. (1980). Student team learning: A manual for teachers. In S. Sharan, P. Hare, C. Webb, & R. Hertz-Lazarowitz (Eds.), *Cooperation in Education*, (pp. 82-135). Provo, UT: Brigham Young University.

Provides a solid overview of student team learning, including: Description of various team techniques (Teams-Games-Tournament, Student Teams-Achievement Divisions, and Jigsaw II), research on team learning and basic skills, the social impact on student relations via the use of teams, implication for teachers, and detailed suggestions on how to implement each strategy.

017.   Slavin, R. E. (1982). *Cooperative learning: Student Teams.*
        Washington, D.C.: National Education Association. 32 pp.

        Succinctly addresses the following: overview of cooperative
        learning; discussion of cooperative learning methods such as
        Student Teams - Achievement Divisions (STAD), Teams-
        Games-Tournaments (TGT), Team-Assisted Instruction (TAI),
        Jigsaw, Learning Together, Group Investigations, etc.; and
        Research on Cooperative Learning regarding academic
        achievement, intergroup relations, mainstreaming, self-esteem,
        etc. Concludes with a bibliography that contains 59 citations.

018.   Slavin, R. E. (1986). Learning together. *American Educator: The
        Professional Journal of the American Federation of Teachers, 10,*
        6-10.

        Briefly discusses the effects of competition upon students
        and offers effective alternatives to competition. One alternative
        discussed is cooperative learning. Even though an emphasis is
        placed on Student-Teams-Achievement Divisions (STAD), the
        author briefly discusses Team Accelerated Instruction (TAI),
        Teams-Games-Tournament (TGT), Cooperative Integrated
        Reading and Composition (CIRC), and Jigsaw by presenting key
        concepts of each strategy and relevant research findings.

019.   Slavin, R. E. (1986). *Student Team Learning: An Overview and
        Practical Guide.* Washington, D.C.: National Education
        Association. 56 pp.

        A lucid, detailed, and extremely useful overview and guide to
        student team learning techniques. The introduction presents
        research evidence vis-a-vis this technique and the practical guide
        section presents step-by-step suggestions regarding the
        development and implementation of the following cooperative
        learning methods: Student Teams-Achievement Divisions
        (STAD), Teams-Games-Tournaments (TGT), Jigsaw II, Team-
        Assisted Individualization (TAI), and other cooperative learning
        methods. The latter section also includes a section entitled
        "Troubleshooting" which provides teachers with helpful hints in
        regard to some of the more common problems they may face
        when incorporating cooperative learning into their classrooms.
        The appendices include information on prorating scores for teams

with two, three or five members, methods to calculate near base scores, instructions for making worksheets/games/quizzes for STAD and TGT, a sample Jigsaw II unit, and sample record forms.

020.   Slavin, R. E. (1986). *Using Student Team Learning*. Baltimore, MD: Center for Research on Elementary and Middle Schools, The Johns Hopkins University. 109 pp.

Provides an outstanding overview of student team learning. Includes an overview of research on student team learning methods, a separate discussion of Student Teams - Achievement Divisions (STAD) and Teams-Game-Tournament (TGT); suggestions on how to make worksheets and quizzes for STAD and TGT; and brief overview of the following cooperative learning strategies: Team Accelerated Instruction, Cooperative Integrated Reading and Composition (CIRC), Jigsaw II, Co-op Co-op, and Group Investigation. Also discusses the Johnsons' methods, informal cooperative learning methods, student team learning and mastery learning, cooperative classroom management, team building, and troubleshooting.

021.   Slavin, R. E., & Hansell, S. (1983). Cooperative learning and intergroup relations: Contact theory in the classroom. In J. L. Epstein and N. Karweit's (Eds.), *Friends in school: Patterns of selection and influence in secondary schools*, (pp. 93-114) New York: Academic Press.

Provides a brief overview of various cooperative learning strategies (Student Teams - Achievement Divisions, Teams-Games-Tournaments, Jigsaw I and Jigsaw II, and Learning Together), discusses the main effects of different cooperative learning strategies on intergroup relations, examines the research on cooperation versus competition, discusses "contact theory," and describes and discusses a causal model vis-a-vis the effects of cooperative learning on intergroup relations.

022.   Slavin, R. E., & Karweit, N. L. (1981). Cognitive and affective outcomes of an intensive student team learning experience. *The Journal of Experimental Education, 50*, 29-35.

Evaluated the use of the strategies known as Student Teams-Achievement Divisions (STAD), Teams-Games-Tournaments (TGT), and Jigsaw, "covering most of students' instructional day, to discover whether student team learning methods can be used to replace traditional methods. Fourth- and fifth-grade students were assigned to experimental or control treatments for a semester. Results indicated that the intensive use of student team learning methods was feasible and produced positive outcomes on student friendships, liking of school, self-esteem, and language and reading achievement."

023.   *Small-group Cooperative Learning*. (1984). The best of ERIC on Educational Management Number 76. (ERIC Document Reproduction Service No. ED 251 915).

Succinct review of twelve major cooperative learning works.

024.   Stewart, W. J. (1988). Stimulating intuitive thinking through problem solving. *Clearing House, 62,* 175-176.

Offers evidence to suggest that intuitive thinking is as important as analytical thinking and that students should be encouraged to solve problems intuitively. Describes a variety of group activities including cooperatively structured ones, that classroom teachers can use to enhance their students' intuitive thinking skills.

B. COOPERATIVE INTEGRATED READING AND COMPOSITION (CIRC)

025.   Madden, N. A., Slavin, R. E., & Stevens, R. J. (1986).
Cooperative Integrated Reading and Composition: Teacher's Manual. Baltimore, MD: Johns Hopkins University Center for Research on Elementary and Middle Schools.

Teacher's manual for a teaching strategy that uses a combination of mixed-ability cooperative groups and skill-based reading groups to teach reading, language arts, and writing in the upper elementary grades.

*   Madden, N. A., Slavin, R. E., Karweit, N. L., & Livermon, B. J. (1989). Restructuring the urban elementary school. *Educational Leadership*, *46*(5), 14-18. (Cited below as Item 245.)

*   Madden, N. A., Slavin, R. E., Karweit, N. L., Livermon, B. J., & Dolan, L. (1988). *Success for All: Effects on Student Achievement, Retentions, and Special Education Referrals*. Baltimore, MD: Johns Hopkins University, Center for Research on Elementary and Middle Schools. (Cited below as Item 246.)

026.   Madden, N. A., Slavin, R. E., Karweit, N. L., Livermon, B., & Stevens, R. J. (1987). *Success for all: Teacher's manual for reading*. Baltimore, MD: Johns Hopkins University, Center for Research on Elementary and Middle Schools.

Partly focuses on the role of Cooperative Integrated Reading and Composition (CIRC) in the Success for All Program, a model of elementary school organization that incorporates much of what is known about effective programs for students at risk.

*   Slavin, R. E. (1986). Learning together. *American Educator: The Professional Journal of the American Federation of Teachers*, *10*, 6-10. (Cited above as Item 018.)

*   Slavin, R. E. (1986). *Using Student Team Learning*. Baltimore, MD: Center for Research on Elementary and Middle Schools,

31

The Johns Hopkins University. 109 pp. (Cited above as Item 020.)

*   Slavin, R. E., & Madden, N. A. (1989). Effective classroom programs for students at risk. In Robert E. Slavin, N. L. Karweit, & N. A. Madden (Eds.), *Effective Programs for Students at Risk,* (pp. 23-51). Boston: Allyn and Bacon. (Cited below as Item 265.)

*   Slavin, R. E., & Madden, N. A. (1989). What works for students at risk: A research synthesis. *Educational Leadership, 46*(5), 4-13. (Cited below as Item 266.)

*   Slavin, R. E., Madden, N. A., & Karweit, N. L. (1989). Effective programs for students at risk: Conclusions for practice and policy. In R. Slavin, N. L. Karweit, & N. A. Madden (Eds.), *Effective programs for students at risk* (pp. 355-372). Boston: Allyn and Bacon. (Cited below as Item 267.)

027.   Stevens, R. J., Madden, N. A., Slavin, R. E., & Farnish, A. M. (1986). *Cooperative integrated reading and composition: A brief overview of the CIRC program.* Baltimore, MD: Center for Research on Elementary and Middle Schools at Johns Hopkins University. 7 pp.

The CIRC program is comprised of three key elements: Basal-related activities, direct instruction in reading comprehension, and integrated language arts writing. "In all of these activities students work in heterogeneous learning teams." This overview presents the following information on this program: The composition of the reading groups and teams, the types of basal-related activities that are used, the focus of the direct instruction in reading comprehension, the methods of integrating language arts and writing, and the program evaluation procedures.

C. STRUCTURED CONTROVERSY

028.   Holubec, E. J., Johnson, D. W, & Johnson, R. T. (in press).
        Structuring controversy in a cooperative context: Studying civil
        disobedience. In C. M. Hurlbert, & S. Totten (Eds.), *Social
        Issues in the English Classroom: Theory and Practice.* Urbana,
        IL: National Council of the Teachers of English.

        Explains how English teachers can use "structured
        controversy," a cooperative learning strategy, to teach about civil
        disobedience. This strategy can be used across the curriculum to
        address any controversial issue.

*   Johnson, D. W. (1970). Cooperation, competition, and conflict
        resolution. In D.W. Johnson, *The Social Psychology of
        Education* (pp. 153-179). New York: Holt, Rinehart and
        Winston, Inc. (Cited above as Item 007.)

029.   Johnson, D. W., Johnson, F. P., & Johnson, R. T. (1976).
        Promoting constructive conflict. *Notre Dame Journal of
        Education, 7,* 163-167.

        Discusses the value of addressing/examining conflict in the
        classroom when handled constructively. Discusses and delineates
        a method for structuring controversy in the classroom through
        the use of a cooperative learning structure. [A condensed version
        of this article appears in the November 1976 issue of *Education
        Digest, 42,* 46-48.]

030.   Johnson, D. W., & Johnson, R. T. (1988). Critical thinking
        through structured controversy. *Educational Leadership, 46*(8),
        58-64.

        Discusses and explains a cooperative learning model
        (structured controversy) for engaging students in academic
        conflicts and controversies. Explains the model, discusses how
        to structure controversy in the classroom as well as prerequisites
        for providing constructive controversy, and the benefits gained by
        the students. Includes an excellent chart on the differences

33

between controversy, debate, concurrence-seeking, and individualistic learning processes as well as a schematic diagram of the structured controversy process. Based on their research, the authors state that the use of structured controversy in the classroom leads to the following: "...[an] increase in students' perspective taking abilities, greater student mastery and retention of the subject and greater ability to generalize the principles learned to a wider variety of situations; higher quality decisions and solutions to problems; the promotion of creative insights by influencing students to view a problem for different perspectives and reformulate it in ways that allow the emergence of new orientations to the problem; and an increase in the number and quality of students' ideas, feelings of stimulation and enjoyment, and originality of expression in problem solving, resulting in greater emotional commitment to solving the problem, greater enjoyment of the process, and more imaginative solutions" (p. 63).

031.   Johnson, D. W., & Johnson, R. T. (1989). Controversy and learning. In D. W. Johnson & R. T. Johnson (Eds.), *Cooperation and Competition: Theory and Research* (pp. 89-106). Edina, MN: Interaction Book Company.

Examines the nature of controversy, some of its outcomes, and how it can be used constructively as a learning experience. Controversy will be present in cooperative situations when the members of the group feel a sense of commitment to some issue being discussed. Controversy within the cooperative group may be constructive if the group is heterogeneous, group members are knowledgeable, and members have good communicative and conflict skills.

*   Johnson, D. W., Johnson, R. T., & Holubec, E. J. (1987). Getting Started with Cooperative Groups. In R. T. Johnson, D. W. Johnson, & E. J. Holubec, (Eds.), *Structuring Cooperative Learning: Lesson Plans for Teachers 1987* (pp. 43-75). Edina, MN: Interaction Book Company, 1987. (Cited below as Item 472.)

032.   Lindow, J. A. Wilkinson, L. C., & Peterson, P. L. (1985). Antecedents and consequences of verbal disagreements during

small-group learning. *Journal of Educational Psychology, 77*(6), 658-667.

Group controversy was investigated in ten mixed-ability, mixed-sex, elementary math groups through analysis of dissension episodes (defined as the interaction that followed a verbal assertion of disagreement about a math answer. Examined was the relation of ability and sex with four dissension variables: initiation, participation, demonstrations, and prevailing answers. These variables were then related to two outcome measures: adjusted achievement and peer nominations of competence. Boys and higher ability students had significantly more prevailing answers and demonstrations. Participation, demonstration, and prevailing answers were positively related to peer competence nominations. Prevailing answers were also positively related to adjusted achievement. Students were able to resolve conflict when it occurred, without having received explicit instructions about how to do so. They usually also reached consensus on the correct answer. Researchers suggested teachers encourage the occurrence of dissension among students in small groups by having them check answers regularly.

033.   Lyons, V. M. (1982). A study of elaborative cognitive processing as a variable mediating achievement in cooperative learning groups. University of Minnesota. *Dissertation Abstracts International, 43*, 1090A.

Compared the effects of cooperative and individualistic learning experiences on achievement, quality and quantity of cognitive processes, and relative amounts of participation by high, middle, and low ability elementary students. Findings revealed that cooperatively structured controversy produced greater achievement and cognitive processing than did individualistic learning structures. "Eighteen percent of the participation in the cooperative controversy condition was by high ability students, fifty-seven percent by middle ability students, and twenty-four percent by low ability students."

034.   Nijhof, W., & Kommers, P. (1985). An analysis of cooperation in relation to cognitive controversy. In R. Slavin, S. Sharan, S. Kagan, R. Hertz-Lazarowitz, C. Webb, & R. Schmuck

(Eds.), *Learning to Cooperate, Cooperating to Learn*, (pp. 125-145). New York: Plenum Press.

Dutch researchers discuss a study that focused on an analysis of the cognitive functioning of students within small groups. The two basic questions examined were: Is the level of communication influenced by group composition or prior knowledge of a task domain? and What is the shift in perspective of the individual members of a group due to a cooperative learning experience?

035.   Smith, K. (1989). *Using controversy to increase students' achievement, epistemic curiosity and positive attitudes toward learning.* University Microfilms Order Number ADG81-02164. 0000.

"Assessed the effects of controversy in cooperative learning groups on achievement, epistemic curiosity, and attitudes....The results of the study showed that achievement and epistemic curiosity were greater and attitudes toward studying controversial issues, arguing, group work and fellow group members were more positive in the cooperative group with controversy conditions than in the cooperative group without controversy condition or the individualistic condition."

036.   Smith, K., Johnson, D. W., & Johnson, R. T. (1981). Can conflict be constructive? Controversy versus concurrence seeking in learning groups. *Journal of Educational Psychology, 73*(5), 651-663.

The study compared the effects of controversy in learning groups, concurrence seeking in learning groups, and individualistic study. Eighty-four sixth-graders were assigned to conditions on a stratified random basis controlling for sex and reading ability. All students studied two controversial issues with materials representing pro and con views. In the controversy condition, each group was divided into halves representing pro and con sides. In the concurrence-seeking condition, each group could study the material any way they wished, but were to avoid arguing. In the individualistic condition, students were to learn the material by themselves. "Results indicated that controversy compared with the other two

conditions promotes higher achievement and retention, greater
search for information, more cognitive rehearsal, accurate
understanding of the material, continuing motivation, and
positive attitudes toward controversy and classmates." The
authors considered the use of controversy to be an important
addition to classroom instruction.

037.   Smith, K., Johnson, D. W., & Johnson, R. T. (1984). Effects of
controversy on learning in cooperative groups. *The Journal of
Social Psychology, 122* 199-209.

Discusses the effects of controversy in cooperative learning
groups. Involved in the study were thirty-six engineering
students who discussed the controversial issues of hazardous
waste (dispose vs. eliminate) and energy production (coal vs.
nuclear). After five days of discussion on each issue, the
students wrote a report, took an achievement test, and completed
an attitude survey. Oral interaction among the group members
was recorded by trained monitors. Results indicate that
controversy did not have a negative effect upon achievement,
attitudes, or self-esteem of the students.

038.   Tjosvold, D., & Johnson, D. W. (1977). Effects of controversy on
cognitive perspective taking. *Journal of Educational
Psychology, 69*(6), 679-85.

A group of thirty undergraduates was chosen to discuss a
moral issue with a confederate who had the same opinion or an
opposing opinion to the one they held. Subjects who were in
the controversy condition indicated more accurately the reasoning
behind the confederate's beliefs than did those in the
noncontroversy condition.

*   Warring, D. F. (1983). Fostering prosocial attitudes in desegregated
schools through cooperative learning (controversy). University
of Minnesota. *Dissertation Abstracts International, 44*, 3334A.
(Cited below as Item 442.)

D. CO-OP CO-OP

*   Bohlmeyer, E. M., & Burke, J. P. (1987). Selecting cooperative learning techniques: A consultative strategy guide. *School Psychology Review, 16*, 36-49. (Cited below as Item 451.)

039.   Gordon, B. A. (1985). Cooperative learning: A comparative study of attitude and achievement of two groups of grade seven mathematics classes. *Dissertation Abstracts International, 47*, 772A. (University Microfilms Order Number ADG86-05385. 8609)

    Attempted to determine if the use of the Co-op Co-op strategy would result in a significant increase in achievement in mathematics and a more positive student attitude toward the study of mathematics.

040.   Kagan, S. (1985). Co-op Co-op: A flexible cooperative learning technique. In R. Slavin, S. Sharan, S. Kagan, R. Hertz-Lazarowits, C. Webb, & R. Schmuck (Eds.), *Learning to cooperate, cooperating to learn* (pp. 437-462). New York: Plenum Press.

    Presents a thorough overview of the philosophy, the elements, and effects (cognitive and affective) of Co-op Co-op. Appendices include "Elicited Student Comments About Co-op Co-op," and a list of "Spontaneous Student Comments."

*   Kagan, S. (1989). *Cooperative Learning: Resources for Teachers.* San Juan Capistrano, CA: Resources for Teachers. 294 pp. (Cited above as Item 011.)

*   Nattiv, A. (1986). The effects of cooperative learning instructional strategies on academic achievement among sixth grade social studies students. *Dissertation Abstracts International, 47*, 3651A. (University Microfilms Order Number ADG86-29488 8704) (Cited below as Item 534.)

*   Slavin, R. E. (1986). *Using Student Team Learning*. Baltimore,
         MD: Center for Research on Elementary and Middle Schools,
         The Johns Hopkins University. 109 pp. (Cited above as Item
         020.)

041.   Wyatt, F. (1988). Rethinking the research project through
         cooperative learning. *Middle School Journal*, 20(1), 6-7.

         Describes research projects that engage the students in an
         adapted version of Co-op Co-op, a cooperative learning strategy
         developed by Spencer Kagan. The key difference, Wyatt says, is
         that "the strategy described here focuses on group rather than
         individual mini-topic presentations as described by Kagan." The
         unit of study discussed here is Energy. One of the primary goals
         for this project was to involve students in a different approach to
         research: students forming research questions, using specific data
         collection techniques, which helps focus on research questions,
         synthesizing this information, and sharing findings through
         group interaction.

E. GROUP INVESTIGATION (GI)

042. Bakke, S. E. (1986). A collaborative exploratory study of the use of the Group Investigation model to improve instruction in elementary schools. *Dissertation Abstracts International, 47,* 3958A. (Copies available exclusively from Micrographics Department, Doheny Library, USC, Los Angeles, CA 90080-0182)

   This dissertation explores and describes elementary teachers' use of the Group Investigation strategy and its effects in the classroom.

*   Bohlmeyer, E. M., & Burke, J. P. (1987). Selecting cooperative learning techniques: A consultative strategy guide. *School Psychology Review, 16,* 36-49. (Cited below as Item 451.)

*   Brubacher, M., Payne, R., and Pickett, K. (Eds.). (1990). *Perspectives on Small Group Learning.* Oakville, Ontario: Rubicon Publishing Co. (Cited below as Item 567.)

*   Graves, T. (1988) Review: Cooper, J. and Sherman, L. Cooperative Learning at the University Level. *The International Association for the Study of Cooperation in Education, 9*(3 and 4), 20-21. (Cited above as Item 004.)

*   Kagan, S. (1989). *Cooperative Learning: Resources for Teachers.* San Juan Capistrano, CA: Resources for Teachers. 294 pp. (Cited above as Item 011.)

*   Lehr, F. (1984). ERIC/RCS: Cooperative learning. *Journal of Reading, 27,* 458-461. (Cited above as Item 013.)

*   O'Brien, M. J. (1984). Critical instructional competencies as perceived and applied by training directors (industry, development). University of Cincinnati. *Dissertation Abstracts International, 45,* 2380A. (Cited below as Item 483.)

043.   Sharan, S., & Hertz-Lazarowitz, R. (1979). A group-investigation
         method of cooperative learning in the classroom. In S. Sharan,
         P. Hare, C. D. Webb, & R. Hertz-Lazarowitz, (Eds.),
         Cooperation in Education (pp. 14-46). Provo, UT: Brigham
         Young University Press.

         Provides an overview of the theoretical underpinnings and
         purposes of the Group Investigation method (e.g., it "attempts to
         combine in one teaching strategy, the form and dynamics of the
         democratic process and the process of academic inquiry"),
         describes the stages of implementation of the strategy (e.g.,
         identifies the topic and how to organize pupils into research
         groups, how to plan the learning task, carry out the
         investigation, prepare a final report, present the final report,
         evaluation), and a discussion of research and a plan for future
         development of the model.

*   Sharan, S., & Kuffell, P. (with collaboration of Brosh, T. & Pelleg,
         R.). (1984). *Cooperative Learning in the Classroom: Research
         in Desegregated Schools.* Hillsdale, NJ: Lawrence Erlbaum
         Associates, Publishers. 176 pp. [Foreword by Seymour
         Sarason.] (Cited below as Item 426.)

*   Sharan, S., Kuffell, P., Hertz-Lazarowitz, R., Bejarano, Y., Raviv,
         S., & Sharan, Y. (1985). Cooperative learning effects on ethnic
         relations and achievement in Israel: Junior-high-school
         classrooms. In R. Slavin, S. Sharan, S. Kagan, R. Hertz-
         Lazarowitz, C. Webb, & R. Schmuck (Eds.), *Learning to
         Cooperate, Cooperating to Learn*, (pp. 313-344). New York:
         Plenum Press. (Cited below as Item 427.)

044.   Sharan, S., & Shachar, H. (1988). *Language and Learning in the
         Cooperative Classroom.* New York: Springer-Verlag. 176 pp.

         Reports the findings of a study of the Group-Investigation
         method that was implemented in five "eighth-grade classrooms in
         a junior high where two-thirds of the student body consisted of
         pupils from Jewish families who came to Israel from Western
         countries, and one-third came from countries of the Middle East.
         Four other 8th grade classes in the same school were taught with
         the traditional Whole-Class methods.... [Among] the salient
         questions asked in this study are as follows: Do pupils who

study in classrooms conducted with the Group-Investigation method achieve more, academically, in both informational (low-level) and analytic/synthetic (higher-level) kinds of knowledge than pupils who study with the Whole Class methods, or are the effects of the Group-Investigation method on achievement primarily with the latter...kinds of knowledge?; Is the effect of cooperative learning on achievement more salient for pupils from the majority or minority ethnic groups?; Do pupils who study with Group-Investigation methods display more extensive verbal interaction with their peers than pupils who study with the Whole-Class method?"

045.   Sharan, Y., & Sharan, S. (1989/1990). Group investigation expands cooperative learning. *Educational Leadership, 47*(4), 17-21.

Provides an overview of the group investigation approach (including stages of implementation). This is an approach that attempts to "combine in one teaching strategy the form and dynamics of the democratic process and the process of academic inquiry." Includes a sample worksheet.

*   Sharan, Y., & Sharan, S. (1989/1990). How effective is group investigation? *Educational Leadership, 47*(4), 18. (Cited below as Item 657.)

*   Sherman, L. W. (1989). A comparative study of cooperative and competitive achievement in secondary biology classrooms: The group investigation model versus and individually competitive goal structure. *Journal of Research in Science Teaching, 26*(1), 55-64. (Cited below as Item 207.)

*   Slavin, R. E. (1982). *Cooperative learning: Student Teams.* Washington, D.C.: National Education Association. 32 pp. (Cited above as Item 017.)

*   Slavin, R. E. (1986). *Using Student Team Learning.* Baltimore, MD: Center for Research on Elementary and Middle Schools, The Johns Hopkins University. 109 pp. (Cited above as Item 020.)

F. JIGSAW

046.   Aronson, E., Blaney, N., Stephan, C., Sikes, J., & Snapp, M.
(1978). *The Jigsaw Classroom.* Newbury Park, CA: Sage
Publications. 197 pp.

Outlines the Jigsaw method for cooperative learning and
teaching. Designed for use with grades four and up. Classrooms
are divided into groups which all study segments of a subject
area. Expert groups then share their knowledge with "home"
groups.

*   Aronson, E., & Goode, E. (1980). Training teachers to implement
jigsaw learning: A manual for teachers. In S. Sharan, P. Hare,
C. D. Webb, & R. Hertz-Lazarowitz (Eds.), *Cooperation
in Education,* (pp. 47-81). Provo, UT: Brigham Young
University Press. (Cited below as Item 447.)

047.   Blaney, N. T., Stephan, C., Rosenfield, D., Aronson, E., & Sikes,
J. (1977). Interdependence in the classroom: A field study.
Journal of Educational Psychology, 69(2), 121-128.

Fifth-grade students spent three class periods per week for
six weeks in interdependent learning groups. Using a jigsaw
method, each student taught other members of his/her group a
portion of the assignment. Results indicated that students in the
interdependent learning groups showed higher self-esteem than
controls and liked groupmates more than other classmates. Black
and Anglo experimentals increased their liking for school more
than control black and Anglos. Authors stress the importance of
cooperative learning teams for use in mitigating school
desegregation problems.

*   Bohlmeyer, E. M., & Burke, J. P. (1987). Selecting cooperative
learning techniques: A consultative strategy guide. *School
Psychology Review, 16,* 36-49. (Cited below as Item 451.)

048.   Clarke, J., & Wideman, R. (1985). *Cooperative Learning: The
Jigsaw Strategy.* Scarborough, Ontario: Board of Education.

An account of the Jigsaw method and strategy. Includes five sample lessons in the content areas.

*   Dishon, D., & O'Leary, P. W. (1984). *A Guidebook for Cooperative Learning: A Technique for Creating More Effective Schools.* Holmes Beach, FL: Learning Publications. [Foreword by David W. Johnson and Roger T. Johnson] (Cited below as Item 584.)

*   Dittman, J. (1986). Join the winning circle. *Illinois Teacher of Home Economics, 30,* 46-49, 53. (Cited below as Item 277.)

*   Ferguson, P. (1988). Modernization in Meiji Japan: A jigsaw lesson. *Social Education, 51,* 393-394. (Cited below as Item 213.)

*   Ferguson, P. (1989/1990, Winter). Cooperative team learning; Theory into practice for the prospective middle school teacher. *Action in Teacher Education. XI* (4):24-28. (Cited below as Item 461.)

049.   Guerrero, M., & Gonzalez, A. (1983). *A Cooperative/Interdependent Approach to Bilingual Education: Jigsaw Teacher's Handbook.* (Available from Hollister School District, Curriculum Center, 761 South St., Hollister, CA 95023).

*   Gunter, M. A., Estes, T. H., & Schwab, J. H. (1990). *Instruction: A Models Approach.* Needham Heights, MA: Allyn & Bacon. 352 pp. (Cited above as Item 005.)

*   Hawley, W. D., Rosenholtz, S. J., Goodstein, H., & Hasselbring, T. (1984). Good "effective teaching" schools: What research says about improving student achievement. *Peabody Journal of Education, 61,* 15-52. (Cited below as Item 468.)

*   Hollifield, J. H. (1984, May). Student team learning. *Middle School Journal, 15,* 6-7. (Cited above as Item 006.)

050.   Jefferies, W. M. (1987). A naturalistic inquiry of cooperative learning using the "Jigsaw" strategy in four LDS church seminary classes in the Northwestern United States during 1986-

1987. Brigham Young University. *Dissertation Abstracts International, 49,* 1685A.

A qualitative study that describes and analyzes the implementation of Jigsaw in seminary classes consisting of high school students. Concludes that cooperative learning should become part of seminary classes, that new strategies tailored to the seminary needs should be developed, and that appropriate in-service programs should be provided.

* Johnson, D. W., Johnson, R. T., & Holubec, E. J. (1987). Getting Started with Cooperative Groups. In R. T. Johnson, D. W. Johnson, & E. J. Holubec (Eds.), *Structuring Cooperative Learning: Lesson Plans for Teachers 1987* (pp. 43-75). Edina, MN: Interaction Book Company, 1987. (Cited below as Item 472.)

* Judge, J. (1978). Student team learning. *American Education, 4,* 28-32. Cited below as Item 079.)

* Kagan, S. (1980). Cooperation -- Competition, culture, and structural bias in classrooms. In S. Sharan, P. Hare, C. D. Webb, & R. Hertz-Lazarowitz (Eds.), *Cooperation in Education,* (pp. 197-211). Provo, UT: Brigham Young University Press. (Cited below as Item 397.)

* Kagan, S. (1989). *Cooperative Learning: Resources for Teachers.* San Juan Capistrano, CA: Resources for Teachers. 294 pp. (Cited above as Item 011.)

* Lazarowitz, R., Hertz, R. L., Baird, J. H., & Bowlden, V. (1988). Academic achievement and on-task behavior of high school biology students instructed in a cooperative small investigative group. *Science Education, 72*(4): 475-487. (Cited below as Item 197.)

* Lehr, F. (1984). ERIC/RCS: Cooperative learning. *Journal of Reading, 27,* 458-461. (Cited above as Item 013.)

* Leighton, M. S. (1990). Cooperative learning. In J. M. Cooper's *Classroom Teaching Skills,* (pp. 307-335). Lexington, MA: D.C. Heath and Co. (Cited below as Item 478.)

*   Leming, J. S. (1985). Research on social studies curriculum and
        instruction: Interventions and outcomes in the socio-moral
        domain. In W. B. Stanley (Ed.) *Review of Research in Social
        Studies Education*. (Bulletin 75). Washington, D.C.: National
        Council for the Social Studies. (Cited below as Item 216.)

051.   Little, D. C. (1986). An investigation of the effects of cooperative
        small-group instruction and the use of advanced organizers on the
        self-concept and social studies achievement of third-grade
        students. The University of Alabama. *Dissertation Abstracts
        International, 47*, 2872A.

        Using four specific advance organizers (summaries, outlines,
        key terms, and questions), the researcher examined the effect that
        Jigsaw learning strategies have upon the self-concept and social
        studies achievement of third-grade students. Findings revealed
        that "the use of summaries and outlines with Jigsaw and the use
        of conventional social studies instruction were effective; the use
        of key terms and questions with Jigsaw was not effective in
        improving the self-concept of students," that "the use of outlines
        and questions with Jigsaw was effective; the use of summaries
        and key terms with Jigsaw and the use of conventional social
        studies instruction were not effective in improving the teacher-
        perceived (inferred) self-concept of students," and "that the use of
        summaries, outlines, key terms, and questions (with Jigsaw) and
        the use of conventional social studies instruction were effective
        in improving the social studies achievement of students."

052.   Male, M. (1986). Cooperative learning for effective jigsaw
        mainstreaming. *Computing Teacher, 14*(1), 35-37.

        Based upon research that supports the effectiveness of
        "students teaching each other, the opportunity to be successful,
        the support and interaction with teammates, and the amount of
        actual engaged time with the task at hand." Gives practical
        classroom examples of Jigsaw and Teams-Games-
        Tournaments(TGT) strategies that can be used effectively to
        mainstream handicapped students. Concludes by offering
        suggestions for creating a cooperative competitive classroom for
        mainstreaming.

*   Male, M., Johnson, R. Johnson, D., & Anderson, M. (1985). *Cooperative Learning and Computers: An Activity Guide for Teachers*. Minneapolis, MN: Cooperative Learning Project. 171 pp. (Cited below as Item 101.)

053.   Mangum, T. M. (1985). Social studies achievement and self-evaluation of performance in jigsaw and cooperative study homogeneous groups. *Dissertation Abstracts International, 46,* 3237A. (University Microfilms Order Number ADG86-00093. 8605)

     Investigated the effects of "the Jigsaw Model Group and the Cooperative Study Group on black high reading level sixth-grade students and their achievement on a social studies task."

*   Maring, G. H., Fruman, G. C., and Blum-Anderson, J. (1985). Five Cooperative learning strategies for mainstreamed youngsters in content area classrooms. *The Reading teacher, 39*(3), 310-317. (Cited below as Item 151.)

054.   Moskowitz, J. M., Malvin, J. H., Schaeffer, G. A., & Schaps, E. (1983). Evaluation of a cooperative learning strategy. *American Educational Research Journal, 20,* 687-696.

     Jigsaw, a cooperative learning strategy, "was evaluated for its effect on students' attitudes and behaviors with regard to themselves, peers, and school. Fifth- and sixth-grade teachers implemented Jigsaw for about two hours each week over a school year. Using a randomized invitation design, these teachers were compared with controls who were willing to be trained in Jigsaw had they been offered it. Few affective gains were found although participants in Jigsaw rated their classes as less competitive and sixth-graders rated their classes as more cooperative. Analyses of exemplary Jigsaw classes revealed similar results and also improved attendance. Results were discussed in terms of problems inherent in the strategy, and the generalizability of the findings."

*   Nattiv, A. (1986). The effects of cooperative learning instructional strategies on academic achievement among sixth grade social studies students. *Dissertation Abstracts International, 47,* 3651A.

(University Microfilms Order Number ADG86-29488 8704) (Cited below as Item 534.)

* Okebukola, P. A. (1985). The relative effectiveness of cooperative and competitive interaction techniques in strengthening students' performance in science classes. *Science Education, 69*(4), 501-509. (Cited below as Item 201.)

* Orlick, T. (1978). *Winning Through Cooperation: Competitive Insanity -- Cooperative Alternatives.* Washington, D. C.: Acropolis. 278 pp. (Cited below as Item 643.)

* Palmer, J. J. (1988). The electoral college: A jigsaw lesson. *Social Education, 52,* 306-307. (Cited below as Item 218.)

* Slavin, R. E. (1980). Student team learning: A manual for teachers. In S. Sharan, P. Hare, C. Webb, & R. Hertz-Lazarowitz (Eds.), *Cooperation in Education,* (pp. 82-135). Provo, UT: Brigham Young University. (Cited above as Item 016.)

* Slavin, R. E. (1981). Cooperative learning and desegregation. *Journal of Educational Equity and Leadership, 1*(3), 145-161. (Cited below as Item 434.)

* Slavin, R. E. (1982). *Cooperative learning: Student Teams.* Washington, D.C.: National Education Association. 32 pp. (Cited above as Item 017.)

* Slavin, R. E. (1986). Learning together. *American Educator: The Professional Journal of the American Federation of Teachers, 10,* 6-10. (Cited above as Item 018.)

* Slavin, R. E. (1986). *Student Team Learning: An Overview and Practical Guide.* Washington, D.C.: National Education Association. 56 pp. (Cited above as Item 019.)

* Slavin, R. E. (1986). *Using Student Team Learning.* Baltimore, MD: Center for Research on Elementary and Middle Schools, The Johns Hopkins University. 109 pp. (Cited above as Item 020.)

*   Slavin, R. E., & Hansell, S. (1983). Cooperative learning and intergroup relations: Contact theory in the classroom. In J. L. Epstein and N. Karweit's (Eds.), *Friends in school: Patterns of selection and influence in secondary schools*, (pp. 93-114) New York: Academic Press. (Cited above as Item 021.)

*   Slavin, R. E., & Karweit, N. L. (1981). Cognitive and affective outcomes of an intensive student team learning experience. *The Journal of Experimental Education, 50*, 29-35. (Cited above as Item 022.)

G. STUDENT TEAMS ACHIEVEMENT DIVISIONS (STAD)

* Allen, W. H., & VanSickle, R. L. (1984). Learning teams and low achievers. *Social Education. 48*, 60-64. (Cited below as Item 209.)

055. Bejarano, Y. (1987). A cooperative small-group methodology in the language classroom. *TESOL Quarterly, 21*, 483-504.

Discusses the results of a study designed to test the effects of cooperative learning techniques, including Discussion Groups and Student-Teams-Achievement Divisions (STAD), upon the achievement of students enrolled in English as a Foreign Language class. Results indicated that students involved in Discussion Groups and STAD treatments experienced greater overall improvement that students receiving traditional whole-class instruction and that students in the Discussion Group classes and the STAD classes experienced no significant difference in overall achievement. Concludes that "both small-group methods proved superior to the whole-class method on these scales, and the two group methods emerged as equally effective."

* Bohlmeyer, E. M., & Burke, J. P. (1987). Selecting cooperative learning techniques: A consultative strategy guide. *School Psychology Review, 16*, 36-49. (Cited below as Item 451.)

* Dittman, J. (1986). Join the winning circle. *Illinois Teacher of Home Economics, 30*, 46-49, 53. (Cited below as Item 277.)

* Graves, T. (1988). Review: Cooper, J. and Sherman, L. Cooperative Learning at the University Level. *The International Association for the Study of Cooperation in Education, 9*(3 and 4), 20-21. (Cited above as Item 004.)

* Gunter, M. A., Estes, T. H., & Schwab, J. H. (1990). *Instruction: A Models Approach*. Needham Heights, MA: Allyn & Bacon. 352 pp. (Cited above as Item 005.)

*   Hansell, S., & Slavin, R.E. (1981). Cooperative learning and the
       structure of interracial friendships. *Sociology of Education*,
       54(2), 98-106.   (Cited below as Item 390.)

*   Hawley, W. D. (1982). Effective educational strategies for
       desegregated schools. *Peabody Journal of Education*, *59*, 209-
       233. (Cited below as Item 392).

*   Hawley, W. D., Rosenholtz, S. J., Goodstein, H., & Hasselbring, T.
       (1984). Good "effective teaching" schools: What research says
       about improving student achievement. *Peabody Journal of
       Education*, *61*, 15-52. (Cited below as Item 468.)

*   Hollifield, J. H. (1984, May). Student team learning. *Middle
       School Journal*, *15*, 6-7. (Cited above as Item 006.)

*   Judge, J. (1978). Student team learning. *American Education*, *4*,
       28-32. Cited below as Item 079.)

*   Kagan, S. (1980). Cooperation -- Competition, culture, and
       structural bias in classrooms. In S. Sharan, P. Hare, C. D.
       Webb, & R. Hertz-Lazarowitz (Eds.), *Cooperation in
       Education*, (pp. 197-211). Provo, UT: Brigham Young
       University Press. (Cited below as Item 397.)

*   Kelly, P., Hall, M. P., & Small, R.C., Jr. (1984). Composition
       through the team approach. *English Journal*, *73*(5), 71-74.
       (Cited below as Item 124.)

*   Lehr, F. (1984). ERIC/RCS: Cooperative learning. *Journal of
       Reading*, *27*, 458-461. (Cited above as Item 013.)

*   Leighton, M. S. (1990). Cooperative learning. In J. M. Cooper's
       Classroom Teaching Skills, (pp. 307-335). Lexington, MA:
       D.C. Heath and Co. (Cited below as Item 478.)

*   Leming, J. S. (1985). Research on social studies curriculum and
       instruction: Interventions and outcomes in the socio-moral
       domain. In W. B. Stanley (Ed.) Review of Research in Social
       Studies Education. (Bulletin 75). Washington, D.C.: National
       Council for the Social Studies. (Cited below as Item 216.)

*   Madden, N. A., & Slavin, R. E. (1983). Effects of cooperative
         learning on the social acceptance of mainstreamed academically
         handicapped students. *The Journal of Special Education, 17*(2),
         171-182. (Cited below as Item 244.)

056.   Meekins, A. S. (1987). Effects of a student team learning technique
         on the academic progress and social acceptance of academically
         handicapped elementary and mainstreamed students. *Dissertation
         Abstracts International, 49*, 421A. (University Microfilms Order
         Number ADG88-08624. 8809)

         Compared the effectiveness of a student team learning
         technique (STAD - Student Teams-Achievement Divisions) and a
         non-student team learning technique on the academic progress of
         academically handicapped elementary mainstreamed students;
         investigated the effects of STAD on the social acceptance of
         academically handicapped elementary mainstreamed students by
         their non-academically handicapped peers; and compared the
         effectiveness of STAD and a non-student team learning technique
         on the academic progress of non-academically handicapped
         elementary students.

*   Okebukola, P. A. (1985). The relative effectiveness of cooperative
         and competitive interaction techniques in strengthening students'
         performance in science classes. *Science Education, 69*(4), 501-
         509. (Cited below as Item 201.)

057.   Ross, J. A., & Raphael, D. (1990). Communication and problem
         solving achievement in cooperative learning groups. *Journal of
         Curriculum Studies, 22*(2), 149-164.

         Using a version of Student Teams-Achievement Divisions
         (STAD), researchers attempted to find out if what students talk
         about in cooperative groups is related to their learning of
         complex cognitive tasks. Results showed strong correlations
         between achievement and communication. Large group
         differences in communication patterns were found between the
         two classes used in the study. Students in the class which
         implemented a highly structured version of the cooperative
         learning program did not learn as much as did students in the
         class that rejected the task structure. Unknown and pre-existing
         differences among teachers and students affected the quality of

inferences to be made about results. An interesting article
highlighting teacher/researcher interactions. The teacher who
rejected the treatment did so in the interest of her students and
did, indeed, achieve better results. Authors hypothesized that, in
the case of the class which completed the highly structured
treatment, the students may have become bored with doing
similar activities repeatedly, and that the STAD design itself was
not at fault.

*   Scott, T. M. (1984). The effects of cooperative learning
        environments on relationships with peers, attitudes toward self
        and school, and achievement in spelling of ethnically diverse
        elementary students. *Dissertation Abstracts International, 46*,
        1503A. (University Microfilms Order Number ADG85-17629.
        8512) (Cited below as Item 140.)

*   Sharan, S., & Kuffell, P. (with collaboration of Brosh, T. & Pelleg,
        R.). (1984). *Cooperative Learning in the Classroom: Research
        in Desegregated Schools*. Hillsdale, NJ: Lawrence Erlbaum
        Associates, Publishers. 176 pp. [Foreword by Seymour
        Sarason.] (Cited below as Item 426.)

*   Sharan, S., Kuffell, P., Hertz-Lazarowitz, R., Bejarano, Y., Raviv,
        S., & Sharan, Y. (1985). Cooperative learning effects on ethnic
        relations and achievement in Israel: Junior-high-school
        classrooms. In R. Slavin, S. Sharan, S. Kagan, R. Hertz-
        Lazarowitz, C. Webb, & R. Schmuck (Eds.), *Learning to
        Cooperate, Cooperating to Learn*, (pp. 313-344). New York:
        Plenum Press. (Cited below as Item 427.)

*   Slavin, R. E. (1977). How student learning teams can integrate the
        desegregated classroom. *Integrated Education, 15*, 56-58. (Cited
        below as Item 430.)

058. Slavin, R. E. (1980). Effects of student teams and peer tutoring on
        academic achievement and time-on-task. *Journal of Experimental
        Education, 48*, 252-257.

        Experiment examined the separate effects on student
        achievement and time on-task of three components of the team
        learning technique, Student Teams-Achievement Division:
        cooperative rewards, group tasks, and a focused schedule of

instruction. The study involved 336 fourth and fifth grade students in fourteen classes who studied language mechanics for nine weeks in one of five treatments. "The results of a curriculum-specific achievement test and behavioral observation of time-on-task indicated significantly greater performance in cooperative than traditional reward structures, but significantly lower performance in group than individual task structures. The focused schedule was found to be an important component of STAD in increasing academic achievement."

* Slavin, R. E. (1980). Student team learning: A manual for teachers. In S. Sharan, P. Hare, C. Webb, & R. Hertz-Lazarowitz (Eds.), *Cooperation in Education*, (pp. 82-135). Provo, UT: Brigham Young University. (Cited above as Item 016.)

* Slavin, R. E. (1981). Cooperative learning and desegregation. *Journal of Educational Equity and Leadership, 1*(3), 145-161. (Cited below as Item 434.)

* Slavin, R. E. (1982). *Cooperative learning: Student Teams.* Washington, D.C.: National Education Association. 32 pp. (Cited above as Item 017.)

059. Slavin, R. E. (1986). Getting started with STAD. *American Educator: The Professional Journal of the American Federation of Teachers, 10*(2), 10-11.

Briefly discusses each step involved in using Student-Teams-Achievement Divisions (STAD). Steps explained are assigning students to teams, determining base scores, preparing resources, scheduling activities, teaching the material, monitoring team study, testing, computing improvement scores, computing team scores, recognizing team accomplishment, and assigning final grades.

* Slavin, R. E. (1986). Learning together. *American Educator: The Professional Journal of the American Federation of Teachers, 10*, 6-10. (Cited above as Item 018.)

* Slavin, R. E. (1986). *Student Team Learning: An Overview and Practical Guide.* Washington, D.C.: National Education Association. 56 pp. (Cited above as Item 019.)

*   Slavin, R. E. (1986). *Educational Psychology: Theory into Practice.*
       Englewood Cliffs, NJ: Prentice-Hall. 672 pp. (Cited below as
       Item 660.)

*   Slavin, R. E. (1986). *Using Student Team Learning.* Baltimore,
       MD: Center for Research on Elementary and Middle Schools,
       The Johns Hopkins University. 109 pp. (Cited above as Item
       020.)

*   Slavin, R. E., & Hansell, S. (1983). Cooperative learning and
       intergroup relations: Contact theory in the classroom. In J. L.
       Epstein and N. Karweit (Eds.), *Friends in school: Patterns of
       selection and influence in secondary schools,* (pp. 93-114). New
       York: Academic Press. (Cited above as Item 021.)

*   Slavin, R. E., & Karweit, N. L. (1981). Cognitive and affective
       outcomes of an intensive student team learning experience. *The
       Journal of Experimental Education, 50,* 29-35. (Cited above as
       Item 022.)

*   Slavin, R. E., & Madden, N. A. (1989). What works for students at
       risk: A research synthesis. *Educational Leadership, 46*(5), 4-13.
       (Cited below as Item 266.)

*   Valentino, V. R. (1988). A study of achievement, anxiety, and
       attitude toward mathematics in college algebra students using
       small-group interaction methods. *Dissertation Abstracts
       International, 50,* 379A. (University Microfilms Order number
       ADG89-05132, 8908) (Cited below as Item 180.)

*   Zahn, G. L., Kagan, S., & Widaman, K. F. (1986). Cooperative
       learning and classroom climate. *Journal of School Psychology,
       24,* 351-362. (Cited below as Item 339.)

H.   TEAM-ASSISTED INDIVIDUALIZATION (TAI)

*   Bryant, R. R. (1981). Effects of team-assisted individualization on the attitudes and achievement of third, fourth and fifth grade students on mathematics. University of Maryland. *Dissertation Abstracts International, 43*, 70A. (Cited below as Item 158.)

060.   Emley, W. P. (1986). The effectiveness of cooperative learning versus individualized instruction in a college level remedial mathematics course, with relation to attitudes towards mathematics and Myers-Briggs Personality Type. *Dissertation Abstracts International, 48*, 70A. (University Microfilms Order Number ADG87-09061 8707)

        Attempted to determine the effectiveness of Team-Assisted Individualization (TAI) versus Individualized Instruction in teaching remedial mathematics at the college level.

061.   Leinhardt, G., & Bickel, W. (1989). Instruction's the thing wherein to catch the mind that falls behind. In R. E. Slavin's (Ed.), *School and Classroom Organization*, (pp. 197-226). Hillsdale, NJ: Lawrence Erlbaum Associates, Publishers.

        Briefly mentions the cooperative learning strategy Team-Assisted Individualization (TAI) in their discussion of grouping (p. 213) and motivation (p. 217).

*   Madden, N. A., Slavin, R. E., Karweit, N. L., Livermon, B. J., & Dolan, L. (1988). *Success for All: Effects on Student Achievement, Retentions, and Special Education Referrals.* Baltimore, MD: Johns Hopkins University, Center for Research on Elementary and Middle Schools. (Cited below as Item 246.)

062.   Oishi, S. S. (1983). Effects of Team-Assisted individualization in mathematics on cross-race and cross-sex interactions of elementary school children (Johns Hopkins; Maryland). University of Maryland. *Dissertation Abstracts International, 44*, 3622A.

Discusses the findings of a sixteen-week experiment designed to examine the socializing effects of team-assisted individualized mathematics program (TAI) in and urban neighborhood school. Findings indicate that TAI has a positive effect upon the socialization of group participants and that it is "effective in improving inter-group ratings of classmates and for increasing reported interactions outside the classroom."

063.   Slavin, R. E. (1970). A theory of school and classroom organization. In R. E. Slavin (Ed.), *School and Classroom Organization*, (pp. 3-21). Hillsdale, NJ: Lawrence Erlbaum Associates, Publishers.

Under his discussion of individualized instruction, Slavin addresses the cooperative learning strategy Team-Assisted Individualization (TAI). (pp. 15-16).

*   Slavin, R. E. (1982). *Cooperative learning: Student Teams*. Washington, D.C.: National Education Association. 32 pp. (Cited above as Item 017.)

*   Slavin, R. E. (1984). *Team-assisted individualization: Cooperative learning and individualized instruction in the mainstreamed classroom*. Remedial and Special Education, 5, 3-42. (Cited below as Item 264.)

064.   Slavin, R. E. (1985). Team-Assisted Individualization: A cooperative learning solution for adaptive instruction in mathematics. In M. C. Wang & H. J. Walberg (Eds.)., *Adapting Instruction to Individual Differences*, (pp. 236-253). Berkeley, CA: McCutchan Publishing Corporation.

Provides a solid overview of the strategy entitled team-assisted individualization (TAI), and its role in regard to adaptive instruction. Briefly discusses the research on TAI, including that which is concerned with academic achievement, attitudes, race relations, and effects on academically handicapped students.

065.   Slavin, R. E. (1985). Team-Assisted Individualization: combining cooperative learning and individualized instruction in mathematics. In R. Slavin, S. Sharan, S. Kagan, R. Hertz-Lazarowits, C. Webb, & R. Schmuck (Eds.), *Learning to*

Cooperate, Cooperating to Learn, (pp. 177-209). New York: Plenum Press.

Addresses the principle features of Team-Assisted Individualization (TAI), describes a series of experiments involving TAI, and presents a summary of results.

*   Slavin, R. E. (1986). Learning together. *American Educator: The Professional Journal of the American Federation of Teachers, 10*, 6-10. (Cited above as Item 018.)

*   Slavin, R. E. (1986). *Student Team Learning: An Overview and Practical Guide*. Washington, D.C.: National Education Association. 56 pp. (Cited above as Item 019.)

*   Slavin, R. E. (1986). *Using Student Team Learning*. Baltimore, MD: Center for Research on Elementary and Middle Schools, The Johns Hopkins University. 109 pp. (Cited above as Item 020.)

066.   Slavin, R. E. (1987, November). Cooperative learning and individualized instruction. *Arithmetic Teacher, 35*, 14-16.

Details the Team-Assisted Individualization (TAI) program. TAI, a program designed primarily for grades 3-6 but also used at higher levels, incorporates the principles of cooperative learning, thus allowing students to "take care of checking and management, help one another with problems, and encourage one another to achieve." Discusses the principal elements of TAI: teams, placement tests, curriculum materials, team-study method, team scores and team recognition, teaching groups, tests and whole-class units. Cites findings from several studies on TAI and concludes that, in addition to increased achievement, "positive effects have been found on such varied outcomes as students' self-esteem in mathematics, liking of mathematics, acceptance of mainstreamed classmates, and race relations."

*   Slavin, R. E., & Karweit, N. L. (1985). Effects of whole class, ability grouped, and individualized instruction on mathematics achievement. *American Educational Research Journal, 22*, 351-367. (Cited below as Item 177.)

*   Slavin, R. E., & Madden, N. A. (1989). Effective classroom programs for students at risk. In Robert E. Slavin, N. L. Karweit, & N. A. Madden (Eds.), *Effective Programs for Students at Risk*, (pp. 23-51). Boston: Allyn and Bacon. (Cited below as Item 265.)

*   Slavin, R. E., & Madden, N. A. (1989). What works for students at risk: A research synthesis. *Educational Leadership, 46*(5), 4-13. (Cited below as Item 266.)

*   Slavin, R. E., Madden, N. A., & Karweit, N. L. (1989). Effective programs for students at risk: Conclusions for practice and policy. In R. Slavin, N. L. Karweit, & N. A. Madden (Eds.), *Effective programs for students at risk* (pp. 355-372). Boston: Allyn and Bacon. (Cited below as Item 267.)

067.   Slavin, R. E., Madden, N. A., & Stevens, R. J. (1989/1990). Cooperative learning models for the 3 r's. *Educational Leadership, 47*(4), 22-28.

      Provides a strong overview of Team-Assisted Individualization (e.g., principal features and research on TAI) and Cooperative Integrated Reading Composition (e.g., principal features of CIRC and research). Argues that these cooperative learning strategies can be "used successfully as the primary instructional method in reading, writing, and mathematics."

I. TEAMS GAMES TOURNAMENTS (TGT)

*   Allen, W. H., & VanSickle, R. L. (1984). Learning teams and low achievers. *Social Education, 48,* 60-64. (Cited below as Item 209.)

*   Bohlmeyer, E. M., & Burke, J. P. (1987). Selecting cooperative learning techniques: A consultative strategy guide. *School Psychology Review, 16,* 36-49. (Cited below as Item 451.)

068.   Dechow, R. R. (1983). A comparison of Teams-Games-Tournaments (TGT) and traditional classroom methods in high school biology. Virginia Polytechnic Institute and State University. *Dissertation Abstracts International, 44,* 3262A.

      Reports the findings of a study designed to answer the following questions: "Would high school students playing teams-games-tournaments have greater academic achievement in a high school biology course than students in classes using traditional classroom methods? Would high school students in TGT classes have greater retention of knowledge after a delayed period of time than those students in classes using traditional classroom methods? Would high school students in TGT have more positive attitudes toward the subject of biology than students in classes using traditional classroom methods? Would high school students like TGT better as a means for studying chapter material than traditional methods?" Findings indicate that TGT had no significant effect on biology achievement scores or on attitudes toward biology but that students in the experimental group did like TGT as a learning strategy.

*   DeVries, D. L., Edwards, K. J., & Slavin, R. E. (1978). Biracial learning teams and race relations in the classroom: Four field experiments using Teams-Games-Tournament. *Journal of Educational Psychology, 70*(3), 356-362. (Cited below as Item 385.)

069.   DeVries, D. L., & Mescon, I. T. (1975). *Teams-Games-Tournament: An effective task and reward structure in the*

elementary grades (Report No. 189). Baltimore: Center for
Social Organization of Schools, Johns Hopkins University.

070.   DeVries, D. L., Edwards, K. J., & Slavin, R. E. (1978). Biracial
         learning teams and race relations in the classroom: Four field
         experiments using Teams-Games-Tournament. Journal of
         Educational Psychology, *70*(3), 356-362.

              Researchers investigated the effects of Teams-Games-
         Tournament (TGT), an instructional strategy employing biracial
         learning teams and instructional games, on cross-racial friendship
         in integrated classes. Four experiments involving 558 students
         in grades 7-12, comparing TGT and control treatments were
         reviewed.
              Sociometric measures assessed TGT effects on the number
         of cross-racial friendship choices and the percentage of cross-
         racial choices over all choices made. Results indicated that TGT
         is an effective means of increasing cross-racial friendships in
         integrated classes, possibly because "race is less of a barrier to
         sociometric choice or as part of a general increase in the number
         of friends and workmates claimed by all students regardless of
         race...If misunderstanding and hostility between racial groups are
         a product of limited communication or friendship between
         members of different races, then TGT and related team techniques
         may -- by increasing the number of cross-race friendships --
         contribute to a diminution of racial tensions in schools."

071.   DeVries, D. L., Edwards, K. J., & Wells, E. H. (1974). *Teams-
         Games-Tournaments in social studies classrooms: Effects on
         academic achievement, student attitudes, cognitive beliefs, and
         classroom climate* (Report No. 173). Baltimore: Center for
         Social Organization of Schools, Johns Hopkins University.

072.   DeVries, D.L., Mescon, I.T., & Shackman, S.L. (1975). *Teams-
         Games-Tournament in the elementary classroom: A replication*
         (Report No. 190). Baltimore: Center for Social Organization of
         Schools, Johns Hopkins University.

073.   DeVries, D. L., Mescon, I. T., & Shackman, S. L. (1975). *Teams-
         Games-Tournament (TGT) effects on reading skills in elementary*

grades (Report 200). Baltimore: Center for Social Organization of Schools, Johns Hopkins University.

074.   DeVries, D. L., Slavin, R. E., Fennessey, G. M., Edwards, K. J., & Lombardo, M. M. (1980). *Teams-Games-Tournament: The Team Learning Approach*. New Jersey: Educational Technology Publications. 87 pp.

A practical resource for teachers who want to use Teams-Games-Tournament (TGT) in their classrooms. The first chapter discusses TGT, explains when TGT is most effective, and tells why the strategy has positive effects upon student achievement, student satisfaction, and cross-racial cooperation. The second chapter presents basic components of TGT. To aid in understanding the strategy, the authors compare TGT with traditional instructional methods. The third chapter presents the steps involved in using TGT. Also included is a day-by-day outline of class activities, including useful charts and diagrams to illustrate various components of TGT. The fourth chapter discusses observed effects of using TGT in classrooms. Chapters five through eight present additional resources and guides that the classroom teacher will find most helpful. This book is an excellent guide for anyone desiring to implement TGT as part of the curriculum.

*   Dittman, J. (1986). Join the winning circle. *Illinois Teacher of Home Economics*, *30*, 46-49, 53. (Cited below as Item 277.)

075.   Edwards, K. J., & DeVries, D. L. (1972). *Learning games and student teams: Their effects on student attitudes and achievement* (Report No. 147). Baltimore: Center for Social Organization of Schools, Johns Hopkins University.

076.   Edwards, K. J., & DeVries, D. L. (1975). *The effects of Teams-Games-Tournaments and two instructional variables on classroom process, student attitudes and student achievement* (Report No. 172). Baltimore: Center for Social Organization of Schools, Johns Hopkins University.

*   Gunter, M. A., Estes, T. H., & Schwab, J. H. (1990). *Instruction: A Models Approach*. Needham Heights, MA: Allyn & Bacon. 352 pp. (Cited above as Item 005.)

*   Hawley, W. D. (1982). Effective educational strategies for
         desegregated schools. *Peabody Journal of Education, 59,* 209-
         233. (Cited below as Item 392.)

*   Hawley, W. D., Rosenholtz, S. J., Goodstein, H., & Hasselbring, T.
         (1984). Good "effective teaching" schools: What research says
         about improving student achievement. *Peabody Journal of
         Education, 61,* 15-52. (Cited below as Item 468.)

*   Hollifield, J. H. (1984, May). Student team learning. *Middle
         School Journal, 15,* 6-7. (Cited above as Item 006.)

077.   Hulten, B. H., & DeVries, D. L. (1976). *Team competition and
         group practice: Effects on student achievement and attitudes*
         (Report 212). Baltimore: Center for Social Organization of
         Schools, Johns Hopkins University.

078.   Janke, R. (1977). *The Teams-Games-Tournament (TGT) method
         and the behavioral adjustments and academic achievement of
         emotionally impaired adolescents.* Paper presented at the Annual
         Convention of the American Educational Research Association,
         Toronto.

079.   Judge, J. (1978). Student team learning. *American Education, 4,*
         28-32.

              Describes an early large-scale study of three Student Team
         Learning strategies (Teams-Games-Tournaments, Student Teams
         Achievement Divisions, and Jigsaw) conducted by the Johns
         Hopkins University Center for Social Organization of Schools.
         Provides a succinct but solid overview of the various strategies
         and their purposes, the results (academic and social) of the
         students, and student reactions regarding their use of the
         strategies.

080.   Lang, N. A. (1983). The effects of a cooperative learning technique,
         Teams-Games-Tournament, on the academic achievement and
         attitude toward economics of college students enrolled in a
         Principles of Microeconomics course. University of Georgia.
         Dissertation Abstracts International, 44, 1517A.

Tested the effects of Teams-Games-Tournament (TGT) upon academic achievement and attitudes of college students toward economics. Findings revealed that TGT had no significant effect upon academic achievement of students in three ability groups upon their attitudes toward economics.

*   Lehr, F. (1984). ERIC/RCS: Cooperative learning. *Journal of Reading, 27*, 458-461. (Cited above as Item 013.)

*   Leighton, M. S. (1990). Cooperative learning. In J. M. Cooper's *Classroom Teaching Skills*, (pp. 307-335). Lexington, MA: D.C. Heath and Co. (Cited below as Item 478.)

*   Leming, J. S. (1985). Research on social studies curriculum and instruction: Interventions and outcomes in the socio-moral domain. In W. B. Stanley (Ed.) *Review of Research in Social Studies Education*. (Bulletin 75). Washington, D.C.: National Council for the Social Studies. (Cited below as Item 216.)

*   Male, M., Johnson, R., Johnson, D., & Anderson, M. (1985). *Cooperative Learning and Computers: An Activity Guide for Teachers*. Minneapolis, MN: Cooperative Learning Project. 171 pp. (Cited below as Item 101.)

081.   Merebah, S. A. A. (1987). Cooperative learning in science: A comparative study in Saudi Arabia. *Dissertation Abstracts International, 48*, 1892A. (University Microfilms Order Number ADG87-15228. 8710)

Compared the effects of the Teams-Games-Tournament (TGT) strategy and the "Traditional Teacher-Center Method" (TTC) used in Saudi Arabia's schools on student's achievement in science, attitudes, and social interaction in class.

082.   O'Neill, J. S., Jr. (1980). The effects of a teams-games-tournaments reward structure on the self-esteem and academic achievement of ninth grade social studies students. *Dissertation Abstracts International, 41*, 5053A. (University Microfilms Order Number ADG81-07937. 0000)

"Hypothesized that the use of student teams and the use of subject correlated game materials would increase academic achievement....[Also] projected that students working together, to gain a common objective, would result in a more positive social climate which would be reflected in higher self-esteem." No significant difference was found between experimental and control groups vis-a-vis academic achievement, but TGT did have a positive effect on the climate of the classroom.

083.   Oishi, S. S., Slavin, R. E., & Madden, N. A. (1983, April). *Effects of student teams and individualized instruction on cross-race and cross-sex friendships.* Paper presented at the annual meeting of the American Educational Research Association, Montreal.

*   Okebukola, P. A. (1985). The relative effectiveness of cooperative and competitive interaction techniques in strengthening students' performance in science classes. *Science Education, 69*(4), 501-509. (Cited below as Item 201.)

084.   Silver, H. F., Hanson, L. R. & Strong, R. W. (1986). *Teaching styles and strategies. Manual #2 in the dealing with diversity series.* Moorestown, NJ: Hanson, Silver, Strong & Associates, Inc. 197 pp.

Presents a discussion of the "Teams Games Tournament" cooperative learning strategy under its presentation of "involvement strategies" (pp. 153-164). Provides a brief overview of the purpose of the strategy, planning procedures, methods of implementation and evaluation, a sample tournament score sheet, and three sample lessons ("Recalling and Defining Language Terms," "Recalling Information About Matter," and "Recognizing Different Thought Patterns").

085.   Slavin, R. E. (1977). A student team approach to teaching adolescents with special emotional and behavioral needs. *Psychology in the Schools, 14*(1), 77-84.

Reports the findings of a study comparing Teams-Games-Tournament (TGT) with individualized instruction in a school for adolescents of normal intelligence experiencing academic and social problems. Testing procedures involved a behavioral observation scale recording student interaction and task behavior and a sociometric instrument. Findings indicate that TGT produces more positive results than individualized instruction in students' attraction to each other, frequency of peer tutoring, and amount of time on task. A five-month follow-up also showed that former TGT participants continued to interact positively with peers. Concludes that TGT is effective for use with special education students.

086.   Slavin, R.E. (1977). *Student learning teams and scores adjusted for past achievement: A summary of field experiments* (Report No. 227). Baltimore: Center for Social Organization of Schools, Johns Hopkins University.

*   Slavin, R. E. (1979). Integrating the desegregated classroom: Actions speak louder than words. *Educational Leadership, 36*(5), 322-324. (Cited below as Item 433.)

*   Slavin, R. E. (1980). Student team learning: A manual for teachers. In S. Sharan, P. Hare, C. Webb, & R. Hertz-Lazarowitz (Eds.), *Cooperation in Education*, (pp. 82-135). Provo, UT: Brigham Young University. (Cited above as Item 016.)

*   Slavin, R. E. (1981). Cooperative learning and desegregation. *Journal of Educational Equity and Leadership, 1*(3), 145-161. (Cited below as Item 434.)

*   Slavin, R. E. (1982). *Cooperative learning: Student Teams.* Washington, D.C.: National Education Association. 32 pp. (Cited above as Item 017.)

*   Slavin, R. E. (1986). Learning together. *American Educator: The Professional Journal of the American Federation of Teachers, 10,* 6-10. (Cited above as Item 018.)

*   Slavin, R. E. (1986). *Student Team Learning: An Overview and Practical Guide.* Washington, D.C.: National Education Association. 56 pp. (Cited above as Item 019.)

*   Slavin, R. E. (1986). *Using Student Team Learning.* Baltimore, MD: Center for Research on Elementary and Middle Schools, The Johns Hopkins University. 109 pp. (Cited above as Item 020.)

*   Slavin, R. E., & Hansell, S. (1983). Cooperative learning and
      intergroup relations: Contact theory in the classroom. In J. L.
      Epstein and N. Karweit's (Eds.), *Friends in school: Patterns of
      selection and influence in secondary schools*, (pp. 93-ll4). New
      York: Academic Press. (Cited above as Item 021.)

*   Slavin, R. E., & Karweit, N. L. (1981). Cognitive and affective
      outcomes of an intensive student team learning experience. *The
      Journal of Experimental Education, 50*, 29-35. (Cited above as
      Item 022.)

087. Wodarski, J. S. (1988). Teams-games-tournaments: Teaching
      adolescents about alcohol and driving. *Journal of Alcohol and
      Drug Education, 33*(3), 46-57.

      Presents a brief review of variables that influence adolescent
      drinking habits. Seeking alternatives to traditional approaches,
      the author presents an in-depth discussion of Teams-Games-
      Tournaments (TGT) by summarizing an alcohol education
      program tested in Georgia. Involved in the state-wide study were
      1365 students who received one of three treatments: TGT
      instruction, traditional instruction, or no instruction. Students
      receiving TGT instruction demonstrated significant increases in
      knowledge about alcohol. The comprehensive article concludes
      that TGT is an effective strategy through which to teach facts
      about alcohol and its effects upon driving behaviors.

088. Wodarski, J. S. (1987). Teaching Adolescents about Alcohol and
      Driving: A Two-Year Follow-up. *Journal of Drug Education,
      17*, (4), 327-344.

      The author used the "Teams, Games, Tournaments (TGT)"
      program as a method for teaching students about drinking and
      driving. Students in the control groups received regular
      classroom instruction or no instruction at all. The students in
      the TGT model reviewed three days of regular instruction,
      followed by a fourth day of preparing worksheets to study from,
      and a fifth day of team question and answer games which served
      to reinforce the week's learning. Two years later, students in the
      TGT group reported remembering and enjoying the learning
      experience, and reported maintaining the knowledge and attitudes
      formed during the instruction. Students in TGT scored

substantially better on a test of alcohol knowledge than either of
the other two groups.

089.   Wodarski, L. A., Adelson, C. L., Todd, M. T., & Wodarski, J. S.
        (1980). Teaching nutrition by Teams-Games-Tournaments.
        Journal of Nutrition Education, 12(2), 61-65.

        Two Teams-Games-Tournament units were developed to test
        the effect of cooperative learning on the teaching of nutrition.
        The unit for elementary students and the unit for secondary
        students both provided a basic introduction to nutrition with
        comprehensive daily lesson plans focused on the application of
        nutrition concepts. Students at both levels were divided into four-
        member heterogeneous groups consisting of one high, two
        average, and one low achiever.
        Results of student responses to questionnaires indicated
        significant increases in nutrition knowledge for both element and
        high school students. Students also indicated that they enjoyed
        the TGT nutrition units. They felt they had learned a lot about
        nutrition and that this knowledge would influence future food
        choices.
        Teachers, in addition to students' improvement in knowledge
        of nutrition, felt students reinforced reading, math, spelling, and
        measurement skills. Some teachers felt middle and lower ability
        students benefited more than higher ability students. Higher
        ability students sometimes seemed frustrated when they received
        lower scores than they were used to.

*   Zahn, G. L., Kagan, S., & Widaman, K. F. (1986). Cooperative
        learning and classroom climate. *Journal of School Psychology,
        24*, 351-362. (Cited below as Item 339.)

Subject Areas

II. SUBJECT AREAS

A. COMPUTERS

090.   Anderson, M. A. (1990). *Partnerships: Developing Teamwork at the Computer*. Arlington, VA: Majo Press. 147 p.

Designed for teachers using computers. It is a cooperative approach to computer lessons for regular, mainstreamed, and special education students in elementary and junior high school. By using software and the included worksheets, and by following the steps outlined in a lesson, a teacher can facilitate the social growth and collaborative skills needed by children to work in groups.

*   Baird, W. E., and Koballa, T. R. (1988). Changes in pre-service elementary teachers' hypothesizing skills following group or individual study with computer simulations. *Science Education*, 72(2), 209-223. (Cited below as Item 448.)

091.   Barlocher, F. (1987). Selfishness and cooperation. *The American Biology Teacher*, 49, 31-33.

Argues that cooperative activities are successful because participants must be accountable to the group. Describes computer games based upon competition vs. cooperation and honesty vs. dishonesty. Indicates that the same principles are applicable to classroom situations, resulting in positive experiences for each partner.

092.   Bennett, R. (1986). *Sentence Building with a Macintosh Microcomputer*. (ERIC Document Reproduction Service No. ED 274 162).

Study used small group activity at the microcomputer, emphasizing cooperative learning, to compare sentence-building skills of two groups of Native Americans.

*   Davidson, N. (Ed.). (1990). *Cooperative Learning in Mathematics:*
           Handbook for Teachers. New York, NY: Addison-Wesley
           Publishing Co. 399 pp. (Cited below as Item 163).

093.   Davies, D. (1988). Computer-supported co-operative learning
           systems: Interactive groups. *Programmed Learning and*
           Educational Technology, 25, 205-215.

           Presents the view that learning is a group process and
           examines computer-assisted co-operative learning. "This paper,
           using a communication-centered analysis, attempts to clarify the
           nature of those difficulties and offers some techniques for the
           design of computer-supported co-operative learning
           environments."

094.   Devoe, M. W., Render, G. F., & Collins, J. R. (1979).
           Microtechnology processes and cooperative behavior of third
           grade children. *The Journal of Experimental Education, 47,* 296-
           301.

           Investigates four variations of a microtechnology process
           and its effect on the development of cooperative behavior in 96
           third grade children. Findings suggest that cooperative behavior
           can be significantly increased by use of microtechnology
           techniques. Describes the problems of the study, results, and
           discussion of three research questions that were posed as the
           focus of the study.

095.   Fazio, R. P., & Berenty, F. J. (1983). Everybody wins in group
           computing. *The Science Teacher, 50,* 56-58.

           Discusses a cooperative computer learning curriculum in
           earth science used in the Fairfax County Public Schools in
           Virginia. Development of the innovative curriculum became
           necessary when the high school received one computer to be used
           with twenty-five to thirty students. "The solution was to design
           science programs that required group investigation based on a
           shared goal, including criteria that would enable students to
           evaluate their work and a means of rewarding their cooperative
           effort."

096.   Johnson, D. W., & Johnson, R. T. (1985). Cooperative learning:
           One key to computer assisted learning. In L. Rathje (Ed.),

*Software selection, evaluation and organization and software
reviews.* Eugene, OR: University of Oregon, International
Council for Computers in Education. (ERIC Document
Reproduction Service No. ED 297 703).

Cooperative learning with computers promotes a number of
educational outcomes including: 1. More and better work; 2.
More successful problem solving; and 3. Higher performance on
factual recognition, application and problem-solving tasks. The
Johnsons note that the combination of cooperative learning and
computer assisted instruction has an especially positive impact
on female students attitudes toward computers. Cooperative
learning not only makes more effective use of a limited number
of computers, but actually enhances learning. Includes rules for
cooperative learning at the computer and descriptions of roles and
responsibilities of cooperative learning group members.

097.   Johnson, D. W., & Johnson, R. T. (1985). Cooperative learning:
        One key to computer assisted learning. *The Computing Teacher*,
        13(2), 11-13.

        Based upon the assumption that "the teaching of computers
        and the interpersonal interaction promoted by cooperative
        learning provides complimentary strengths." Offers practical
        cooperative learning activities for teachers to use in a computer
        course. Concludes with two sample lesson plans for use in
        elementary classrooms.

098.   Johnson, R. T., Johnson, D. W., & Stanne, M. B. (1985). Effects
        of cooperative, competitive, and individualistic goal structures on
        computer-assisted instruction. *Journal of Educational
        Psychology*, *77*(6), 668-677.

        The study compared the relative efficacy of computer-assisted
        cooperative, competitive, and individualistic learning in
        promoting high achievement, oral interaction among students,
        perceptions of status, and positive attitudes toward subject area
        and instructional methods. Seventy-three eighth-graders were
        randomly assigned to conditions stratified for sex and ability.
        Students in all experimental conditions completed the same
        computer-assisted instructional unit. The results indicated that
        computer-assisted cooperative instruction promotes greater
        quantity and quality of daily achievement, more successful

problem solving, and higher performance on factual recognition, application, and problem-solving test items than did the computer-assisted competitive or individualistic learning. The authors were particularly concerned that the competitive condition seemed to be detrimental to the achievement of girls. "If educators wish to promote girls' success in using computers and positive attitudes toward working with computers, computer-assisted cooperative learning situations should be emphasized."

099.   Johnson, R. T., Johnson, D. W., & Stanne, M. B. (1986). Comparison of computer-assisted cooperative, competitive, and individualistic learning. *American Educational Research Journal*, *23*, 382-392.

"The effects of computer-assisted cooperative, competitive, and individualistic instruction were compared on achievement, student-student interaction, and attitudes. Seventy-four eighth grade students were randomly assigned to conditions, stratifying for sex and ability. Computer-assisted instruction promoted greater quantity and quality of daily achievement, more successful problem solving, more task-related student-student interaction, and increased perceived status of female students.

100.   MacGregor, S. K. (1988). Structured walk-through. *The Computing Teacher*, *15*(9), 7-10.

Describes the results of a project designed to improve students' programming practice. "The method is a variation of a program development procedure known as the structured walk-through (SWT). The method differs from traditional approaches in that it provides specific coding and design milestones and requires collaboration among students. The outcomes of the project were positive: Students' programming performance and attitude toward programming improved." Provides a strong research base for using a collaborative learning environment. "A collaborative learning environment may serve several purposes including the facilitation of cooperative learning skills, maximizing use of limited equipment, and reducing the demands placed on the teacher to answer questions." Stresses that cooperative learning promotes "more and better work, more successful problem solving, and higher performance on factual recognition, applications, and problem solving tasks." Points out that in a cooperative situation, students must have a clearly

defined cooperative goal structure to maximize achievement.
Concludes by addressing some of the major concerns of teachers
who implement cooperative learning strategies.

101.   Male, M., Johnson, R. Johnson, D., & Anderson, M. (1985).
        *Cooperative Learning and Computers: An Activity Guide for
        Teachers.* Minneapolis, MN: Cooperative Learning Project. 171
        pp.

        Includes the following chapters: An Introduction to
        Cooperative Learning and Computers; Essential Ingredients of
        Cooperative Computer Lessons; General Design Principles for
        Three Cooperative Learning Strategies (Learning Together,
        Jigsaw, and Teams-Games-Tournaments); Sample Lessons:
        Learning Together; Sample Lessons: Jigsaw; Sample Lessons:
        Teams-Games-Tournaments; Software Descriptions and
        Simplified Reference Cards; and Suggestions for Dividing
        Students into Teams. The appendices include: A lesson plan
        guide, sample team recognition certificates, sample observation
        forms, and sample scoring systems.

102.   Malouf, D. B., Wizer, D. R., Pilato, V. H., & Grogan, M. M.
        (1990). Computer-assisted instruction with small groups of
        mildly handicapped students. *Journal of Special Education,
        24*(1), 51-68.

        A compilation of two studies of mildly handicapped students
        using computer assisted instruction and cooperative learning
        groups.

103.   McDonald, P. (1989). *Cooperation at the Computer - A Handbook
        for Using Software with Cooperative Learning Groups.* Quincy,
        IL: Looking Glass Learning Products. 26 pp.

        A useful resource for teachers of all disciplines. Contains a
        wide variety of lesson plans, including suggestions for
        cooperative learning activities, effective establishment of groups,
        and follow-up activities.

104.   Oh, H. A. (1988). *The effects of individualistic, cooperative task
        and cooperative incentive structures on college student
        achievement in computer programming in BASIC.* Illinois State
        University. *Dissertation Abstracts International, 49,* 1688A.

Reports that task structure and incentive structure are basic components of cooperative learning strategies. Compares these two structures with each other "as well as with individualistic structure in terms of their effectiveness on students achievement" in BASIC programming. Found no significant differences in student achievement among the three groups.

105.   Rathje, L. (Ed.). (1985). *Software selection, evaluation and organization and software reviews.* Eugene, OR: University of Oregon, International Council for Computers in Education. (ERIC Document Reproduction Service No. ED 297 703).

Collection of reprints from the *Computing Teacher.* Contains eleven articles on the selection, evaluation, and organization of software published between August 1983 and March 1986, as well as more than twenty reviews of Software packages published between December 1982 and June 1986. Each review includes the name of the software program, the name of the reviewer and producer, target audience, hardware requirements, and cost. "Cooperative Learning: One Key to Computer Assisted Learning" written by Johnson & Johnson explains how cooperative learning with computers promotes a number of positive educational outcomes.

106.   Reglin, G. L. (1990). The effects of individualized and cooperative computer assisted instruction of mathematics achievement and mathematics anxiety for prospective teachers. *Journal of Research on Computing in Education, 22*(4), 404-412.

Study found that prospective minority teachers who worked cooperatively significantly outperformed those who worked individually in mathematics achievement. Math anxiety scores did not significantly increase or decrease for either group. Females, however, significantly increased their anxiety scores.

107.   Sengends, A. B. K. (1987). The effects of computer-assisted cooperative learning on the science achievement and attitudes of American Indian students. University of Kansas. *Dissertation Abstracts International, 49,* 1435A.

"The purpose of this study was to investigate the effects of Computer-Assisted cooperative learning on the science achievement and retention, and attitudes of American Indian students. Sex-by-treatment interaction effects as well as correlations between achievement and attitudes were also investigated." Findings indicate that Computer-Assisted Individualistic Learning resulted in higher science achievement than Computer-Assisted Cooperative Learning. "For nurturing positive interpersonal attitudes and attitudes toward school, Computer-Assisted Cooperative Learning was better for males while Computer-Assisted Individualistic Learning was better for females."

108. Stannard, W. A. (1984). "Guess and check" problem solving strategy plus computer programming equals a tool to solve word problems. *School Science and Mathematics, 84*, 453-458.

To meet two basic goals of the National Council of Teachers of Mathematics (to teach problem solving and to utilize calculators and computers), the article recommends using cooperative teams to write computer programs. Included are sample problems and programs.

109. Underwood, G., & McCaffrey, M. (1990). Gender differences in a cooperative computer-based language task. *Educational Research, 32*(1), 44-49.

While mixed-gender groups were reported to be preferred by teachers over single-gender groups, girls tended to be dominated by boys in computer-based tasks. Measures of performance in this study using ten to eleven-year-old students showed single-gender pairs improved in comparison with individuals working alone, but mixed pairs did not. Informal observations indicate that "single sex pairs tended to share parts of the task and discuss possible solutions, whereas mixed gender pairs tended to separate the task components and work on each other's instructions." Authors recommend that cross-gender discussion and negotiation be encouraged if students work in mixed-gender pairs.

110. Webb, N. W. (1984). Microcomputer learning in small groups: Cognitive requirements and group processes. *Journal of Educational Psychology, 76*(6), 1076-1088.

"This study investigated the cognitive abilities, cognitive styles, and student demographic characteristics that predicted learning of computer programming in small groups; the group process variables that predicted learning of computer programming; and the student characteristics that related to group processes. Thirty-five students aged eleven and fourteen learned LOGO for one week in three-person groups that were homogeneous with respect to previous experiences with computers. Different profiles of abilities predicted different programming outcomes. Mathematics ability was the best predictor of knowledge of syntax, interpreting graphics programs, and generating relations programs; spatial ability was the best predictor of knowledge of basic commands; and a combination of spatial ability and field independence best predicted generating graphics programs." Five out of eleven group process variables were found to predict programming outcomes. Positively related to outcomes were 1. receiving explanations in response to errors, and 2. time at the keyboard. Negatively related process variables were 1. receiving explanations in response to questions; 2. receiving no explanation after an error; and 3. receiving no response to a question. The author discusses implications for group work with computers.

111.   Wilcox, R. E. (1988). Using CASE software to teach undergraduates systems analysis and design. *Technological Horizons in Education, 15,* 71-73.

Describes a college course designed for information systems students who utilize a Computer-Aided Software Engineering Course (CASE). Among the topics discussed are class assignments, cooperative learning activities, and student attitudes. With regard to cooperative activities, the author stated, "The quality level and thoroughness of each team's work was far above any project work in systems analysis that I had ever experienced."

112.   Yates, B. C., & Moursund, D. (1988). The computer and problem solving: How theory can support classroom practice. *The Computing Teacher, 16*(4), 12-16.

Focuses on the impact that using computers can have upon problem solving strategies. In a brief section on cooperative learning, the authors point out that small-group cooperative problem solving is much more effective than large-group activities that involve computers.

B. LANGUAGE ARTS

Reading and Composition

* Bernagozzi, T. (1988, February). The new cooperative learning. *Learning88*, pp. 38-43. (Cited below as Item 450.)

113. Dansereau, D. F. (1987). Transfer from cooperative to individual studying. *Journal of Reading, 30*(7), 614-619.

      The author compares two types of cooperative learning. In the first, the children read the same material and correct each other's summaries. In the second, the children learn different material and teach each other. He found that the second type was slightly better than the first in terms of academic achievement. He also found that the students learn study skills by watching others and that such skills carry over into individual studying. The author also video-taped students interacting in order to teach better cooperative skills. He advocates immediate shift to dyad in schools.

114. Davey, B. (1987). Team for success: Guided practice in study skills through cooperative research reports. *Journal of Reading, 30*(8), 701-705.

      The author discusses need for practice in study skills and the benefits of practicing in dyads and research teams. She gives steps in implementing such a program: topic selection, planning, researching, organizing, and writing. The author discusses how feedback from other team members and being able to observe others using study skills carry over into individual study skills.

115. Duin, A. H. (1984, May). *Implementing cooperative learning groups in the writing curriculum: What research shows and what you can do.* Paper presented at the Annual Meeting of the Minnesota Council of Teacher of English, Mankato, MN. (ERIC Document Reproduction Service No. ED 251 849).

In a paper presented at the Annual Meeting of the Minnesota
Council of Teachers of English, Duin reviewed the results of
over 800 studies of cooperative learning. She found that students
who studied in cooperative learning groups--as compared to
competitive or individualized learning--achieve more
academically, have more positive attitudes toward school, subject
areas, and teachers, are more positive about each other, regardless
of ability, race, or handicap, and are more effective
interpersonally. Students who learn cooperatively actively
discover knowledge and direct their own learning. Cooperative
learning strategies can help student writers practice invention
techniques, share writing, revise, edit, and discuss material.
Discusses the requirements for cooperative learning (group
interdependence and individual accountability) and explains their
implementation in the composition class. Appendices include
several activities adapted for group use.

116.   Duin, A. H. (1986). Implementing cooperative learning groups in
        the writing curriculum. *Journal of Teaching Writing, 5*, 315-
        323.

        Based upon the hypothesis that students who work
        cooperatively experience greater achievement than students who
        work competitively and individually, the article outlines
        cooperative learning activities designed to teach the writing
        process. Concludes by challenging writing instructors to
        incorporate cooperative learning activities in their curriculum as
        a means of achieving "better communication and better writing
        skills."

117.   Ediger, M. (1984). Grouping students in reading. *The Education
        Quarterly, 36*(4), 17-21.

        The article summarizes several grouping methods:
        homogeneous, interage, heterogeneous, programmed,
        individualized, and language experience. The author suggests
        that homogeneous grouping should remain flexible in order to
        allow for students who progress at a different rate than others in
        their initial group. Interage grouping stimulates actual societal
        relationships, where people of similar ability are not always of
        the same age. Heterogeneous grouping also allows for each
        group member to benefit from the others, but may also limit the
        leadership opportunities of slower learners. The other methods

mentioned are for individualized learning; the author expresses no preference.

*   Frew, T. W., & Wiggins, A. (1979). Teacher preparation and communication arts. *Childhood Education, 56,* 80-83. (Cited below as Item 148.)

118.   Glatthorn, A. A. (1973). Cooperate and create: Teaching writing through small groups. *English Journal, 62* (9), 1274-1275.

Explains use of scenarios to study and write poetry. A scenario involves a group of five students, each playing a different role: leader, sound and light specialist, director, writer, or reader. Students use music and poetry or prose read by the "reader," to establish a mood. Elements of the scenario guide students through a series of steps which help students write creative original poems. Scenarios are teacher-made, structured, but open-ended. Final "act" of the scenario involves performing the finished poem. Examples of scenarios are not included in the article.

119.   Graner, M. H. (1987). Revision workshops: An alternative to peer editing groups. *English Journal, 76* (3), 40-45.

Graner offers an effective alternative to peer editing to those English teachers who feel uncomfortable with its limitations -- including unskilled and uncritical editorial comments, lack of student preparation, and loss of classroom control. He argues that students improve their writing through analysis of other students' work, not necessarily by receiving feedback on their own work. On revision workshop days, Graner has students evaluate two themes from another class using a teacher-prepared checklist. He then leads a class discussion to determine consensus on each item.

When compared, peer editing students and revision workshop students both made significant gains from initial to final draft with no significant difference between the two. He emphasized that revision workshop is an effective technique in which teachers are not required to surrender classroom control.

120.   Greenbaum, L. A., and Schmerl, R. B. (1967). A team learning approach to freshman English. *College English, 29*(2), 135-152.

The authors conducted freshman English classes in which the students worked to produce a single monograph over the semester. They began with a single group topic; their paper was then edited by another group, added to if necessary, edited again by a third group, and prepared for publication by a fourth. As the semester progressed, students were placed in other groups as well, and given multiple tasks at various stages of the process. The course was designed to make the students comfortable with the writing process, expose them to the ideas of others, and to stimulate actual group writing projects in the professional world. The instructors note that the topic must be carefully chosen, and an efficiently run course can be costly.

121.   Hawkins, T. (1976). Group inquiry techniques for teaching writing. *College English, 37*(4), 637-646.

The author outlines three methods of group learning. The first, "The Parceled Classroom," divides the class into groups with a chair and a secretary. The secretary takes notes on discussion of readings and writing topics. The students agree on their essay topics with the chair making decisions in a stalemate. In "Peer Criticism," students' papers are discussed with and evaluated by peers and then teachers, and rewritten by the student. The "Task-Making" method involves assigning specific tasks to a group which must agree on and submit the solutions.

122.   Jacobson, J. M. (1990). Group vs. Individual Completion of a cloze passage. *Journal of Reading, 33* (4), 224-250.

The author conducted a study in which the graduate and undergraduate students completed a cloze passage first as individuals and then in a group. The cloze passage was taken from a journal and had 68 words deleted. Although the groups scored better than the individuals, the author found no major relationship between the group score and an individual score. She did find that the groups produced more responses, worked with larger parts of the text at one time, and were able to utilize every possible clue. The author suggests that college students who use cloze may be able to retain important ideas better.

123.   James, D. R. (1981). Peer teaching in the writing classroom. *English Journal, 70*(7), 48-50.

Explains the value of shifting the responsibility of learning how to write from the teacher to the student through peer evaluation. Offers a realistic solution to every writing teachers' problem -- too many papers to grade. Includes a bibliography for those interested in learning more about peer evaluation in writing.

*   Johnson, R. T., Johnson, D. W., & Holubec, E. J. (Eds.). (1987). *Structuring Cooperative Learning: Lesson Plans for Teachers 1987*. Edina, Minnesota: Interaction Book Company. 339 pp. (Cited above as Item 010.)

124.   Kelly, P., Hall, M. P., & Small, R. C., Jr. (1984). Composition through the team approach. *English Journal, 73*(5), 71-74.

Writing teachers used Slavin's Student Teams-Achievement Division (STAD) cooperative learning technique to improve composition. A step-by-step explanation is given for setting up a unit in composition using teams. When compared with other classes who did not use the STAD approach, yet who studied the same content and wrote the same papers, teachers found that STAD students improved their writing twice as often. In addition to improving writing skills, students and teachers both said they enjoyed class more. Teachers felt the team approach was no more difficult to manage than a traditional class once the routine was established.

125.   Larson, C. O., & Dansereau, D. F. (1986). Cooperative learning in dyads. *Journal of Reading, 29*, 516-520.

Discusses a dyad form of learning that encompasses certain (e.g., interdependence and role assignments) but not all components of cooperative learning for use in mastering academic information. A major weakness in this so-called cooperative learning lesson is that it does not include individual or group accountability.

*   Madden, N. A., Slavin, R. E., & Stevens, R. J. (1986). *Cooperative Integrated Reading and Composition: Teacher's Manual*. Baltimore, MD: Johns Hopkins University Center for Research on Elementary and Middle Schools. (Cited above as Item 025.)

126.   Madden, N. A., Stevens, R. J., & Slavin, R. E. (1986, November).
        *Reading instruction in the mainstream: A cooperative learning
        approach.* (Report No. 5). Baltimore, MD: Center for Research
        on Elementary and Middle Schools, Johns Hopkins University.
        47 pp.

127.   Madden, N. A., Stevens, R. J., & Slavin, R. E. (1986). *A
        comprehensive cooperative learning approach to elementary
        reading and writing: Effects on student achievement.* (Report No.
        2). Center for Research on Elementary and Middle Schools,
        Johns Hopkins University. 24 pp.

128.   Montague, M., & Tanner, M. L. (1987). Reading strategy groups
        for content area instruction. *Journal of Reading*, *30*(8), 716-723.

        The authors discuss ways to improve reading and
        understanding of material. A section discusses the use of
        cooperative learning groups organized around "preferred reading"
        strategies. Such methods include SQR3 (survey, question, read,
        react, review), DRTA (Directed Reading and Thinking Activity),
        and MULTIPASS (survey, size-up, and sort-out). They also
        discuss Slavin's cooperative methods and dyads, and importance
        of cooperative groups in allowing many ability levels to
        function in one classroom.

129.   Perrino, J. A. (1988). Utilize media and literature to promote
        research and cooperative skills. *Middle School Journal*, *20*(2),
        30-31.

        Discusses a research project for secondary level students that
        combines the use of literature, video technology, and elements of
        cooperative learning. Includes a lesson plan for a research project
        undertaken by eighth grade students. Emphasizes meeting the
        learning styles of different students, and assisting the students in
        acquiring both the academic content and the development of
        social skills.

130.   Radebaugh, M., and Kazemek, F. E. (1989). Cooperative learning
        in college reading and study skills class. *Journal of Reading*, *32*,
        414-418.

        A section discusses the use of cooperative learning groups
        organized around "preferred reading" strategies. The authors

assert that students often do not know the social aspects of
learning. In their college study skills groups, they have students
work together. Groups are permanent throughout the semester
and are a mixture of male and female, leader and followers, able
and less able students. They meet outside of class to work on
projects and study as well as work together in class. Groups
share information such as good places to study, and study for
exams together. Groups are assigned a project near the end of the
semester. The authors claim that the students benefit from the
multitude of sources other than the instructor and from the
positive feelings generated from working in a group.

131.   Rasinski, T. V. (1988). Caring and cooperation in the reading
        curriculum. *Reading Teacher*, *41*(7), 632-634.

        Rasinski argues for more cooperative learning amongst
        students. The current isolated structure of our classrooms
        reinforces very little interaction between students. Rasinski
        supports the contention that our society values social
        responsibility, cooperation and caring among people; however,
        these values are not supported nor are they taught in classroom
        communities.

132.   Stevens, R. J., Madden, N. A., Slavin, R. E., & Farnish, A. M.
        (1987). *Cooperative integrated reading and composition: Two
        field experiments*. (Report No. 10A). Baltimore, MD: Center for
        Research on Elementary and Middle Schools, Johns Hopkins
        University. 20 pp.

133.   Stevens, R. J., Madden, N. A., Slavin, R. E., & Farnish, A. M.
        (1987, March). *Cooperative integrated reading and composition:
        Two field experiments*. (Report No. 10). Baltimore, MD:
        Center for Research on Elementary and Middle Schools, Johns
        Hopkins University. 47 pp.

134.   Stevens, R. J., Madden, N. A., Slavin, R. E., & Farnish, A. M.
        (1989). *Cooperative Integrated Reading and Composition: A
        Brief Overview of the CIRC Program*. Baltimore: Center for
        Research on Elementary and Middle Level Schools, Johns
        Hopkins University. 47 pp.

        Discusses the following: Composition of teams, basal-
        related activities, partner reading, story grammar and story related

writing, word mastery list, word meaning, story retell, spelling, partner checking tests, direct instruction in reading comprehension, integrated language arts and writing, independent reading, and program evaluation. Concludes with lists of resources and materials available for implementing such a program.

135.   Stevens, R. J., Slavin, R. E., Farnish, A. M., & Madden, N. A. (1988, April). *The effects of cooperative learning and direct instruction in reading comprehension strategies on main idea identification.* Paper Presented at the annual convention of the American Educational Research Association, New Orleans.

136.   Williamson, R., & Osborne, D. C. (1988). *Using conceptional analysis in the classroom: a writing process approach.* (ERIC Document Reproduction Service No. ED 292 119).

        Focuses on the composing process to enhance conceptual analysis. Encourages the use of cooperative learning strategies, critical thinking skills, and interdisciplinary teaming. Students write "cases," stories which illustrate a concept without identifying the concept in the text. Does not emphasize cooperative learning, but explains a strategy for writing that will make use of cooperative learning techniques.

137.   Woo, K. J. (1987). Fostering cooperative learning in middle and secondary level classrooms. *Journal of Reading, 31*(1), 10-18.

        The author discusses the benefits of a cooperative classroom over a competitive classroom, including increased self-esteem and better feelings toward peers. Claims that only 7-20% of classrooms use some type of cooperative activity. Suggests several ways to implement cooperative activities in the classroom: group retellings, associational dialogue, dyadic learning, needs grouping through testing, the buddy system, cybernetic session (children move from station to station in groups), research grouping, tutorial grouping, random grouping, social grouping (children choose who to work with), team grouping, and base grouping.

*   Wooster, A. (1986). Social skills training and reading gain. *Educational Research, 28*(1), 68-71. (Cited below as Item 337.)

Spelling

138.   Augustine, D. K., Gruber, K. D., & Hanson, L. R. (1989/1990).
         Cooperative spelling groups. *Educational Leadership, 47*(4), 6.

         A five-part procedure for using cooperative learning to teach
         spelling.

*   Frew, T. W., & Wiggins, A. (1979). Teacher preparation and
         communication arts. *Childhood Education, 56*, 80-83. (Cited
         below as Item 148.)

139.   Higgins, T. S., Jr. (1982). A comparison of two methods of
         practice on the spelling performance of learning disabled
         adolescents. Georgia State University. *Dissertation Abstracts
         International, 43*, 1926A.

         Investigated the effects of "peer tutoring and independent
         study on increasing the spelling performance of eight adolescents
         in a self-contained class for students with learning disabilities"
         and the effects "on spelling performance of serving as a tutor
         compared to serving as a tutee." Findings revealed that both peer
         tutoring and independent study were effective in increasing
         spelling performance and that students learned more as a tutor
         than as a tutee.

140.   Scott, T. M. (1984). The effects of cooperative learning
         environments on relationships with peers, attitudes toward self
         and school, and achievement in spelling of ethnically diverse
         elementary students. *Dissertation Abstracts International, 46*,
         1503A. (University Microfilms Order Number ADG85-17629.
         8512)

         Investigated the social and academic effects of Cooperative
         Learning Environments (CLEs). "Utilized the interdependent
         learning strategies of Student Teams-Achievement Divisions
         (STAD) to determine the effects of relationships with peers,
         attitudes toward self and school, and achievement in spelling."

141.   Shevin-Shapon, M. (1978). Cooperative instructional games:
        Alternatives to the spelling bee. *The Elementary School
        Journal*, 79(2), 81-87.

        The author suggests that cooperative games lessen the
        competitive emphasis in most instructional games which leads
        to self-consciousness or gloating, and provides for little actual
        learning. Cooperative games teach students to work together for
        a common goal or reward. A "sequence game," in which
        students receive a card with a cue and an instruction on it
        (thereby every member has a responsibility, but must work with
        the others for success), encourage the students to be attentive to
        each other while requiring specific tasks that contribute to the
        group being rewarded. The acquired skills foster more productive
        social interactions and develop practical collaborating skills.

142.   Turco, T. L., & Elliot, S. N. (1990). Acceptability and
        effectiveness of group contingencies for improving spelling
        achievement. *Journal of School Psychology*, 28(1), 27-37.

        Study using fifth graders to assess how individual or group
        task structures and interdependent, dependent, or no-incentive
        reward structure affected spelling achievement, peer-nominated
        social status, and treatment acceptability. While all spelling
        performances of all teams increased, no significant increases in
        weekly spelling achievement were found in any of the treatment
        teams as a result of either the incentive or the task structure. All
        teams except the dependent individual team rated their treatment
        significantly less acceptable at the posttreatment than they had at
        the pretreatment. In dependent individual teams, individuals
        studied alone, but scores over a certain percentage earned awards
        for the entire team.

143.   van Oudenhoven, J. P., van Berkum, G., Swen-Koopmans, T.
        (1987). Effect of cooperation and shared feedback on spelling
        achievement. *Journal of Educational Psychology*, 79(1), 92-94.

        Using third grade students, traditional spelling instruction
        was compared with two different forms of cooperative learning,
        one involving individual feedback and one with shared feedback.
        As rated by their teachers, both cooperative methods had positive
        effects on spelling achievement and on students' effort. Shared
        feedback did not produce at a significant level better spelling than

did individual feedback, but did show a slight increase. It is possible that shared feedback (letting all group members know each others' scores) alone is a very mild incentive for greater effort to learn.

Authors indicated that it took four weeks before the third graders were used to the new working method. They also thought that cooperative learning may offer a solution for big classes, in which it is difficult for teachers to give students individual attention.

English as a Second Language (ESL)

* Brubacher, M., Payne, R., and Pickett, K. (Eds.). (1990). *Perspectives on Small Group Learning*. Oakville, Ontario: Rubicon Publishing Co. (Cited below as Item 567.)

* Cohen, E. G. (1986). *Designing groupwork: Strategies for the heterogeneous classroom*. New York: Teachers College Press. 208 pp. (Cited below as Item 379.)

144. Ebel, C. W. (1985). The teacher as a coach in the ESL classroom. *NASSP Bulletin, 69*(479), 77-81.

Asserts that English as an second language (ESL) students learn English more easily through cooperative activities in which students take responsibility for the actions of their peers and in which the teacher serves as a facilitator. Summarizes the components of a successful ESL program in Virginia. Concludes that the "transition to the mainstream English classroom might even be easier, for the bilingual student will have already experienced contributing to the learning of others."

145. Gonzalez, M. A. (1986). Effects of cooperative and individual learning groups on the second language achievement of limited-English-proficient students (natural approach, peer interaction). Fordham University. *Dissertation Abstracts International, 47,* 2436.A

Reports the findings of a study that investigated the effects of cooperative and individual learning groups on the oral language acquisition of limited-English-proficient students in third grade through an English as a Second Language (ESL)

Module. Findings revealed that significant differences in
achievement and interpersonal relationships existed.

146.   Pierce, L.V. (Ed.). (1987). *Cooperative Learning: Integrating
Language and Content-Area Instruction.* Wheaton, MD: National
Clearinghouse for Bilingual Education. (ERIC Document
Reproduction Service No. 291 245).

A review of research on language minority students'
academic success preceeds the presentation of a bilingual,
content-based curriculum which uses cooperative learning
techniques. The Finding Out/Descubrimiento Approach (FO/D)
developed by Edward A. De Avila, S. E. Duncan, and Cecelia J.
Navarrete is described and its curriculum outlined. FO/D is an
integrated language skills program for oral and written
communication mastery in English and Spanish within a
cooperative learning environment used in second to fifth grades,
it is designed to involve students with diverse cultural, academic,
and linguistic backgrounds in learning by focussing on their
natural interest in how the world works. Introduction to social
aspects of cooperative learning and supervised content-learning
activities comprise the two phases of the program. Methods and
materials for program implementation are discussed and several
specific activities are explained in detail.

147.   Tikunoff, W. J., & Vazquez-Faria, J. A. (1982). Successful
instruction for bilingual schooling. *Peabody Journal of
Education, 59,* 234-271.

Deals with various components of effective classroom
instruction for students with no or limited English language
proficiency. The paper is organized into four major sections: an
overview of bilingual education, components of effective
instruction, effective teacher characteristics, and recommendations
for establishing policy to achieve effective instruction. One brief
section discusses the effectiveness of using cooperative learning
techniques in bilingual classrooms.

General Language Arts Skills

*   Bejarano, Y. (1987). A cooperative small-group methodology in the
language classroom. *TESOL Quarterly, 21,* 483-504. (Cited
above as Item 055.)

*   Bennett, R. (1986). *Sentence Building with a Macintosh Microcomputer*. (ERIC Document Reproduction Service No. ED 274 162). (Cited above as Item 092.)

*   Fehring, H. (1987). *Cooperative learning strategies applied in the language classroom*. (Reading Around Series No. 1). Adelaide, Australia: Australian Reading Association. (ERIC Document Reproduction Service No. ED 285122). (Cited below as Item 347.)

148.   Frew, T. W., & Wiggins, A. (1979). Teacher preparation and communication arts. *Childhood Education, 56*, 80-83.

    Describes a communication arts course designed to reach reading and language arts to atypical learners through the use of cooperative groups. A descriptive analysis of the course revealed that "the cooperative learning that has progressed within it has been positive, revealing that many aspects of communication arts were embellished and expanded by the teacher in the regular classroom." Gives examples of proven classroom activities used to teach creative dramatics, reading, listening, and spelling.

149.   Golub, J. (Chair) and the Committee on Classroom Practices: Busching, B. A., de Dwyer, C. G., Hornburger, J. M., Lalley, J. C., & Phelan, P. (1988). *Focus on collaborative learning. Classroom practices in teaching English, 1988*. (Stock No. 17538-015). Urbana, IL: National Council of Teachers of English. (ERIC Document Reproduction Service No. ED 297 338).

    Series of essays written by successful English teachers on the effective use of collaborative learning in the language arts classroom. Titles range from ""Group Presentations of Poetry" by Muriel Ridland to "Cooperative Learning in the Literature Classroom" by Rex Easley. Not all essays are pure cooperative learning, as several simply focus on group learning techniques.

*   Johnson, R. T., Johnson, D. W., & Holubec, E. J. (Eds.). (1987). *Structuring Cooperative Learning: Lesson Plans for Teachers 1987*. Edina, Minnesota: Interaction Book Company. 339 pp. (Cited above as Item 010.)

150.   Kincaid, G. L. (1972). Curriculum for the '70s: Cooperation is the
         name of the game. *English Journal, 61*(5), 723-727.

         Kincaid tries to prove through quoting such authors as Alvin
         Toffler (*Future Shock*), Paul Ehrlich (*Population Bomb* and *How
         To Be a Survivor*), and Ramsey Clark (*Crime in America*) that
         the switch from competitive learning to cooperation must be
         made. He argues that a successful future can only be assured by
         improving communication skills. Communication skills are
         best improved by cooperative learning, cooperative planning, and
         cooperative effort. He proposes that while human nature can't be
         changed, human behavior can be.

*   Madden, N. A., Slavin, R. E., & Stevens, R. J. (1986).
         *Cooperative Integrated Reading and Composition: Teacher's
         Manual.* Baltimore, MD: Johns Hopkins University Center for
         Research on Elementary and Middle Schools. (Cited above as
         Item 025.)

*   Male, M., & Anderson, M. (1990). *Fitting In: Cooperative
         Learning in the Mainstream Classroom.* Arlington, VA: Majo
         Press. 181 p. (Cited below as Item 247.)

151.   Maring, G. H., Fruman, G. C., & Blum-Anderson, J. (1985). Five
         cooperative learning strategies for mainstreamed youngsters in
         content area classrooms. *The Reading teacher, 39*(3), 310-317.

         The authors recommend placing students of different abilities
         together. Rules should be given for group behavior. They
         discuss several strategies for learning. In the Jigsaw method,
         students research topics and then teach other students. In "list-
         group" level, students group words that relate to each other. In
         this method there is no wrong answer. In "small group
         structured overview," groups select important terms from their
         textbooks. In "survey, predict, read, revise" method, groups
         predict what information might appear under certain headings.
         They then read the pages and revise their previous ideas. In
         "translation reading," the students produce a smaller version of
         their textbooks.

152.   Nelson, K. A. (1990). Gender Communication through Small
         Groups. *English Journal, 79*(2). pp. 58-61.

Students working in cooperative learning groups can learn to view gender issues as "thought-provoking and exciting" as they study various pieces of literature. Nelson recommends a variety of literary works appropriate to gender issues and suggests methods for adopting them to cooperative learning situations.

* Owens, L., & Barnes, J. (1982). The relationships between cooperative, competitive, and individualized learning preferences and students' perceptions of classroom learning atmosphere. American Educational Research Journal, 19, 182-200. (Cited below as Item 368.)

153. Riley, R., & Schaffer, E. (1975). Testing without tears. *English Journal*, *64*(3), 64-68.

Gives suggestions for conducting and evaluating a variety of group discussions. Uses many elements of cooperative learning to set up discussion groups. Explains the "four-stage rocket" discussion method developed by Charlotte Epstein, Temple University, and includes group evaluation forms from Gene Sanford and Albert Roark's book *Human Interaction in Education*. Briefly explains how a number of other activities can be used in place of traditional evaluation. Included are "four-stage rocket," student observers, feedback forms, sociometric diagrams, "where are we now?" questions, instant replay, fishbowl, roleplaying, gaming, debate and panel discussions, interviews, drawing and interpreting cartoons, brainstorming, orienteering, drama, sensitivity modules, and high school internship.

* Sharan, S., Kussell, P., Hertz-Lazarowitz, R., Bejarano, Y., Raviv, S., & Sharan, Y. (1985). Cooperative learning effects on ethnic relations and achievement in Israel: Junior-high-school classrooms. In R. Slavin, S. Sharan, S. Kagan, R. Hertz-Lazarowitz, C. Webb, & R. Schmuck (Eds.), *Learning to Cooperate, Cooperating to Learn*, (pp. 313-344). New York: Plenum Press. (Cited below as Item 427.)

* Shirley, O. L. B. (1988). The impact of multicultural education on the self-concept, racial attitude, and student achievement of black and white fifth and sixth graders. University of Mississippi. *Dissertation Abstracts International*, *49*, 1364A. (Cited below as Item 428.)

*   Slavin, R. E. (1980). Effects of student teams and peer tutoring on
         academic achievement and time-on-task. *Journal of Experimental
         Education, 48*, 252-257. (Cited above as Item 058.)

154.   Uttero, D. A. (1988) Activating comprehension through cooperative
         learning. *The Reading Teacher, 41*(4), 390-394.

         The author presents several methods for implementing
         cooperative learning techniques in the classroom. She discusses
         three phases. In connection, the first phase, the students work in
         small groups, brainstorming, categorizing, and comparing and
         contrasting. In the second phase, students read independently,
         answer questions, outline and paraphrase. In the follow-up
         phase, they prepare to take test using summarization and
         mnemonic strategies. The author discusses the benefits of this
         approach. It helps evaluate progress during the learning stage
         and promotes a positive attitude.

C. MATHEMATICS

155.   Artzt, A. (1979). Student teams in mathematics class. *Mathematics Teacher, 72*, 505-508.

A second grade mathematics teacher discusses her use of cooperative learning groups. Included are suggestions about grouping procedures and evaluating individual and group achievement. Concludes with a list of conditions that support maximum student achievement.

156.   Behounek, K. J., Rosenbaum, L. J., Brown, L., & Burcalow, J. V. (1988). Our class has twenty-five teachers. *Arithmetic Teacher, 36*(4), 10-13.

Distinguishes between cooperative groups and ability-based groups. Offers suggestions for setting up cooperative groups in the elementary classroom. Gives examples to show why cooperative learning is effective in a mathematics classroom. Lists benefits of cooperative learning and stresses that "when we set up cooperative teams, each child becomes a teacher, helping to monitor and keep others on task."

157.   Brophy, J. (1986). Teaching and learning mathematics: Where research should be going. *Journal for Research in Mathematic Education, 17*, 323-346.

Points out "several lines of research on teaching that have not been conducted with a specific interest in mathematics instruction." Among the numerous topics discussed is cooperative learning. "It remains to be seen whether they [the positive results] will hold up when the novelty wears off and the methods become institutionalized as an expected part of mathematics instruction in certain schools."

158.   Bryant, R. R. (1981). Effects of team-assisted individualization on the attitudes and achievement of third, fourth and fifth grade students on mathematics. University of Maryland. *Dissertation Abstracts International, 43*, 70A.

Discusses an eight-week study designed to evaluate the effects of Team-Assisted Individualization (TAI) that combined student team learning and individualized interaction and Rapid Progress Mathematics (RPM) upon the mathematical achievement of elementary school children. Students in the TAI experimental group revealed greater achievement than did students in the RPM groups. Both experimental groups experienced more achievement than did students in the control group.

159.   Cobb, P., Yackel, E., Wood, T., Wheatly, G., and Merckel, G. (1988). Research into Practice: Creating a Problem-Solving Atmosphere. *The Arithmetic Teacher*, *36*(1), 46-47.

The teachers involved divided their classrooms into small groups, allowing fifteen to twenty minutes for the groups to work, and then involved the whole class in a discussion of the solution(s) of each group. The teachers emphasize that cooperation among the group members, at times encouraged by the teacher, and explaining alternate solutions in class discussion, are essential for successfully creating a "problem-solving atmosphere."

160.   Cook, M. (1986). *Scavenger Hunts for Math*. Balboa Island, CA: Marcy Cook Math. 28 pp.

Contains a variety of mathematical activities for cooperative groups of two to four. Mathematical skills stressed are estimating, approximating, computing, and visualizing. These are designed for elementary and junior high students.

161.   Cook, M. (1987). *Talk It Over*. Balboa Island, CA: Marcy Cook Math.

A collection of 90 problems which are meant to involve a "pursuit" instead of routine. The problems are meant for upper elementary and junior high students and are designed for cooperative groups of two to four.

162.   Davidson, N. (1985). Small-group learning and teaching in mathematics: A selective review of the research. In R. Slavin, S. Sharan, S. Kagan, R. Hertz-Lazarowitz, C. Webb, & R. Schmuck (Eds.), *Learning to cooperate, cooperating to learn*, (pp. 177-209). New York: Plenum Press.

Addresses main effects of small groups methods; research on internal dynamics of cooperative learning; group testing, brainstorming, cooperative development, and recommendations for research.

163.   Davidson, N. (Ed.). (1990). *Cooperative Learning in Mathematics: Handbook for Teachers*. New York, NY: Addison-Wesley Publishing Co. 399 pp.

Major resource on cooperative learning in mathematics. Includes the following essays: "The Math Solution: Using Groups of Four" by Marilyn Burns; "Finding Out about Complex Instruction: Teaching Math and Science in Heterogeneous Classrooms" by Rachel A. Lotan and Joan Denton; "Student Team Learning and Mathematics" by Robert E. Slavin; "Using Cooperative Learning in Math" by David and Roger Johnson; "Cooperative Learning and Computers in the Elementary and Middle School Math Classroom" by Mary Male; "Cooperation in the Mathematics Classroom: A User's Manual" by Roberta L. Dees' "Small-Group Learning in the Secondary Mathematics Classroom" by Calvin D. Crabill; "Real Maths in Cooperative Groups in Secondary Education" by Jan Terwell; "Integrating Computers as Tools in Mathematics Curricula (Grades 9-13): Portraits of Group Interaction" by Charlene Sheets and M. Kathleen Heid. "Cooperative Learning Using a Small-Group Laboratory Approach" by Julian Weissglass; "The Small-Group Discovery Method in Secondary- and College-Level Mathematics" by Neil Davidson; and "Implementing Group Work: Issues for Teachers and Administrators" by Laurel Robertson, Nancy Graves, and Patricia Tuck.

*   DeVries, D. L., & Edwards, K. J. (1973). Learning games and student teams: Their effects on classroom process. *American Educational Research Journal, 10*, 307-318. (Cited below as Item 739.)

164.   Downie, D., Slesnick, T., & Stenmark, J. (1981). *Math for Girls and Other Problem Solvers*. Berkeley, CA: Lawrence Hall of Science. 108 pp.

A collection of over 73 activities designed to reduce "math anxiety" by offering a hands-on approach to problem solving and logical thinking. These activities were designed for small groups or classes and strive to create a cooperative atmosphere.

*   Edwards, K. J., DeVries, D. L., & Snyder, J. P. (1972). Games and teams: A winning combination. *Simulation and Games, 3*, 247-269. (Cited below as Item 740.)

*   Emley, W. P. (1986). The effectiveness of cooperative learning versus individualized instruction in a college level remedial mathematics course, with relation to attitudes towards mathematics and Myers-Briggs Personality Type. *Dissertation Abstracts International, 48*, 70A. (University Microfilms Order Number ADG87-09061 8707) (Cited above as Item 060.)

165. Fremont, H. (1977). Organizing a learning cooperative: Survival groups. *National Council of Teachers of Mathematics Yearbook*, 98-112.

      Offers practical suggestions for the establishment, use and evaluation of cooperative groups. Among topics discussed are student/teacher roles, group procedures and guidelines, testing, and evaluation. Concludes that "students can learn to assume responsibility, to be considerate, and to acquire mathematical concepts and skills more effectively. The beginning of a lifelong process of learning may be started."

166. Gilbert-Macmillan, K., & Leitz, S. J. (1986). Cooperative small groups: A method for teaching problem solving. *The Arithmetic Teacher, 33*(7), 9-11.

      The authors discuss methods for training a small group (ideally four children) to work well together. The goals of the group must be specified, the individual talents of each member must be made use of, the responsibilities of listening, encouraging and participating must be emphasized, and this training should proceed gradually as the children experience working together. They also point out that children must be allowed to talk through extra information in a problem in order to facilitate the development of problem solving skills.

167. Good, T. L., Reys, B. J., Grouws, D. A., & Mulryan, C. M. (Dec.1989/Jan 1990). Using work-groups in mathematics instruction. *Educational Leadership, 47*(4), 56-62.

A descriptive analysis of "how teachers who use work-groups actually employ these formats and to explore, in a preliminary way, the possible advantages and disadvantages of using these groups." Observed strengths include active learning, interesting mathematical activities, increased peer interaction, increased critical thinking exercises. Weaknesses included the lack of group dependency, lack of clarity in assigning student roles, student passivity, and lack of accountability. Includes practical lesson examples, including possible problem areas. "Obviously, the effectiveness of a work-group depends on students' mathematical knowledge and their experience in cooperative settings, as well as the teacher's instructional goals."

*   Gordon, B. A. (1985). Cooperative learning: A comparative study of attitude and achievement of two groups of grade seven mathematics classes. *Dissertation Abstracts International, 47,* 772A. (University Microfilms Order Number ADG86-05385. 8609) (Cited above as Item 039.)

*   Graybeal, S. S., & Stodolsky, S. S. (1985). Peer work groups in elementary schools. *American Journal of Education, 93,* 409-428. (Cited below as Item 214.)

168.   Johnson, D. W., & Johnson, R. T. (1989). Cooperative learning in mathematics education. In P. R. Trafton & A. P. Shulte (Eds.), *New Directions for Elementary School Mathematics* (pp. 234-245). Reston, VA: The National Council of Teachers of Mathematics.

A very broad overview that addresses the following: The nature of cooperative learning, a few basic concerns vis-a-vis cooperative learning and learning mathematics, basic elements of cooperative learning, and the teacher's role in implementing cooperative learning.

*   Johnson, L. C. (1985). The effects of the groups of four cooperative learning models on student problem-solving achievement in mathematics. *Dissertation Abstracts International, 47,* 403A (University Microfilms Order Number ADG86-07019. 8608). (Cited below as Item 517.)

*   Johnson, R. T., Johnson, D. W., & Holubec, E. J. (Eds.). (1987). *Structuring Cooperative Learning: Lesson Plans for Teachers*

1987. Edina, Minnesota: Interaction Book Company. 339 pp. (Cited above as Item 010.)

*   Lindow, J. A., Wilkinson, L. C., & Peterson, P. L. (1985). Antecedents and consequences of verbal disagreements during small-group learning. *Journal of Educational Psychology, 77*(6), 658-667. (Cited above as Item 032.)

*   Male, M., & Anderson, M. (1990). *Fitting In: Cooperative Learning in the Mainstream Classroom.* Arlington, VA: Majo Press. 181 p. (Cited below as Item 247.)

169.   *Mathematics Framework for California Public Schools, Kindergarten through Grade Twelve.* (1985). Sacramento, CA: California State Department of Education, Bureau of Publications. (ERIC Document Reproduction Service No. ED 269 250).

Gives directions for development of a mathematics program in California schools. The third chapter mentions cooperative learning, among other learning strategies, as a way to effectively deliver instruction to students.

170.   Noddings, N. (1989). Theoretical and Practical Concerns about Small Groups in Mathematics. *The Elementary School Journal, 89*(5), 607-625.

The author notes that most discussion of group learning is divided between those concerned with what is learned, and those concerned with how the material is learned. She suggests more theoretical goal descriptions by both groups to elicit productive discussion. The author also suggests research into the materials needed for "student-centered" (students developing social skills and problem-solving techniques on their own) vs. "teacher-centered" (students learning from the teacher and then working as a group) groups. The groups should remain flexible to allow students to advance or review as necessary. Grading procedures, the role of the teacher, curricula, and homogeneous vs. heterogeneous grouping all need to be further explored and evaluated.

*   Oishi, S. S. (1983). Effects of Team-Assisted individualization in mathematics on cross-race and cross-sex interactions of elementary school children (Johns Hopkins; Maryland).

University of Maryland. *Dissertation Abstracts International*, *44*, 3622A. (Cited above as Item 062.)

*   Owens, L., & Barnes, J. (1982). The relationships between cooperative, competitive, and individualized learning preferences and students' perceptions of classroom learning atmosphere. *American Educational Research Journal*, *19*, 182-200. (Cited below as Item 368.)

171.   Pagni, D. L. (1989). A television programming challenge: A cooperative group activity that uses mathematics. *Arithmetic Teacher*, *36*(5), 7-9.

Designed for junior high students to apply mathematical principles to the real world, the Television Programming Challenge consists of the following tasks: to conduct a survey of junior high school students to determine how much television they watch, the types of shows that they watch, and the types of advertisements that captured their attention; to prepare a report of the survey; and to prepare a suggested week of television shows. To complete the assignment, students were divided into cooperative groups. The article details the instruction and procedures for the project.

*   Pierce, L. V. (1987). *Cooperative Learning: Integrating Language and Content-Area Instruction. Teacher Resource Guide Series, Number 2*. Wheaton, MD: National Clearinghouse for Bilingual Education. (Cited below as Item 420.)

*   Rees, R. D. (1990). Station break: A mathematical game using cooperative learning and role playing. *Arithmetic Teacher*, *37*(8), 8-12. (Cited below as Item 755.)

*   Reglin, G.L. (1990). The effects of individualized and cooperative computer assisted instruction of mathematics achievement and mathematics anxiety for prospective teachers. *Journal of Research on Computing in Education*, *22*(4), 404-412. (Cited above as Item 106.)

172.   Rosenbaum, L. J., Behounek, K. J., Brown, L., & Burcalow, J. V. (1989). Step into problem solving with cooperative learning. *Arithmetic Teacher*, *36*(7), 7-11.

Offers suggestions about using small, cooperative groups to teach problem solving to primary-level students. States that "cooperative grouping can give pupils an opportunity to practice problem-solving skills in a low-risk environment." Gives practical classroom activities for use in cooperative groups and lists five tricks for success: Teach strategies, rehearse technique, involve everyone, cooperate to solve problems, keep groups small, and share ideas.

*   Salend, S. J., and Washin, B. (1988). Team-assisted individualization with handicapped adjudicated youth. *Exceptional Children*, *55*, 174-180. (Cited above as Item 259.)

*   Schielack, D. J. F. (1988). A cooperative learning laboratory approach in a mathematics course for prospective elementary teachers. Texas A & M University. *Dissertation Abstracts International*, *49*, 2672A. (Cited below as Item 494.)

173.   Sherman, L. W. (1986, November). *Cooperative learning strategies in secondary mathematics and science classes: Three comparative studies*. Papers presented at the Annual Meeting of the School Science and Mathematics Association, Lexington, KY.

Results of three cooperative learning studies are presented. Results of a general mathematics class study comparing cooperative learning with an individualistic goal structure found the cooperative learning group of students achieved significantly higher posttest scores. Results of the remedial mathematics study comparing cooperative learning with individualistic learning found students who used cooperative learning to have significantly higher posttest scores. No significant difference was found among posttest scores of two biology classes, one using a cooperative method and the other using an individually competitive structure.

*   Slavin, R. E. (1984). Team assisted individualization: Cooperative learning and individualized instruction in the mainstreamed classroom. *Remedial and Special Education*, *5*, 3-42. (Cited below as Item 264.)

174.   Slavin, R. E. (1985). Team-assisted individualization: A cooperative learning solution for adaptive instruction in mathematics. In M. C. Wang & H. J. Walberg (Eds.), *Adapting*

Instruction to Individual Differences, (pp. 236-253). Berkeley, CA: McCutchan Publishing Corporation.

Provides a solid overview of the strategy entitled team-assisted individualization (TAI), and its role in regard to adaptive instruction. Briefly discusses the research on TAI, including that which is concerned with academic achievement, attitudes, race relations, and effects on academically handicapped students.

175.   Slavin, R. E. (1987). Cooperative learning and individualized instruction. *Arithmetic Teacher*, *35*, 14-16.

Discusses Team-Assisted Individualization (TAI), which applies principles of cooperative learning to an individualized program. Examines team composition, placement tests, curriculum materials, team scores and recognition, and teaching groups. Concludes that "Research on TAI has amply justified our expectation that if the management, motivational, and direct instructional problems of individualized instruction can be solved, the approach could considerably improve students' mathematics achievement. In six carefully controlled studies in grades 3-6, TAI classes gained an average of twice as many grade equivalents as control classes on standardized tests. Results in mathematic concepts and applications have been less dramatic but are still positive as are results on such varied outcomes as students' self-esteem in mathematics, liking of mathematics, acceptance of mainstreamed classmates, and race relations."

176.   Slavin, R. E., & Karweit, N. L. (1984, Winter). Mastery learning and student teams: A factorial experiment in urban general mathematics classes. *American Educational Research Journal*, *21*, 725-736.

"The mathematics achievement effects on principal components of mastery learning and student team learning were evaluated in a year-long randomized experiment in urban ninth grade general mathematics classes. The components were formative tests, corrective instruction for nonmasters, summative tests (Mastery), and practice in four-member heterogeneous teams and teams rewards (Teams). A 2x2 (Mastery by Teams) factorial experiment compared Mastery, Teams, Teams + Mastery, and a control treatment. All methods used the same materials and schedule of teaching, worksheets, and test. A nested analysis of

covariance indicated significant achievement main effects for
Teams but not for Mastery. No Mastery by Teams or pretest by
treatment interactions were found."

177.   Slavin, R. E., & Karweit, N. L. (1985). Effects of whole class,
ability grouped, and individualized instruction on mathematics
achievement. *American Educational Research Journal, 22,* 351-
367.

One of the strategies (Team-Assisted Individualization)
examined in this study is a cooperative learning strategy.
"Achievement and attitudinal effects of three mathematics
instruction methods directed in varying degrees toward
accommodating diversity in student performance levels were
compared in two randomized field experiments. Treatments
included an individualized model, Team-Assisted Individualization
(TAI); an ability grouped model, Ability Grouped Active
Teaching (AGAT); a group-paced model, the Missouri
Mathematics Program (MMP); and in Experiment 2 only,
untreated Control classes. Analysis of Comprehensive Test of
Basic Skills (CTBS) Computation scores adjusted for pretests
indicated that in both experiments, TAI and AGAT exceeded
MMP. TAI, AGAT, and MMP also exceeded control. No effects
on CTBS Concepts and applications were found, and there were
no treatment by prior achievement interactions on either scale.
Effects on Liking of Math Class and Self-Concept in Math
generally favored TAI."

*   Slavin, R. E., Madden, N. A., & Stevens, R. J. (1989/1990).
Cooperative learning models for the 3 r's. *Educational
Leadership, 47*(4), 22-28. (Cited above as Item 067.)

*   Stannard, W. A. (1984). "Guess and check" problem solving
strategy plus computer programming equals a tool to solve word
problems. *School Science and Mathematics, 84,* 453-458.
(Cited above as Item 108.)

178.   Suydam, M. N. (1985, April). Research report: Individualized or
cooperative learning. *Arithmetic Teacher, 32,* 39.

Briefly describes the results of a study done by Robert E.
Slavin, Marshall B. Leary, and Nancy A. Wadden that found
"that individualization of mathematics instruction using

programmed materials with individual or cooperative learning teams can be effective and manageable by a single teacher without an aide."

179.   Taylor, R. (1989). The potential of small group mathematics instruction in grades four through six. *The Elementary School Journal, 89*(5), 633-643.

   The author advocates the use of small-group learning to develop problem solving skills and to increase the understanding of concepts through verbalization. Heterogeneous groups (based on ethnicity and gender) increase a sense of social equity. Teachers need to be instructed in group learning methods, and have a better understanding themselves of mathematical concepts and problem solving. In homogeneous (by ability) grouping, the author warns against setting expectations too low for slower groups, and leaving the student without productive activities while working with other groups. The author notes that teachers need more training in cooperative learning in order to implement it effectively.

180.   Valentino, V. R. (1988). A study of achievement, anxiety, and attitude toward mathematics in college algebra students using small-group interaction methods. *Dissertation Abstracts International, 50*, 379A. (University Microfilms Order number ADG89-05132, 8908)

   Compared the effects of cooperative learning (an adaption of Slavin's Student Teams Achievement Division strategy) and lecture/discussion on the levels of achievement, math anxiety, and attitude towards mathematics in two sections of college algebra. "The group instruction method produced significantly better results in the areas of successful completion of a mathematics course, math anxiety, and attitudes toward mathematics but produced no significant differences in the level of achievement."

181.   Webb, N. M. (1982). Group composition, group interaction, and achievement in cooperative small groups. *Journal of Educational Psychology, 74*(4), 475-484.

   Ninety-six junior high school students learned a 1-week unit on consumer mathematics in mixed-ability or uniform-ability groups. The variable related most strongly to achievement was asking a question and receiving no response; there was a negative relationship to achievement. Group interaction was predicted by group composition and student personality. The frequency of asking a question and receiving no response was higher among extroverted students and among uniform-ability groups.

182.   Webb, N. M. (1982). Peer interaction and learning in cooperative small groups. *Journal of Educational Psychology*, 74(5), 642-655.

Seventy-seven students in two junior high school mathematics classrooms learned a two-week unit on exponents and scientification in mixed-ability or uniform-ability groups. Three types of interactions were related to achievement: receiving no explanation in response to a question or error was negatively related; giving explanations and receiving explanations were positively related; achievement and interaction in the group were related to group composition, sex, ability, and personality. Medium-ability students achieved better in uniform-ability groups. Boys achieved better than girls. Introverted students outperformed extroverted students, but extroverted students received more explanations.

*   Webb, N. M. (1984). Stability of small group interaction and achievement over time. *Journal of Educational Psychology*, 76(2), 211-224. (Cited below as Item 550.)

183.   Weissglass, J. (1979). *Exploring Elementary Mathematics: A Small Group Approach for Teaching*. Santa Barbara, CA: Tri-Country Math Project. 289 pp.

A textbook which teaches teachers how to use laboratories effectively while teaching cooperative mathematics groups in elementary schools.

184.   Williams, M. S. (1988). The effects of cooperative team learning on student achievement and student attitude in the algebra classroom. University of Alabama. *Dissertation Abstracts International*, 49, 3611A.

Discusses the findings of a study that compared the effectiveness of cooperative team learning strategies with that of traditional instructional methods in increasing student achievement and in improving student attitudes in Algebra I classes. Results showed that students involved in STAD and TGT learning structures exhibited a significant increase in individual achievement but no change in attitudes.

D. SCIENCE

185.   Bonnstetter, R., & Pedersen, J. (1990). S/T/S for students. *Science Scope*
         13(4), 49.

         Presents an interesting, effective method for using cooperative
         controversy to teach science, technology, and societal issues. Written a
         conversation between a son and his mother, the article provides good
         reading for any teacher or parent interested in cooperative learning.

186.   Cline, M. (1990). Inventing in the classroom. *Science Scope,*
         13(4), 16-18.

         Points out that since "many of today's technological
         advancements are made by university-trained professionals
         working in cooperative teams, schools should prepare students to
         meet those challenges by promoting creativity and imagination
         in the classrooms." Offers helpful suggestions for
         interdisciplinary, cooperative activities.

187.   Crouch, N. R. (1990). Learning cells. *Science Scope, 13*(5), 9-10.

         Presents a lesson plan that includes information about
         materials, advance preparation, procedures, benefits, and limits
         designed to teach the concept of cells. A unique feature of the
         lesson is the use of cooperative groups to design model cells.

188.   Crowell, S. (1989). A new way of thinking: The challenge of the
         future. *Educational Leadership, 47*(4), 60-63.

         Noting that "science is forcing us to change our view of the
         world," Crowell examines the implications that has for citizens
         today and in the future. In doing so, he addresses "compatible
         educational practices," including cooperative learning and
         "complex instruction" (a variation of cooperative learning in
         which "groups are arranged to work through discovery activities
         with both individual and group outcomes expected"). He
         provides a brief overview of the methods involved with

cooperative learning and then succinctly discusses the efficacy of such methods.

*   Dechow, R. R. (1983). A comparison of Teams-Games-Tournaments (TGT) and traditional classroom methods in high school biology. Virginia Polytechnic Institute and State University. *Dissertation Abstracts International*, *44*, 3262A. (Cited above as Item 068.)

189.   Fazio, R. P., & Berenty, F. J. (1983). Everybody wins in group computing. *Science Teacher*, *50*, 56-58.

Suggests that cooperative learning projects are ideal when there is only one classroom computer available in a science class. They discuss a program which which correlates sedimentary rock layers through cross-sectional analysis. The article includes pedagogical strategies and academic objectives for this module program.

190.   Gardner, A. L., Mason, C. L., & Matyas, M. L. (1989). Equity, excellence, and 'just plain good teaching.' *The American Biology Teacher*, *51*, 72-77.

Stresses that excellence and equity in the science classroom do not exist independently; they are partners. Offers practical guidelines for selecting teaching strategies and materials that enhance both equity and excellence in the biology classroom. Points out that lecture and large-group discussion are used most frequently in classrooms but that "cooperative small group work is a more effective strategy both for achievement and motivation, especially for female students." Stresses that small-group activities give students opportunities to teach and to listen. Concludes that "by including small group work in the curriculum, students of both sexes and of all racial/ethnic groups have greater opportunities to participate, to gain hands-on skills and to increase their confidence in their science abilities."

191.   Hannigan, M. R. (1989/1990). Cooperative learning in elementary science. *Educational Leadership*, *47*(4), 25.

Discusses "Science for Life and Living: Integrating Science, Technology, and Health," a new science program for elementary students that emphasizes concrete experiences and is one in which cooperative learning is a central strategy.

192.   Hanshaw, L. G. (1982). Test Anxiety, Self Concept, and the Test Performance of Students Paired for Testing and the Same Students Working Alone. *Science Education, 66*(1), 15-24.

The subjects in this study were college students enrolled in Fundamentals of Science. They were paired randomly and assigned to take part of a test together. On the other part of the test, they worked alone. Some pairs worked together on part 1 of the test, and some worked together on part two. Pairs performed better than individuals but there was no difference in test anxiety. The author recommends that more research be done and that college students be allowed to work more in pairs.

193.   Jaffe, R., Cadeux, M., & Appel, G. (1982). *The Growing Classroom: Book 1 -- Becoming a Farmer; Book 2 -- Science; Book 3 -- Nutrition.* Capitola, CA: Life Lab Science Program. 419 pp.

Designed for cooperative group learning in grades 2-6 through the use of science. Students have a garden and participate in outdoor activities from which they learn cooperative group problem solving skills.

194.   Johnson, R. T., & Johnson, D. W. (1979). Cooperative learning, powerful science. *Science and Children, 17*(3), 26-27.

Answers basic questions about cooperative learning: 1. Does cooperation produce a more positive outcome in science classes than individualism or competition does? 2. What is cooperative learning? 3. How should teachers set up cooperative groups, including the assignment and monitoring of cooperative tests? Concludes that "Science, with its emphasis on experimenting and critical thinking, is an excellent place to start cooperative interaction and teach the skills which will make students more effective in working with each other."

195.   Johnson, R. T., & Johnson, D. W. (1986). Action research: Cooperative learning in the science classroom. *Science and Children, 24*(2), 31-32.

Emphasizes the need for studies testing the effectiveness of cooperative learning activities within science classrooms. Written for teachers who desire to conduct research, the article discusses three types of studies that can be done by classroom teachers: replication, refining, and extending. "Classroom research can replicate the classic studies, comparing cooperative learning with competitive or individualistic learning; it can be refinement research, which examines specific parts of the cooperative model; or it can be research designed to extend the theory." Concludes that teachers who do cooperative learning research will gain valuable experience and knowledge that will enhance their teaching skills.

*   Johnson, R. T., & Johnson, D. W. (1986). *Encouraging Student/Student Interaction. Research Matters...to the Science Teacher.* National Association for Research in Science Teaching. (ERIC Document Reproduction Service No. ED 266 960). (Cited below as Item 364.)

*   Johnson, R. T., Johnson, D.W., DeWeerdt, N., Lyons, V., & Zaidman, B. (1983). Integrating severely adaptively handicapped seventh-grade students into constructive relationships with nonhandicapped peers in science class. *American Journal of Mental Deficiency, 87*(6), 611-618. (Cited below as Item 234.)

*   Johnson, R. T., Johnson, D. W., & Holubec, E. J. (Eds.). (1987). *Structuring Cooperative Learning: Lesson Plans for Teachers 1987.* Edina, Minnesota: Interaction Book Company. 339 pp. (Cited above as Item 010.)

196.   Lazarowitz, R., Baird, H., Bowlden, V., & Hertz-Lazarowitz, R. (1982). *Academic achievements, learning environment, and self-esteem of high school students in biology taught in cooperative-investigative small groups.* Unpublished manuscript, The Technion, Haifa, Israel.

197.   Lazarowitz, R., Hertz, R. L., Baird, J. H., & Bowlden, V. (1988). Academic achievement and on-task behavior of high school biology students instructed in a cooperative small investigative group. *Science Education, 72* (4): 475-487.

A modified Jigsaw method combined with the investigative group approach was used to teach two biology units (cells and plants) to tenth graders. An individualized mastery training approach was used for the control group. Results showed that the experimental group displayed a larger amount of on-task behavior during and after the experiment than did the control groups. Results regarding academic achievement were inconclusive. The cooperative learning group showed higher achievement while studying the unit on cells. The control group showed higher achievement while studying the unit on plans. The cell unit was found to be more investigative in nature, requiring more inquiry and high level thinking skills. The plant unit required more information gathering and observation. Differences in the two units of study may have contributed to the conflicting results.

Authors concluded that while academic results were inconclusive, improvement in time-on-task behaviors caused by cooperative learning may lead to better attitudes toward science, less absenteeism, and higher student expectations.

*   Male, M., & Anderson, M. (1990). *Fitting In: Cooperative Learning in the Mainstream Classroom*. Arlington, VA: Majo Press. 181 p. (Cited below as Item 247.)

198.   Martens, M. L. (1990). Getting a grip on groups. *Science and Children*, 27(5), 18-19.

After a brief analysis of an unsuccessful cooperative science activity for second-graders, the author offers practical suggestions for making cooperative learning techniques effective. Included are brief sections on establishing productive groups, monitoring the groups, and setting realistic class rules. Concludes that cooperative learning does produce a variety of positive results and that it "has filled her [the second-grade teacher] classroom with a clear sense of purpose and greater respect among the students."

*   Merebah, S. A. A. (1987). Cooperative learning in science: A comparative study in Saudi Arabia. *Dissertation Abstracts International*, 48, 1892A. (University Microfilms Order Number ADG87-15228. 8710). (Cited above as Item 081.)

199.   Musgrave, A. J. (1986). Team participation in environmental biology. *American Biology Teacher*, 31, 429-434.

Gives step-by-step instructions for cooperative learning
activities found to be effective in environmental biology classes.
Explains the value of team learning and makes suggestions for
evaluating the work of cooperative groups.

200.   O'Donnell, A. M., Dansereau, D. F., Rocklin, T. R., Hythecker, V.
        I., Young, M. D., Hall, R. H., Skaggs, L. P., & Lambiotte, J.
        G. (1988). Promoting functional literacy through cooperative
        learning. *Journal of Reading Behavior*, *20*, 339-356.

Discusses the results of an experiment that examines the
efficacy of various cooperative learning strategies in facilitating
the enactment and recall of medical procedures. Consisting of
one hundred and twenty-three college students, the participants
were random assigned to groups in one of four experimental
conditions: No-strategy, baseline strategy, prompting strategy,
and planning strategy. Results indicate that the prompting group
had the best overall performance with the planning group scoring
best on recall procedures.

201.   Okebukola, P. A. (1985). The relative effectiveness of cooperative
        and competitive interaction techniques in strengthening students'
        performance in science classes. *Science Education*, *69*(4), 501-
        509.

Compared the effectiveness on students' performance in
science classes of two "pure" cooperative (Johnsons' technique
and jigsaw), two cooperative-competitive (Teams, Games,
Tournament and Student Teams-Achievement Division), and one
"pure" competitive learning technique (student has own set of
learning materials, studies independently, and competes for first,
second, and third place within the class).
Results showed that cooperative-competitive methods had
greater positive effects on student performance when compared to
"pure" cooperative and "pure" competitive methods. STAD and
TGT techniques also caused students to perform significantly
better on higher cognitive skills. Okebukola concluded that a
combination of cooperation and competition may be considered
to be the best method of instruction in science classes to increase
student achievement.

202.   Okebukola, P. A. (1986). Cooperative learning and students'
         attitudes to laboratory work. *School Science and Mathematics*,
         86, 582-590.

         Discusses the results of a study designed to test the effects of
         cooperative learning upon the attitudes of ninth-grade biology
         students toward laboratory work. Findings revealed that students
         in the experimental cooperative learning groups had significantly
         better attitudes toward laboratory activities than did students in
         the control groups. Concludes that "cooperative learning,
         featuring intergroup competition, is a potent way of assisting
         students in developing favorable attitudes toward laboratory
         work."

203.   Okebukola, P. A. (1986). Reducing anxiety in science classes: An
         experiment involving some models of class interaction.
         Educational Research, *28*(2), 146-149.

         Explained the effects of cooperative learning and indirect
         teacher interaction (involved praising and avoiding making
         criticisms) on the anxiety levels of science students. One
         hundred sixty-three ninth graders in Nigeria were randomly
         assigned to one of four groups: cooperative, indirect teacher,
         cooperative-indirect teacher, and control. Results showed no
         significant difference between pre- and posttests of control group.
         All three experimental groups showed significant differences.
         Indirect teacher interaction reduced anxiety more than cooperative
         learning did. Cooperative-indirect teacher interaction resulted in
         the greatest reduction of anxiety, possibly caused by a
         combination of the advantages of the other strategies.

204.   Okebukola, P. A. (1986). The influence of preferred learning styles
         on cooperative learning in science. *Science Education*, *70*(5),
         509-517.

         Rural and urban Nigerian ninth graders were compared to
         determine if preferred learning styles (cooperative or competitive)
         influenced degree of achievement in science. Rural students
         preferred cooperative work while urban students seemed to prefer
         competitive work, supporting the contention that economic-
         cultural factors do influence students preferences for cooperative
         or competitive work. Results showed that students who preferred
         cooperative work and who were made to work in a cooperative

learning setting achieved significantly better in biology than students who were "mis-matched." Results also showed that students did equally well in cooperative or competitive conditions as long as they were placed in a setting that "matched" their preference. Okebukola suggested that further studies of cooperative learning strategies be structured to allow for eco-cultural influences within various communities.

205.   Okebukola, P. A., & Ogunniyi, M. B. (1984). Cooperative, Competitive and Individualistic Science Laboratory Interaction Patterns-Effects on Students Achievement and Acquisition of Practice Skills. *Journal of Research in Science Education, 21*(9), 875-889.

Four schools for every method were used in this study. The teachers participating underwent training in whatever method they were assigned. The authors found that cooperative groups achieved more than mixed-ability competitive groups, but in the gaining of practical skills and abilities, competitive groups did the best. They conclude that the effectiveness of different types of groups depend on the type of activity to be performed.

*   Pierce, L. V. (1987). *Cooperative Learning: Integrating Language and Content-Area Instruction. Teacher Resource Guide Series, Number 2.* Wheaton, MD: National Clearinghouse for Bilingual Education.   (Cited below as Item 420.)

*   Prague, S. A. V. (1988). Identifying social skills important to junior high school science students working in cooperative groups. Texas A & M University. *Dissertation Abstracts International, 49,* 3285A. (Cited below as Item 325.)

206.   Sachse, T. P. (1989). Making science happen. *Educational Leadership, 47*(3), 18-21.

Discusses how cooperative learning strategies are outstanding for use with "constructivist teaching" and an ideal way to engage students in "interactive learning."

*   Sengends, A. B. K. (1987). The effects of computer-assisted cooperative learning on the science achievement and attitudes of American Indian students. University of Kansas. *Dissertation Abstracts International, 49,* 1435A. (Cited above as Item 107.)

*   Sherman, L. (1986, November). *Cooperative learning strategies in secondary mathematics and science classes: Three comparative studies.* Papers presented at the Annual Meeting of the School Science and Mathematics Association, Lexington, KY. (Cited above as Item 173.)

207.   Sherman, L. W. (1989). A comparative study of cooperative and competitive achievement in secondary biology classrooms: The group investigation model versus and individually competitive goal structure. *Journal of Research in Science Teaching, 26*(1), 55-64.

          This study was done in a mainly white middle class rural school. It explores the success of GI (Group Investigation). Over a 35 day period, the children participated in small groups, researching a topic. The children divided the work among themselves. Pre-tests showed that the experimental group was similar to the control group, taught by the traditional methods. The study found that both groups showed gains and that neither one was superior to the other. The author suggests that the way in which the study was carried out may have had bearing on the results. Not everyone in the cooperative group participated fully and the time in the school year may have had some effect.

*   Shirley, O. L. B. (1988). The impact of multicultural education on the self-concept, racial attitude, and student achievement of black and white fifth and sixth graders. University of Mississippi. *Dissertation Abstracts International, 49*, 1364A. (Cited below as Item 428.)

208.   Tjosvold, D., & Santamria, P. (1978). Effects of cooperation and teacher support on student attitudes toward decision making in the elementary science classroom. *Journal of Research in Science Education, 15*(5), 381-385.

          Four groups of fourth and fifth graders were used in this study. One group was cooperative with a supportive teacher. The second was cooperative with a non-supportive teacher. The third group was competitive with a supportive teacher. The final group was competitive with a non-supportive teacher. Supportive teachers told their class that they were capable of making a decision about what to study next. Non-supportive teachers told the students that they were not capable of making a good decision. Students rated their own decision making skills on how committed they were to their decision and their expectations on enjoying the decision making process. Supportive outranked nonsupportive. Cooperative outranked competitive in expectation of enjoyment but not in commitment to decision.

*   Watson, S. B. (1988). *Cooperative learning and group educational modules: Effects on cognitive achievement of high school biology students*. University Microfilms Order Number ADG89-07658. 8907. (Cited below as Item 548.)

E. SOCIAL STUDIES

209.   Allen, W. H., & VanSickle, R. L. (1984). Learning teams and low achievers. *Social Education, 48*, 60-64.

Discusses research on "the effects of student team learning on low-achieving social studies students' self-concepts and academic achievement" [as well as the effort] "to identify those effects in the context of classes composed primarily of low-achieving students." Includes discussion of their review of the research, procedures of the research (including sample, instruments, treatment conditions), data analysis, and conclusions. Their final conclusion is: "This inquiry provides grounds for generalizing the positive achievement effect on the team learning techniques, particularly Teams-Games-Tournament and Student-Achievement Divisions, to homogeneously grouped low-achieving classes in social studies."

210.   Arnstine, D., & Arnstine, B. (1987). Teaching democracy through participation: The crucial role of student interest. *Educational Forum, 51*, 377-392.

Using the analogy of a democratic government, the authors argue that student participation in the educational process should be required. Believes that group participation occurs because of common interests or need for social interaction. Concludes that the "classroom must be reconceived as a place where several learning groups cooperatively pursue a variety of activities in the pursuit of related yet distinctly different learning goals."

211.   Bump, E. (1989). Utilizing cooperative learning to teach social studies in the middle school. *Social Science Record, 26*(2), 32-36.

A social studies supervisor's insight as to why and how cooperative learning can be used in middle school social studies programs to attempt to meet the needs of "transescents" and to make the study of social studies more interesting.

212.   DeVries, D. L., Edwards, K. J., & Wells, E. H. (1974). *Teams-Games-Tournaments in social studies classrooms: Effects on academic achievement, student attitudes, cognitive beliefs, and classroom climate.* (Report No. 173). Baltimore, MD: Center for Social Organization of Schools, The Johns Hopkins University.

213.   Ferguson, P. (1988). Modernization in Meiji Japan: A jigsaw lesson. *Social Education, 51*, 393-394.

        Provides a step-by-step procedure for teaching a jigsaw lesson on modernization in Meiji, Japan. It also provides the actual information and directions needed by the students in order to complete the jigsaw exercise.

214.   Graybeal, S. S., & Stodolsky, S. S. (1985). Peer work groups in elementary schools. *American Journal of Education, 93*, 409-428.

        "This study investigated the use of peer work groups (PWGs) in fifth-grade math and social studies classrooms. Social studies PWGs were more frequent than math PWGs and involved a broader variety of student behaviors and cognitive levels. Classification according to a purposed PWG typology revealed that the majority of social studies groups was cooperative in both task and reward structures. Helping task structures, with individualistic reward structure, were more common in math. Competitive reward structures occurred only in math. For both subjects, student involvement was highest in cooperatively task-structured groups." Includes a discussion on the various types and features of cooperative and/or peer work groups.

*   Johnson, R. T., Johnson, D. W., & Holubec, E. J. (Eds.). (1987). *Structuring Cooperative Learning: Lesson Plans for Teachers 1987.* Edina, Minnesota: Interaction Book Company. 339 pp. (Cited above as Item 010.)

215.   Kobus, D. K. (1982). *The Developing Field of Global Education: A Review of the Literature.* 38 pp. (ERIC Document Reproduction Series No.227 037).

Definition, scope, and nature of global education are discussed in this review of developmental research. It is suggested that a certain age span is appropriate for teaching awareness of other notions and environmental research. Children between seven and twelve seem to be particularly open to learning about others and to developing patriotism without chauvinism. Research suggests the most effective teaching approach is an analysis of cultural differences within the context of universal needs and characteristics. Two relationships central to this review of the literature are a positive relationship between concept attainment and cooperative goal structures, and the occurrence of greater perspective-taking ability as a result of students engaging in cooperative learning activities. In addition to cooperative learning, classroom climate and teacher credibility appear to be important factors in developing positive attitudes toward global education.

216.   Leming, J. S. (1985). Research on social studies curriculum and instruction: Interventions and outcomes in the socio-moral domain. In W. B. Stanley (Ed.) *Review of Research in Social Studies Education.* (Bulletin 75). Washington, D.C.: National Council for the Social Studies.

Analyzes the research on a diverse number of approaches (including cooperative learning) in relation to socio-moral or values education. Describes the nature of cooperative learning, a number of key methods (e.g., Student Teams-Achievement Divisions, Teams-Games-Tournament, and Jigsaw I and II), describes the research findings of the effects of cooperative learning in general, and discusses three studies that have been conducted in social studies classes. Concludes that "Cooperative learning appears to be a promising method by which social studies teachers can simultaneously achieve both academic and socio-moral objectives. To date, the research has not examined whether the results achieved persist over time. Also, there has been little research conducted with high school students. Nevertheless, the findings are sufficiently promising to warrant future serious consideration by social studies teachers and researchers."

*   Little, D. C. (1986). An investigation of the effects of cooperative small-group instruction and the use of advanced organizers on the self-concept and social studies achievement of third-grade

students. The University of Alabama. *Dissertation Abstracts International*, *47*, 2872A. (Cited above as Item 051.)

217.   Lyman, L. K., & Foyle, H. C. (1988). *Cooperative learning: Experiencing the constitution in action.* Paper presented at the Rocky Mountain Regional Conference of the National Council for the Social Studies, Salt Lake City, UT. (ERIC Document Reproduction Service No. ED 293 791).

Ten basic steps for implementation of cooperative learning are identified.   Sample cooperative learning lesson plans include "Creating a Classroom Bill of Rights" for 4-6th graders and "The United States Constitution: Powers of Congress" for 7-12th graders. Encourages use of cooperative learning by social studies teachers because it motivates students and encourages social and academic interaction among students.

*   Male, M., & Anderson, M. (1990). *Fitting In: Cooperative Learning in the Mainstream Classroom.* Arlington, VA: Majo Press. 181 p. (Cited below as Item 247.)

*   Mangum, T. M. (1985). Social studies achievement and self-evaluation of performance in jigsaw and cooperative study homogeneous groups. *Dissertation Abstracts International*, *46*, 3237A. (University Microfilms Order Number ADG86-00093. 8605) (Cited above as Item 053.)

*   O'Neill, J. S., Jr. (1980). The effects of a teams-games-tournaments reward structure on the self-esteem and academic achievement of ninth grade social studies students. *Dissertation Abstracts International*, *41*, 5053A. (University Microfilms Order Number ADG81-07937. 0000) (Cited above as Item 082.)

218.   Palmer, J. J. (1988). The electoral college: A jigsaw lesson. *Social Education*, *52*, 306-307.

A jigsaw lesson for high school students. Addresses what the electoral college is and how it works.

F. STUDENTS WITH SPECIAL NEEDS

219. Anderson, M. A. (1985). Cooperative group tasks and their relationship to peer acceptance and cooperation. *Journal of Learning Disabilities, 18*(2), 83-86.

Discusses the results of a study designed to test the effects of cooperative learning activities upon peer acceptance and cooperation among learning-disabled boys. A sociogram was used to measure peer acceptance, and cooperation was measured by forced choice card tasks. Results indicated improvement in both peer acceptance and cooperation. Concludes that the use of cooperative learning activities may be helpful in promoting peer acceptance and cooperation among learning-disabled children.

* Anderson, M. (1990). *Partnerships: Developing Teamwork at the Computer*. Arlington, VA: Majo Press. 147 pp. (Cited above as Item 090.)

220. Armstrong, B., Johnson, D. W., & Balow, B. (1981). Effects of cooperative vs individualistic learning experiences on interpersonal attraction between learning-disabled and normal-progress elementary school students. *Contemporary Educational Psychology, 6*, 102-109.

The effects of cooperative and individualistic learning experiences were compared on 1. interpersonal attraction between on handicapped fifth- and sixth-grade elementary school students and learning-disabled peers and 2. achievement. Concludes that cooperative activities promote interpersonal attraction between students and that these activities also facilitate the learning of greater quantities of material without any loss of accuracy than do individualistic activities.

* Augustine, D. K., Gruber, K.D., & Hanson, L.R. (1989/1990). Cooperation Works! *Educational Leadership, 47*(4), 3. (Cited below as Item 557.)

221.   Bender, W. N. (1987). Learning characteristics suggestive of
       teaching strategies in secondary mainstream classes. *The High
       School Journal, 70*, 217-223.

       Under his discussion of "Social Behavior and Peer
       Relationships," Bender discusses how research by Johnson and
       Johnson "indicated that the co-operative learning condition
       resulted in much more cross-handicapped interaction."

222.   Bina, M. J. (1986). Social skills development through cooperative
       group learning strategies. *Education of the Visually Handicapped,
       18*(1), 27-40.

       Describes the use of cooperative learning strategies with
       visually handicapped (VH) students in order to improve
       socialization skills and integration with nonhandicapped peers.
       Looks at reasons for poor social skills of handicapped students:
       1. inadequate time to teach social skills; 2. overreliance on
       individualized or competitive learning; 2. social skills not
       assigned a high priority by teachers. Contains a brief overview
       of cooperative learning and various cooperative learning
       strategies, then reports how it has been used effectively with
       visually impaired students. Gives concrete and useful
       suggestions for implementing cooperative learning with
       handicapped students. Discusses potential problems in
       implementation with visually handicapped students and offers
       solutions.

*   Blau, B., & Raferty, J. (1970). Changes in friendship status as a
       function of reinforcement. *Child Development, 41*, 113-121.
       (Cited below as Item 288.)

223.   Bryan, T., Donahue, M., & Pearl, R. (1981). Learning disabled
       children's peer interactions during a small-group problem-solving
       task. *Learning Disability Quarterly, 4*(1), 13-23.

       The study investigated the behavior of learning disabled
       children in a group task. The LD students were found to become
       less involved in discussion, speak less critically of others, and
       were less defensive of their own choices. They were less
       "persuasive" overall, easily accepting the choices of others. The
       authors conclude that their lack of ability to persuade others is at
       least partially due to their "lack of assertiveness" and different

"communicative strategies," since the learning disabled students made suggestions similar to those of the other group members, and spoke (though irrelevant remarks were usually made) as frequently.

224. Carlson, H. L., Ellison, D., & Dietrich, J. E. (1984). *Servicing Low Achieving Pupils and Pupils with Learning Disabilities: A Comparison of Two Approaches.* 39 p. (ERIC Document Reproduction Service No. ED 283 341).

A process-consultation system was used as an alternative service delivery model for serving both low-achieving and learning disabled students. The effects on both students and teachers were studied with focus being on groups of pupils in an in-class team approach. Regular and special education teachers worked together with heterogeneous groups of students to help students learn social skills as they completed academic tasks. Seven teams of teachers were trained in teaming skills and cooperative learning to work with twenty-one learning disabled and twenty-four low-achieving elementary and secondary school students. Students in the experimental model made significant gains in reading, comprehension, math computation and math reasoning when compared to the control groups (taught in a traditional removal model). Students in the process-consultation model felt more satisfaction and felt that the work was less difficult. Teachers in the experimental model spent more time offering feedback to small groups, had more interactions with each other, and had better attitudes.

225. Cosden, M., Pearl, R. & Bryan, T. E. (1985). The effects of cooperative and individual goal structures on learning disabled and nondisabled students. *Exceptional Children, 52*(2), 103-114.

Subjects in this study worked with same-sex partners who had IQ's within 10 points. Some were paired Learning Disabled to Non-Learning Disabled. Others were paired LD to LD, and NLD to NLD. The scores of learning disabled students did not change. Differences in cooperative behavior according to gender was observed. Girls were more likely to help each other than boys were.

226. Cuban, L. (1989). At-risk students: What teachers and principals can do. *Educational Leadership,* 46(5), 29-32.

Under the subtitle "Options for Instruction," Cuban
discusses the point that "cooperative learning approaches that
target culturally different children have demonstrated an array of
positive outcomes including test scores."

*   Edwards, K. J., & DeVries, D. L. (1972). *Learning games and
       student teams: Their effects on student attitudes and achievement*
       (Report No. 147). Baltimore: Center for Social Organization of
       Schools, Johns Hopkins University. (Cited above as Item 075.)

*   Edwards, K. J., & DeVries, D. L. (1975). *The effects of Teams-
       Games-Tournaments and two instructional variables on
       classroom process, student attitudes and student achievement*
       (Report No. 172). Baltimore: Center for Social Organization of
       Schools, Johns Hopkins University. (Cited above as Item 076.)

227.   Guinagh, B. (1980). The social integration of handicapped children.
       Phi Delta Kappan, 62(1), 27-29.

Argues that integration of handicapped children into the
mainstream of schooling should not be left to chance, and
suggests that cooperative learning activities make social
integration more likely. Discusses research of Johnson and
Johnson and their associates, and Slavin and his associates, etc.

*   Harper, G., Sacca, K., & Mahedy, L. (1988). Classwide peer
       tutoring in a secondary resource room program for the mildly
       handicapped. *Journal of Research and Development in
       Education, 21*(3), 76-83. (Cited below as Item 688.)

*   Hooker, S. K. R. (1988). Cooperative learning with four gifted and
       talented students: A case study focusing on interpersonal skills.
       Dissertation Abstracts International, 50, 921A. (University
       Microfilms Order Number ADG89-07959. 8910) (Cited below as
       Item 302.)

*   Hulten, B. H., & DeVries, D. L. (1976). *Team competition and
       group practice: Effects on student achievement and attitudes*
       (Report 212). Baltimore: Center for Social Organization of
       Schools, Johns Hopkins University. (Cited above as Item 077.)

228. Jacobs, N. (1989). Nontraditional students: The new ecology of the classroom. *Educational Forum, 53*, 329-336.

> Discusses the problems found in an intergenerational classroom. Suggests that the best technique for resolving conflicts is cooperative and/or collaborative learning. Working in groups to achieve common goals, students of all ages can make appropriate life-related contributions.

* Janke, R. (1977). *The Teams-Games-Tournament (TGT) method and the behavioral adjustments and academic achievement of emotionally impaired adolescents.* Paper presented at the Annual Convention of the American Educational Research Association, Toronto. (Cited above as Item 078.)

229. Johnson, D.W. (1982). *Experiments to attain full participation of handicapped students in the regular classroom.* Final report. Minneapolis, MN: Minnesota University, Cooperative Learning Project. (ERIC Document Reproduction Service No. ED 245 514).

> Reprints of seventeen studies on approaches for involving handicapped student in regular classroom activities. The studies, carried out over a three-year period, included severely handicapped, hearing impaired, mildly retarded, and learning disabled students. Johnson examined the evidence on the efficacy of mainstreaming, emphasizing the role of competitive, cooperative, and individualistic learning on several types of interactions among handicapped and nonhandicapped students, including friendship, interpersonal attraction, performance, and achievement. Cooperative learning was found to be valuable in activities involving handicapped students in classroom activities and resulted in benefits for both handicapped and nonhandicapped students.

230. Johnson, D. W., & Johnson, R. T. (1981). The integration of the handicapped into the regular classroom: Effects of cooperative and individualistic instruction. *Contemporary Educational Psychology, 6*, 344-353.

> Details a study that compares the "effects of cooperative and individualist learning experience on interpersonal attraction between handicapped and nonhandicapped fourth-grade students.

Result indicated that cooperative learning experiences, compared with individualistic ones, promote more cross-handicapped interaction during both instructional and free-time situations and more interpersonal attraction between handicapped and nonhandicapped students." Concludes that cooperative learning activities are effective when handicapped students are mainstreamed into the regular classroom.

231.   Johnson, D. W., & Johnson, R. T. (1984). Building acceptance of differences between handicapped and nonhandicapped students: The effects of cooperative and individualistic instruction. *The Journal of Social Psychology, 122*, 257-267.

Several social psychological theories have suggested that when individuals of different ability levels join there will be conflict (e.g.., contact theory, frustration-aggression theory). This study examines the interaction of handicapped and nonhandicapped students placed in either cooperative or individualistic situations in order to test these theories. Forty-eight fourth graders from an inner city school served as subjects. Twelve of these students met the requirements for being either learning disabled or emotionally disturbed. There were 36 nonhandicapped students. Subjects were assigned to either a cooperative or individualistic learning situation stratifying for handicap condition, sex, social class, and ability level.

Students participating in the cooperative situation, in general, had more cross-handicap interactions. Handicapped and nonhandicapped students spent more time together, helped each other more, and played together more than students in individualistic conditions. This study contradicts previous theories claiming that students of different ability cannot get along. This study strongly supports the idea of mainstreaming. The study appears to answer the issue it chose to address. However, several methodological flaws limit the results. The measures taken on the subjects are not presented, described or validated. What was the measure of ability used? How were observations conducted and coded? Was reliability of coding obtained? One also wonders why the number of handicapped and nonhandicapped students was not the same.

*   Johnson, D. W., & Johnson, R. T. (1987). The high achieving student in cooperative learning groups. In R. T. Johnson, D. W. Johnson, & E. J. Holubec (Eds.), *Structuring Cooperative*

Learning: Lesson Plans for Teachers 1987 (pp. 3-11). Edina, MN: Interaction Book Company, 1987. (Cited above as Item 008.)

232.   Johnson, D. W., & Johnson, R. T. (1989). Cooperative learning: What special education teachers need to know. *Pointer, 33*(2), 5-10.

Paper seeks to identify what cooperative learning is and the basic factors within it that make cooperative learning effective. Also examines the importance of the teacher in constructing cooperative learning groups, various ways groups may be utilized, how the learning outcome is affected by cooperation, and teaching methods which can be used in placing handicapped and non-handicapped students in the same groups.

*   Johnson, D. W., Johnson, R. T., & Maruyama, G. (1983). Interdependence and interpersonal attraction among heterogeneous and homogeneous individuals: A theoretical formulation and a meta-analysis of the research. *Review of Educational Research, 53*(1), 5-54. (Cited below as Item 315.)

233.   Johnson, R. T., & Johnson, D. W. (1981). Building friendships between handicapped and nonhandicapped students: Effects of cooperative learning and individualistic learning. *American Educational Research Journal, 18*, 415-423.

"The effects of cooperative and individualistic learning experiences were compared on interpersonal attraction between handicapped and non-handicapped third-grade students. Forty students were assigned to conditions on a stratified random basis controlling for handicap, ability, sex, and peer popularity. Students participated in an instructional math unit for 25 minutes a day for 16 instructional days. Type of interaction within the instructional situation, interpersonal attraction, and frequency of interaction in a free-choice, postinstructional situation were measured. Three attitude scales were also given. The results indicate that cooperative learning experiences, compared with individualistic ones, promote more cross-handicapped interaction during instruction; promote interaction characterized by involving handicapped students in the learning activities, giving them assistance, and encouraging them to achieve; promote more cross-handicap friendships; and promote

more cross-handicap interaction during post instructional free-
time."

234.   Johnson, R. T., Johnson, D. W., DeWeerdt, N., Lyons, V. M., &
        Zaidman, B. (1983). Integrating severely adaptively handicapped
        seventh-grade students into constructive relationships with
        nonhandicapped peers in science class. *American Journal of
        Mental Deficiency, 87*(6), 611-618.

        Cooperative learning and individualistic learning modes were
        compared on interactions and relationships between severely
        handicapped and nonhandicapped seventh grade students. Forty-
        eight students were assigned to conditions controlling for
        handicap, sex, and ability level. Students worked together in
        learning groups for ten days studying a science unit on digestion.
        Nonhandicapped students were given strategies for interacting
        with the handicapped students.
              Results of the cooperative learning condition showed: 1.
        achievement of nonhandicapped students was unaffected; 2.
        handicapped students did not withdraw from interaction with
        nonhandicapped peers; 3. handicapped students participated in
        more tasks, management, and social interactions with
        nonhandicapped than in the individualistic condition; and 4.
        handicapped felt they "belonged" more.
              Authors recommend cooperative learning procedures be used
        when mainstreaming severely handicapped students, but warn
        that nonhandicapped students must be given instruction in
        strategies to effectively work with them and must give
        nonhandicapped students feedback as to how well they are
        working with handicapped students.

235.   Johnson, R. T., Johnson, D. W., & Rynders, J. (1981). Effect of
        cooperative, competitive, and individualistic experiences on self-
        esteem of handicapped and nonhandicapped students. *Journal of
        Psychology, 108*(1), 31-34.

        A study of self-esteem and personal acceptance by teachers of
        eighteen non-handicapped and twelve handicapped (trainable
        retarded) students. The students were studied in a mainstream
        junior high setting. It was found that those students in the
        cooperative condition had the highest self esteem and the most
        personal acceptance. It was also found that handicapped students
        had a higher reported self-esteem than non-handicapped.

236.　Johnson, R. T., Rynders, J., Johnson, D. W., Schmidt, B., & Haider, S. (1979). Interaction between handicapped and nonhandicapped teenagers as a function of situational goal structuring: Implications for mainstreaming. *American Educational Research Journal, 16*, 161-167.

"The effects of cooperative, individualistic, and laissez faire goal structures were compared on interpersonal interaction and attraction between nonhandicapped junior high school students and high trainable mentally retarded peers participating in six weekly sessions of a bowling class." The results indicate that considerably more positive interactions took place between the nonhandicapped and the handicapped students in the cooperative condition than in the individualistic or laissez faire conditions.

237.　Kopple, H. (February, 1976). Competition, cooperation, and individualization in Title I classes: Which is most effective? *Affective Education Newsletter*.

Discussion of the impact of various goal structures on student learning in the public schools of Philadelphia.

238.　Lew, M., Mesch, D., Johnson, D. W., & Johnson, R. T. (1986). Components of cooperative learning: Effects of collaborative skills and academic group contingencies on achievement and mainstreaming. *Contemporary Educational Psychology, 11*, 229-239.

"The effects of four conditions were investigated: (a) opportunity to interact with classmates, (b) positive goal interdependence, (c) positive goal interdependence with a collaborative-skills group contingency, and (d) positive goal interdependence with both contingencies." Findings "indicate that positive goal interdependence with both collaborative-skills and academic group contingencies promoted the most positive skills, and the highest achievement." Concludes that the first step in successful integration of isolated students into the educational process is to structure learning cooperatively.

239.　Lew, M., Mesch, D., Johnson, D. W., & Johnson, R. (1986). Positive interdependence, academic and collaborative-skills group

"The effects of (a) opportunity to interact with classmates, (b) positive goal interdependence, (c) positive goal and positive reward interdependence, and (d) positive goal and reward interdependence with an added contingency for the use of collaborative skills were investigated. The dependent measures were achievement, interpersonal attraction, and the voluntary use of collaborative skills by socially withdrawn and isolated students. Four socially isolated and withdrawn sixth-grade students (two male and two female) were studied in a reading class. The results indicate that both positive goal and reward interdependence are needed to maximize student achievement and the interpersonal attraction between socially withdrawn and nonhandicapped students. The specific reinforcement for engaging in collaborative skills was required to maximize the voluntary engagement in the skills by socially withdrawn and isolated students."

240.   Lloyd, J. W., Crowley, E. P., Kohler, F. W., & Strain, P. S. (1988). Redefining the applied research agenda: Cooperative learning, preferral, teacher consultation, and peer-mediated interventions. *Journal of Learning Disabilities, 21*(1), 43-51.

While regarding cooperative learning optimistically, the authors note that studies have not proven its effectiveness to be greater than that of other methods. They emphasize the need for research on the effectiveness of cooperative education on mainstreamed high-incidence handicapped students, its social consequences, and its comparison with other methods. They discuss "sharing reinforcement, non-academic peer management, academic peer-tutoring, and peer modeling" and stress the need for research into the effects of these methods on the peers, the effects over time, the behaviors appropriate for peer intervention, and the costs.

241.   Luckner, J. L. (1987). *Enhancing Self-Esteem of Special Needs Students*. Paper presented at the Annual Meeting of the Council for Exceptional Children, Chicago, IL. (ERIC Document Reproduction Service No. ED 288 344).

Uses outdoor adventure education--an education vehicle for self discovery and personal growth. Program places an important emphasis on a cooperative rather than a competitive learning environment. Lists possible reasons for effectiveness of the program: 1. connection: a feeling of being related to other, being part of a team; 2. uniqueness; 3. power; 4. models; and 5. accomplishment.

242.   Madden, N. A. (1980). Effects of cooperative learning on the social acceptance of mainstreamed academically handicapped students. *Dissertation Abstracts International, 41*, 2332B. (University Microfilms Order Number ADG80-27386. 0000)

"Examined the use of a cooperative classroom structure to facilitate social acceptance and reduce rejection of mildly handicapped students. The cooperation was structured around an academic task, mathematics instruction....The results indicated that special students in the cooperative treatment were less frequently rejected than were students in the control treatment. However, there were no differences in friendship choices."

243.   Madden, N. A., & Slavin, R. E. (1982). *Count me in: Academic achievement and social outcomes of mainstreaming students with mild academic handicaps.* (Report No. 329). Baltimore, MD: Johns Hopkins University, Center for the Study of Social Organization of Schools. (ERIC Document Reproduction Service No. ED 227 643).

Reviews research on the effects of placement in full-time special education classes, part-time regular classes with resource support and full-time regular classes on mildly handicapped students. Research favors full- or part-time regular class placement for achievement, self-esteem, behavior, and emotional adjustment. A combination of cooperative learning and individualized instruction had particularly strong effects on social acceptance of mildly academically handicapped students, as well as on the achievement of all students.

244.   Madden, N. A., & Slavin, R. E. (1983). Effects of cooperative learning on the social acceptance of mainstreamed academically handicapped students. *The Journal of Special Education, 17*(2), 171-182.

An attempt to discover if the social acceptance of mildly-academically handicapped children enrolled in regular classes would improve as a result of cooperative learning. Over seven weeks, two instructional methods were used to teach 183 third,

fourth, and sixth graders a structured math curriculum. Forty
students were identified as special education (two grade levels
behind age expectations). An adaptation of Students Teams-
Achievement Division (STAD) was used as the cooperative
intervention. In the control condition, students studied
individually and were given feedback individually.

While cooperative learning did not result in increased
friendships between academically handicapped and normal-
progress children, it did cause a significant decrease in rejection
of handicapped students. Both groups showed greater academic
achievement and self concept as a result of cooperation.   The
authors believe that if cooperation had been used for a longer
time period, friendships may also have grown between the two
groups.

245.   Madden, N. A., Slavin, R. E., Karweit, N. L., & Livermon, B. J.
        (1989). Restructuring the urban elementary school. *Educational
        Leadership*, *46*(5), 14-18.

        Discusses how the "Success for All" program has improved
        achievement of students at an inner-city elementary school by
        producing immediate intensive interventions when learning
        problems occur. Briefly touches on the strategy called
        "Cooperative Integrated Reading and Composition" (CIRC),
        which "provides cooperative learning activities built around story
        structure, prediction, summarization, vocabulary building,
        decoding practice, writing, and direct instruction in reading
        comprehension and language skills."

246.   Madden, N. A., Slavin, R. E., Karweit, N. L., Livermon, B. J., &
        Dolan, L. (1988). *Success for All: Effects on Student
        Achievement, Retentions, and Special Education Referrals.*
        Baltimore, MD: Johns Hopkins University, Center for Research
        on Elementary and Middle Schools.

        Discusses a model of elementary school organization that
        incorporates much of what is known about effective programs for
        students at risk. This model makes solid use of such cooperative
        learning strategies as Team-Assisted Individualization (TAI), and
        Cooperative Integrated Reading and Composition (CIRC). The
        Success for All program was initially piloted and evaluated at
        one Baltimore City elementary school during the 1987-1988

school year, and has been expanded to additional schools in subsequent years.

*   Male, M. (1986). Cooperative learning for effective jigsaw mainstreaming. *Computing Teacher*, 14(1), 35-37. (Cited above as Item 052.)

247.   Male, M., & Anderson, M. A. (1990). *Fitting In: Cooperative Learning in the Mainstream Classroom*. Arlington, VA: Majo Press. 181 p.

Authors envision classrooms where differences are viewed as strengths to draw on, with cooperative learning strategies as the catalyst for allowing each student to discover a place to fit in. Text includes lessons and worksheets for grades K-12 in language arts, math, science, health, and social studies.

*   Malouf, D. B., Wizer, D. R., Pilato, V. H., & Grogan, M. M. (1990). Computer-assisted instruction with small groups of mildly handicapped students. *Journal of Special Education*, 24(1). (Cited above as Item 102.)

248.   Margolis, H., McCabe, P., & Schwartz, E. (February 1990). Using cooperative learning to facilitate mainstreaming in the social studies. *Social Education*, 54(2), 111-114, 120.

Provides an overview and rationale for the use of cooperative learning, discusses how its use enriches instruction and how it can be used for facilitating mainstreaming, and provides examples of its power to positively influence attitudes of nonhandicapped students towards handicapped students.

249.   Margolis, H., & Schwartz, E. (1989). Facilitating mainstreaming through cooperative learning. *The High School Journal*, 72, 83-88.

Broad overview as to why the use of cooperative learning may facilitate mainstreaming. Also provides suggested guidelines for implementation.

250.   Maring, G. H., Fruman, G. C., and Blum-Anderson, J. (1985). Five cooperative learning strategies for mainstreamed

youngsters in content area classrooms. *The Reading Teacher*, *39*(3), 310-313.

Highlights learning strategies for implementing cooperative learning techniques for main-streamed youngsters in content area classrooms. Small groups of students (4-8) at various instructional levels are placed in a non-competitive environment of working together toward a common goal. The article describes effective cooperative strategies such as jigsaw strategy, list-groups-label strategy, small group structures, survey, predict, read, revise, and translation writing in developing cooperative learning strategies for mainstreamed students.

251.   Martino, L., & Johnson, D. W. (1979). Cooperative and individualistic experiences among disabled and normal children. *The Journal of Social Psychology*, *107*, 177-183.

Reports the findings of a study that examined the "effects of cooperative and individual learning experiences on friendly and hostile interaction between normal-progress and learning-disabled children in free-choice, postinstructional situations." Results "indicate that more friendly interactions in the postinstructional, free-swim periods occurred in the cooperative compared to the individual condition. More hostile interactions occurred in the individual condition. Learning-disabled students were ignored by their normal-progress peers more in the individual condition. Learning-disabled students in the cooperative condition learned more swimming skills than did their counterparts in the individual condition."

252.   Meadows, N. B. W. (1988). The effects of individual, teacher-directed and cooperative learning instructional methods on the comprehension of expository text. *Dissertation Abstracts International*, *50*, 407A. (University Microfilms Order Number ADG89-06928. 8908)

"Data was analyzed to determine whether the instructional methods had differential effects on comprehension for students of differing academic and social abilities and for mainstreamed disabled students....Cooperative learning was found to be equally as effective for all students when literal and inferential comprehension was measured."

*   Meekins, A. S. (1987). Effects of a student team learning technique on the academic progress and social acceptance of academically handicapped elementary and mainstreamed students. *Dissertation Abstracts International, 49,* 421A. (University Microfilms Order Number ADG88-08624. 8809) (Cited above as Item 056.)

253.   Nevin, A. (1984). The impact of cooperative learning in a regular classroom. *Pointer, 28*(3), 19-21.

         Describes a consultative approach using heterogeneous cooperative learning groups with mainstreamed special students. Significant improvement was found in social attitudes and achievement.

*   Polloway, E. A., Cronin, M. E., & Patton, J. R. (1986). The Efficacy of Group versus One-to-One Instruction: A Review. *Remedial and Special Education, 7*(1), 22-30. (Cited below as Item 701.)

254.   Putnam, J. W. (1983). Social integration of moderately handicapped students through cooperative goal structuring: Influence of teacher instruction on cooperation. University of Minnesota. *Dissertation Abstracts International, 44,* 2736A.

         Compares the effectiveness of two types of cooperative learning techniques with moderately mentally handicapped and nonhandicapped students. In the first condition the teacher did not instruct the students in the basic of cooperation, whereas in the second condition the teacher instructed the students in desired cooperative behaviors. Dependent variables measured were social interaction and attitudes of nonhandicapped students toward handicapped persons. Findings support the conclusion that "instructing students on cooperative skills can increase positive social interaction during cooperative learning activities and noninstructional free play activities, particularly those directed toward handicapped peers by nonhandicapped students."

255.   Rajendran, B. (1987). The effect of cooperative and conventional classroom environments on the on-task behavior and attitude toward learning of secondary learning-disabled students. University of Oregon. *Dissertation Abstracts International, 49,* 718A.

Reports the results of a study that tested the effectiveness of
cooperative learning techniques within an "academic
departmentalized program for learning disabled high school
students on Guam." Findings revealed that "on-task behavior
gains scores of learning disabled students increased three to four
times as much in experimental classes as in the control classes."
Significant increases in attitude were also noted by students in
the experimental classes. Concludes that cooperative learning
techniques are effective for disabled high school students.

256.   Rath, C. C. (1989). The integration of handicapped students in the
        middle school: The principal's view. Boston University.
        Dissertation Abstracts International, 50, 1166A.

A qualitative study that focused on the efforts of eight
principals to integrate educationally handicapped students into
regular classroom settings. The use of cooperative learning
groups is one example of successful integrative structures.

257.   Reisberg, L., & Wolf, R. (1986). Developing a consulting program
        in special education: Implementation and interventions. *Focus
        on Exceptional Children, 19*(3), 1-14.

The authors briefly discuss cooperative learning as an
"effective approach for fostering both academic achievement and
improving the social integration of mildly handicapped students."
The four elements of CL stressed are "positive interdependence,"
"face-to-face interaction," "individual accountability," and use of
"interpersonal skills." Peer and Cross-Age tutoring are also
discussed using a "model-lead-test-sequence" for the peer teachers.
They suggest tutoring be used to reinforce, rather than expand,
the curriculum.

258.   Reynolds, M. C. (1989). Students with special needs. In M. C.
        Reynolds (Ed.) *Knowledge base for the beginning teacher* (pp.
        129-142). New York: Pergamon Press.

Under a section entitled "Positive Interdependence Among
Students," Reynolds suggests that the use of cooperative group
strategies for part of the day may be a way to achieve a decent
environment for students who "show wide diversity in
characteristics." Discusses achievement advances when
cooperative learning is used with inner city pupils, children from

low-income families, black students, mentally retarded, and others. Also discusses "gains in appreciation and acceptance among students who are diverse in racial and ethnic backgrounds and children with handicaps."

259.   Salend, S. J., & Washin, B. (1988). Team-assisted individualization with handicapped adjudicated youth. *Exceptional Children, 55,* 174-180.

The subjects in this study were males in the New York State Division for Youth. All were enrolled in remedial math classes. Teams of 2-3 members with both high, average, and low ability mixed, checked each other's answers and made team decisions. Reinforcement was delivered to the team as a whole. The study observed an increase in on-task behavior but no large gains in academic skills. The subjects preferred working in groups over traditional classroom activities.

260.   Schniedewind, N., & Salend, S. J. (1987). Cooperative learning works. *Teaching Exceptional Children, 19,* 22-25.

"This article presents special educators with practical guidelines for designing and implementing cooperative learning strategies in their classroom, along with examples of how these guidelines are used by teachers in mainstreamed, resource room, and self-contained classroom settings." Topics discussed are the following: Selecting a cooperative learning format, establishing guidelines for cooperating activities, forming cooperative groups, arranging the classroom, developing cooperative skills, and confronting problems. Even though the article targets special education teachers, it will serve as a valuable resource for all teachers interested in cooperative learning.

261.   Searcy, S. K. (1986). The behavioral effects of teaching supportive and task-related behaviors to behaviorally disordered students in combination with cooperative learning strategies (social skills). University of Kansas. *Dissertation Abstracts International, 47,* 2124A.

Discusses the findings of a study that investigated the effects of cooperative learning social skills upon group behavior of adolescents with behavioral disorders. Students in the experimental group were first taught selected social skills and were then instructed to work in cooperative groups; while completing a task, the students were asked to observe, record, and provide feedback. No significant differences were found in any of the three supportive behaviors. On-task behavior was the only variable positively influenced by cooperative learning strategies.

262.   Sherborne, V. (1989). Movement and the integration of exceptional children. *Educational Forum, 54*, 105-116.

Discusses appropriate instructional methods for mainstreaming special learners into a movement program. Advocates cooperative learning activities that promote mutual regard and respect between exceptional and mainstream students. "The best arrangement for exceptional children is to collaborate with mainstream children in physical activities that are not competitive, in which everyone can be successful."

263.   Slavin, R. E. (1977). A student team approach to teaching adolescents with special emotional and behavioral needs. *Psychology in Schools, 14,* 77-83.

Proposes that the Team-Games-Tournament (TGT) strategy be used as an alternative classroom structure for students with special needs. TGT and individualized instruction were compared in a school for adolescents of normal intelligence expressing problems with human relationships and academic tasks. "The results confirmed the hypothesis that TGT would exceed individualized instruction on students' attraction to one another...A five-month follow up showed former TGT students distributed among six new classes to be still interacting with their peers both on and off task more than control students."

*   Slavin, R. E. (1982). *Cooperative learning: Student Teams.* Washington, D.C.: National Education Association. 32 pp. (Cited above as Item 017.)

*   Slavin, R. E. (1983). *Cooperative Learning.* NY: Longman. 147 pp. (Cited below as Item 659.)

264.   Slavin, R. E. (1984). Team assisted individualization: Cooperative learning and individualized instruction in the mainstreamed classroom. *Remedial and Special Education, 5*, 3-42.

Slavin discusses Team-Assisted Individualization (TAI), a mathematics program that combines cooperative learning and individualized instruction to accommodate the social and academic needs of mainstreamed academically handicapped students. It was found to improve both the social and academic behavior of these students. In one of two studies, the program was found to increase mathematics achievement more than traditional methods. Achievement and behavior of nonhandicapped students also improved. Effects of mainstreaming are also discussed.

265.   Slavin, R. E., & Madden, N. A. (1989). Effective classroom programs for students at risk. In Robert E. Slavin, N. L. Karweit, & N. A. Madden (Eds.), *Effective Programs for Students at Risk*, (pp. 23-51). Boston: Allyn and Bacon.

Includes a section entitled "Cooperative Learning" (pp. 39-42) that discusses Team Accelerated Instruction (TAI) and Cooperative Integrated Reading and Composition (CIRC).

266.   Slavin, R. E., & Madden, N. A. (1989). What works for students at risk: A research synthesis. *Educational Leadership, 46*(5), 4-13.

A section of this article (pp. 8-10) examines the value of cooperative learning strategies in regard to the student at risk. The researchers found that "While many cooperative learning methods have been successfully applied in many subjects, only four meet the inclusion criteria applied in this article: Team Accelerated Instruction, Cooperative Integrated Reading and Composition, Student Teams-Achievement Divisions, and Companion Reading."

267.   Slavin, R. E., Madden, N. A., & Karweit, N. L. (1989). Effective programs for students at risk: Conclusions for practice and policy. In R. Slavin, N. L. Karweit, & N. A. Madden (Eds.), *Effective programs for students at risk* (pp. 355-372). Boston: Allyn and Bacon.

Briefly discusses how Cooperative Integrated Reading and Composition (CIRC) and Team-Assisted Individualization (TAI) have been incorporated into a model of elementary school organization and "Success for All," an effective educational program for students at risk.

268.   Slavin, R. E., Madden, N.A., & Leavey, M. (1982). *Combining cooperative learning and individualized instruction: Effects on the social acceptance, achievement and behavior of mainstreamed students.* Paper presented at the annual meeting of the American Educational Research Association.

269.   Strom, R. D. (1983). Expectations for educating the gifted and talented. *Educational Forum, 47*, 279-303.

Focuses on five major questions concerning gifted education: 1. How can the school programs be more meaningful? 2. How can teachers increase their effectiveness? 3. What types of social interaction should be encouraged? 4. How can parents facilitate the learning process? 5. What are the obligations of society in the educational process? The third question targets cooperative learning structures and the effects that they have upon gifted students. Citing a study by Torrance that involved 1700 students who acknowledged that they were not good at group or team activities, Strom concludes that peer instruction is a vital part of gifted education. After the experiment, 98% of the 1700 students admitted that peer instruction is not only effective but also exciting. Strom also points out that peer teaching allows gifted students to enhance their social skills and to "define success in terms of the goals of others as well as their own goals."

270.   Tateyama-Sniezek, K. M. (1990). Cooperative learning: Does it improve the academic achievement of students with handicaps? *Exceptional Children, 56*, 426-437.

Presents a review of the "research on the effects of cooperative learning on the achievement of students with handicaps." To be included in this review, studies must have included handicapped students as part of the sample. In addition, achievement had to be the dependent variable and cooperative learning the independent variable. As a result, only twelve studies met the criteria and were included for review purposes. Findings were inconsistent among the twelve studies, indicating a need for more research in this area before teachers are encouraged to use cooperative learning methods with mainstreamed special education students.

271.   Torrey, R. D. (1956). Citizenship education for the gifted
        adolescent. *Progressive Education, 33*, 78-84.

        Argues that many gifted/talented programs ignore the fact
        that intellectually gifted students are future civil leaders.
        According to Torrey, homogeneous grouping does not fulfill the
        purposes of citizenship education. Challenges educators to use
        instructional methods, including cooperative groups, that
        challenge gifted/talented students.

272.   Watson, D. L., & Rangel, L. (1989). Don't forget the slow learner.
        Clearing House, 62, 266-268.

        Discusses the learning styles of slow learners, including
        their preference for group work, their need to have teachers check
        assignments, and their desire for peer approval. By summarizing
        research conducted in a sixth-grade class, the authors argue that
        cooperative learning will meet the needs of slow learners. Offers
        suggestions for initial implementation of cooperative learning in
        content areas and outlines the role of the principal in the
        planning process.
        "Cooperative learning provides an excellent tool for bridging
        the gaps between the students' learning styles and the teaching
        requirements of the classroom."

273.   Wilcox, E. S., & Nevin, A. (1987). Cooperative learning groups
        aid integration. Teaching *Exceptional Children, 20*, 61-63.

        Describes ways in which a regular classroom teacher used
        cooperative learning groups to involve a severely handicapped
        first-grade girl in class activities. Includes a discussion of the
        planning stage, the eight steps involved in implementing the
        program, and the evaluation procedures and results." Based upon
        data collected and classroom observations, the teacher concluded
        that the handicapped child was accepted as "just another member
        of the class."

274.   Womack, S. T. (1989). Modes of instruction. *Clearing House, 62*,
        205-210.

        Discusses four modes of instruction (expository,
        demonstration, inquiry, and individualization) by presenting
        assumptions about the learners, roles of both teacher and

learners, helpful resources, evaluation procedures, and
weaknesses. Suggests using cooperative learning with students
who have learning difficulties.

275. Yager, S. O., Johnson, R. T., Johnson, D. W., & Snider, B.
(1985). The effect of cooperative and individualistic learning
experiences on positive and negative cross-handicap
relationships. *Contemporary Educational Psychology, 10*, 127-
138.

"The effects of cooperative and individualistic learning
contingencies on interpersonal attraction, social acceptability,
and self-esteem between handicapped and nonhandicapped fourth-
grade students were tracked and compared." Findings revealed
that "continued use of cooperative learning contingencies
promotes positive growth in interpersonal attraction, social
acceptability, and self-esteem between handicapped and
nonhandicapped students. The results also indicate that when
cooperative learning contingencies are replaced with individual
learning contingencies, decrease in the above-mentioned variables
occurs." Concludes that cooperative learning procedures are
effective in mainstreamed classrooms.

G.   VOCATIONAL EDUCATION

276.   Bell, J., Clark, V., Gebo, E., & Lord, S. (1989). FHA: Achieving excellence through cooperative learning. *NASSP Bulletin, 73,* 114-117.

Reviews the findings of studies on cooperative learning conducted by Johnson and Johnson. Explains ways in which vocational student organizations, especially Future Homemakers of America, teach these skills in conjunction with academic content of courses. Outlines a five-step planning process involved in establishing cooperative activities. Concludes with suggestions for administrators about how to support and encourage increased cooperation.

277.   Dittman, J. (1986). Join the winning circle. *Illinois Teacher of Home Economics, 30,* 46-49, 53.

Begins with a comprehensive description of cooperative learning by comparing cooperative learning groups to traditional classroom groups and by defining, through the use of relevant research, the key components of cooperative learning. Also included are practical suggestions for using Student Teams Achievement Divisions (STAD), Jigsaw II, and Teams-Games-Tournament(TGT) within home economics classrooms. A useful article for home economics teachers who desire to implement cooperative learning in their classrooms.

278.   Dow, D. M., & Dow, H. (1972). Cooperative learning. *School Shop, 32,* 64-65.

A short, descriptive article that discusses cooperative learning activities within Michigan public schools. "Cooperation is the key word, in this venture" that involves the learning of basic print skills.

279.   Gerard, J. (1988). Helping troubled youth be somebody - Pre-vocational agricultural education. *Agricultural Education Magazine, 60,* 21-22.

Discussed five strategies for assisting youth in vocational training: 1. the use of a pre-vocational concept in curriculum development, 2. the development of good work habits, 3. the use of nonverbal instruction, 4. the use of cooperative learning to build self-esteem, and 5. the encouragement to try new ideas. "Implementing the cooperative learning learning technique not only builds-up students, but helps reduce the instructor's workload."

280.   Helm, G. R. (1987). Relationships--Decisions through life cycle: A course to stimulate thinking skills. *Illinois Teacher of Home Economics*, *30*, 127-128, 133.

Describes a home economics course at a Nebraska high school designed to teach thinking skills and decision-making skills. Three features of the program are the development of thinking and decision making skills, the use of simulations, and the use of older people as role models. To accomplish the objective of the course, instructors utilizes cooperative learning strategies. Although practical in nature, the article contains a limited amount of discussion on the use of cooperative learning strategies.

281.   Johnson, D.W. (1987). *Human Relations and Your Career: A Guide to Interpersonal Skills* (2nd ed.). Englewood Cliffs, New Jersey: Prentice-Hall, Inc. 330 pp.

Designed to teach students in career training programs the interpersonal and group skills they need to be successful. Experiential learning procedures are used to help students learn practical interpersonal skills. Each chapter begins with a questionnaire introducing the terms, concepts, and skills to be learned. Exercises are followed by relevant theory in social psychology to help students reach conclusions about their experiences.

The role of the teacher is explained and instruction and suggestions given for organizing students into cooperative groups. Students use learning contracts and participate in competitive tournaments. Evaluation and grading are explained. Indexed.

An informative, readable, practical book. If not used as a class text, should be included in a career education teacher's professional library.

282.   Michaelson, L. K., & Obenshain, S. (1983). Developing professional competence. *New Directions for Teaching and Learning, 4*, 41-55.

Describes a program in medicine at the University of New Mexico and a program in business at the University of Oklahoma. The number of participants involved in cooperative groups in the New Mexico project was small. Students involved in the groups exhibited a more positive attitude toward school and their peers, but a slightly lower understanding of basic concepts. Students enrolled in business education at the University of Oklahoma exhibited better attitude and increased academic performance. Concludes the article by stating that cooperative group structures help to relieve anxiety about mistakes, problem-solving, and unfamiliar settings.

283.   Perreault, R. J., Jr. (1982). An experimental comparison of cooperative learning to noncooperative learning and their effects on cognitive achievement in junior high industrial arts laboratories. University of Maryland. *Dissertation Abstracts International, 43*, 3830A.

Compared the effects of cooperative structures with those of noncooperative structures upon achievement at the knowledge and comprehension levels of Bloom's taxonomy. Significant effects of cooperative structures at the knowledge and comprehension levels were revealed, but no significant difference was found at the application level.

284.   Rhinehart, R. R. (1989). Experiencing team responsibility in class. *Chemical Engineering Education, 23*(1), 38-43.

Describes a junior-level engineering course that incorporates cooperative learning activities designed to teach project management and interpersonal skills. Includes project guidelines, lists of suggested activities, and group evaluation form.

General Topics

III. GENERAL TOPICS

A. CLASSROOM CLIMATE AND SOCIAL NEEDS OF STUDENTS

*   Anderson, M. A. (1985). Cooperative group tasks and their relationship to peer acceptance and cooperation. *Journal of Learning Disabilities, 18*(2), 83-86. (Cited above as Item 219.)

*   Arnstine, D., & Arnstine B. (1987). Teaching democracy through participation: The crucial role of student interest. *Educational Forum, 51,* 377-392. (Cited above as Item 210.)

285.   Benne, K. D. (1957). Group processes in education. *Progressive Education, 34,* 37-43.

> Praises small-group activities. Discusses two essential components: 1. Students and teachers must be wise in their evaluations of the activities; 2. Maintenance, as well as problem solving, is essential to a positive group experience. The author bases much of his discussion upon the following quotation by W. H. Kilpatrick in 1919: "It is cooperative purposeful activity in group affairs that has perhaps most to do with building healthy social character with its spirit of give and take, its like-mindedness, its tendency to prefer the group and its welfare to one's private and personal welfare."

286.   Berkowitz, L. (1957). Effects of perceived dependency relationships upon conformity to group exceptions. *Journal of Abnormal and Social Psychology, 55,* 350-354.

> Reports the findings of a study designed to test the effects of interdependent reward structures upon individual and group behavior. Results indicated that interdependence has a positive effect upon motivation and completion of assigned group tasks.

287.   Berndt, T. J., Perry, T. B., & Miller, K. E. (1988). Friends' and classmates' interactions on academic tasks. *Journal of Educational Psychology, 80*(4), 506-513.

Sixty third graders and seventy seventh graders were paired with friends and with other classmates to determine the effects of existing social relationships on interactions during cooperative learning tasks. No significant difference between pairs of friends and pairs of classmates was found. Friends did not talk more with each other than other classmates did, and the content of friends' and classmates' conversation was similar. Seventh graders made more comments, asked more questions, and gave fewer commands and directives during interactions than did third graders.

There seems to be no disadvantage to pairing students with their close friends--they did not distract each other. The authors suggest pairing of non-friends to draw all students into social relationships.

*   Bina, M. J. (1986). Social skills development through cooperative group learning strategies. *Education of the Visually Handicapped, 18*(1), 27-40. (Cited above as Item 222.)

*   Blaney, N. T., Stephan, C., Rosenfield, D., Aronson, E., & Sikes, J. (1977). Interdependence in the classroom: A field study. *Journal of Educational Psychology, 69*(2), 121-128. (Cited above as Item 047.)

288. Blau, B., & Raferty, J. (1970). Changes in friendship status as a function of reinforcement. *Child Development, 41*, 113-121.

Study involving preschoolers shows that friendships develop from reasons other than personality similarities and that they are susceptible to reward contingencies. Points out that cooperatively structured groups may be beneficial in improving the social status of disadvantaged and disturbed children.

*   Brubacher, M., Payne, R., and Pickett, K. (Eds.). (1990). *Perspectives on Small Group Learning.* Oakville, Ontario: Rubicon Publishing Co. (Cited below as Item 567.)

289. Byrnes, D. A. (1984). Social isolates and the teacher. *Educational Forum, 48*, 373-381.

Discusses the effects of social isolation upon students. Arguing that cooperative groups and goal structures have a positive influence upon the social development of students,

Byrnes summarizes the findings of several studies, including those by Cave, Hallinana and Tuma, and Johnson and Johnson. Her conclusion is that "joint cooperative activity in behalf of a supportive goal" fosters positive social relationships.

290. Carson, L., & Hoyle, S. (1989/1990). Teaching social skills: A view from the classroom. *Educational Leadership, 47*(4), 31.

A useful piece by two high school teachers on effective methods for teaching social skills -- modelling the skill, taking social skills one at a time, easing students into using social skills, and rewarding groups in which all members in the group practice/display the social skill.

291. Clark, M. L. (April, 1985). *Gender, race, and friendship research.* Paper presented at the Annual Meeting of the American Educational Research Association, Chicago, IL. (ERIC Document Reproduction Service No. ED 259 053).

Reviews studies that have included either gender or race as a variable in assessing the nature of friendships of children and adolescents. Also discusses the impact which women and minorities have had on friendship research. Female friendships seem based on loyalty and commitment while achievement and status form the basis for male friendships. Intergroup hostility is highest in racially balanced schools where no one group is clearly in control. Black and white children made more cross-race friendships in classes when they were in the minority. Gender and grade point average were better predictors of academic and social acceptance than race for blacks and whites. Heterogeneous cooperative learning groups experienced increased cross-race friendships. Though these were weak relationships, the experimenter felt that cooperative learning techniques carried out over a longer period of time would lead to improved interrace relationships.

292. Co-operative College of Canada. (1980). *Co-operation and Community Life.* Toronto, Canada: Ontario Institute for Studies in Education.

Designed to help seven- to fourteen-year-olds understand themselves and others through cooperative groups.

293.   Co-operative College of Canada. (1983). *Co-operative Outlooks.*
        Toronto, CA: Ontario Institute for Studies in Education.

        Designed to help high school students through cooperative
        economics.

294.   Cooper, L., Johnson, D. W., Johnson, R., & Wilderson, F. (1980).
        The effects of cooperative, competitive, and individualistic
        experiences on interpersonal attraction among heterogeneous
        peers. *The Journal of Social Psychology, 111,* 243-252.

        Reports the findings of a study that compared the effects of
        cooperative, competitive, and individualistic experiences on
        "cross-ethnic, cross-sex, and cross-ability interpersonal
        attraction." The study involved sixty seventh-grade, lower-class
        students from an inner-city junior high school. "The results
        indicate that when students who were initially prejudiced against
        one another were present in the same situation, cooperative
        experiences promoted more interpersonal attraction than did
        competitive or individualistic experiences, and competitive
        experiences promoted more interpersonal attraction than did
        individualistic experiences." In addition, the results indicate that
        "cooperative experiences promote greater feelings of being
        accepted by peers than do competitive experiences and that more
        mutual helping among heterogeneous peers results from
        cooperative rather than competitive or individualistic
        experiences."

*   Crary, E. (1984). *Kids Can Cooperate.* P.O. Box 2002, Santa
        Barbara, CA 93120: Animal Town Game Co. 112 pp. (Cited
        below as Item 573.)

295.   Dembo, M. H., & McAuliffe, T. J. (1987). Effects of perceived
        ability and grade status on social interaction and influence in
        cooperative groups. *Journal of Educational Psychology, 79*(4),
        415-423.

        Authors examined how a natural status characteristic (grade
        level) and an experimentally induced status characteristic (ability)
        combined to affect group interaction and interpersonal perception
        in homogeneous and heterogeneous groupings.
        The social interaction of 80 male fifth and sixth graders who
        had been randomly assigned to groups of four was videotaped.

Groups were made into homogeneous or heterogeneous "ability" groups on the basis of a bogus aptitude test.

High status students dominated group interaction, were more influential, and were more likely to be perceived as leaders. High-status students were more likely than lower status students to give help to lower status students or to the group. Data indicates that inducing higher status may lead to increased helping behavior. High ability students received more help than "average" students from students at any status level. "High ability" students tended to receive more negative as well as more positive reactions to help given, possibly due to their domination of group interaction.

*   DeVries, D. L., & Edwards, K. J. (1974). Student teams and learning games: Their effects on cross-race and cross-sex interaction. *Journal of Educational Psychology*, 66(5), 741-749. (Cited below as Item 384.)

296.   Doescher, S. M., & Sugawara, A. I. (1989). Encouraging prosocial behavior in young children. *Childhood Education*, 65, 213-216.

Discusses cooperative learning activities that encourage prosocial behavior in young children. One strategy is to arrange the classroom to facilitate interactions between children. "An environment with a limited but reasonable amount of supplies requires children to work together on projects." A positive result is that children learn to respect each other and attempt to reach mutually beneficial goals.

297.   Eastwood, L. E. (1988). A case study of a cooperative learning project at an elementary school in Los Angeles County (California). Pepperdine University. *Dissertation Abstracts International*, 50, 196A.

"The purpose of this study was to determine if the implementation of cooperative learning instruction for all students at an elementary school site over an extended period of time did significantly change students sense of self-esteem, attitude toward school and respect for others, as well as improve their academic achievement." Results indicate that the use of cooperative learning had a significant effect on students' self-esteem, their attitude toward others, and their attitude toward school, but no significant effect on students' academic achievement.

298.   Gigante, T. (1990). Ricki the rebel. *Learning, 18*, 56-58.

A first-person account of one teacher's successful efforts to involve a rebellious student in classroom activities through the use of cooperatively structured teams. After much frustration on the part of Ricki and the other group members, "Ricki could see for herself that her contribution made a difference, and she started to put her intelligence to use. Her group began to succeed, and she liked being a winner."

299.   Graves, T. D. (1988). Review: Armendi, R.A. The Effects of Cooperative Games on Preschool Children's Prosocial Behavior. Quezon City, Philippines: St, Joseph's College Graduate School. *The International Association for the Study of Cooperation in Education, 9*(3 and 4), 18.

This master's thesis summarizes a study in which cooperative games were played by one kindergarten class, while another played competitive games. A test of 20 questions to measure attitude was administered before and after the test, as well as a "Donation Task pretend game" in which children indicated how many of nine lollipops they would share with others. Over the seven month test period, both groups made four times the gain. The author concludes that "a cooperative games program is potentially more productive in developing prosocial attitudes and spontaneous cooperative behavior in children than traditional competitive games."

*   Gunderson, B., & Johnson, D. (1980). Building positive attitudes by using cooperative learning groups. *Foreign Language Annals, 13*, 39-43. (Cited below as Item 467.)

300.   Hall, B. W., Villeme, M. G., & Burley, W. W. (1986). Humanistic orientation and selected teaching practices among 1st-year teachers. *Journal of Humanistic Education and Development, 25*(1), 12-17.

The article concentrates on the practices of teachers who "value both humanistic and academic outcomes for children." It was found that the teachers value cooperative learning over

competitive practices, which received the lowest rating of
importance (using praise received the highest rating). Other
practices given high ratings were "the teaching of social values"
and "attention to the socioemotional development of students."

*   Hansell, S., & Slavin, R.E. (1981). Cooperative learning and the
        structure of interracial friendships. *Sociology of Education*,
        54(2), 98-106.   (Cited below as Item 390.)

301.   Hill, W. F. (1977). *Learning through Discussion: Guide for
        Leaders and Members of Discussion*. Newbury Park: CA: Sage
        Publications. 58 pp.

        A guide for teachers which presents strategies for
        maximizing group interaction as a learning tool.

302.   Hooker, S. K. R. (1988). Cooperative learning with four gifted and
        talented students: A case study focusing on interpersonal skills.
        Dissertation Abstracts International, *50*, 921A. (University
        Microfilms Order Number ADG89-07959. 8910)

        Examined changes in four gifted nine and ten year olds'
        interpersonal skills and their attitudes toward school, self, and
        others. Favorable results were evident in all areas.

303.   Johnson, D. W. (1980). Constructive peer relationships, social
        development, and cooperative learning experiences: Implications
        for the prevention of drug abuse. *Journal of Drug Education*,
        10(1), 7-24.

        Explores ways in which the socialization of children can be
        achieved through adopting social roles and having meaningful
        relationships with adults, peers, and children and through direct
        learning. Discusses methods to improve students' psychological
        health and responsible decision-making as a means of preventing
        drug abuse.

304.   Johnson, D. W. (1980). Group processes: Influences of student-
        student interaction on school outcomes. In J. McMillan (Ed.),
        The Social Psychology of School Learning (pp. 123-168). New
        York: Academic Press.

Discusses the development of student-students relationships
and the effects of group dynamics on interaction among students.
Focuses on the importance of peer interaction and the teacher's
role and function in ensuring positive peer relationships to
improve achievement, appropriate behavior, and social skills
among students.

*   Johnson, D. W., Falk, D., Martino, L., & Purdie, S. (1976). The
evaluation of persons seeking and volunteering information under
cooperative and competitive conditions. *The Journal of
Psychology*, *92*, 161-165. (Cited below as Item 604.)

305.   Johnson, D. W., & Johnson, R. T. (August, 1982). *Having your
cake and eating it too: maximizing achievement and cognitive-
social development and socialization through cooperative
learning*. Paper presented at the Annual Convention of the
American Psychological Association, Washington, DC. (ERIC
Document Reproduction Service No. ED 227 408).

A review of research on cooperative, competitive,
individualistic, and traditional instructional methods on a range
of educational outcomes. Cooperative learning strategies can
eliminate the need to choose either academic achievement or
cognitive development and socialization (educators can "have
their cake and eat it, too"). Cooperative learning methods have
been found to promote, simultaneously, academic achievement,
student/students relationships, positive attitudes towards school,
teachers, and subject areas, critical thinking skills, cooperative
behaviors, and psychological health. Results of this meta-
analysis of studies involving effects of cooperative learning on
achievement and interpersonal relationships are detailed.
Approaches to the development of cooperative learning strategies
are described and future directions of research on cooperative
learning and schooling are discussed. Mentions problems with
previous research.

306.   Johnson, D. W., & Johnson, R. T. (1983). Social interdependence
and perceived academic and personal support in the classroom.
The Journal of Social Psychology, *120*, 77-82.

Discusses a study involving the responses of 859 students to
a classroom climate instrument. The students were in grades 5-9
in three Midwestern school districts. Results were based upon

correlational analyses of "relationships between scales measuring attitudes toward social interdependence and attitudes towards relationships with peers and teachers." Students who frequently participated in cooperative learning groups were compared with those who had few cooperative learning experiences. Results indicate that "cooperativeness and frequently participating in cooperative learning situations were positively related to perceptions of support, help, and friendship from teachers and peers."

307.   Johnson, D.W., & Johnson, R. T. (1985). *Supportive Peer Relationships: A Necessity Not a Luxury.* Minneapolis, MN: Cooperative Learning Center, University of Minnesota. 31 pp.

Highlights the major factors involved in fostering productive peer relationships with an emphasis on cooperative learning experiences.

308.   Johnson, D. W., & Johnson, R. T. (1989). Social interdependence. In D.W. Johnson & R.T. Johnson (Eds.), *Cooperation and Competition: Theory and Research* (pp. 23-38). Edina, MN: Interaction Book Company.

Examines social interdependence and how it is affected by a cooperative, competitive, or individualistic situation. Findings show that there is a positive correlation between cooperative groups and individual fulfillment of goals. There is a negative correlation between competitive situations and attainment of individual goals. In the individual situation, no correlation was found.

309.   Johnson, D. W., & Johnson, R. T. (1989). Social interdependence and interpersonal attraction. In D. W. Johnson & R. T. Johnson (Eds.), *Cooperation and Competition: Theory and Research* (pp. 107-130). Edina, MN: Interaction Book Company.

Analyzes interpersonal relationships and discusses the formation of positive relationships as well as cross-ethnic and homogeneous relationships. Findings show that cooperative situations promote greater interpersonal attraction than competitive or individualistic ones.

310.   Johnson, D. W., & Johnson, R. T. (1989). Social interdependence
        and psychological health. In D. W. Johnson & R. T. Johnson
        (Eds.), *Cooperation and Competition: Theory and Research* (pp.
        141-154). Edina, MN: Interaction Book Company.

        Compares the relationship between cooperative,
        competitive, and individualistic situations to psychological
        health. Results indicate that there is a positive correlation
        between the cooperative situation and psychological health,
        positive and negative correlation between competition and
        psychological health, and negative correlation between
        individualistic situations and psychological health.

311.   Johnson, D. W., & Johnson, R. T. (1989). Social interdependence
        and self-esteem. In D. W. Johnson & R. T. Johnson (Eds.),
        Cooperation and Competition: Theory and Research (pp. 155-
        168). Edina, MN: Interaction Book Company.

        Defines self-esteem and explains its importance. The
        authors argue that a relationship exists between self-esteem and
        cooperation, competition, and individualism. The three
        conditions have all been found or hypothesized to be self-esteem
        builders. Findings indicate, however, that higher self-esteem is
        promoted in the cooperative situation than in the competitive or
        individualistic. Along with the cooperative situation come self-
        acceptance and greater self-esteem, whereas in the competitive
        situation, self-esteem is conditional and in the individualistic,
        self-esteem is turned to self-rejection.

312.   Johnson, D. W., & Johnson, R. T. (1989). Social interdependence
        and social support. In D. W. Johnson & R. T. Johnson (Eds.),
        Cooperation and Competition: Theory and Research (pp. 131-
        140). Edina, MN: Interaction Book Company.

        Examines social support and its effect on people. Social
        support was tested in three conditions: cooperative, competitive,
        and individualistic. Findings show that in the cooperative
        situation, greater social support is promoted.

313.   Johnson, D. W., & Johnson, R. T. (1989/1990). Social skills for
        successful group work. *Educational Leadership, 47*(4), 29-33.

An excellent piece on the value of teaching social skills and methods for doing so. Includes sections on teaching cooperative learning skills, using bonus points, long-term outcomes, and a discussion as to why teaching social skills is as important as teaching academic content.

314. Johnson, D. W., Johnson, R. T., Buckman, L. A., & Richards, T. S. (1985). The effects of prolonged implementation of cooperative learning on support. *Journal of Psychology, 119*(5), 405-411.

Article supports the theory that cooperative learning activities associated with interrelationships among students socially provides a setting for greater learning in the classroom.

* Johnson, D. W., Johnson, R. T., Johnson, J., & Anderson, D. (1976). Effects of cooperative versus individualized instruction on student prosocial behavior, attitudes toward learning, and achievement. *Journal of Educational Psychology, 68*(4), 446-452. (Cited below as Item 358.)

315. Johnson, D. W., Johnson, R. T., & Maruyama, G. (1983). Interdependence and interpersonal attraction among heterogeneous and homogeneous individuals: A theoretical formulation and a meta-analysis of the research. *Review of Educational Research, 53*(1), 5-54.

A review of the literature and a presentation of a theoretical framework to support the conditions that lead to positive or negative relationships when students interact in the classroom setting. Groups of students studied were homogenous groups, ethnically diverse groups and handicapped and nonhandicapped groups. Findings derived from the review of studies through a meta-analysis indicated that cooperative learning strategies can be an important instructional tool to foster positive relationships among ethnically diverse, handicapped students in homogenous classroom settings.

316. Johnson, R. T., & Johnson, D. W. (1985). *Cooperative Learning: Warm-Ups, Grouping Strategies, and Group Activities*. Edina, MN: Interaction Book Company. 91 pp.

An activity booklet filled with exercises designed to reinforce and build on previous ideas for group work activities. Contains a wide assortment of lessons including warm-ups, grouping strategies, and cooperative group activities.

317.   Kagan, S. (1985). Learning to cooperate. In R. Slavin, S. Sharan, S. Kagan, R. Hertz-Lazarowitz, C. Webb, & R. Schmuck (Eds.), *Learning to Cooperate, Cooperating to Learn* (pp. 365-370). New York: Plenum Press.

A fascinating essay on the need to incorporate cooperative, prosocial socialization experiences in schools especially in light of "the modern socialization void, the negative consequences of this void, and projected and economic needs."

318.   Karsg, N. B. (1980). Effects of preaching, practice, and helpful evaluations on third graders' collaborative work. In E. Pepitone (Ed.), *Children in cooperation and competition*, (pp. 365-388). Mass.: D.C. Heath.

Tested the effects of cooperative treatments upon "group-oriented behavior on the task performance of small group interdependent children. The treatment included group discussion of cooperative skills, task performance in cooperative groups, evaluation, and feedback. Results indicated that students in cooperative groups exhibited positive interpersonal skills. Concludes that if students are placed in classrooms "where freedom to interact with peers exists, and where most academic skills are taught in just this way, the results might prove startling" and that "the needs of our society could be beneficially served by such a change."

319.   Kinney, M., & Hurst, J. B. (1980). Developing a supportive classroom. *The Social Studies, 71*, 178-182.

Defines the concepts underlying a supportive group climate and suggests practical ways to develop such a cooperative atmosphere in classrooms. Discusses concepts of "supportiveness" and "defensiveness" as well as "teacher as role model." Ideas are applicable across the curriculum.

320.   Knight, G. P., Dubro, A. F., & Chao, Chia-Chen. (1985). Information processing and the development of cooperative,

competitive, and individualistic social values. *Developmental Psychology, 21*(1), 37-45.

This study was designed to find out if the developmental difference in social values is associated with the development of information-processing capabilities. One hundred and nine three-to ten-year-old children completed a central-incident memory measure, an assessment of social values, and a free-recall word list task. Results indicated that age, sex, and memory were all significantly related to the expression of social values.

*   Leming, J. S. (1985). Cooperative learning processes - some advantages. *NASSP Bulletin, 69*, 63. (Cited below as Item 629.)

321.   Leming, J. S. (1985). School curriculum and social development in early adolescent. *Childhood Education, 61*, 257-263.

Reviews relevant research concerning the effect of values clarification, moral development, and cooperative learning on the social development of early adolescents. Concerning cooperative learning, the author points out that "to the extent that early adolescents are denied experiences in cooperative activities with peers, important opportunities for social development are missed."

*   Lew, M., Mesch, D., Johnson, D. W., & Johnson, R. T. (1986). Positive interdependence, academic and collaborative-skills group contingencies, and isolated students. *American Educational Research Journal, 23*, 476-488. (Cited above as Item 239.)

*   Madden, N. A. (1980). Effects of cooperative learning on the social acceptance of mainstreamed academically handicapped students. *Dissertation Abstracts International, 41*, 2332B. (University Microfilms Order Number ADG80-27386. 0000) (Cited above as Item 242.)

*   Martens, M. L. (1990). Getting a grip on groups. *Science and Children, 27*(5), 18-19. (Cited above as Item 198.)

*   Merebah, S. A. A. (1987). Cooperative learning in science: A comparative study in Saudi Arabia. *Dissertation Abstracts*

International, 48, 1892A. (University Microfilms Order Number ADG87-15228. 8710) (Cited above as Item 081.)

322.   Mesch, D., Lew, M., Johnson, D. W., & Johnson, R. T. (1986, July). Isolated teenagers, cooperative learning, and the training of social skills. *The Journal of Psychology, 120*(4), 323-334.

Examined the effects of individual and group contingencies on the achievement and social skills of learning-disabled students in an isolated setting.

*   Morgan, B. M. (1987). Cooperative learning: Teacher use, classroom life, social integration, and student achievement. *Dissertation Abstracts International, 48*, 3043A. (Copies available exclusively from Micrographics Department, Doheny Library, USC, Los Angeles, CA 90089-0182) (Cited below as Item 417.)

323.   Nelson, J. (1981). *Positive Discipline. Teaching Children Self Discipline, Responsibility, Cooperation, and Problem-Solving Skills.* Fair Oaks, CA: Sunrise Press.

This book looks at creating democracy and cooperative groups within the classroom for better classroom management.

324.   O'Donnell, A. M., Dansereau, D. F., Hall, R. H., & Rocklin, T. R. (1987). Cognitive, social/affective, and metacognitive outcomes of scripted cooperative learning. *Journal of Educational Psychology, 79*(4), 431-437.

Ninety-three introductory psychology students participated in a two-session experiment using combinations of free recall tests and subjective graphing methods to assess three kinds of outcomes. During the first session, students were assigned to (a) scripted dyads; (b) unscripted dyads; or (c) a group of individuals. During the second session, all students were assigned to new partners and worked together as unscripted dyads. (In a script for a cooperative learning group, the roles played by the members of the group and the sequence of activities engaged in by the group are specified to a greater or lesser extent.)

Dyads recalled more than individuals. Scripted dyads were more positive about their second partners than unscripted dyads, were more accurate in rating their performance, and viewed the activity as less anxiety-provoking than did individuals. Participants who were low in public self-consciousness recalled significantly more information and expressed less anxiety on the initial task than did those who were high in public self-consciousness.

*   Oishi, S. S. (1983). Effects of Team-Assisted individualization in mathematics on cross-race and cross-sex interactions of elementary school children (Johns Hopkins; Maryland). University of Maryland. *Dissertation Abstracts International*, *44*, 3622A. (Cited above as Item 062.)

*   O'Neill, J. S., Jr. (1980). The effects of a teams-games-tournaments reward structure on the self-esteem and academic achievement of ninth grade social studies students. *Dissertation Abstracts International*, *41*, 5053A. (University Microfilms Order Number ADG81-07937. 0000) (Cited above as Item 082.)

*   Orlick, T. D. (1981). Positive socialization via cooperative games. *Developmental Psychology*, *17*(4), 426-429. (Cited below as Item 751.)

*   Parker, R. E. (1985). Small-group cooperative learning - improving academic learning, social gains in the classroom. *NASSP Bulletin*, *69*, 48-57. (Cited below as Item 645.)

325.   Prague, S. A. V. (1988). Identifying social skills important to junior high school science students working in cooperative groups. Texas A & M University. *Dissertation Abstracts International*, *49*, 3285A.

         "The purpose of this qualitative research was for junior high school science students, in grades six, seven and eight, to identify and define in their own terminology the social skills considered important to them while working in cooperative groups." Study consisted of interviews with their students and administration of questionnaires to six teachers and 465 students. Identified social skills that are necessary for successful implementation of cooperative learning techniques: cooperate, listen, explain well, involve everyone, follow directions, divide jobs fairly, work effectively, be creative, be courteous, be patient, discuss, involve the non-worker, encourage, question, and prompt.

326.   Ritchie, A. (1989). Learning to share: A moral necessity. *Educational Forum*, *53*, 365-378.

        Argues that the concept of sharing should be taught to all young children. Citing Dewey's work as the basis for her conclusion, Ritchie insists that schools must provide shared learning opportunities. Positive results of cooperative learning activities include the development of good self-concept and a respect for peers.

327.   Schaps, E., & Solomon, D. (1988). The child development project. *Newsletter. The International Association for the Study of Cooperation in Education*, *9*(3, 4), 15-16.

        The study's approach to cooperative learning is to emphasize "intrinsic reasons for engaging in group tasks," rather than giving group rewards or grades. Result so far indicate that "the greater the teacher's implementation of the program, the more prosocially the students behave." Students in the program also had a more positive attitude toward the program and toward other students than control groups. Increases (after 3 or 4 years in the program) in "assertion responsibility," "willingness to compromise," and "equality of representation and participation" were reported. The authors conclude that the results indicate a "self-other balance" where students are concerned with the opinions of others as well as their own opinions, and are willing to compromise.

328.   Schmuck, R. A., & Schmuck, P.A. (1974). *A Humanistic Psychology of Education. Making the School Everybody's House*. Palo Alto, CA: Mayfield Publishing Co.

        A guide to creating a climate within the school which is caring through the use of cooperative groups.

329.   Schultz, J. L. (1989/1990). Cooperative learning: Refining the process. *Educational Leadership*, *47*(4), 43-45.

        Emphasizes the crucial need for teachers to give adequate attention to monitoring and teaching social skills if they are to introduce cooperative learning successfully. Addresses the author's initial difficulty and final triumph after some reflection, monitoring, and adjustment on his part.

* Sharan, S., & Shachar, H. (1988). *Language and Learning in the Cooperative Classroom.* New York: Springer-Verlag. 176 pp. (Cited above as Item 044.)

* Sharan, Y., & Sharan, S. (1989/1990). How effective is group investigation? *Educational Leadership, 47*(4), 18. (Cited below as Item 657.)

* Slavin, R. E. (1983). *Cooperative Learning.* NY: Longman. 147 pp. (Cited below as Item 659.)

330. Slavin, R. E. (1977). *Student learning team techniques: Narrowing the achievement gap between the races* (Report No. 228). Baltimore: Center for Social Organization of Schools, Johns Hopkins University.

331. Slavin, R. E. (1978). Student teams and comparison among equals: Effects on academic performance and student attitudes. *Journal of Educational Psychology, 70*(4), 532-538.

> The independent effects of level of reward (recognition based on the performance of a four- to five-member cooperative learning team vs. recognition based on individual performance) and comparison of student quiz scores (comparison with ability-homogeneous groups vs. comparison with entire class) on student achievement and attitudes. Subjects were 205 seventh-grade students in eight English classes.
> Slavin found that participation in the team treatments increased the percentage of time students spent on tasks but did not increase their academic achievement. The predicted positive effects of team reward on mutual concern, peer norms supporting academic performance, and motivation were in evidence. This last finding is of importance for use in settings which are in need of improving student concern for others, as in schools for disturbed adolescents and racially integrated schools.

* Slavin, R. E., & Hansell, S. (1983). Cooperative learning and intergroup relations: Contact theory in the classroom. In J. L. Epstein and N. Karweit (Eds.), *Friends in school: Patterns of selection and influence in secondary schools*, (pp. 93-114). New York: Academic Press. (Cited above as Item 021.)

332.   Tjosvold, D., Johnson, D. W., & Johnson, R. T. (1981). Effect of
         partner's effort and ability on liking for partner after failure on a
         cooperative task. *The Journal of Psychology, 109*, 147-152.

         Fifty-two Canadians participated in a study to determine the
         effects of perceived effort and ability between group members on
         a cooperative task. Results indicate that cooperative experiences
         in relation to interpersonal liking was desirable in social setting
         when working with high-effort partners.

*   Tyrrell, R. (1990, January). What teachers say about cooperative
         learning. *Middle School Journal, 21*(3), 16-19. (Cited below as
         Item 497.)

333.   Vacha, E., McDonald, W., Coburn, J. & Black, H. (1979).
         Improving Classroom Social Climate: Teacher's Handbook.
         New York, NY: Rinehart & Winston.

         A collection of exercises that can be used in the classroom
         of fourth through sixth graders in order to deal with such areas as
         leadership, communication, attraction, classroom cohesion, and
         expectations. All exercises are based on the principles that were
         developed by Dick and Pat Schmuck.

334.   Webb, N. (1988). Small group problem solving: Peer interaction
         and learning. Newsletter. *The International Association for the
         Study of Cooperation in Education, 9*(3,4), 11-12.

         The author finds that in terms of giving (and receiving)
         appropriate help to other students, mid-ability students give and
         receive the most help in homogeneous groups. ("In wide range
         heterogeneous groups, the highs and lows [ability] and to form a
         'teacher-student' relationship while ignoring the needs of those in
         the middle." Training students in explaining, question-asking,
         and in understanding the needs of others is suggested. The author
         suggests using equal numbers of girls and boys to "help equalize
         participation in the group." Also notes that if introverted
         students are the students of highest ability in a group, they will
         participate more.

335.   Wood, K. (1988). Meeting the social needs of adolescents through
         cooperative learning. *Middle School Journal, 20*(1), 32-34.

Discusses the significance of meeting the social needs of adolescents, and describes a variety of so-called cooperative learning strategies that are easily implemented and appropriate for all subject areas: Group retellings, buddy system, research grouping, cybernetic sessions, tutorial groupings, social grouping, and interest grouping. Some of the methods suggested are not truly cooperative learning since they lack such key components as group accountability and individual accountability.

336. Wood, K. (1988). Meeting the social needs of adolescents. *Middle School Journal, 20*(2), 21-23.

A continuation of the article described in annotation number 337, this piece describes the additional strategies for incorporating what is rather loosely termed "cooperative learning" into middle school classrooms: Dyadic learning, group communal writing, associational dialogue, generic lesson grouping, random grouping, base grouping, and needs grouping. Each strategy is described and suggestions for implementation in various subject areas are made.

337. Wooster, A. (1986). Social skills training and reading gain. *Educational Research, 28*(1), 68-71.

The study was developed to see if an improvement in social skills would increase reading skills. Nineteen ten-year-olds engaged in a series of exercises designed to teach a range of human relations skills. Students were encouraged to help themselves and each other in pairs and in small and large groups.

The experimental group showed a significant change in reading ability. No significant change was shown in control group scores. The experimental group significantly changed their willingness to accept responsibility for their shortcomings, but did not improve in their willingness to accept credit for their academic successes. The control groups showed no changes in either area. Experimental group expressed more interest in school, improved attendance, and increased number of friendships.

338. Zaccaro, S. J., & Loew, C. A. (1988). Cohesiveness and performance on an additive task: Evidence for

multidimensionality. *The Journal of Social Psychology, 128,*
547-558.

"This experiment contrasted two predictions regarding the
effects of two types of cohesiveness on the performance of
American students. Task-based cohesion and interpersonal
cohesion were manipulated independently. Results show that
high task cohesion facilitated performance, whereas interpersonal
attraction had no apparent effect on production. Increases in
interpersonal cohesion did, however, result in higher task
commitment and more frequent interactions among group
members.

339.   Zahn, G. L., Kagan, S., & Widaman, K. F. (1986). Cooperative
learning and classroom climate. *Journal of School Psychology,*
24, 351-362.

Examines the impact of Student Teams-Achievement
Divisions and Teams-Games-Tournament on classroom climate
as compared to traditional whole-class format. "Thirty-five
student teachers were randomly assigned to one of the three
classroom structures. Their pupils were 864 second- through
sixth-grade students, including 288 non-Anglo (black and
Mexican-American) students. A new measure of classroom
climate, the Classroom Attitudes Scale, was developed that
produced two attitude factors: Social Relations and School-work.
Cooperative techniques generally produced a slightly more
favorable climate on both dimensions, and especially for females
on Social Relations. Of the cooperative methods, Teams-
Games-Tournament produced a significantly more favorable
climate for Anglo-American students. The results support the
conclusion that choice of classroom structure can bias classroom
climate in favor of or against different ethnic groups."

B. COMPARISONS OF LEARNING CONDITIONS (COOPERATIVE, COMPETITIVE, INDIVIDUALISTIC)

340. Ahlgren, A. (1983). Sex differences in the correlates of cooperative and competitive school attitudes. *Developmental Psychology, 19* (6), 881-888.

> To determine sex differences in attitudinal patterns, attitudes toward cooperation and competition in school were correlated with other school attitudes: personal worth, external motivation, behavior control, internal motivation, non-communication, academic press (stress), and external loss of control. Participants included 2,130 boys and girls in grades two through twelve. Significant differences were found at all grade levels. As students get older, cooperation becomes a positive construct for both boys and girls, but girls identify it more with their own personal worth. Early in school, boys lose the negative correlates of competition while girls retain some. In high school, boys showed little correlation between cooperation and self-worth, while girls showed for the first time correlations of competition with self-worth and internal motivation.
>
> Ahlgren urged caution when comparing attitudes of boys and girls toward cooperation and competition. He felt a comparison of the gender patterns over the years correlated with cooperative and competitive attitudes may be more valuable than simple comparisons of means between boys and girls.

* Alvarez, C. M., & Pader, O. F. (1979). Cooperative and competitive behavior of Cuban-American and Anglo-American children. *The Journal of Psychology, 101*, 265-271. (Cited below as Item 377.)

341. Ames, C. (1981). Competitive versus cooperative reward structures: The influence of individual and group performance factors on achievement attributions and affect. *American Educational Research Journal, 18*, 273-287.

> "This study examined the effects of cooperative and competitive reward structures on children's attributions and

175

affective reactions to success and failure. Eighty sixth-grade children performed at a high or low level at an achievement task under competitive or cooperative reward contingencies. The cooperative structure included both group success and group failure. Results showed that competitive contingencies accentuated the differences in self-other perceptions and cooperative contingencies minimized these differences. Within a cooperative structure, the success of the cooperative group was a major factor affecting self and interpersonal evaluations. The results are discussed within an attribution and self-worth theory of motivated behavior."

342.   Ames, C., & Ames, R. (1978). The Thrill of Victory and the Agony of Defeat: Childrens' Self and Interpersonal Evaluations in Competitive and Non Competitive Learning Environments. *Journal of Research and Development in Education*, *12*, 79-87.

The authors conducted two studies. In the first, children attempted to solve puzzles which were either solvable or not. In the first group, the child who solved the most puzzles received a prize. In the second group, all children received a prize. In the competitive groups, the children who lost had more negative feelings towards themselves than the children who lost in other groups. In the competitive groups, the winning children felt more deserving than the children who lost. In the second study, children listened to a story about children solving puzzles in order to receive an individual reward, competitive award or cooperative award. The findings were repeated; children who failed in competitive groups were viewed as less deserving than failed children of other groups.

343.   Azmita, M. (1988). Peer interaction and problem problem solving: When are two heads better than one? *Child Development*, *59*, 87-96.

Addresses the findings of three questions: 1. Does group work and cooperative activities lead to greater learning than independent study? 2. Does group and/or cooperative team learning generalize to later independent situations? 3. What characteristics of group interaction facilitate learning? Azmita found that preschool children are "more likely to acquire cognitive skills when they work with a more expert partner," that "only novices who worked with an expert generalized their skills to the individual posttest," and that "observational learning and guidance by an expert mediated learning."

344. Bar-Tal, D., & Geser, D. (1980). Observing cooperation in the classroom group. In S. Sharan, P. Hare, C. D. Webb, C. D., & R. Hertz-Lazarowitz (Eds.), *Cooperation in Education*, (pp. 212-225). Provo, UT: Brigham Young University Press.

"Reports on the development of a conceptualization and operationalization of cooperation, allowing for a qualitative and quantitative examination in various groups under natural situations, including the classroom content. [In doing so, it] includes a report on a small-scale study to demonstrate the application of the conceptual model and the use of the research instrument designed to measure cooperative behavior."

* Bruning, J. L., Sommer, D. K., & Jones, B. R. (1966). The motivational effects of cooperation and competition in the means-independent situation. *The Journal of Social Psychology, 68,* 269-274. (Cited below as Item 568.)

* Delgado, M. T. (1987). The effects of a cooperative learning strategy on the academic behavior of Mexican-American children. *Stanford University, 48,* (6). (Cited below as Item 383.)

345. Dunn, R. E., & Goldman, M. (1966). Competition and non-competition in relationship to satisfaction and feelings toward own-group and nongroup members." *The Journal of Social Psychology, 68,* 299-311.

"One purpose of this study was to evaluate the relative satisfaction of small-discussion-group members under four conditions of reward: (a) rewards given individually on a noncompetitive basis (individual merit), (b) rewards given equally among a group on a noncompetitive basis (group merit), (c) rewards given individually on a competitive basis (individual competitive), and (d) rewards given equally among a group on a competitive basis (group competition). A second purpose of the study was to compare the group-merit and group-competition treatment with respect to the acceptance or the rejection of own-group and nongroup members." Findings revealed that group members experience greater satisfaction when they share the rewards for achievement than when given individual awards.

Subjects receiving mutual rewards revealed greater acceptance of both own-group and nongroup members. Results "emphasize the advantage of having group members share rewards while making mutual contributions on a competitive basis, competing neither against each other nor against other groups."

346.   Farivar, S. H. (1985). Developing and implementing a cooperative learning program in a middle elementary classroom: A comparative study of innovative and traditional teaching and learning strategies. *Dissertation Abstracts International, 46,* 1823A. (University Microfilms Order Number ADG85-19093. 8601)

An exploratory study that describes a cooperative class (one that uses cooperative learning) and a quasi-experimental study that compares the cooperative class with a traditional one.

347.   Fehring, H. (1987). *Cooperative learning strategies applied in the language classroom.* (Reading Around Series No. 1). Adelaide, Australia: Australian Reading Association. (ERIC Document Reproduction Service No. ED 285122).

Compares individual, competitive, and cooperative learning, then discusses key features of a cooperative learning environment. Several examples of practical lessons using cooperative learning strategies are included: a one-lesson unit for year three on the creative use of synonyms, a three-week story writing unit for year 6, a one-term unit called "the making of a video" for year nine, a one to three lesson unit on clear thinking for year eleven. A final section suggests a method for organizing a one-unit lesson and lists helpful hints for implementing cooperative learning.

348.   Garibaldi, A. M. (1979). Affective contributions of cooperative and group goal structures. *Journal of Educational Psychology, 71*(6), 788-794.

Ninety-two high school students were randomly assigned to one of four experimental conditions involving the playing of two games. Students were then asked to assess the affective benefits of using cooperative and group goal structures on problem-solving tasks. Results showed that students who worked in groups (cooperation and intergroup competition) performed better on tasks, expressed greater certainty about their answers, and indicated more enjoyment of tasks than did students who worked alone (interpersonal competition and individualization). "Pure" cooperation also improved interpersonal attraction and influenced more positive ratings towards tasks than did intergroup competition. These results support findings by Johnson and Johnson (1974) in favor of cooperation and group goal structures and contest the review of Michaels (1977) who favored the efficiency of competition and individual reward contingencies.

The major implication for teachers, says Garibaldi, is that cooperative and group goal structures should be considered more often in the classroom. The study suggests that "students not only feel better about their learning when they work in groups but also show greater liking toward peers and regard learning exercises more favorably in cooperatively structured activities."

349.   Georgas, J. (1986). Cooperative, competitive, and individualistic goal structure with seventh-grade Greek children: Problem-solving effectiveness and group interactions. *The Journal of Social Psychology, 126,* 227-236.

Details a study testing the hypothesis that "the problem-solving effectiveness and types of group interactions of cooperative, competitive, and individualistic goal structures might be affected by sex and academic grades." The study involved 90 seventh-grade Greek students who were divided into "30 three-person groups, half male and half female, with three academic grade (A, B, and C) levels." Using Mastermind and Questions problems, the researcher found that "problem-solving effectiveness of the cooperative goal structure did not differ from average individual, nor did the cooperative goal structure from the competitive. Low academic grades resulted in lower problem-solving effectiveness, but academic grades did not interact with goal structures. Group interactions differed in cooperative and competitive goal structure but were not affected by grades or sex."

*   Goldman, M. (1965). A comparison of individual and group performance for varying combinations of initial ability. *Journal of Personality and Social Psychology, 1,* 210-216. (Cited below as Item 509.)

*   Gottheil, E. (1955). Changes in social perception contingent upon
         competing and cooperating. *Sociometry, 18*, 132-137. (Cited
         below as Item 686.)

350.   Griffin, R. (1988). Cooperation, competition, individualism --
         students need all three. *Clearing House, 62*, 52.

         A short article that presents the necessity, as well as the
         merits, of providing students a wide range of learning activities,
         including cooperative, competitive, and individual learning
         activities.

*   Grossack, M. M. (1954). Some effects of cooperation and
         competition upon small group behavior. *Journal of Abnormal
         and Social Psychology, 49*, 341-348. (Cited below as Item
         687.)

351.   Henderson, R. W., & Hannelore, H. (1979). Relationships among
         cooperation-competition and locus of control in social and
         academic situations among children in traditional and open
         classrooms. *Contemporary Educational Psychology, 4*, 121-
         131.

         Discusses the findings of a study that compares the
         relationships among cooperation and competition, perceptions of
         focus of control in social situations, and perceptions of locus of
         control in intellectual-academic situations of students in
         traditional and open classrooms. Students in the open setting
         displayed more cooperative characteristics and made significant
         gains in cooperative behavior. "Traditional students displayed
         significantly higher internality for locus of control in academic
         settings, while perception of locus of control in social settings
         did not differ for the two groups. Academics and social locus of
         control judgments were significantly correlated for the open
         education students, but not for the students from traditional
         classrooms." States that conclusions based upon the findings of
         the study must be examined carefully because the validity of one
         of the instruments has not been demonstrated.

352.   Hertz-Lazarowitz, R., Sharan, S., & Steinberg, R. (1980).
         Classroom learning style and cooperative behavior of elementary
         school children. *Journal of Educational Psychology, 72*(1), 99-
         106.

The cooperative behavior of 243 elementary students who studied in cooperative small groups was compared to that of 150 elementary students who were taught with whole-class instruction. In experiment one, a version of Madsen's domino game was used to assess students' altruistic, cooperative, or competitive behavior. In experiment two, groups of five students were asked to construct new words from the letters appearing in an epigram. They were allowed to work alone or to collaborate with others. The authors found students from small-group classrooms to be more cooperative on both judgmental and behavioral measures than students from traditional classrooms.

353.   Hill, G. W. (1982). Group versus individual performance: Are N + 1 heads better than one? *Psychological Bulletin, 91*(3), 517-539.

A review of findings about comparison of groups and individuals. Studies were analyzed on four dimensions (task, process, individual differences, and methodology) using four types of group versus individual comparisons (group vs. individual, group vs. the most competent member, groups vs. statistical pooled responses, and group vs. math models).
Results show: 1. When a task was difficult, group members pooled and integrated their resources and corrected each other's errors. 2. When a task was easy, one competent member often determined performance. 3. Statistical pooling of individual responses frequently produced a larger number of unique ideas than did group interaction when brainstorming. Individuals seem to be able to produce a greater number of ideas when working separately. 4. Group performance was usually superior to individual performance, but was not as good as that of statistical pooling models.
The review supports the concept of process loss in groups as described in I.D. Steiner's theory of group productivity.

354.   Johnson, D. W., & Johnson, R. T. (1978). Cooperative, competitive, and individualistic learning. *Journal of Research and Development in Education, 12*(1), 3-15.

A review of the findings of studies on cooperative, competitive, and individualistic learning and their effects on student motivation, self-concept, attitudes, and psychological health. The authors conclude that all three can be effectively used in the classroom.

*   Johnson, D. W., & Johnson, R. T. (1981). Effects of cooperative
         and individualistic learning experiences on inter-ethnic
         interaction. *Journal of Educational Psychology*, *73*(3), 444-449.
         (Cited below as Item 394.)

*   Johnson, D. W., & Johnson, R. T. (1981). The integration of the
         handicapped into the regular classroom: Effects of cooperative
         and individualistic instruction. *Contemporary Educational
         Psychology*, *6*, 344-353. (Cited above as Item 230.)

*   Johnson, D.W., & Johnson, R.T. (1984). Building acceptance of
         differences between handicapped and nonhandicapped students:
         The effects of cooperative and individualistic instruction. *The
         Journal of Social Psychology*, *122*, 257-267. (Cited above as
         Item 231.)

355.   Johnson, D. W., & Johnson, R. T. (1985). The internal dynamics
         of cooperative learning groups. In R. Slavin, S. Sharan, S.
         Kagan, R. Hertz-Lazarowitz, C. Webb, & R. Schmuck (Eds.),
         Learning to Cooperate, Cooperating to Learn, (pp. 103-124).
         New York: Plenum Press.

             In their discussion of "the internal processes within
         cooperative learning groups that mediate or moderate the
         relationship between cooperation and productivity as well as
         interpersonal attraction among students," the Johnsons address
         the following: Theory of social interdependence, their research
         efforts and procedures, social interdependence and achievement,
         social interdependence and relationships among students, and
         various variables that illustrate internal dynamics of cooperative
         learning groups (e.g., type of task, quality of learning strategy,
         controversy versus concurrence seeking, time on task, cognitive
         processing, peer support, active mutual involvement in
         learning, ability levels of groups members, psychological
         support and acceptance, attitudes toward subject areas, fairness of
         grading, etc.).

*   Johnson, D. W., & Johnson, R. T. (1987). *Learning Together &
         Alone: Cooperative, Competitive, & Individualistic Learning*.
         Englewood Cliffs, NJ: Prentice-Hall. 193 pp. (Cited below as
         Item 610.)

*   Johnson, D. W., & Johnson, R. T. (1988). Critical thinking
            through structured controversy. *Educational Leadership*, *46*(8),
            58-64. (Cited above as Item 030.)

356.   Johnson, D. W., & Johnson, R. T. (1989). Motivational processes.
            In D. W. Johnson & R. T. Johnson (Eds.), *Cooperation and
            Competition: Theory and Research* (pp. 77-88). Edina, MN:
            Interaction Book Company.

            Discusses motivation and its determinants which cause
            different levels of achievement. Results indicate that in the
            cooperative condition, achievement levels are high and positive
            in regard to success expectation, commitment, persistence,
            incentive to achieve, curiosity, and interest. In the competitive
            and individualistic conditions, results were low or negative in all
            areas except ability.

*   Johnson, D. W., & Johnson, R. T. (1989). Social interdependence.
            In D.W. Johnson & R.T. Johnson (Eds.), *Cooperation and
            Competition: Theory and Research* (pp. 23-38). Edina, MN:
            Interaction Book Company. (Cited above as Item 308.)

*   Johnson, D. W., & Johnson, R. T. (1989). Social interdependence
            and interpersonal attraction. In D. W. Johnson & R. T.
            Johnson (Eds.), *Cooperation and Competition: Theory and
            Research* (pp. 107-130). Edina, MN: Interaction Book
            Company. (Cited above as Item 309.)

357.   Johnson, D.W., & Johnson, R. T. (1989). Social interdependence
            and productivity/achievement. In D.W. Johnson & R.T.
            Johnson (Eds.), *Cooperation and Competition: Theory and
            Research* (pp. 39-56). Edina, MN: Interaction Book Company.

            Compares the outcomes of cooperative, competitive, and
            individualistic situations in regard to productivity and
            achievement. Findings show that in the cooperative situation,
            higher achievement is observed as well as greater productivity.
            Cooperative situations promote more frequent reasoning and
            learning than competitive or individualistic situations.

*   Johnson, D. W., & Johnson, R. T. (1989). Social interdependence
            and psychological health. In D. W. Johnson & R. T. Johnson
            (Eds.), *Cooperation and Competition: Theory and Research* (pp.

141-154). Edina, MN: Interaction Book Company. (Cited above as Item 310.)

*   Johnson, D. W., & Johnson, R. T. (1989). Social interdependence and self-esteem. In D. W. Johnson & R. T. Johnson (Eds.), *Cooperation and Competition: Theory and Research* (pp. 155-168). Edina, MN: Interaction Book Company. (Cited above as Item 311.)

*   Johnson, D. W., & Johnson, R. T. (1989). Social interdependence and social support. In D. W. Johnson & R. T. Johnson (Eds.), *Cooperation and Competition: Theory and Research* (pp. 131-140). Edina, MN: Interaction Book Company. (Cited above as Item 312.)

*   Johnson, D. W., Johnson, R. T., & Anderson, D. (1978). Student cooperative, competitive, and individualistic attitudes, and attitudes toward schooling. *The Journal of Psychology, 100*, 183-199. (Cited below as Item 615.)

358.   Johnson, D. W., Johnson, R. T., Johnson, J., & Anderson, D. (1976). Effects of cooperative versus individualized instruction on student prosocial behavior, attitudes toward learning, and achievement. *Journal of Educational Psychology, 68*(4), 446-452.

Thirty fifth-grade students matched on previous achievement in language arts were assigned to cooperative and individualized conditions for learning language arts for 45 to 60 minutes a day for a seventeen-day period. Results indicate that cooperative learning resulted in more altruism, more positive attitudes toward classroom life, and higher achievement. Authors warned that while results supported past research, due to limitations of the study, results should be tentatively accepted.

*   Johnson, D. W., Johnson, R. T., & Skon, L. (1979). Student achievement on different types of tasks under cooperative, competitive, and individualistic conditions. *Contemporary Educational Psychology, 4*, 99-106. (Cited below as Item 514.)

*   Johnson, D. W., Maruyama, G., Johnson, R. T., Nelson, D. & Skon, L. (1981). Effects of cooperative, competitive, and individualistic goal structure on achievement: a meta-analysis.

Psychological Bulletin, 89(1), 47-62. (Cited below as Item 516.)

359.   Johnson, D. W., & Norem-Hebeisen, A. A. (1979). A measure of cooperative, competitive, and individualistic attitudes. *The Journal of Social Psychology, 109*, 253-261.

"Six studies involving over 600 students from kindergarten through college were sequenced over a period of years to develop three relatively independent self-report scales with substantial internal reliability to measure attitudes toward cooperative, competitive, and individualistic interdependence between oneself and others in educational settings. The purpose of the scale development was to provide a research tool for social scientists interested in social interdependence. In addition, evidence was gathered, and some additional evidence indicating a change in conceptions of the three types of social interdependence in junior high was found." Based upon student responses, the cooperative scale was divided into two parts: liking to cooperate and valuing cooperative learning. Results of cooperative learning experiences include learning from other students and sharing ideas and materials with others.

360.   Johnson, D. W., Skon, L., & Johnson, R. T. (1980). Effects of cooperative, competitive, and individualistic conditions on children's problem-solving performance. *American Educational Research Journal, 17*, 83-93.

"The effects of interpersonal cooperation, competition, and individualistic efforts were compared on a categorization and retrieval, a spatial-reasoning, and a verbal problem-solving task. Forty-five first-grade children were randomly assigned to conditions stratified on the basis of sex and ability, so that an approximately equal percentage of males and females and high, medium, and low ability children were included in each condition. The results indicate that on all three tasks students in the cooperative condition achieved higher than did those in the competitive condition. There were no significant differences between the competitive and individualistic condition. Students in the cooperative condition used higher quality strategies on the three tasks than did those in the other two conditions, and they perceived higher levels of peer support and encouragement for learning. High ability students in the cooperative condition generally achieved higher than did the high ability students in the competitive and individualistic conditions."

361.   Johnson, D. W., McCarty, K., & Allen, T. (1976). Congruent and contradictory verbal and nonverbal communications of cooperativeness and competitiveness in negotiations. *Communication Research: An International Quarterly*, *3*(3), 275-292.

Examines congruency of verbal and nonverbal messages, relative impact of verbal and nonverbal messages, and expression of cooperative or competitive intentions as the three issues which are thought to leave an effect on the negotiation of an agreement in mixed-motive conflict.

362.   Johnson, R. T., Bjorkland, R., & Krotee, M. L. (1984). The effects of cooperative, competitive, and individualistic student interaction patterns on the achievement and attitudes of students learning the golf skill of putting. *Research Quarterly for Exercise and Sport*, *55*(2), 129-134.

A discussion of three specific types of student-student learning (cooperative, competitive, and individualistic) which can be used in the learning process of certain physical skills. The golf skill of putting was learned and demonstrated by students while they were observed in order to determine which interaction pattern best promoted learning.

*   Johnson, R. T., & Johnson, D. W. (1979). Cooperative learning, powerful science. *Science and Children*, *17*(3), 26-27. (Cited above as Item 194.)

363.   Johnson, R. T., & Johnson, D. W. (1979). Type of task and student achievement and attitudes in interpersonal cooperation, competition, and individualization. *The Journal of Social Psychology*, *108*, 37-48.

"The effects of interpersonal cooperation, competition, and individualization were compared on drill-review, problem-solving, specific-knowledge acquisition, and specific-knowledge retention instructional tasks." The study involved sixty-six fifth graders. "The results indicate that cooperation generally produced more positive attitudes than did either individualization or competition. Cooperation resulted in higher achievement than did competition and individualization on both the problem-solving and retention tasks, higher achievement than competition and just as high achievement as individualization on the drill-review task, and higher achievement than individualization and just as high achievement as competition on the specific-knowledge-acquisition task."

*   Johnson, R.T., & Johnson, D. W. (1981). Building friendships between handicapped and nonhandicapped students: Effects of cooperative learning and individualistic learning. *American Educational Research Journal, 18,* 415-423. (Cited above as Item 233.)

364. Johnson, R. T., & Johnson, D. W. (1986). *Encouraging Student/Student Interaction. Research Matters...to the Science Teacher.* National Association for Research in Science Teaching. (ERIC Document Reproduction Service No. ED 266 960).

Results of a study of over 600 research studies comparing cooperative, competitive, and individualistic goals structure find that cooperative learning is the most powerful of the three. Findings suggest that science teachers should use small, heterogeneous, cooperative groups most of the time during instruction.

*   Johnson, R. T, & Johnson, D. W. (1985). Student-student interaction: Ignored but powerful. *Journal of Teacher Education, 34,* 22-26. (Cited below as Item 473.)

*   Johnson, R. T., Johnson, D.W., DeWeerdt, N., Lyons, V., & Zaidman, B. (1983). Integrating severely adaptively handicapped seventh-grade students into constructive relationships with nonhandicapped peers in science class. *American Journal of Mental Deficiency, 87*(6), 611-618. (Cited above as Item 234.)

*   Johnson, R.T., Johnson, D.W. & Rynders, J. (1981). Effect of cooperative, competitive, and individualistic experiences on self-esteem of handicapped and nonhandicapped students. *Journal of Psychology, 108*(1), 31-34. (Cited above as Item 235.)

*   Johnson, R. T., Johnson, D. W., & Stanne, M. B. (1985). Effects of cooperative, competitive, and individualistic goal structures on computer-assisted instruction. *Journal of Educational Psychology*, *77*(6), 668-677. (Cited above as Item 098.)

*   Johnson, R. T., Johnson, D. W., & Stanne, M. B. (1986). Comparison of computer-assisted cooperative, competitive, and individualistic learning. *American Educational Research Journal*, *23*, 382-392. (Cited above as Item 99.)

*   Johnson, R.T., Johnson, D.W., & Tauer, M. (1979). The effects of cooperative, competitive, and individualistic goal structures on students' attitudes and achievement. *The Journal of Psychology*, *102*, 191-198. (Cited below as Item 519.)

*   Johnson, R., Rynders, J., Johnson, D. W., Schmidt, B., & Haider, S. (1979). Interaction between handicapped and nonhandicapped teenagers as a function of situational goal structuring: Implications for mainstreaming. *American Educational Research Journal*, *16*, 161-167. (Cited above as Item 236.)

*   Kagan, S. (1980). Cooperation -- Competition, culture, and structural bias in classrooms. In S. Sharan, P. Hare, C. D. Webb, C. D., & R. Hertz-Lazarowitz (Eds.), *Cooperation in Education*, (pp. 197-211). Provo, UT: Brigham Young University Press. (Cited below as Item 397.)

*   Kagan, S. (1989/1990). The structural approach to cooperative learning. *Educational Leadership*, *47*(4), 12-15. (Cited above as Item 012.)

*   Kagan, S., Zahn, G. L., Widaman, K. F., Schwarzwald, J., & Tyrrell, G. (1985). Classroom structural bias: Impact of cooperative and competitive classroom structures on cooperative and competitive individuals and groups. In R. Slavin, S. Sharan, S. Kagan, R. Hertz-Lazarowitz, C. Webb, & R. Schmuck (Eds.), *Learning to Cooperate, Cooperating to Learn*, (pp. 227-312). New York: Plenum Press. (Cited below as Item 401.)

*   Kenderski, C. M. (1983). Interaction processes and learning among third grade Black and Mexican-American students in cooperative small groups. University of California at Los Angeles. *Dissertation Abstracts International*, *45*, 1216A. (Cited below as Item 402.)

*   Knight, G. P., & Kagan, S. (1982). Siblings' birth order and
        cooperative-competitive social behavior: A comparison of
        Anglo-American and Mexican-American children. *Journal of
        Cross-Cultural Psychology, 13*(2), 239-49. (Cited below as Item
        404.)

*   Lyons, V. M. (1982). A study of elaborative cognitive processing
        as a variable mediating achievement in cooperative learning
        groups. University of Minnesota. *Dissertation Abstracts
        International, 43*, 1090A. (Cited above as Item 033.)

*   Luckner, J. L. (1987). *Enhancing Self-Esteem of Special Needs
        Students.* Paper presented at the Annual Meeting of the Council
        for Exceptional Children, Chicago, IL. (ERIC Document
        Reproduction Service No. ED 288 344). (Cited above as Item
        241.)

*   Madsen, M. C. (1967). Cooperative and competitive motivation of
        children in three Mexican subcultures. *Psychology Reports, 20*,
        1307-1320. (Cited below as Item 409.)

*   May, M., & Doob, L. W. (1937). *Competition and cooperation.
        Social Science Research Council Bulletin.* New York: Social
        Science Research Council. (Cited below as Item 692.)

365.   Miller, L. K., & Hamblin, R. L. (1963). Interdependence,
        differential rewarding and productivity. *American Sociological
        Review, 21*, 768-778.

            Argues that cooperative incentive structures are most
        effective for interdependent tasks, while competitive or
        individualistic incentive structures are most effective for
        independent tasks. Over the years there has been considerable
        disagreement with this finding. Johnson and Johnson (1974)
        argued that cooperative incentive structures are best for all but
        the most mechanical-like tasks, such as speed drills.

366.   Napier, S. (1968). Individual versus group learning on three
        different tasks. *The Journal of Psychology, 69*, 249-257.

            Verbal, motor, and a complex coordination task are used in a
        series of experiments to evaluate differences between individuals
        and groups. No convincing evidence was found that a group

achieves more than the pooling of behavior results of a similar number of individual acting alone.

367.   Nowicki, S., Jr., Duke, M. P., & Crouch, M. P. D. (1978). Sex differences in locus of control and performance under competitive and cooperative conditions. *Journal of Educational Psychology*, *70*(4), 482-486.

Locus of control (external or internal) was determined for 60 volunteers taken from two social sororities and 20 females and 80 males selected from the subject pool of an introductory psychology course. Median age of subjects was 19 years. Subjects were asked to compete against or cooperate with same- or opposite-sex partners. Internally controlled males increased their achievement more than did externally controlled males. Internally controlled females increased their performance when competing against males or cooperating with females. The authors interpreted their results to mean that "females may require more complex models to describe their behavior in general and the locus of control/achievement relation in particular." While males respond in a fairly consistent manner, "the type of situation and the type of participants in that situation may have a significant effect on how an internal as opposed to an external female responds."

*   Okebukola, P. A., & Ogunniyi, M. B. (1984). Cooperative, Competitive and Individualistic Science Laboratory Interaction Patterns-Effects on Students Achievement and Acquisition of Practice Skills. *Journal of Research in Science Education*, *21*(9), 875-889. (Cited above as Item 205.)

*   Okebukola, P. A. (1985). The relative effectiveness of cooperative and competitive interaction techniques in strengthening students' performance in science classes. *Science Education*, *69*(4), 501-509. (Cited above as Item 201.)

*   Orlick, T. (1978). *Winning Through Cooperation: Competitive Insanity -- Cooperative Alternatives*. Washington, D. C.: Acropolis. 278 pp. (Cited below as Item 643.)

368.   Owens, L., & Barnes, J. (1982). The relationships between cooperative, competitive, and individualized learning preferences

and students' perceptions of classroom learning atmosphere. *American Educational Research Journal, 19*, 182-200.

"Learning preferences and perceptions of classroom learning atmosphere were compared for a sample of 279 Sydney secondary school students in grades seven and eleven. Students completed both the Learning Preference Scale-Students and the Classroom Learning Atmosphere Scale -- secondary twice, once for their English classes and once for their mathematics classes. Grade eleven students prefer both more cooperative and more competitive contact than do Grade seven students. English generally is seen as more appropriate for cooperative contact than is mathematics, though girls prefer competing in English more than boys do, and boys prefer competing in mathematics more than girls do. Personal cooperative learning preferences are clearly related to perceptions of actual classroom emphasis on interpersonal relationships and personal development in three of the four Year X Subject groups. Grade eleven mathematics differs in that both students with high cooperative learning preferences and students with low cooperative learning preferences perceive classroom atmosphere similarly. Discussion concentrates on the study of mathematics by girls and the efficacy of cooperative learning."

369.   Owens, L., & Straton, R. G. (1980). The development of a cooperative, competitive, and individualized learning preference scale for students. *The British Journal of Educational Psychology*, 50, 147-161.

Discusses the Learning Preference Scale-Students (LPSS) which was developed "with a sample of 1,653 Sydney [Australia] school-children." The authors state that "Internal consistency, test-retest stability, sub-scale inter-correlations, and factor analysis show that the LPSS has considerable promise as a valid and reliable instrument" to assess the preference of the student for a learning mode, i.e., cooperative, individualized, or competitive. States that "results show clear and significant difference between the preferences of boys and girls over the range of grades from Year Four to Year Eleven." Discusses the following: definitions, review of research, method of study, sample, administration of the tests, and the results. Also includes a copy of the scale.

*   Pepitone, E. A. (Ed.) (1980). *Children in Cooperation and
         Competition*. Lexington, MA: Lexington Books. (Cited below
         as Item 646.)

370.   Pepitone, E. A. (1985). Children in cooperation and competition:
        Antecedents and consequences of self-orientation. In R. Slavin,
        S. Sharan, S. Kagan, R. Hertz-Lazarowitz, C. Webb, & R.
        Schmuck (Eds.), *Learning to Cooperate, Cooperating to Learn*,
        (pp. 17-65). New York: Plenum Press.

        "Considers several theoretical issues on the
        conceptualization of competition and cooperation..., and presents
        a series of related studies of elementary school children from
        different socioeconomic backgrounds in which the emphasis is
        on the children's interpersonal behavior and performance as they
        worked under experimentally controlled competitive and
        cooperative conditions."

*   Pepitone, E. A. (1980). Facilitation of interdependencies in role-
        related cooperative conditions. In E.A. Pepitone (Ed.), *Children
        in Cooperation and Competition*, (pp. 187-208). Lexington,
        Mass: D. C. Heath. (Cited below as Item 696.)

*   Pepitone, E. A. (1980). Major trends in research on competition and
        cooperation, 1897-1980. In E. A. Pepitone (Ed.), *Children in
        Cooperation and Competition*, (pp. 3-65). Lexington, MA:
        D. C. Heath. (Cited below as Item 697.)

*   Pepitone, E. A. (1980). Theoretical orientation. In E. A. Pepitone
        (Ed.), *Children in Cooperation and Competition*, (pp. 67-104).
        Lexington, MA: D. C. Heath. (Cited below as Item 698.)

*   Pepitone, E. A., & Vanderbilt, C. E. (1980). Sharing in
        kindergarten children. In E.A. Pepitone (Ed.), *Children in
        Cooperation and Competition*, (pp. 175-186). Lexington, MA:
        D. C. Heath. (Cited below as Item 699.)

*   Pepitone, E. A., Loeb, H. W., & Murdock, E. M. (1980). Age and
        socioeconomic status in children's behavior and performance in
        competition and cooperative working conditions. In E.A.
        Pepitone (Ed.), *Children in Cooperation and Competition*, (pp.
        209-250). Lexington, MA: D. C. Heath. (Cited below as Item
        700.)

*   Perreault, R. J., Jr. (1982). An experimental comparison of cooperative learning to noncooperative learning and their effects on cognitive achievement in junior high industrial arts laboratories. University of Maryland. Dissertation Abstracts International, 43, 3830A. (Cited above as Item 283.)

371.   Perry, L. R. (1975). Competition and cooperation. *British Journal of Educational Studies, 23,* 127-133.

         While this piece does not address cooperative learning per se, its insights into the nature of cooperative learning and competition in the classroom are thought-provoking. The upshot of this piece is that educators need to face the fact that "people co-operate competitively and compete co-operatively, and the neglect of planning educational circumstances with this thought in mind is plainly seen."

372.   Peterson, P. L., & Janicki, T. C. (1979). Individual characteristics and children's learning in large-group and small-group approaches. *Journal of Educational Psychology, 71*(5), 677-687.

         Aptitude-treatment interactions in fourth-, fifth-, and sixth-grade students' learning of a two-week fractions unit. Each of two elementary teachers taught the unit to two classes of randomly assigned students, with each class receiving only one approach. Aptitude measures were administered at the beginning of the study and achievement, attitude, and retention measures at the end. Regression analyses showed significant aptitude-treatment interactions for approach and for ability. Students who initially preferred small groups actually did worse in that approach than in the large-group approach and visa-versa, supporting previous research by Cronbach and Snow that assigning students to the instructional approach they prefer does not improve learning and tends to be detrimental. High ability students did better and had more positive attitudes in the small group because they benefited from "teaching." Low ability students did better and had more positive attitudes in the large group. No one teaching method was found to be best for all students, and authors recommended that teachers take individual needs of students into consideration when planning instruction.

*   Schick, C., & McGlynn, R. P. (1976). Cooperation versus competition in group concept attainment under conditions of

information exchange. *The Journal of Social Psychology, 100*, 311-312. (Cited below as Item 705.)

*   Shapira, A., & Madsden, M. C. (1969). Cooperative competitive behavior of kibbutz and urban children in Israel. *Child Development, 40*, 609-617. (Cited below as Item 425.)

*   Sherman, L. W. (1989). A comparative study of cooperative and competitive achievement in secondary biology classrooms: The group investigation model versus and individually competitive goal structure. *Journal of Research in Science Teaching, 26*(1), 55-64.   (Cited above as Item 207.)

*   Silverthorne, C., Chelune, C., & Imada, A. (1974). The effects of competition and cooperation on level of prejudice. *The Journal of Social Psychology, 92*, 293-301. (Cited below as Item 429.)

*   Simmons, C. H., King, C. S., Tucker, S. S., & Wehner, E. A. (1986). Success strategies: Winning through cooperation or competition. *The Journal of Social Psychology, 126*, 437-444. (Cited below as Item 708.)

*   Simmons, C. H., Wehner, E. A., Tucker, S. S., & King, C. S. (1988). The cooperative/competitive strategy scale: A measure of motivation to use cooperative or competitive strategies for success. *The Journal of Social Psychology, 128*, 199-205. (Cited below as Item 709.)

373.   Skon, L., Johnson, D. W., & Johnson, R. T. (1981). Cooperative peer interaction versus individual competition and individualistic efforts: Effects on the acquisition of cognitive reasoning strategies. *Journal of Educational Psychology, 73*(1), 83-92.

Reasoning strategies involved in categorization and retrieval, language development, and mathematical tasks were examined by comparing the relative effects of cooperative, competitive, and individualistic goal structures on achievement and the acquisition of high-level reasoning strategies.

Eighty-six first grade students were randomly assigned to conditions stratified by sex and academic ability. In the cooperative conditions, students worked with peers of equal or diverse abilities. In the competitive condition, students competed with peers of equal or diverse abilities.

Cooperative interaction, when compared with competitive and individualistic learning, promoted higher achievement and the discovering of superior cognitive reasoning strategies. Results seem to indicate that it is the discussion with one's peers that promotes the higher cognitive reasoning and not the ability of the members of one's cooperative group. When high academic performance based on the use of high quality cognitive reasoning strategies is desired, cooperative interaction is to be preferred over competitive and individualistic instruction.

*   Smith, K., Johnson, D. W., & Johnson, R. T. (1981). Can conflict be constructive? Controversy versus concurrence seeking in learning groups. *Journal of Educational Psychology, 73*(5), 651-663. (Cited above as Item 036.)

374.   Smith, S. A. (1965). Conformity in cooperative and competitive groups. *The Journal of Social Psychology, 65*, 337-350.

"This investigation reports on an experiment designed to find the effects upon conformity of varying subjects' set, in terms of different degrees of competition and cooperation. The aim is to find under what conditions of competition and cooperation conformity is the more strongly represented." The experiment involved four groups: a cooperative group, a competitive group, and two control groups. Findings support the hypothesis that people in cooperative groups will conform more than people in a competitive setting.

375.   Solomon, D., Watson, M., Battistich, V., Schaps, E., Tuck, P., Solomon, J., Cooper, C., & Ritchey, W. (1985). A program to promote interpersonal consideration and cooperation in children. In R. Slavin, S. Sharan, S. Kagan, R. Hertz-Lazarowitz, C. Webb, & R. Schmuck (Eds.), *Learning to Cooperate, Cooperating to Learn*, (pp. 371-401). New York: Plenum Press.

Describes a project whose purpose is to develop and evaluate the effectiveness of a comprehensive school- and home-based program (Child Development Program) to enhance pro-social tendencies in young children. Discusses the theoretical model used, the program, evaluation of the program, significance of the program, and future directions.

*   Tjosvold, D., & Santamria, P. (1978). Effects of cooperation and
           teacher support on student attitudes toward decision making in
           the elementary science classroom. *Journal of Research in
           Science Education, 15*(5), 381-385. (Cited above as Item 208.)

376.   Valiant, G., Glachan, M., & Emler, N. (1982). The stimulation of
           cognitive development through co-operative task performance.
           The British Journal of Educational Psychology, 52, 282-288.

           "Seventy-eight children, identified as pre-operational with
           respect to multiple classification skills and understanding of left-
           right relations, were provided with one of three forms of training.
           Two of these involved children working in pairs on classification
           problems (collective conditions), the difference between the two
           conditions being where each child stood in relation to the other
           and to the task. In the third form of training, children attempted
           the same problems but worked alone (individual condition).
           During post-tests, children trained in collective conditions
           progressed significantly more than those trained in the individual
           condition with respect to both multiple classification skills and
           conceptions of left-right relations. Results are discussed in terms
           of the role of social interaction in cognitive development."

*   Warring, D., Johnson, D. W., Maruyama, G., & Johnson, R.
           (1985). Impact of different types of cooperative learning on
           cross-ethnic and cross-sex relationships. *Journal of Educational
           Psychology, 77*(1), 53-59. (Cited below as Item 443.)

*   Workie, A. (1974). The relative productivity of cooperation and
           competition. *The Journal of Social Psychology, 92,* 225-230.
           (Cited below as Item 682.)

C.   CULTURAL AND ETHNIC DIFFERENCES

377.   Alvarez, C. M., & Pader, O. F. (1979). Cooperative and competitive behavior of Cuban-American and Anglo-American children. *The Journal of Psychology*, *101*, 265-271.

An examination of cultural differences in the cooperative and competitive behaviors of American children. One hundred forty-four six to eight year-old boys and girls were compared in their performance on the Madsen Cooperation Board. Under group reward instructions, all three groups performed cooperatively, with Anglo-American students averaging higher numbers of circles crossed than Cuban students. All groups decreased in cooperation when instructions changed to individual reward, but only the Anglo-Americans showed a significant increase in competitiveness. Results seemed to show that Cuban-American children were less competitive than Anglo-American children when individually rewarded.

378.   Blanchard, F. A., Weigel, R. H., & Cook, S. W. (1975). The effect of relative competence of group members upon interpersonal attraction in cooperative interracial groups. *Journal of Personality and Social Psychology*, *32*, 519-530.

"This experiment examined the effects of competence of group members and group success-failure on interpersonal attraction of white subjects for both white and black males in cooperative interracial groups." Results indicated that participants exhibited decreased attraction for black participants who performed incompetently, whereas no parallel effect was observed for white participants. Concludes that the success or failure of a group influences the degree of liking and respect among participants of interracial groups.

*   Blau, B., & Raferty, J. (1970). Changes in friendship status as a function of reinforcement. *Child Development*, *41*, 113-121. (Cited above as Item 288.)

*   Clark, M. L. (April, 1985). *Gender, race, and friendship research.*
         Paper presented at the Annual Meeting of the American
         Educational Research Association, Chicago, IL. (ERIC
         Document Reproduction Service No. ED 259 053). (Cited above
         as 291.)

379.   Cohen, E. G. (1986). *Designing groupwork: Strategies for the
         heterogeneous classroom.* New York: Teachers College Press.
         208 pp.

         A guide for designing and encouraging participation in group
         activities regardless of race, sex, academic achievement, or socio-
         economic class. The book may be an effective tool in teaching
         bilingual classes. Not specifically cooperative learning, but
         includes adaptable material.

380.   Conrad, B. D. (1988). Cooperative learning and prejudice reduction.
         Social Education, 52(4), 283-286.

         Conrad presents key research by Kagan, Johnson and
         Johnson, Glasser, Deutsch, Kohn, and Slavin in arguing that
         teachers can assist students "in reducing their prejudices by
         allowing them to learn cooperatively and encouraging them to
         value one another." Readers would be wise to go to the original
         sources for an examination of the actual studies by the
         aforementioned researchers, not all of whom are in agreement
         with one another.

381.   Cook, H., & Chi, C. (1984). Cooperative behavior and locus of
         control among American and Chinese-American boys. *The
         Journal of Psychology, 118*(2), 169-177.

         One hundred thirty-nine American and Chinese-American
         boys aged eight to ten years old were paired into internal,
         external, and mixed locus-of-control dyads. Each pair played a
         cooperative board game. Results showed that, overall, Chinese-
         Americans were more external than Americans and, when
         matched on locus of control, were more cooperative than
         Americans. External dyads were more cooperative than internal
         or mixed dyads. In mixed dyads, Chinese-Americans were more
         cooperative than Americans. Results suggest that cultural
         factors play an essential role in influencing cooperative behavior.

382.   Cook, S. W. (1980). *Unresolved issues of cooperative learning.*
         (ERIC Document Reproduction Service No. ED 220 558).

         While research suggests pessimistic outcomes for cross-
         racial relationships in cooperative-learning oriented classrooms,
         actual measures of friendship choices and classmate ratings show
         consistently improving cross-racial relations. Competitiveness
         and the presence of relationships where whites usually tutor
         minorities can be expected to negatively affect relationships.
         Cook concludes that conflicting findings indicate need for more
         research.

*   Cooper, L., Johnson, D. W., Johnson, R., & Wilderson, F. (1980).
         The effects of cooperative, competitive, and individualistic
         experiences on interpersonal attraction among heterogeneous
         peers. *The Journal of Social Psychology, 111,* 243-252. (Cited
         above as Item 294.)

*   Cuban, L. (1989). At-risk students: What teachers and principals
         can do. *Educational Leadership, 46*(5), 29-32. (Cited above as
         Item 226.)

383.   Delgado, M. T. (1987). The effects of a cooperative learning
         strategy on the academic behavior of Mexican-American children.
         Stanford University, 48, (6).

         "The main goal of the present study was to compare a form
         of cooperative learning- paired learning - to individual learning of
         division instruction in fifth-grade Mexican American students."
         Findings revealed that the use of cooperative learning strategies
         provided no significant changes in achievement, attitude toward
         mathematics, or time on task.

384.   DeVries, D. L., & Edwards, K. J. (1974). Student teams and
         learning games: Their effects on cross-race and cross-sex
         interaction. *Journal of Educational Psychology, 66*(5), 741-749.

         "Although many public school are nominally desegregated,
         the interaction among students of varying racial and ethnic
         backgrounds is minimal." One hundred and ten seventh-graders
         (43% blacks and 47% males) were randomly assigned to four
         treatment conditions: 1. Individual quiz; 2. Individual game; 3.
         Team quiz; 4. Team game. The authors found that placing

students on heterogeneous four-member student teams created
significantly greater cross-race and cross sex helping and
friendship. The team-game combination considerably increased
the incidence of cross-race and cross-sex interaction over that of
game alone. Other results were marginal.

385.   DeVries, D. L., Edwards, K. J., & Slavin, R. E. (1978). Biracial
        learning teams and race relations in the classroom: Four field
        experiments using Teams-Games-Tournament. *Journal of
        Educational Psychology, 70*(3), 356-362.

        Researchers investigated the effects of Teams-Games-
        Tournament (TGT), an instructional strategy employing biracial
        learning teams and instructional games, on cross-racial friendship
        in integrated classes. Four experiments involving 558 students
        in grades 7-12, comparing TGT and control treatments were
        reviewed.
        Sociometric measures assessed TGT effects on the number
        of cross-racial friendship choices and the percentage of cross-
        racial choices over all choices made. Results indicated that TGT
        is an effective means of increasing cross-racial friendships in
        integrated classes, possibly because "race is less of a barrier to
        sociometric choice or as part of a general increase in the number
        of friends and workmates claimed by all students regardless of
        race...If misunderstanding and hostility between racial groups are
        a product of limited communication or friendship between
        members of different races, then TGT and related team techniques
        may--by increasing the number of cross-race friendships--
        contribute to a diminution of racial tensions in schools."

386.   Downing, L. L., & Bothwell, K. H., Jr. (1979). Open-space
        schools: Anticipation of peer interaction and development of
        cooperative interdependence. *Journal of Educational Psychology,
        71*(4), 478-484.

        Forty-two same-sex pairs of eighth graders of varied racial
        composition were selected in each of two matched schools, open-
        versus closed-space architectural styles. Open-space students
        were more inclined to choose seats expecting social interaction
        and closed-space students to choose seats indicating little
        interaction with each other, i.e. facing the teacher. A Sex x Race
        x Trial Blocks interaction effect showed that females of either
        race learned to cooperate in same-race pairs and to compete in

mixed-race pairs. White males learned to cooperate and black
males to compete independent of their partner's race. External
locus of control scores were not related to schools, but were
higher for blacks than for whites.

387.   Enters, L. M. (1987). Desegregation: A legal success, an empirical
        failure. Cooperative learning: A promising educational
        intervention. *Dissertation Abstracts International, 48,* 2822A.
        (University Microfilms Order Number ADG88-00172. 8805)

        Discusses the role of cooperative learning in regard to
        fostering better interracial relations.

388.   Gaertner, S. L., Mann, J., Murrell, A., & Dovidio, J. F. (1989).
        Reducing intergroup bias: The benefits of recategorization.
        Journal of Personality and Social Psychology, 57(2). 239-249.

        Using a social categorization approach, two strategies for
        reducing intergroup bias were tested. Three hundred and sixty
        undergraduates participated in small groups. The recategorization
        treatments caused members of two three-person groups to think
        of both memberships as one six-person group or as six separate
        individuals. Results showed that both conditions as compared
        with the control group reduced intergroup bias and in different
        ways. The one-group representation seemed to increase the
        attractiveness of former out-group members, while the separate-
        individuals representation primarily decreased the attractiveness of
        former in-group members. Implications of these findings are
        discussed, including implications for structuring cooperative
        learning groups in the classroom.

389.   Hallinan, M. T., & Teixeira, R. A. (1987). Students' interracial
        friendships: Individual characteristic, structural effects, and racial
        differences. *American Journal of Education, 95,* 563-583.

        Examines the "effects of individual, dyadic, group, and
        classroom level variable on cross-race friendship choices." With
        regard to cooperative classroom structures, the findings indicate
        that "it is the opportunity to get to know black peers better
        through working in the same groups with them that motivates a
        white student's choice of a black best friend." Points out that
        this finding is consistent with earlier research by Robert E.
        Slavin on cooperative work groups. Reveals that the interaction

and shared activities within groups may lead to "discovery of attractive personal characteristics that become a basis of friendship."

390.   Hansell, S., & Slavin, R.E. (1981). Cooperative learning and the structure of interracial friendships. *Sociology of Education, 54*(2), 98-106.

An attempt to determine whether "intensive, regular, cooperative contact between races mandated by the cooperative group experience would stimulate strong interracial friendships." Four hundred and two seventh and eighth graders in twelve inner city language arts classrooms studied a ten-week language mechanics unit on grammar, punctuation, and English usage. Classes were randomly designated as controls or to cooperative team learning treatments.

Using Student Teams-Achievement Divisions (STAD), students were assigned to four or five member learning teams. Each team contained a mix of black and white students, girls and boys, and a range of academic achievement. Results indicated that new cross-race friendships tended to be reciprocated rather than unreciprocated. New cross-race friends were among the first six chosen on socio-metric questionnaires. Cooperative learning increased cross-race friendships equally for students of different sexes, races, and achievement levels.

The authors suggest that cooperative learning in the classroom is a way to improve interracial relations both in and out of class.

391.   Hare, B. R., & Levine, D. U. (1985). Effective schooling in desegregated settings: What do we know about learning styles and linguistic differences? *Equity and Choice, 1*, 13-18.

Discusses various reasons for low academic performance of many low-status students, especially minorities. Suggests instructional strategies that have proved to be effective for use in multicultural/desegregated classrooms. Among the strategies discussed are cooperative learning and individualized instruction.

392.   Hawley, W. D. (1982). Effective educational strategies for desegregated schools. *Peabody Journal of Education, 59*, 209-233.

In the first of two major sections, the article identifies four general conditions that may affect the quality of education in desegregated schools: diversity of student abilities, potential for interracial conflict, discontentment between home and school, and multidimensional change. The second section identifies and discusses in detail twelve strategies for responding to the conditions involved in desegregated schooling. One of the suggested strategies is to "employ instructional strategies that retain heterogeneous classes and work groups"; specifically cited as an example is cooperative learning in a desegregated classroom. Also included are a brief review of related literature, advantages of cooperative learning techniques, and findings of research studies involving cooperative learning strategies, including TGT and STAD.

393. Hernandez, N. G., & Descamps, J. A. (1986). *Review of factors affecting learning of Mexican-Americans.* Paper presented at the National Association for Chicano Studies, El Paso, TX. (ERIC Document Reproduction Service No. ED 267 946).

A review of more than 500 empirical studies conducted since 1970 on the achievement of Mexican-Americans. Cooperative learning environments were found to produce greater academic gains than competitive or individualistic learning environments for all students.

394. Johnson, D. W., & Johnson, R. T. (1981). Effects of cooperative and individualistic learning experiences on inter-ethnic interaction. *Journal of Educational Psychology, 73*(3), 444-449.

Behavioral measures were taken for cross-ethnic interaction within the instructional situation and during daily free-time period of 51 fourth-grade students who had been assigned to conditions which had been controlled for ethnic membership, ability, and sex.

In the cooperative condition, there was an average of 38 cross-ethnic interactions per hour; in the individualistic condition, there was an average of two cross-ethnic interactions per hour.

Results indicate that cooperative learning experiences, compared with individualistic experiences, promote greater interaction between minority and majority students during instruction. This interaction is characterized by greater perceived

helping between minority and majority students and stronger
beliefs that students encourage and support each other's efforts to
learn, that students know each other and are friends, that students
think through the rationale for their answers and apply and use
what they know in new situations, that students work together
and help each other, and that students do not work alone, without
interacting with other students.

Findings also provide behavioral evidence that the cross-
ethnic relationships created in cooperative learning groups do
generalize to free-time, free-choice situations.

*   Johnson, D. W., & Johnson, R. T. (August, 1982). *Having your
        cake and eating it too: maximizing achievement and cognitive-
        social development and socialization through cooperative
        learning.* Paper presented at the Annual Convention of the
        American Psychological Association, Washington, DC. (ERIC
        Document Reproduction Service No. ED 227 408). (Cited
        above as Item 305.)

*   Johnson, D. W., & Johnson, R. T. (1989). Social interdependence
        and interpersonal attraction. In D. W. Johnson & R. T.
        Johnson (Eds.), *Cooperation and Competition: Theory and
        Research* (pp. 107-130). Edina, MN: Interaction Book
        Company. (Cited above as Item 309.)

*   Johnson, D. W., Johnson, R. T., & Maruyama, G. (1983).
        Interdependence and interpersonal attraction among heterogeneous
        and homogeneous individuals: A theoretical formulation and a
        meta-analysis of the research. *Review of Educational Research,
        53*(1), 5-54. (Cited above as Item 315.)

395.   Johnson, D. W., Johnson, R. T., Tiffany, M., & Zaidman, B.
        (1984). Cross-ethnic relationships: The impact of intergroup
        cooperation and intergroup competition. *Journal of Educational
        Research, 78*(2), 75-79.

        Compares and contrasts intergroup cooperation and
        competition in order to see if consistent differences exist between
        classes (majority and minority) that were prompted by such
        groupings. Findings indicate that intergroup cooperation
        produces more cross-ethnic or interclass relationships than does
        competition.

396.   Johnson, D.W., Johnson, R. T, Tiffany, M., and Zaidman, B.
         (1983). Are low achievers disliked in a cooperative situation? A
         test of rival theories in a mixed ethnic situation. *Contemporary
         Educational Psychology, 8*, 189-200.

         Several social psychological theories have suggested that
there will be conflict when individuals of different ability levels
join (e.g., contact theory, frustration-aggression theory). This
study examines the interaction between majority and minority
students in two different learning situations, cooperative and
individualistic. The social interactions of these students are
observed to test the above theories.
         Forty-eight fourth graders from an inner city school served
as subjects. There were twenty minority students (eighteen
black, one American Indian, one Hispanic) and 28 white
students. All students were randomly assigned to cooperative or
individualistic conditions stratifying for ethnic membership, sex,
social class, and ability (from teacher reports).
         Cooperative groups were asked to master a set of materials
insuring that all understood. Praise was given on a group level.
In the individualistic condition, subjects were instructed to learn
the materials on their own and praise was given to individuals.
Conditions were held for 55 minutes over fifteen days.
Achievement was measured after five, ten, and fifteen days. The
social interactions of the students were observed. Observations
in the classroom examined directives, suggestions, support,
feedback, task-related questions, off task behavior, and rejecting
statements. Free time observations examined proximity.
Subjects were then asked who they would like to spend time
with in the class, with whom they would like to spend free time,
and who helped them in class. Students' attitudes about peer
helping, peer academic support, and perceived personal success
were obtained by students ranking of statements.
         In cooperative situations, students made more cross-ethnic
choices for free time play. Students in cooperative situations
also were more proximate to students from other ethnic
backgrounds and had more interactions with cross-ethnic
students, except for off task behavior, than students in
individualistic situations. Cooperative learning situations also
increased student reports of liking to receive help from peers.

         This study contradicts previous theories claiming that
students of different ethnic memberships cannot get along.

Cross-ethnic relationships were facilitated in cooperative learning situations.

The study nicely demonstrates that different types of students work together given the right environment. However, several methodological flaws limit the results. Measuring ability based on teacher report is not the best way to obtain an ability rating. How were observations conducted and coded? Was reliability of coding obtained? Why wasn't the number of different ethnic students equated? In addition, the authors report many trends without specifying that they are trends.

397.   Kagan, S. (1980). Cooperation -- Competition, culture, and structural bias in classrooms. In S. Sharan, P. Hare, C. D. Webb, & R. Hertz-Lazarowitz (Eds.), *Cooperation in Education*, (pp. 197-211). Provo, UT: Brigham Young University Press.

The basic thesis of this paper is that significant "interactions exist between culturally determined individually differences in cooperative and competitive social orientation and the effects of classroom situation variables." The major implication of the study is that "the data strongly suggest that the educational system in the United States (and probably in other countries as well) is systematically biased against certain low-income and minority groups and are primarily competitive in their social orientation." Discusses the Jigsaw and Students Teams-Achievement Divisions in regard to this thesis.

398.   Kagan, S., & Knight, G. P. (1981). Social motives among Anglo-American and Mexican-American children: Experimental and projective measures. *Journal of Research in Personality*, *15*(1), 93-106.

A study of Anglo-American and Mexican-American children and the relationships between competitiveness and achievement, cooperativeness and affiliation, and cultural differences in cooperation-competition, and those in affiliation and achievement.

399.   Kagan, S., & Madsen, W. C. (1972). Experimental analyses of cooperation and competition of Anglo-American and Mexican children. *Developmental Psychology*, *6*(1), 49-59.

Discusses the results of four different experiments which were conducted on Anglo-American and Mexican American children, comparing the behavior of each.

400.   Kagan, S., Zahn, G. L., & Gealy, J. (1977). Competition and school achievement among Anglo-American and Mexican-American children. *Journal of Educational Psychology*, *69*(4), 432-41.

A study of competition, individualism, field experience, and school achievement in Mexican-American and Anglo-American children. The students were taken from semi-rural, low-income elementary schools. Findings show that the Mexican-American children were more prosocial and less competitive.

401.   Kagan, S., Zahn, G. L., Widaman, K. F., Schwarzwald, J., & Tyrrell, G. (1985). Classroom structural bias: Impact of cooperative and competitive classroom structures on cooperative and competitive individuals and groups. In R. Slavin, S. Sharan, S. Kagan, R. Hertz-Lazarowitz, C. Webb, & R. Schmuck (Eds.), *Learning to Cooperate, Cooperating to Learn*, (pp. 227-312). New York: Plenum Press.

The express purpose of this essay is to present empirical evidence that addresses the hypothesis that "classroom structures common in the U.S. public schools discriminate against the achievement, the cultural values, and well-being of Mexican-American and black students (or the structural bias hypothesis)." Discusses the theory of structural bias, the [University of California's] Riverside Cooperative Learning Project, empirical evidence of structural bias, and conclusions.

402.   Kenderski, C. M. (1983). Interaction processes and learning among third grade Black and Mexican-American students in cooperative small groups. University of California at Los Angeles. *Dissertation Abstracts International*, *45*, 1216A.

Investigated 1. the effects of group composition upon cooperation and its relationship to achievement, group interaction, and selected individual characteristics and 2. the construct validity of three measures of cooperative learning styles. "The variables that significantly related to achievement included group competition or cooperation, sex, individual

competition, three interaction variables - gives requested
information, detects an error without an explanation, and shows
off-task behavior- and attitude toward mathematics. Ethnic
background, individual competition, individual individualization,
and self-concept did not relate to achievement." Variables that
"significantly related to group interaction included individual
cooperation, individual competition, individualization, ethnic
background, self-concept, and attitude toward mathematics."

403.   King, J. (1982). The role of the psychologist in school
         desegregation: A plan for action. *Psychology in the Schools,
         19*, 72-77.

         Reviews the "historical role of social science in
         desegregation and reviews some of the current research on
         cooperative learning in the desegregated classroom." With regard
         to cooperative learning and its effect upon desegregation, the
         author gives a brief overview of the work of three groups: Elliott
         Aronson and his colleagues, Roger and David Johnson, and
         David DeVries and Robert Slavin. Shows how various
         cooperative learning strategies meet the criteria for fostering
         positive race relationships as outlined in the social science brief,
         a document resulting from litigation during the Brown vs. Board
         of Education of Topeka, Kansas, (1954) court battle.

404.   Knight, G. P., & Kagan, S. (1982). Siblings' birth order and
         cooperative-competitive social behavior: A comparison of
         Anglo-American and Mexican-American children. *Journal of
         Cross-Cultural Psychology, 13*(2), 239-49.

         Analyzes the hypothesis which credits the larger family size
         of Mexican Americans with cooperative-competitive social
         behavior differences between Mexican Americans and Anglo
         Americans. Findings indicate that significantly different
         behavior remained between the two groups even after the number
         of siblings and birth order were controlled.

405.   Knight, G. P., Nelson, W., Kagan, S., & Gumbiner, J. (1982).
         Cooperative - competitive social orientation and school
         achievement among Anglo-Americans and Mexican-American
         children. *Contemporary Educational Psychology, 7*, 97-106.

Reports the results of a study that tested the "relative contribution of cooperative - competitive social orientation as a personality predictor of school achievement." Findings indicate 1. competitiveness is positively related to school achievement among the Anglo-American children but not the Mexican-American children; 2. among the Anglo-American children competitiveness is a better predictor of school achievement than field independence, locus of control, and self-esteem; 3. the personality variables are moderately but not independently related to school achievement within both cultural groups; and 4. the between-culture variance in the personality variable does not account for the between-culture variance in school achievement.

406.   Lacy, W. B., Mason, E. J., & Middleton, E. (1983). Fostering constructive intergroup contact in desegregated schools: Suggestions for future research. *The Journal of Negro Education, 52*, 130-141.

Focuses on both group contingency rewards and on the promising effects of cooperative learning for fostering positive intergroup contact in desegregated schools. Also suggests numerous areas that are in need of additional research (e.g., the long-term effects of group contingency rewards and other aspects of cooperative learning on achievement and positive intergroup relations, etc.).

407.   Lawless, K. (1986). *Class Acts: Instructional Strategies and Classroom Materials That Work. Harvesting the Harvesters.* Book 5. Potsdam, NY: Potsdam College, School of Professional Studies. (ERIC Document Reproduction Service No. ED 279 470).

Discusses teaching methods including cooperative learning in this fifth in a series of ten study units for a Migrant Educators' National Training OutReach (MENTOR) correspondence course.

408.   Little Soldier, L. (1989). Cooperative learning and the Native American student. *Phi Delta Kappan, 71*(2), 161-163.

Discusses how cooperative learning can be used to upgrade the quality of education for Native American children while remaining sensitive to cultural issues. Claims that cooperative learning matches traditional Indian values and behaviors such as

respect for the individual, development of an internal locus of
control, cooperation, sharing, and harmony. Also provides a
discussion of how to use cooperative learning, mentions a few
research studies, and potential benefits of cooperative learning for
Native American students.

409.   Madsen, M. C. (1967). Cooperative and competitive motivation of
children in three Mexican subcultures. *Psychology Reports*, *20*,
1307-1320.

Discusses the findings of a study designed to "assess
cooperative and competitive motivation under four experimental
conditions: (1) simple altruism, (2) work output, (3) solution of
a problem in which competition minimized individual reward,
and (4) solution of a problem in which competition maximized
individual reward." Samples represented Mexican urban middle-
class, Mexican urban poor, and rural Mexican Indians. Overall
results of the study indicate that urban middle-class children are
more competitive than their rural and urban poor counterparts.
Specifically, results of Experiment III indicate that when rewards
are contingent on individual success with groups, cooperation
breaks down and gradually becomes competition.

410.   Madsen, M. C., & Shapira, A. (1970). Cooperative and competitive
behavior of urban Afro-American, Anglo-American, Mexican-
American and Mexican village children. *Developmental
Psychology*, *3*(1), 16-20.

The findings of a study involving a variety of ethnic groups
indicate that competitive behavior is common among U. S.
groups and that cooperation is common among Mexican
subjects. One experiment discussed in the article involved the
introduction of individual rewards within the group setting, a
modification that resulted in a higher degree of cooperation
within each of the ethnic groups. Concludes that group rewards,
not individual ones, lead to increased cooperation among
subjects.

411.   Majority Staff, Committee on Education and Labor, U.S. House of
Representatives. (1988). *Educational policies and practices:
their impact on education, on at-risk students, and on minority
teachers*. (Staff Report, One Hundredth Congress, Second
Session). Washington, D.C.: Congress of the U.S., House

Committee on Education and Labor. (ERIC Document
Reproduction Service No. ED 296 042).

Discusses the impact of educational policies and practices on
at risk students and minority teachers. Higher standards and
expectations have not been matched with adequate resources to
meet the special needs of these two groups. A review of the
research is included. Issues are identified and discussed: 1. The
organization of schooling into elementary and secondary levels;
2. Restructuring the high school; 3. How reform effects
disadvantaged students; 4. The effective schools movement; 5.
The teacher shortage; 6. Teacher testing policies; and 7. Reform
of the teaching profession. Research based outcomes of
cooperative learning are listed. A movement has begun to
expand cooperative learning beyond the classroom to all levels of
education.

412.   Metz, M. H. (1983). Sources of constructive social relationships in
        an urban magnet school. *Journal of Education*, 9, 202-245.

Discusses a study conducted in a racially diverse urban
middle school with the majority of students below average in
achievement. The school was a magnet school; however, it
exhibited some unique features that contributed to fewer
interracial conflicts that are often found in other comparable
settings. Argues that one of the major contributing factors was
the use of cooperative learning groups. Concludes that
interdependence, a necessary element of cooperative learning,
transcends racial barriers and creates a learning climate free of
tension as students work toward a common goal.

413.   Miller, N. (1983). Peer relations in desegregated schools. In J. L.
        Epstein & N. Karweit (Eds.), *Friends in Schools: Patterns of
        Selection and Influence in Secondary Schools*, (pp. 201-217).
        New York: Academic Press.

Briefly discusses various cooperative learning strategies and
their impact of peer acceptance and influence. Miller states, in
part, that "Although many researchers believe that cooperative
activity is important in the desegregated setting and that it
promotes intergroup acceptance, they have not systematically
determined the variables that account for its effectiveness.
Furthermore, many of the specific procedures developed to

stimulate cooperation into the daily school program...contain elements that may interfere with the development of cross-racial acceptance, despite the fact that the advocates of such procedures specifically cite increased intergroup acceptance as a by-product..." Also raises numerous concerns/problems that merit additional research.

414.   Miller, N., Brewer, M. B., & Edwards, K. J. (1985). Cooperative interaction in desegregated settings: a laboratory analogue. *Journal of Social Issues, 41*(3), 63-79.

Discusses the negative effects of some cooperative learning methods on ethnic relationships in desegregated schools. Argues that cooperative task structure alone is not sufficient to guarantee personalized interaction within heterogeneous groups or to assure that positive effects will generalize to new situations. In order to achieve positive outcomes from cooperative interventions, two conditions were proposed as necessary for success: 1. The nature of the cooperative interaction promotes an interpersonal orientation rather than a task orientation toward fellow team members; and 2. The basis for assignment to teams or to roles within teams is perceived to be category independent. (Social categories may be differentiated by culture, economics, linguistics, and physical features.)

Outlines a program of research designed to test subtle effects of implementation condition of alternative versions of cooperative learning methods on intergroup acceptance. Findings suggest that the Johnson methods (e.g. Learning Together), Jigsaw, Sharan methods (Group Investigation), STAD, and TAI are likely to be superior to Teams Games Tournament intervention for increasing intergroup acceptance. Teachers are warned to avoid explicit or implicit use of racist or ethnic identity as a basis for team assignment.

415.   Minnis, B. I. (1986). An analysis of the effects of a cooperative learning team on cross-race, cross-sex, and cross-socioeconomic status relationships of middle school students in a desegregated setting (Kentucky). *Dissertation Abstracts International, 48*, 272A. (University Microfilms Order Number ADG87-05281. 8708)

Used effects of Teams-Games-Tournament (TGT) strategy for the study.

416.   Moore, H. A. (1988). Effects of gender, ethnicity, and school equity
        on students' leadership behaviors in a group game. *The
        Elementary School Journal, 88*(5), 515-529.

        Students in group activities were evaluated on the number of
        times they exhibited "leadership behaviors," and whether their
        school was "high-" or "low equity" in terms of integration. The
        high equity schools showed greater interaction, with white males
        showing more physical leadership behaviors, and Hispanic males
        controlling the cards used for the activity. The white females
        were more vocal than Hispanic females. In low-equity schools
        the Hispanic females controlled the cards to "balance the verbal
        interruptions" of the white females. Professional observers rated
        leadership qualities similar for all students, while teachers
        consistently rated Hispanics in low-equity schools to exhibit
        fewer leadership behaviors.

417.   Morgan, B. M. (1987). Cooperative learning: Teacher use,
        classroom life, social integration, and student achievement.
        Dissertation Abstracts International, 48, 3043A. (Copies
        available exclusively from Micrographics Department, Doheny
        Library, USC, Los Angeles, CA 90089-0182)

        Concludes that "students in classrooms where cooperative
        learning strategies are used at least 30% of the time have a more
        positive view of classroom life, and their achievement scores
        reflect more growth than students in low use classrooms. There
        were no differences in perceptions of social interaction."

418.   Munroe, R. L., & Munroe, R. H. (1977). Cooperation and
        competition among East African and American children. *The
        Journal of Social Psychology, 101,* 145-146.

        Reports the findings of a study that compared the
        cooperative and competitive characteristics of East African
        children with those of United States students. Based upon a
        board game that required cooperation to reach a specified goal
        with an appropriate reward system, the findings revealed that
        African children participate in cooperative groups more
        effectively than do American students. Reported that African
        children "frequently assist others, with no immediate tangible
        reward for themselves" and that they "frequently assist in tasks
        with immediate and tangible but shared rewards."

*   Nelson, L., & Madsen, M.C. (1969). Cooperation and competition
         in four-year-olds as a function of reward contingency and
         subculture. *Developmental Psychology, 1*(4), 340-344. (Cited
         below as Item 694.)

*   Okebukola, P. A. (1986). The influence of preferred learning styles
         on cooperative learning in science. *Science Education, 70*(5),
         509-517. (Cited above as Item 204.)

419.   Pairs, B. R. (1985). Effects of cooperative learning on race/human
         relations: Study of a district program. *Spectrum, 3*, 37-43.

            Details a study designed to test the effects of cooperative
         learning upon acceptance rates, self-esteem, academic
         achievement, and classroom perceptions of elementary and
         secondary students. Results indicated that cooperative learning
         produced statistically insignificant effects upon each of the
         variables.

*   Pierce, L.V. (Ed.). (1987). *Cooperative Learning: Integrating
         Language and Content-Area Instruction.* Wheaton, MD:
         National Clearinghouse for Bilingual Education. (ERIC
         Document Reproduction Service No. 291 245). (Cited above as
         Item 146.)

420.   Pierce, L. V. (1987). *Cooperative Learning: Integrating Language
         and Content-Area Instruction. Teacher Resource Guide Series,
         Number 2.* Wheaton, MD: National Clearinghouse for Bilingual
         Education.

            Provides insights gained from experience and research on
         "language minority students' (grades 2-5) academic success" with
         a curriculum that was bilingual, content-based, and one that used
         cooperative learning techniques. Rationale, curriculum, and
         methods are discussed. Science and math activities drawn from
         the curriculum are listed and numerous sample activities are
         outlined in detail.

*   Rajendran, B. (1987). The effect of cooperative and conventional
         classroom environments on the on-task behavior and attitude
         toward learning of secondary learning-disabled students.

University of Oregon. *Dissertation Abstracts International*, *49*,
718A. (Cited above as Item 255.)

421.   Rash, T. E., & Thompson, S. (1988). Legacy's 'Global Village.'
Camping Magazine, *60*, 10-15.

Discusses principles of cooperative learning and conflict
resolution, reviews of scientific studies, and descriptions of
practical applications. Analyzes a summer program sponsored
by Legacy International designed to teach multicultural
understanding, leadership, communications, and other practical
skills. Because "cooperative learning has been central to Legacy
since its inception" in 1977, many proven cooperative learning
strategies are presented.

*   Reynolds, M. C. (1989). Students with special needs. In M. C.
Reynolds (Ed.) *Knowledge base for the beginning teacher*, (pp.
129-142). New York: Pergamon Press. (Cited above as Item
258.)

422.   Scanlan, P. A. (1988). Student talk in cooperative learning groups.
Dissertation Abstracts International, *50*, 868A. (University
Microfilms Order Number ADG89-13229. 8910)

An ethnographic study whose results showed that student
talk in cooperative groups was "significantly different from the
typical patterns of classroom discourse described in research
literature by Bellack, et al.," and others.

423.   Schofield, J. W. (1980). Cooperation as social exchange: Resource
gaps and reciprocity in academic work. In S. Sharan, P. Hare,
C. D. Webb, & R. Hertz-Lazarowitz (Eds.), *Cooperation in
Education*, (pp. 160-181). Provo, Utah: Brigham Young
University Press.

Basically analyzes factors affecting cooperative behavior.
The paper grew out of a three-year research project on the
"development of social relations between students in a
desegregated school." Scholfield concludes that "the widespread
and successful use of planned cooperative team-learning
techniques suggests that effective interracial cooperation in the
classroom is possible."

*   Sengends, A. B. K. (1987). The effects of computer-assisted
           cooperative learning on the science achievement and attitudes of
           American Indian students. University of Kansas. *Dissertation
           Abstracts International, 49*, 1435A. (Cited above as Item 107.)

424.   Serow, R. C., & Solomon, D. (1979). Classroom climates and
           students' intergroup behavior. *Journal of Educational
           Psychology, 71*(5), 669-676.

               Observations were conducted in 25 desegregated elementary
           schools (K-6) in order to determine the relationship between
           classroom conditions and pupils' interracial behaviors. Results
           of factor and regression analyses indicated that two types of
           interracial behavior were associated with different classroom
           environments: (1) positive intergroup contacts were more likely
           to occur when teachers emphasized interpersonal concerns; (2)
           while businesslike environments impeded overall cross-racial
           association, they had no effect on more purposeful intergroup
           contacts, which were facilitated by teacher patience and by
           diversity in instructional arrangements. Serow and Solomon said
           that findings suggest that "tensions between the social and
           academic objective of multiracial education might be resolved by
           emphasizing purposeful interactions among children of different
           racial backgrounds."

425.   Shapira, A., & Madsen, M. C. (1969). Cooperative competitive
           behavior of kibbutz and urban children in Israel. *Child
           Development, 40*, 609-617.

               Reports the results of a study involving Israeli children who
           participated in experiments assessing cooperative and competitive
           behavior. In an experiment involving group rewards, all children
           cooperated. When individual rewards replaced group rewards, the
           urban children began to compete with each other. Concludes that
           group rewards are an important part of cooperative activities.

426.   Sharan, S., & Kuffell, P. (with collaboration of Brosh, T. & Pelleg,
           R.). (1984). *Cooperative Learning in the Classroom: Research
           in Desegregated Schools*. Hillsdale, NJ: Lawrence Erlbaum
           Associates, Publishers. 176 pp. [Foreword by Seymour
           Sarason.]

This text presents the findings of a major study on "the effects of three instructional methods on seventh grade pupils' academic learning and social relations...The three teaching methods were: The Group-Investigation (G-I) method...; Student Teams and Academic Divisions (STAD); and Traditional Whole-class Instruction (W-C)."

The titles of the five chapters in this volume are: "Cooperative Learning: Background and Implementation of this Study"; "Achievement in English Language and in Literature"; "Cooperative and Competitive Behavior"; "Social Attitudes"; and "Cooperative and Traditional Training: An Overview of Results." Its discussion of the teacher training component of the study is highly engaging and informative.

427.   Sharan, S., Kuffell, P., Hertz-Lazarowitz, R., Bejarano, Y., Raviv, S., & Sharan, Y. (1985). Cooperative learning effects on ethnic relations and achievement in Israel: Junior-high-school classrooms. In R. Slavin, S. Sharan, S. Kagan, R. Hertz-Lazarowitz, C. Webb, & R. Schmuck (Eds.), *Learning to Cooperate, Cooperating to Learn*, (pp. 313-344). New York: Plenum Press.

Describes a field experiment conducted in desegregated junior high schools in Israel which compared the effects of three teaching models (Group-Investigation, Student Teams-Achievement Divisions, and traditional whole-class instruction) on the pupil's academic learning, cooperative behavior, and attitudes toward peers of their own and of the other ethnic group. Describes the three teaching methods, the teachers and pupils, sources of teachers' resistance to the new strategies they were required to implement, the teacher training program, processes of implementation, dependent variables, academic achievement in English and literature, cooperative behavior that took place, and impact on social relations.

428.   Shirley, O. L. B. (1988). The impact of multicultural education on the self-concept, racial attitude, and student achievement of black and white fifth and sixth graders. University of Mississippi. *Dissertation Abstracts International, 49*, 1364A.

"The impact of a multicultural curriculum in English, social studies, and reading on self-concept, racial attitude, and student achievement was researched." Cooperative learning techniques were integrated into the multicultural curriculum, with teachers involved in the experimental groups receiving weekly training sessions. No significant differences were found in the self-concepts and the academic achievement levels of students in the experimental groups when compared to students in the control groups. Significant increases in positive racial attitudes of white students in the experimental group occurred when compared to attitudes of students in the control group.

429.   Silverthorne, C., Chelune, C., & Imada, A. (1974). The effects of competition and cooperation on level of prejudice. *The Journal of Social Psychology, 92,* 293-301.

"This study investigated the effects on prejudice of either a cooperative or competitive strategy adopted by either a white or black partner. It indicated that involvement in a game situation led to a reduction in prejudice when a white S had a white partner who cooperated or competed, or a black partner who cooperated." Findings support the general hypothesis that cooperative group participation leads to a decrease in prejudice.

430.   Slavin, R. E. (1977). How student learning teams can integrate the desegregated classroom. *Integrated Education, 15,* 56-58.

Reports the results of an experiment designed to test the effects of Student-Teams-Achievement Divisions (STAD) upon racial relationships and academic achievement. After a brief discussion of the basic elements of STAD, the author discusses a study that was done in Baltimore. During the nine-week treatment period, the experimental class was taught language mechanics through the use of STAD. The control group received traditional instruction. At the conclusion of the treatment, students were administered a sociometric instrument and content-related language arts tests. "The results of this study indicate that STAD is an effective team learning technique, both for increasing cross-racial friendship and for increasing academic achievement, at least among blacks."

431.   Slavin, R. E. (1977). *Student Learning Team Techniques: Narrowing the Achievement Gap between the Races.* (Report No. 228). Baltimore, MD: Center for Social Organization of Schools, The Johns Hopkins University.

432.   Slavin, R. E. (1979). Effects of biracial learning teams on cross-
        racial friendships. *Journal of Educational Psychology, 71*(3),
        381-387.

            Argues that cross-racial friendship choices can be increased
            through the use of biracial learning teams. Two hundred ninety-
            four seventh and eighth graders (170 whites and 124 blacks) in
            twelve English classes participated in the study. Experimental
            students completed worksheets in four or five member groups
            and received recognition based on the sum of members' quiz
            scores. Control groups worked individually and received
            individual quiz scores only. Experimental students increased
            both in the number of cross-racial friendship choices and in the
            percentage of cross-racial choices over all choices. A follow-up
            sample nine months later showed the effects of the experimental
            treatment to have been maintained over time.

433.   Slavin, R. E. (1979). Integrating the desegregated classroom:
        Actions speak louder than words. *Educational Leadership, 36*(5),
        322-324.

            Claims that certain cooperative learning strategies (e. g.
            Teams-Games-Tournaments) have been used in an attempt to
            improve race relations, and the results were "phenomenal." Also
            states that the use of such strategies improved learning.
            Concludes that "Our research has shown that the action that is
            most likely to produce results is the creation of multiracial,
            cooperative learning teams in classrooms."

434.   Slavin, R. E. (1981). Cooperative learning and desegregation.
        Journal of Educational Equity and Leadership, 1(3), 145-161.

            Reviews cooperative learning strategies that appear to have
            significant positive effects on race relations and academic
            achievement in desegregated schools. Included are discussions of
            the key elements of Student-Teams-Achievement Divisions
            (STAD), Teams-Games-Tournaments (TGT), and Jigsaw. Also
            included is a detailed literature review of the positive effects of
            cooperative learning upon race relations and achievement.
            Concludes that "the research done to date justifies optimism that
            cooperative learning may be a significant step toward finally
            achieving the potential of integrated education."

435.   Slavin, R. E. (1985). Cooperative learning: Applying contact
         theory in desegregated schools. *Journal of Social Issues, 41* (3),
         45-62.

         Allport's contact theory of intergroup relations is used to
         evaluate seven cooperative-learning methods in the classroom.
         An attempt is made to understand the changes in both classroom
         organization and student friendship patterns when cooperative,
         integrated learning teams are used. With few exceptions, research
         on cooperative learning showed that when Allport's conditions
         for positive effects of desegregation on race relations are met in
         the classroom, students are more likely to have friends outside
         their own racial groups. Allport's conditions are cooperation
         across racial lines, equal status roles for students of different
         races, contact across racial lines during which students learn
         about each other as individuals, and teacher support for interracial
         contact.
             Cooperative learning methods discussed were the Johnson
         methods, Group Investigation, STAD, TGT, TAI, and Jigsaw.
         STAD, TGT, and TAI were found to have positive effects on
         student achievement in addition to improving intergroup
         relations.

436.   Slavin, R. E., & Madden, N. A. (1979). School practices that
         improve race relations. *American Educational Research Journal,
         16*, 169-180.

         "This study used questionnaire data collected by the
         Educational Testing Service in 51 high schools to discover
         which school practices improved racial attitudes and behaviors in
         desegregated schools. Data were analyzed at school and
         individual levels using multiple regressions. Results for whites
         indicated strong, positive effects on racial attitudes and behaviors
         of assigning students of different races to work together and
         through individual participation on a sports team with students
         of another race. Weaker effects were found for class discussions
         of race. For blacks, assignment of students of different races to
         work together and teacher workshops on race relations had effects
         on one behavioral variable, and individual participation in
         biracial work groups or sports teams had strong, positive effects
         on racial behavior and attitudes. Few effects for either race were
         found for teacher workshops, use of multiethnic texts, or
         tracking. Results were interpreted to indicate that programs

involving cooperative interaction between students of different races are most likely to improve race relations in desegregated schools" (p. 169).

437.   Slavin, R.E., & Oickle, E. (1981). Effects of cooperative learning teams on student achievement and race relations: Treatment by race interactions. *Sociology of Education, 54*(3), 174-180.

An attempt to find out if cooperative learning benefits one race more than another, the study discusses implications for understanding black and white interactions in traditional schooling and cooperative learning. Two hundred and seventy students in sixth, seventh, and eighth grades (33.0% black) were divided by classes into team or non-team treatment conditions. Students were taught the same language mechanics curriculum for twelve weeks. Results indicated that cooperative learning groups made significantly more academic progress than did the control groups, due mainly to the substantial gains made by black students. A marginally significant positive main effect of cooperative learning on cross-racial friendships was due to a disproportionate number of whites gaining black friends.

438.   Strickland, D. S., & Cooper, E. J. (Eds.). (1987). *Educating black children: America's challenge.* Washington, D.C.: Bureau of Educational Research. (ERIC Document Reproduction Service No. ED 298 188).

A series of papers on effectively educating black children. In Section II, Robert E. Slavin ("Cooperative Learning and the Education of Black Students") discusses the use of cooperative learning as a successful strategy for increasing student achievement in both desegregated and majority-black schools. He finds that cooperative learning methods seem to be particularly effective for black students regardless of achievement level, possibly because black students are known to be more favorable toward cooperation with their peers than are white students. In addition to increased achievement, cooperative learning also causes students to have improved attitudes toward their classmates, particularly those of different ethnicities. Slavin emphasizes that the students themselves can be the most powerful, free instructional resource available in any school, when effectively involved in cooperative learning activities.

439.   Tackaberry, S. N. (1980). Cooperation versus competition: Effects
         on Hispanic and Anglo children. *Dissertation Abstracts
         International, 41*, 2395B. (University Microfilms Order Number
         ADG80-27733. 0000)

         Results supported two of the major hypotheses: 1.
         Cooperative learning reduced negative cross-ethnic nominations
         for playmates and 2. competition increased the number of
         unwanted cross-ethnic peers in math work groups...When
         children were asked to name desirable playmates, friends, and
         work group members, the cooperative intervention did not
         increase cross-ethnic choices.

440.   Thomas, D. R. (1978). Cooperation and competition among
         children in the Pacific Islands and New Zealand. *Journal of
         Research and Development in Education, 12*(1), 88-96.

         The author compared the cooperative behavior among
         Polynesian children and rural Maori children with that of urban
         Maori and European children using a drawing board.
         Cooperation was necessary to complete the task and to receive
         the reward. The author found that rural Maori and Cook Islanders
         were more cooperative than the urban Maori and Europeans. The
         author discussed gender and class differences in the urban Maori
         and Europeans. He recommends that cultural differences be taken
         into account when planning educational or social changes.

441.   Towson, S. (1985). Melting pot or mosaic: Cooperative education
         and interethnic relations. In R. Slavin, S. Sharan, S. Kagan, R.
         Hertz-Lazarowitz, C. Webb, & R. Schmuck (Eds.), *Learning to
         Cooperate, Cooperating to Learn*. New York: Plenum Press.

         Explores the idea that research on the use of cooperative
         learning as a teaching strategy "to facilitate positive interethnic
         relations has been profoundly affected by the two ideologies that
         have dominated North American thought on this issue: the
         melting pot and the mosaic -- or, more prosaically, assimilation
         and pluralism."

442.   Warring, D. F. (1983). Fostering prosocial attitudes in desegregated
         schools through cooperative learning (controversy). University
         of Minnesota. *Dissertation Abstracts International, 44*, 3334A.

"Hypotheses concerning the effects of structured academic controversy, debate, and individualistic learning were compared." Findings revealed that controversy promotes more interaction than debate among group members.

443.   Warring, D. F., Johnson, D. W., Maruyama, G., & Johnson, R. T. (1985). Impact of different types of cooperative learning on cross-ethnic and cross-sex relationships. *Journal of Educational Psychology, 77*(1), 53-59.

The effects of different levels of cooperation on cross-sex and cross-ethnic relationships were compared in two studies: 1. 74 sixth graders were randomly assigned to three conditions (cooperative controversy, cooperative debate, and individualistic) stratifying for sex, ability level, and ethnic membership; 2. 51 fourth graders were randomly assigned to two conditions (intergroup cooperation and intergroup competition) stratifying for sex, ability, and ethnic membership.

Both cooperative controversy and cooperative debate promoted more cross-sex and cross-ethnic relationships than did individual learning. Intergroup cooperation promoted more positive cross-sex and cross-ethnic relationships than did intergroup competition. Relationships among heterogeneous students within cooperative learning situations did tend to transfer into noninstructional classroom, school, and home activities.

These two studies are among the first attempts to move beyond simple comparisons of cooperative, competitive, and individualistic learning activities into an examination of pure cooperative with mixed cooperative and competitive instructional situations.

444.   Weigel, R. H., Wiser, P., & Cook, S. W. (1975). The impact of cooperative learning experiences on cross-ethnic relations and cultures. *Journal of Social Issues, 31*, 219-244.

Discusses the impact that cooperative learning has on relationships between students of different ethnic backgrounds.

445.   Ziegler, S. (1981). The effectiveness of cooperative learning teams for increasing cross-ethnic friendship: Additional evidence. *Human Organization, 40*(3), 264-268.

A Canadian replication of a small, cooperative learning team study to determine the effectiveness of cooperative learning teams for increasing cross-ethnic friendships. The team strategy was found to be very effective in increasing both casual and close cross-ethnic friendships. Analysis showed no main or interaction effects by ethnic group. This was contrary to many American studies which often show positive effects for whites but not for blacks. Recommends the use of cooperative learning teams to improve ethnic relations even in areas where inter-ethnic relations may not be a problem.

* Zahn, G. L., Kagan, S., & Widaman, K. F. (1986). Cooperative learning and classroom climate. *Journal of School Psychology*, *24*, 351-362. (Cited above as Item 339.)

D. TEACHER EDUCATION/STAFF DEVELOPMENT

*   Altenhein, M. R. (1955). The activity program on the college level. *Progressive Education*, *32*, 12-13, 16. (Cited below as Item 683.)

446.   Armstrong, D. G., & Savage, T. V. (1990). *Secondary Education: An Introduction*. New York: Macmillan Publishing Co.

          This text for pre-service secondary teachers includes a section on cooperative learning that addresses the following: General characteristics; preparation for cooperative learning; information on Student Teams - Achievement Divisions, Teams-Games-Tournaments, Jigsaw, and Learning Together; Implementing Cooperative Learning; and Debriefing (pp. 257-260).

447.   Aronson, E., & Goode, E. (1980). Training teachers to implement jigsaw learning: A manual for teachers. In S. Sharan, P. Hare, C. D. Webb, & R. Hertz-Lazarowitz (Eds.), *Cooperation in Education*, (pp. 47-81). Provo, UT: Brigham Young University Press.

          An overview of why and how the jigsaw strategy was developed as well as the "jigsaw classroom" (including how to implement team-building, constructing the jigsaw materials, teaching the jigsaw to students, a question and answer section on the jigsaw), and information about teacher training workshops on the jigsaw.

*   Augustine, D. K., Gruber, K.D., & Hanson, L.R. (1989/1990). Cooperation Works! *Educational Leadership*, *47*(4), 3. (Cited below as Item 557.)

448.   Baird, W. E., and Koballa, T. R. (1988). Changes in pre-service elementary teachers' hypothesizing skills following group or individual study with computer simulations. *Science Education*, *72*(2), 209-223.

The authors discuss the importance of teaching hypothesizing skills to pre-college students. The subjects in their study were elementary education teachers. All groups used a computer game to learn skills. Two of the groups used a computer simulation of the game; one was cooperative and one was competitive. The other two groups simply used computer text; again one group worked together and in the other group each student worked apart. The study found no real difference in gains between groups using simulation and those using text. They did find that cooperative groups using simulation did the best and individuals using text did the least best.

449.   Beeley, C. L. (1989). A study of the relationship between K - 12 teachers' ability to model collegiality and their use of cooperative learning in their classrooms. State University of New York at Buffalo. *Dissertation Abstracts International, 50*, 1638A.

Reveals that "teachers who model a high degree of collegiality with their peers, will also use cooperative learning with their students to a higher degree than low ranking collegial teachers." Concludes that teachers should be trained to use cooperative learning techniques and should be taught effective modeling skills.

450.   Bernagozzi, T. (1988, February). The new cooperative learning. *Learning88*, pp. 38-43.

First hand account about the year Bernagozzi and his third grade class spent as part of a Johns Hopkins pilot program in cooperative learning. Discusses setting up teams, managing the scoring system, teaching cooperative skills, using cooperative learning to teach reading and writing, and pitfalls and benefits.

451.   Bohlmeyer, E. M., & Burke, J. P. (1987). Selecting cooperative learning techniques: A consultative strategy guide. *School Psychology Review, 16*, 36-49.

A comprehensive article that presents "a classification scheme for cooperative learning techniques. This scheme can be utilized by consulting psychologists when collaborating with teachers to select cooperative learning techniques that are compatible with their styles of teaching and specific instructional objectives." Included in the article are detailed descriptions of each category within the classification scheme: type of subject matter, nature of student interdependence, interaction among cooperative groups, method of grouping students, basis for evaluation and reward, and practical requirements for implementation. Nine cooperative learning strategies (Jigsaw, Group Investigation, STAD, TGT, Jigsaw II, Co-op Co-op, Circles of Learning (Learning Together), Small-Group Mathematics, and TAI) are discussed and classified according to the classification scheme. Concludes with general guidelines for implementing cooperative learning. This is an article that anyone interested in cooperative learning should read.

452. Bowman, R. F., Jr. (1984). Relationship educates: An interactive instructional strategy. *Contemporary Education, 55*, 101-103.

Discusses several key elements of cooperative learning activities, including the necessity of redefining teacher-student roles. Also describes undergraduate education classes at Moorhead State University that incorporate cooperative learning activities into the curriculum. Concludes that "if education is a process for living, then schools must provide explicit opportunities for learners to grow through interdependent roles and relationships involving significant others."

453. Bowman, R. F., Jr. (1985). Teaching in tomorrow's classrooms. *Educational Forum, 49*, 241-247.

Discusses six aims that should be integrated into the classrooms of the future. A discussion of the first aim, to prepare students to assume the roles of tomorrow's citizens, targets the effects of cooperative learning. In their groups students benefit from peer evaluation, shared problem solving, and discovery. In addition, they develop interpersonal skills, including acceptance of diversity, trust, and collaboration.

454. Bruffee, K.A. (1973). Collaborative learning: Some practical models. *College English, 34*(5), 634-643.

The author emphasizes the role of the teacher in collaborative learning as that of "organizer of people" rather than a center of authority. Also stressed are the direction by the teacher (the teacher must keep the discussion on track), and the freedom of the student (students must be allowed to change group is not beneficial). In teaching collaboration, the author suggests posing specific questions to groups, and then more general questions, or no questions, as the students learn to work together.

455.   Burns, M. (September, 1981). Groups of four: Solving the management problem. *Learning*, pp. 46-51.

Discusses an elementary teacher's use of a method called "groups of four," -- a hybrid-like cooperative learning activity. Addresses the following: reorganization of the classroom, getting started, the teacher's role, and benefits to learning. Also includes a section entitled "Questions Teachers Ask," and succinct answers to each of the questions. A useful article for elementary teachers.

456.   Calvert, S. (1972). On cooperative learning with teachers as facilitators. *ETC: A Review of General Semantics, 29,* 206-209.

A first-person account of a teacher who, because of his love for teaching and his security in the classroom, is able to maximize the effects of cooperative learning groups. Based upon his personal observations, the author lists several positive results of cooperative learning: quality of learning, enthusiasm, self-motivation, self-control, self-esteem, positive interpersonal relationships, and desire to learn.

*   Cohen, E. G. (1986). *Designing groupwork: Strategies for the heterogeneous classroom.* New York: Teachers College Press. 208 pp. (Cited below as Item 570.)

*   Cole, C. C., Jr. (1982). *Improving Instruction: Issues and Alternatives for Higher Education.* (AAHE-ERIC/ Higher Education Research Report No. 4). Washington, D. C.: American Association for Higher Education. (Cited below as Item 571.)

*   Dishon, D., & O'Leary, P. W. (1984). *A Guidebook for Cooperative Learning: A Technique for Creating More Effective Schools.* Holmes Beach, FL: Learning Publications.

[Foreword by David W. Johnson and Roger T. Johnson] (Cited below as Item 584.)

457.   Edwards, C., & Stout, J. (1989/1990). Cooperative learning: The first year. *Educational Leadership, 47*(4), 38-41.

Two elementary teachers who use cooperative learning offer practical suggestions (e.g., pacing the program, assigning groups, determining group size, forming new groups, group responsibilities, and deciding when to use cooperative learning) to other educators.

458.   Ellis, S. (1985). Introducing cooperative learning groups: A district-wide effort. *Journal of Staff Development, 6*, 52-59.

Ellis describes the efforts of the Greenwich, Connecticut, public school system to train administrators and teachers in the use of cooperative learning strategies. She describes the components of the staff development program, the specific cooperative learning strategies that were taught, and the impact on the students and teachers vis-a-vis the use of such strategies.

459.   Ellis, S. (1989/1990). Introducing cooperative learning. *Educational Leadership, 47*(4), 34-37.

Discusses a successful teacher training program in cooperative learning. Addresses issues such as local support, district support, expanded opportunities for training, in-district expertise, and tips on implementing cooperative learning.

460.   Fenton, R. J. (1988). *The effects of training in small group instruction.* Paper prepared for the Convention of the Western Speech Road. Anchorage, AK. (ERIC Document Reproduction Service No. ED 293 827).

Reviews results of training more than 2,000 teachers in cooperative learning strategies. Comparisons were made between teachers with less than fifteen hours of training and teachers with more than fifteen hours. Both teachers and students were very positive about small group instruction. Teachers with more training tended to use group assignments in a variety of ways, to require students to work cooperatively, and to use cooperative learning more frequently. Students of teachers with less than fifteen hours of training made a 60% greater gain in academic growth, however, than those who were in the classes of more trained teachers. Low achievers made the most academic gains, and made more gains when there was greater use of cooperative learning. Most teachers thought cooperative small group learning was good for their students.

461.   Ferguson, P. (1989/1990, Winter). Cooperative team learning: Theory into practice for the prospective middle school teacher. *Action in Teacher Education, XI* (4):24-28.

Discusses why and how cooperative learning is ideal for use with middle level students, describes an effort to employ a cooperative learning strategy (Jigsaw) as a vehicle for helping prospective middle school teachers enrolled in a social studies methods course translate theory into practice, and makes recommendations for the broader implementation of cooperative learning in middle school teacher education programs.

462.   Finkel, D. L., & Monh, G. S. (1983). Teachers and learning groups: Dissolutions of the Atlas complex. *New Directions for Teaching and Learning, 4,* 83-97.

Offers suggestions, including the use of cooperatively structured groups, for modifying traditional teaching strategies. States that most teachers "start with a small change, which enables them to experience their teaching in a different way and enriches their view of their course as a social system containing diverse teaching functions." Refers to the Atlas complex as descriptive of teachers who are "caught in the middle of their classes by the best of mysterious forces -- hidden assumptions." Gives a case study of a professor who is present in class, but not caught in the middle.

463.   Glass, R. M., & Putnam, J. W. (1988-1989). Cooperative learning in teacher education: A case study. *Action in Teacher Education, 10,* 47-52.

This case study describes several ways in which cooperative learning can be used in teacher education courses as well as how students view their own learning and performance during cooperative learning activities. In doing so, it discusses the following: Definitions of cooperative learning; why and how cooperative learning can be used in teacher education programs; an overview of such cooperative learning strategies as Jigsaw, informal resource groups, study teams, group projects; and an analysis of a cooperative learning survey the authors administered to a sampling of their undergraduate and graduate students at the University of Maine, Farmington.

464. Gordon, T. (1974). *Teacher Effectiveness Training.* New York: Longman, Inc.

Text designed to help teachers improve communication skills in order to implement cooperative learning methods in the classroom.

465. Gorman, G. E. (1982). Making it happen, model for training teachers of gifted and talented. *Roeper Review, 4*(4), 31-32.

This author uses the Ranzulli Enrichment Triad to teach the method to education students. "General Exploratory" and "Group Training" activities are completed in class; "Individual and Small Group Investigations of Real Problems" are worked on out of class. The instructor serves at each stage as a facilitator of materials. At each stage students are encouraged to share their ideas and discuss their work. In this way, the future teachers learn the method by having actually participated in it themselves.

466. Graves, N. B., & Graves, T. D. (1985). Creating a cooperative learning environment: An ecological approach. In R. Slavin, S. Sharan, S. Kagan, R. Hertz-Lazarowitz, C. Webb, & R. Schmuck (Eds.), *Learning to Cooperate, Cooperating to Learn* (pp. 403-436). New York: Plenum Press.

Presents a theoretical basis for the "ecological approach" (e.g., "that learning in general, but particularly cooperative small-group learning, which involves coordination of effort with others, emerges out of the total social and physical environment within which the person is immersed") and delineates a program for implementing cooperative learning in a series of sequential steps within a restructured classroom setting. Also includes a section on fostering growth in cooperative skills.

467.   Gunderson, B., & Johnson, D. W. (1980). Building positive
        attitudes by using cooperative learning groups. *Foreign
        Language Annals, 13*, 39-43.

            Describes a descriptive analysis of a teacher's role in
        teaching junior high school introductory French classes through
        the use of cooperative learning groups. The article also presents
        the results of a study designed to test the effect of cooperative
        learning groups upon "1. the students' attitudes toward French, 2.
        their relationship with peers and the teacher, and 3. the perceived
        impact of the cooperative learning experience on their motivation
        to learn French, the personal benefits they received from the
        group experiences, and their attitudes toward learning in groups."
        Results indicated that cooperative learning experiences had a
        significant positive effect upon all of the variables.

468.   Hawley, W. D., Rosenholtz, S. J., Goodstein, H., & Hasselbring, T.
        (1984). Good "effective teaching" schools: What research says
        about improving student achievement. *Peabody Journal of
        Education, 61*, 15-52.

            The second of seven chapters in a monograph on improving
        student achievement, this article argues that types of
        instructional strategies have a great effect on student
        achievement. Based on a review of related research, the authors
        point out that "effective teachers do the following: (A) optimize
        academic learning time, (B) reward achievement in appropriate
        ways, (C) utilize interactive teaching practices, (D) hold and
        communicate high expectations for student performance, and (E)
        select the appropriate unit of instruction."
            Concerning rewards, the authors discuss competitive,
        cooperative, and independent structures. Concludes that
        cooperative reward structures have more positive effect upon the
        achievement of lower-level students than upon the achievement
        of high-level. Also states that cooperative goals and rewards are
        "most appropriate when teachers seek to promote retention,
        application and transfer of factual information, concepts,
        principles; mastering of concepts and principles; verbal abilities;
        problem solving ability and success; cooperative skills; creative
        ability; divergent and risk-taking thinking and productive
        controversy; awareness and utilization of one's capabilities; and
        role taking abilities."

The article also summarizes various cooperative team
learning strategies, including Teams-Games-Touraments (TGT),
Student-Teams-Achievement Divisions (STAD) and Jigsaw.
Provides a summary of the findings of 28 field projects in
cooperative learning. The use of TGT and STAD positively
influenced academic achievement, race relations and mutual
respect among students, whereas the use of Jigsaw had little
effect on achievement. Concludes that TGT appears to be the
most successful team strategy and that it is more successful in
math, language, and reading than in social studies.

469.   Johnson, D. W. (1979). *Educational Psychology.* Englewood
        Cliffs, New Jersey: Prentice-Hall, Inc., 592 pp.

        A text for use in college educational psychology classes.
        Written to help teachers at every stage of their careers understand
        more fully how to implement teaching strategies based on
        psychological knowledge. The book assumes no prior
        knowledge of psychology, explaining all technical terms as they
        are used. Using an eclectic approach, no single stance is adopted.
        Different points of view are balanced and opposing theories are
        presented. Activities are included in each chapter. Contents are
        arranged around the technical and cooperative competencies
        needed for teaching. Includes glossary, several pages of
        references, and an index. Johnson adds a touch of humor
        throughout the book that makes for engaging reading.

470.   Johnson, D. W., & Johnson, R. T. (1984). Cooperative small-
        group learning. *Curriculum Report, 14*(1), 1-6.

        A brief but detailed overview of the theory and practice of
        cooperative learning. Initially defines key elements of
        cooperative learning and then delineates principles of
        implementation along with nineteen specific steps of
        implementation. Also provides guidelines and tips in regard to
        how principals can most successfully promote and support
        cooperative learning in their schools. Concludes with
        descriptions of two district-wide cooperative learning programs.

471.   Johnson, D.W., & Johnson, R. T. (1987). Implementing
        cooperative learning: The teachers' role. In R.T. Johnson, D.W.
        Johnson, & E.J. Holubec (Eds.), *Structuring Cooperative
        Learning: Lesson Plans for Teachers 1987* (pp. 12-41). Edina,
        MN: Interaction Book Company, 1987.

Learning: Lesson Plans for Teachers 1987 (pp. 12-41). Edina, MN: Interaction Book Company, 1987.

Explains five sets of strategies included in the teacher's role when implementing cooperative learning: 1. clearly specifying objectives for the lesson; 2. making decisions about placing students in groups before teaching the lesson; 3. clearly explaining the task, goal structure, and learning activity to students; 4. monitoring effectiveness of groups and intervening to provide task assistance or to increase students' interpersonal and group skills; and 5. evaluating students' achievement and helping students discuss success with elaboration. The strategies are broken down into eighteen practical steps which elaborate upon and detail a procedure for structuring cooperative learning.

472.   Johnson, D. W., Johnson, R. T., & Holubec, E. J. (1987). Getting Started with Cooperative Groups. In R. T. Johnson, D. W. Johnson, & E. J. Holubec (Eds.), *Structuring Cooperative Learning: Lesson Plans for Teachers 1987* (pp. 43-75). Edina, MN: Interaction Book Company, 1987.

Discusses the stages teachers often go through as they learn to implement cooperative learning in their classrooms. Contains practical suggestions and advice on assigning students to learning groups and quick cooperation starters. Outlines the jigsaw method and lists a variety of roles which may be assigned to student working in groups. Also includes a skills checklist for students, a checklist for teachers' role in cooperative learning, an observation form, and two generic cooperative lesson plan forms. A section on structuring academic controversies in the classroom wraps up the article.

473.   Johnson, R. T., & Johnson, D. W. (1985). Student-student interaction: Ignored but powerful. *Journal of Teacher Education, 34*, 22-26.

Reviews the research on three goal structures (cooperative, competitive, and individualistic) and discusses the implications for teacher education programs. Argues that "research indicates that cooperation should be the dominant interaction pattern in the classroom and researchers cite advantages of a predominantly cooperative setting over a predominantly competitive or individualistic setting."

474.   Johnson, R. T., & Johnson, D. W. (1987). Monitoring Groups
        Effectively. In R. T. Johnson, D. W. Johnson, & E. J. Holubec
        (Eds.), *Structuring Cooperative Learning: Lesson Plans for
        Teachers 1987* (pp. 3-11). Edina, MN: Interaction Book
        Company, 1987. 3-11.

        Explains the tasks related to monitoring students as they
        work cooperatively. Providing task assistance, collecting data on
        students' behavior in the groups, and intervening to teach specific
        cooperative skills were identified as the three most important
        monitoring tasks for teachers. Simple rules for intervening in
        groups are suggested.

475.   Joyce, B. (1975). Learning strategies for learning centers.
        Educational Leadership, 32(6), 388-391.

        While this article is not about cooperative learning per se,
        the issues it addresses are relevant vis-a-vis cooperative learning.
        More specifically, Joyce states that his "stance is that
        competence in teaching is the possession of the range of teaching
        models to: Achieve a range of educational goals, help reach
        learners of widely different learning styles, help learners acquire
        an expanded repertoire of learning strategies, and keep ourselves
        from becoming routine and dull."

476.   Joyce, B., Showers, B., & Rolheiser-Bennett, C. (1987). Staff
        development and student learning: A synthesis of research on
        models of teaching. *Educational Leadership, 45*(2) 11-23.

        The authors assert that it is now possible "to design staff
        development programs around teaching approaches with potential
        for increasing student learning." Among the topics addressed are:
        sources of promising practices, the concept of effect size, models
        of teaching (social models, information process models, personal
        models, and behavioral systems models), specific teaching
        practices applicable across models and styles, and designing staff
        development to increase student learning. The section on social
        models discusses cooperative learning at some length (pp. 14-
        17). The authors state that "Cooperative learning approaches,
        representing social models of teaching, yield effect sizes from
        modest to high. The more complex the outcomes -- higher
        order thinking, problem solving, social skills and attitudes -- the
        greater are the effects."

*   Kagan, S. (1989). *Cooperative Learning: Resources for Teachers.*
        San Juan Capistrano, CA: Resources for Teachers. 294 pp.
        (Cited above as Item 011.)

477.   Kindsvatter, R., Wilen, W., & Ishler, M. (1988). *Dynamics of
        Effective Teaching.* New York: Longman.

        This text for preservice secondary teachers briefly describes
        several purposes of cooperative learning and some general
        research findings (pp. 248-249), and in a subsequent section
        describes cooperative learning in more detail by addressing the
        following: Purpose, focus, role of the teacher, methodology,
        role of the learner, structure, evaluation, and appropriate subjects
        and types of learners (pp. 257-260).

478.   Leighton, M. S. (1990). Cooperative learning. In J. M. Cooper,
        Classroom Teaching Skills, (pp. 307-335). Lexington, MA:
        D.C. Heath and Co.

        Provides a succinct, but strong overview of the philosophy
        behind cooperative learning, the key components inherent in all
        cooperative learning strategies, and information on three
        cooperative learning strategies (Student Teams-Achievement
        Divisions, Teams-Games-Tournament, and Jigsaw II). Includes
        learning activities and mastery tests which were designed for use
        in teacher education courses.

*   Lemlech, J. K. (1990). *Classroom Management: Methods and
        Techniques for Elementary and Secondary Teachers*, 2nd ed.
        White Plains, NY: Longman, Inc. 339 pp. (Cited below as
        Item 630.)

479.   Lloyd, J. W., Crowley, E. P., Kohler, F. W., & Strain, P. S.
        (1988). Redefining the applied research agenda: Cooperative
        learning preferral, teacher consultation, and peer-mediated
        interventions. *Journal of Learning Disabilities*, *21*, 43-52.

        Reviews research published on four intervention strategies,
        one of which is cooperative learning. Includes an easy-to-
        interpret chart of relevant studies, including descriptions of
        subjects tested, independent variables, and results. Realizing that
        many questions about the effectiveness of cooperative learning
        strategies still exist, the authors offer practical suggestions for

future studies designed to test the effects of cooperative learning upon atypical learners.

480.   Lounsbury, J. H. (1956). Professor Gray and group work. *Progressive Education, 33*, 16-18.

Presents an argument for more cooperative group work at the college level, especially in teacher education programs. Written in conversational style, the article stresses that more educators believe that individuals cannot attain their full potential except in interaction with others and that participation in cooperative groups prepare individuals for life in an interdependent world.

*   Lyons, V. M. (Ed.). (1980). *Structuring Cooperative Learning Experiences in the Classroom: The 1980 Handbook.* University of Minn. A Cooperation Network Publication. (Cited below as Item 633.)

481.   Manera, E. S., & Glockhamer, H. (1988-1989). Cooperative learning: Do students "own" the content? *Action in Teacher Education, 10*, 53-56.

Presents a brief but cogent examination as to why cooperative learning has not been implemented on a wide scale in elementary through college classrooms, and then provides descriptions of an English as a Second Language (ESL) course and an undergraduate humanities course that illustrate that "cooperative learning activities work well with adults, can promote higher levels of thinking and mastery of content, and can be used as a student evaluation vehicle."

*   Michaelson, L. K. (1983). Team learning in large classes. *New Directions for Teaching and Learning, 14*, 13-22. (Cited below as Item 634.)

*   Michaelson, L. K., Cragin, J. P., & Watson, W. E. (1981). Grading and anxiety: A strategy for coping. *Exchange: The Organizational Behavior Teaching Journal, 6*, 32-36. (Cited below as Item 533.)

482.   Moorman, C., Dishon, D., & O'Leary, P. W. (1984). An overview of cooperative learning. In J. Reinhartz (Ed.), *Perspectives on*

Effective Teaching and the Cooperative Classroom. Analysis and Action Series. (Stock No. 1691-2) Washington, D.C.: National Education Association, NEA Professional Library. (ERIC Document Reproduction Service No. ED 250 279).

Offers a rationale for teaching cooperation and describes the differences between cooperative groups and typical classroom groups.

*   Myers, C. B., & Myers, L. K. (1990). *An Introduction to Teaching and Schools.* Orlando, FL: Holt, Rinehart and Winston, Inc. 629 pp. (Cited below as Item 638.)

483.   O'Brien, M. J. (1984). Critical instructional competencies as perceived and applied by training directors (industry, development). University of Cincinnati. *Dissertation Abstracts International, 45,* 2380A.

Reports the findings of a qualitative study that involved corporate training directors and that sought to determine "what competencies training directors thought were critical for the role of instructor" and "what models of instruction did they use to make instructional decisions." Among the six known models of instruction that were determined to be useful organizers for the subjects' views about instructional competency was Group Investigation, a form of cooperative team learning.

*   O'Leary, P. W., & Dishon, D. (1985). Cooperative learning. In A. Costa (Ed.) *Developing Minds: A Resource Book for Teaching Thinking,* (pp. 179-180). Alexandria, VA: Association for supervision and curriculum Development. (Cited below as Item 642.)

484.   Parker, R. (1984). Small-group cooperative learning in the classroom. *OSSC Bulletin.* Eugene, Oregon: Organ School Study Council. ED242 065.

Provides an introduction to cooperative learning programs in schools. Includes a detailed discussion of what takes place in a classroom where cooperative learning is implemented. Addresses the difficulties teachers may face but also provides suggestions for facilitation of this process -- including how to make organizational changes and group assignment techniques. Also includes interesting comments by actual teachers who have used cooperative learning and found its use to be positive. Final section identifies four principles for successfully implementing cooperative learning in schools: systemization and long-range staff development, a school-wide rather than an individual-specific approach, the development of support groups during the early stages of implementation, and long-term training for teachers involved in cooperative learning programs.

485. Peck, G. (1989). Facilitating cooperative learning: A forgotten tool gets it started. *Academic Therapy, 25*, 145-150.

After answering the question "Why Cooperative Learning?" by reviewing basic research findings, the author points out that "an integral part of successfully implementing cooperative learning is the formation of cooperative groups." One systematic approach to group formation is a class sociogram. "Teachers who balance cooperative groups with high group status children and mutual choice pairs enhance the effectiveness of the cooperative learning method." Concludes that "few other methods of grouping for instruction have both the academic and social benefits of cooperative learning."

486. Prescott, S. (1989/1990, Winter). Teachers' perceptions of factors that affect successful implementation of cooperative learning. *Action in Teacher Education, XI*(4):30-34.

A thought-provoking article that examines comments from 30 elementary and twenty-one secondary teachers in regard to factors that contribute to and interfere with successful implementation of cooperative learning. Among the factors discussed are the following: reward systems, composition of team members, teaching/management skills, activity design, readiness phase, student evaluation, and student characteristics.

487. Pusch, L, McCabe, J., & Pusch, W. (1985). Personalized on-site coaching. *Education Canada, 25*(3), 36-39.

An inservice program was developed to help teachers incorporate cooperative learning into their classes. Three "coaches" provided group inservice sessions, then worked individually with teachers. The program's objectives for teachers were: 1. to acquire the theoretical background of cooperative learning; 2. to be able to demonstrate cooperative learning teaching strategies; and 3. to view the "coaching for implementation" plan a success. Formal and informal interviews with the teachers indicated that teachers met these objectives. Teachers said their coaches gave them the confidence in skills and the knowledge needed as well as the motivation to pursue the cooperative learning strategy in their classrooms.

488.   Pusch, L., McCabe, J., & Pusch, W. (1985). From awareness to personalized on-site coaching. *The Journal of Staff Development*, *6*, 88-92.

Discusses the role and importance of peer coaching in cooperatively structured settings. Outlines one six-month staff development program implemented for the purpose of helping teachers "to acquire the basic theoretical background of the cooperative-learning method of teaching, of being able to demonstrate the cooperative-learning teaching strategies in the classroom, and of viewing peer coaching "as a valuable process for assisting transfer of a new teaching model into the classroom." Reports that the objectives were satisfactorily met mainly because of the peer coaching element.

489.   Putnam, J. W., & Barnes, H. (1984). *Applications of classroom management research findings*. Research series no. 154. (ERIC Document Reproduction Service No. ED 256 752).

Investigated teachers' uses of cooperative learning strategies, group-development, and student outcomes. Examined the long-term effects of providing a research-based approach to classroom management. A two-phase staff development process was designed to help teachers learn to establish and maintain effective classroom groups.

Analysis of data showed that teachers who were motivated to learn to work with cooperative groups were more successful than those who were not. Teachers who used cooperative learning to increase student responsibility, accountability, and productivity were more successful than those who used it merely as a means of classroom management. Teachers who worked together in the initial stage of implementation were more successful. Teachers who had access to a teacher educator were also more successful.

490. Putnam, J. W., Markovchick, K., & Fogg, M. (1988). Using peer coaching, cooperative learning and effective instruction strategies to promote social integration and mainstreaming of middle school and junior high exceptional students." *Alternative Futures for Rural Special Education. Proceedings of the Annual ACRES National Rural Special Education Conference.* Bellingham, WA: Western Washington University, American Council on Rural Special Education. 705 pp. (ERIC Document Reproduction Service No. ED 299 726).

Paper presents an overview of cooperative learning, describes approach to staff development, and discusses project activities and evaluation procedures. "Cooperative learning activities provide an ideal context for instruction in the mainstream because they afford opportunities for meaningful social interaction." The extent of teachers' use of cooperative learning techniques and effects of peer coaching were assessed through questionnaires, self-ratings, and structured interviews. Results indicated that using a cooperative approach to staff development (including teacher support teams, teacher decision making and peer coaches) is likely to produce the best results when imparting skills in cooperative learning.

491. Redman, G., & Willie, R. (1980). Cooperative learning in a continuing educational program: A case study. *Educational Research Quarterly, 5,* 80-87.

A study to ascertain "selected effects" of cooperative learning in a continuing education program for educators. The hypothesis investigated was: "Cooperative learning fosters greater learner satisfaction with the program, the instructor, and/or self in human relations for in-service teachers, than does individualistic learning."

492. Reinhartz, J. (Ed.) (1984). *Perspectives on Effective Teaching and the Cooperative Classroom.* Analysis and Action Series. National Education Association, Washington, D.C. (ERIC document Reproduction Service No. 250 279).

First six chapters deal with broader aspects of effective teaching and the cooperative classroom. Seventh chapter prepares teachers to implement cooperative learning ideas in the classrooms.

*   Rhodes, J., & McCabe, M. (1985). *Simple Cooperation in the
         Classroom. Beginner's Guide to Establishing Cooperative
         Groups*. Willits, CA: ITA Publication. (Cited below as Item
         649.)

493.   Sapon-Shevin, M., & Schniedewind, N. (1989/1990). Selling
         cooperative learning without selling it short. *Educational
         Leadership, 47*(4), 63-65.

         Urges teachers to be more reflective vis-a-vis their use of
         cooperative learning and to consider such issues as: Reflecting
         on content, making content and process compatible, coordinating
         the approach with other classroom values, giving teachers and
         students a voice, eliminating competition, and promoting
         cooperative learning appropriately.

494.   Schielack, D. J. F. (1988). A cooperative learning laboratory
         approach in a mathematics course for prospective elementary
         teachers. Texas A & M University. *Dissertation Abstracts
         International, 49*, 2672A.

         Reports the findings of a study that investigated the effects
         of a lecture/demonstration approach, a lecture/laboratory
         approach, and a lecture laboratory approach with a cooperative
         learning component upon a mathematics course for pre-service
         elementary teachers. Findings revealed no significant differences
         between treatment groups toward the course, in attitude toward
         mathematics, in achievement, and in concept representation
         ability. It did appear, however, that "the lecture/demonstrating
         approach tended to be less effective than the cooperative
         laboratory approach (for both of the specialist groups) except in
         achievement for the nonmathematics specialist and attitude
         toward mathematics for the mathematics specialist" and that the
         "cooperative laboratory approach, while not as effective for the
         mathematics specialists in some areas, was more effective for the
         non-mathematics specialist than were the other approaches,
         except in achievement."

*   Schmuck, R., & Schmuck, P. A. (1983). *Group Processing in the
         Classroom*. Dubuque, IA: William C. Brown Co. 384 pp.
         (Cited below as Item 652.)

*   Schultz, J. L. (1989/1990). Cooperative learning: Refining the
         process. *Educational Leadership, 47*(4), 43-45. (Cited above as
         Item 329.)

*   Schniedewind, N., & Davidson, E. (1987). *Cooperative Learning,
         Cooperative Lives: A Sourcebook of Learning Activities for
         Building a Peaceful World.* Dubuque, Iowa: Wm. C. Brown
         Company Publishers. 538 pp. (Cited below as Item 653.)

495.   Sharan, Y., & Sharan, S. (1987). Training teachers for cooperative
         learning. *Educational Leadership, 45*(3), 20-25.

              Focuses on how creating a cooperative learning
         situation/classroom for themselves in a workshop setting is
         valuable preparation for teachers who wish to foster norms of
         helping and sharing among their students. At the outset the
         Sharans, professors in Israel and noted researchers/proponents of
         cooperative learning, discuss the "experiential learning model"
         and then cogently delineate how to design and implement a
         cooperative learning experiential workshop.

*   Slavin, R. E. (1980). Student team learning: A manual for teachers.
         In S. Sharan, P. Hare, C. Webb, & R. Hertz-Lazarowitz (Eds.),
         Cooperation in Education, (pp. 82-135). Provo, UT: Brigham
         Young University. (Cited above as Item 016.)

*   Slavin, R. E. (1989/1990). Here to stay - or gone tomorrow?
         Educational Leadership, 47(4), 3. (Cited below as Item 667.)

*   Slavin, R. E. (1990). *Cooperative Learning: Theory, Research, and
         Practice.* Englewood Cliffs, NJ: Prentice Hall. 173 pp. (Cited
         below as Item 668.)

496.   Thew, D. (1980). Teacher education for cooperative learning. In S.
         Sharan, P. Hare, C. D. Webb, & R. Hertz-Lazarowitz
         (Eds.), *Cooperation in Education,* (pp. 235-259). Provo, UT:
         Brigham Young University Press.

              Describes a plan for assisting elementary preservice teachers
         to acquire the skills to promote inter-student cooperative
         learning.

497.   Tyrrell, R. (1990, January). What teachers say about cooperative
        learning. *Middle School Journal, 21*(3), 16-19.

             Argues that cooperative learning is an ideal strategy that
        builds on the learning styles of early adolescents and one that
        lends itself to a climate that is more conducive to the needs of
        such students. Also discusses how and why the training of
        teachers in cooperative learning was implemented in the Program
        of Studies for Teachers of Emerging Adolescents at Cleveland
        State University as well as the outcomes that ensued.

*   Ward, B. A. (1987). *Instructional Grouping in the Classroom*.
        Portland, OR: Northwest Regional Educational Laboratory.
        (ERIC Document Reproduction Service ED 291 145). (Cited
        below as Item 675.)

498   Wilson, M. T. (1989). The effects of cooperative learning on self-
        perceptions of teachers' careers and behaviors. State University
        of New York at Buffalo. *Dissertation Abstracts International,
        50*, 1611A.

             Examines the effects of a staff development program of
        cooperative learning upon teachers' perceptions, of their careers,
        explains and critiques Dewey's theory of intelligence, analyzes
        teacher interviews about Dewey's theory, and re-examines the
        philosophical and pedagogical foundations of cooperative
        learning. Findings revealed that teachers with strong
        professional self-concepts are more willing to experiment with
        instructional strategies than those who are detached from their
        careers. Revealed that Dewey's theory of intelligence and
        cooperative learning techniques are compatible.

499.   Winston, D. M. (1988). The effects of training in the use of
        cooperative learning structures on the performance of student
        teachers. University of Kansas. *Dissertation Abstracts
        International, 49*, 3338A.

             Discusses the findings of a study "designed to determine if a
        treatment intervention could facilitate the use of cooperative
        grouping structures by pre-service elementary teachers." The
        treatment involved four components: a videotaped demonstration,
        a lecture and as related handout, guided pictures, and an in-school
        assignment. Found that significant differences did exist in the
        number of times per week the student teachers used cooperative
        learning techniques. "An analysis of a hypothetical classroom
        simulation did not find differences between the two groups, but
        did find a significant difference between the pre- and post-test
        scores."

E. ACADEMIC ACHIEVEMENT

500.   Ames, C., and Felker, D. (1979). An examination of children's attributions and achievement-related evaluations in competitive, cooperative, and individualistic reward structures. *Journal of Educational Psychology*, *71*(4), 413-420.

Children's achievement-based judgements of success and failure outcomes are strongly dependent upon the social context of the setting. An achievement situation describing two children successfully and unsuccessfully performing a task in competitive, cooperative, and individualistic reward structures is presented to 400 children across five grade levels. Competitive and individualistic structures accentuate perceptions of individual differences and the value placed on achievement outcomes. Data supports the Johnson and Johnson suggestion that American children are so sensitized to a competitive orientation that the value associated with performing a task well is far exceeded by the value placed on winning over another person. Positive outcomes bought about by cooperation seemed to evolve mainly from groups that were successful in their goal accomplishment.

501.   Apurlin, J. S., Dansereau, D. F., Larson, C. O., & Brooks, L. W. (1984). Cooperative learning strategies in processing descriptive text: Effects of role and activity level of the learner. *Cognition and Instruction*, *1*(4), 451-463.

Used cooperative dyads to analyze the effects of interaction strategies on the acquisition of scientific knowledge. One hundred and twenty-six general psychology students were assigned to one of five groups: fixed role/summary plus facilitation activity, fixed role/summary only activity, alternating role/summary plus facilitation activity, alternating role/summary only activity, and individual study method.
Results showed that students who were assigned to fixed recaller role had significantly higher recall scores for main ideas than students who were assigned the fixed listener role. The mean score of the alternate group (each member alternated

245

between being listener and recaller) was about halfway between the scores of the fixed recaller and of the fixed listener group. The more verbal summarization produced by the students, the better the recall performance. Summary/facilitation listener activity groups outperformed summary only groups on free recall of main ideas. Authors suggest that "the active listener may help the partner to process the information on deeper semantic levels through elaborative activity. A subjective evaluation showed alternative groups to enjoy the experience more than recallers or listeners.

*   Archer, J. A. (1988). Feedback effects on achievement, attitude, and group dynamics of adolescents in interdependent cooperative groups for beginning second language and culture study. University of Minnesota. *Dissertation Abstracts International*, *49*, 3658A. (Cited below as Item 556.)

*   Artzt, A. (1979). Student teams in mathematics class. *Mathematics Teacher*, *72*, 505-508. (Cited above as Item 155.)

*   Augustine, D. K., Gruber, K.D., & Hanson, L.R. (1989/1990). Cooperation Works! *Educational Leadership*, *47*(4), 3. (Cited below as Item 557.)

502.   Azmita, M. (1988). Peer interaction and problem solving: When are two heads better than one? *Child Development*, *59*, 87-96.

Addresses the findings of three questions: 1. Does group work and cooperative activities lead to greater learning than independent study? 2. Does group and/or cooperative team learning generalize to later independent situations? 3. What characteristics of group interaction facilitate learning? Azmita found that preschool children are "more likely to acquire cognitive skills when they work with a more expert partner," that "only novices who worked with an expert generalized their skills to the individual posttest," and that "observational learning and guidance by an expert mediated learning."

503.   Cavanagh, B. R. (1984). Effects of interdependent group contingencies on the achievement of elementary school children. University of Maryland. *Dissertation Abstracts International*, *46*, 1558A.

Presents the findings of a study designed to test the effects of group and individual contingencies upon the mathematical achievement of second, third, and fourth graders. "Results indicated that there was a significant difference in favor of rewarded students in amount of work output over the students who had no specific reward contingencies. Students who worked with interdependent group contingencies demonstrated significantly higher achievement than students working with individual reward contingencies." No significant differences in attitude were found.

504.   Collins, C. (1989). Administrators can increase their students' higher-level thinking abilities. *Clearing House*, *62*, 391-396.

Argues that students will improve their performance on achievement tests if they are taught higher order thinking skills. Outlines programs that assist teachers with implementation and evaluation of objectives. Includes cooperative learning activities that enhance higher-order thinking skills.

505.   Dalton, D. W. (1990). The effects of cooperative learning strategies on achievement and attitudes during interactive video. *Journal of Computer-based Instruction*, *17*(1), 8-16.

Study examined effects of gender pairing and locus of control on learner achievement, attitudes, and interactions during an interactive video-based cooperative learning program. Results suggest interactive video may provide an "effective and enjoyable means of promoting cooperation, while minimizing off-task behavior." Lessons should be designed, however, to take into consideration differences in competitiveness between males and females. Male/male teams completed their lessons significantly faster than either male/female or female/female teams. More competitive males had a tendency to race for solutions to "beat" their partners or neighboring teams. Authors suggest designing studies and lesson plans to build in explicit instructions on working cooperatively.

506.   Davis, R. G. (1988). A study on the effects of students' use of selected group process skills on student achievement and attitude during a seventh grade cooperative learning mathematics problem solving unit. *Dissertation Abstracts International*, *49*, 3263A. University Microfilms Order Number.

Investigated whether there were significant differences in attitude and achievement of students who used the group process skills of "think aloud" and "oral summaries" in a series of cooperative learning lessons. The "results of this study indicate that there were no statistically significant differences in student achievement or student attitude between the two conditions. The observational data revealed differences in students' interaction patterns between the treatment and control groups. Students using the specified group process skills were more verbal, interacted more with other group members, demonstrated more concern for other group members, and had more process-oriented explanations for word problems being solved during group work than the other students functioning without the specified teacher-directed group process skills."

* Delgado, M. T. (1987). The effects of a cooperative learning strategy on the academic behavior of Mexican-American children. *Stanford University, 48*, (6). (Cited above as Item 383.)

* Duin, A. H. (1986). Implementing cooperative learning groups in the writing curriculum. Journal of Teaching Writing, 5, 315-323. (Cited above as Item 116.)

507. Elliott, J. L., Jr. (1988). A review of literature on the relationship between motivational techniques and academic achievement. Saint Louis University. *Dissertation Abstracts International, 49*, 1737A.

Covering 1967 through 1985, the study consists of 496 reviews of literature that focused on the relationship between motivational techniques and academic achievement. Reviews are classified under four headings with appropriate subheadings, including cooperative learning. Also contains an extensive bibliography for additional reference.

508. George, P. S. (1983). Instruction: Ten tarnished truths. *Educational Forum, 48*, 34-42.

His conclusions applicable only to low achieving students and to basic skills instruction, the author discusses ten "truths" of education that have been questioned by educational research. The author divides the tarnished beliefs into two categories: "Truths about Classroom Management and Achievement" and

"Teaching Style and Achievement." Points out that the use of individualized instruction and cooperative grouping may be inferior to large groups and teacher-directed instruction when teaching basic skills to below-average learners.

509. Goldman, M. (1965). A comparison of individual and group performance for varying combinations of initial ability. *Journal of Personality and Social Psychology, 1*, 210-216.

Describes a study that compared the performance of subjects working in cooperative groups with that of subjects working alone. Results indicated that the group participants improved significantly when compared to students working individually. Also found that low-level ability students experienced greater gains than all other students.

*   Graves, T. (1988). Review: Cooper, J., and Sherman, L. Cooperative Learning at the University Level. *The International Association for the Study of Cooperation in Education, 9*(3 and 4), 20-21. (Cited above as Item 004.)

510. Hall, R. H., Rocklin, T. R., Dansereau, D. F., Skaggs, L. P., O'Donnell, A. M., Lambiotte, J. G., & Young, M. D. (1988). The role of individual differences in the cooperative learning of technical material. *Journal of Educational Psychology, 80*(2), 172-178.

Situations involving students studying alone and in dyads were used to examine individual differences in the recall of procedural and structural/functional information. Subjects completed a series of nine individual difference measures, learned a four-step study strategy (read, recall, detection of errors by dyad partner, and elaboration where partners work together to develop analogies, images, etc. to help remember the material), and then studied passages that included both structural/functional and procedural material either in a dyad or alone.
Results indicate that the general effectiveness of cooperative learning may be much stronger for certain types of individuals (i. e. those high in cognitive ability and social orientation). Cooperative learning also appears to be an effective learning method with both structural/functional information and well-learned and automatized procedures.

*   Hare, B. R., & Levine, D. U. (1985). Effective schooling in
          desegregated settings: What do we know about learning styles
          and linguistic differences? *Equity and Choice, 1*, 13-18. (Cited
          above as Item 391.)

*   Hawley, W. D., Rosenholtz, S. J., Goodstein, H., & Hasselbring, T.
          (1984). Good "effective teaching" schools: What research says
          about improving student achievement. *Peabody Journal of
          Education, 61*, 15-52. (Cited above as Item 468.)

*   Hernandez, N. G., & Descamps, J. A. (1986). *Review of factors
          affecting learning of Mexican-Americans.* Paper presented at the
          National Association for Chicano Studies, El Paso, TX. (ERIC
          Document Reproduction Service No. ED 267 946). (Cited above
          as Item 393.)

511.   Holton, R. T. (1988). A study of the value of academic competition
          in the K - 12 school curriculum. Central Michigan University.
          Masters Abstracts International, 26, 363A.

          A qualitative study that investigated the positive and
          negative values of academic competition. One of the findings is
          that "the most positive form of competition occurs when
          cooperative learning is also stressed."

*   Johnson, D. W., & Johnson, R. T. (August, 1982). *Having your
          cake and eating it too: maximizing achievement and cognitive-
          social development and socialization through cooperative
          learning.* Paper presented at the Annual Convention of the
          American Psychological Association, Washington, DC. (ERIC
          Document Reproduction Service No. ED 227 408). (Cited above
          as Item 305.)

512.   Johnson, D. W., & Johnson, R. T. (1987). The high achieving
          student in cooperative learning groups. In R. T. Johnson, D. W.
          Johnson, & E. J. Holubec (Eds.), *Structuring Cooperative
          Learning: Lesson Plans for Teachers 1987* (pp. 317-322).
          Edina, MN: Interaction Book Company.

          Gives several practical suggestions for encouraging high
          ability students to work cooperatively in groups. Cites research
          showing improved grades, higher-level reasoning strategies,
          higher creativity, development of friendships and social skills.

513.   Johnson, D. W., & Johnson, R. T. (1989). *Cooperation and Competition: Theory and Research*. Hillsdale, NJ: Lawrence Erlbaum. 258 pp.

A comprehensive review of cooperative learning studies. Three hundred and fifty-two studies have been meta-analyzed and the results reduced to a single analysis. When all studies were included in the analysis, the average student in a cooperative situation performed at about 2/3 a standard deviation above average students in a competitive learning situation and 3/4 a standard deviation above average students in an individualistic situation. In other words, students at the 50th-percentile in a cooperative learning situation will perform at the 75th-percentile of students learning in a competitive situation or an individualistic situation. When the results of "pure" cooperative learning strategies were compared with "mixed" strategies (i.e. original Jigsaw, Teams-Games-Tournaments, Team-Assisted-Instruction, and Student-Teams-Achievement-Divisions), "pure" operationalizations consistently produced significantly higher achievement. Results of the meta-analysis are reported and discussed for a number of other areas, including motivation, emotional involvement in learning, achievement and productivity, social skills, attitudes, and critical thinking competencies. Discusses limitations of many of the studies. Contains Items 031, 310, 311, 312, 313, 314.

*   Johnson, D. W., & Johnson, R. T. (1989). Motivational processes. In D. W. Johnson & R. T. Johnson (Eds.), *Cooperation and Competition: Theory and Research* (pp. 77-88). Edina, MN: Interaction Book Company. (Cited above as Item 356.)

*   Johnson, D.W., & Johnson, R. T. (1989). Social interdependence and productivity/achievement. In D.W. Johnson & R.T. Johnson (Eds.), *Cooperation and Competition: Theory and Research* (pp. 39-56). Edina, MN: Interaction Book Company. (Cited above as Item 357.)

*   Johnson, D. W., Johnson, R. T., Johnson, J., & Anderson, D. (1976). Effects of cooperative versus individualized instruction on student prosocial behavior, attitudes toward learning, and achievement. *Journal of Educational Psychology, 68*(4), 446-452. (Cited above as Item 358.)

514.   Johnson, D. W., Johnson, R. T., & Skon, L. (1979). Student achievement on different types of tasks under cooperative, competitive, and individualistic conditions. *Contemporary Educational Psychology, 4*, 99-106.

"The effects of interpersonal cooperation, competition, and individualistic efforts were compared on math and reading drill-review, study problems, sequencing, triangle identification, and visual sorting according to attributes tasks." Findings reveal that on all six tasks students involved in cooperative activities had greater achievement than students involved in individualistic activities. "In general, subjects in the cooperative condition felt that the tasks were easier than did the subjects in the competitive and individualistic conditions." Concludes that classroom tasks are more effective if they are structured cooperatively and that teacher education programs may desire to increase their emphasis upon the importance of cooperative learning activities.

515.   Johnson, D. W, Johnson, R. T., & Yager, S. (1985). Oral discussion, group-to-individual transfer, and achievement in cooperative learning groups. *Journal of Educational Psychology, 77*, 60-66.

In the first study noted, students were placed in one of three groups: conventional classroom, cooperative learning (CL) groups, and CL groups with 5 minutes of "group processing" at the end of each lesson. Scores on a retention test given three weeks after the unit were as follows (pretest average: 50%): conventional class scored 65%, CL groups scored 75%, and CL groups with group processing scored 87%. In addition, the gap between scores of students of different "ability" levels decreased. In a second study, discussion was "structured" with students assuming a role of "learning leader" or active questioner. Retention scores for conventional , CL, and structured discussion CL groups were 49%, 70%, and 95% respectively.

516.   Johnson, D. W., Maruyama, G., Johnson, R. T., Nelson, D., & Skon, L. (1981). Effects of cooperative, competitive, and individualistic goal structure on achievement: a meta-analysis. *Psychological Bulletin, 89*(1), 47-62.

This review of 122 studies yielded 286 findings. Meta-analysis procedures used were voting methods, effect-size method, and z-score methods. Results indicated that cooperative learning is much more effective than competition and individual work, that cooperation with between groups competition is better than interpersonal competition and individual work, and that no significant difference exists between interpersonal competitive and individualistic efforts. Used results of meta-analyses to argue that educators may want to include more cooperative learning strategies in their curriculums and that group reward systems may increase productivity in industry.

*   Johnson, D. W., Skon, L., & Johnson, R. T. (1980). Effects of cooperative, competitive, and individualistic conditions on children's problem-solving performance. *American Educational Research Journal, 17,* 83-93. (Cited above as Item 360.)

517.   Johnson, L. C. (1985). The effects of the groups of four cooperative learning models on student problem-solving achievement in mathematics. *Dissertation Abstracts International, 47,* 403A (University Microfilms Order Number ADG86-07019. 8608).

Examined the effects of the Group of Four strategy on "student post-achievement and the degree of model implementation in the classroom."

518.   Johnson, R. T., & Johnson, D. W. (1979). Type of task and student achievement and attitudes in interpersonal cooperation, competition, and individualization. *The Journal of Social Psychology, 108,* 37-48.

"The effects of interpersonal cooperation, competition, and individualization were compared on drill-review, problem-solving, specific-knowledge acquisition, and specific-knowledge retention instructional tasks." The study involved sixty-six fifth graders. "The results indicate that cooperation generally produced more positive attitudes than did either individualization or competition. Cooperation resulted in higher achievement than did competition and individualization on both the problem-solving and retention tasks, higher achievement than competition and just as high achievement as individualization on the drill-review task, and higher achievement than individualization and just as high achievement as competition on the specific-knowledge-acquisition task."

*   Johnson, R. T., Johnson, D. W., & Stanne, M. B. (1986).
        Comparison of computer-assisted cooperative, competitive, and
        individualistic learning. *American Educational Research Journal*,
        23, 382-392. (Cited above as Item 99.)

519.   Johnson, R.T., Johnson, D.W., & Tauer, M. (1979). The effects of
        cooperative, competitive, and individualistic goal structures on
        students' attitudes and achievement. *The Journal of Psychology*,
        102, 191-198.

            Sixty-nine male and female fourth, fifth, and sixth graders
        were randomly and equally assigned to cooperative, competitive,
        and individualistic conditions. In the cooperative condition,
        students were assigned to groups of five and instructed to work
        together as a group. The competitive condition tried to
        maximize the constructive and appropriate use of competition.
        In the individualistic condition, students were instructed to work
        on their own, seeking help and receiving rewards only from the
        teacher. Results from an attitude questionnaire and achievement
        test showed that cooperation promoted the strongest perceptions
        of teacher academic and personal support, strongest perceptions
        of peer academia and personal support, and the highest academic
        achievement of the three conditions. Competition resulted in
        higher achievement and stronger perceptions of teacher academic
        support than did individual learning.

*   Kagan, S., & Knight, G.P. (1981). Social motives among Anglo-
        American and Mexican-American children: Experimental and
        projective measures. *Journal of Research in Personality*, *15*(1),
        93-106. (Cited above as Item 398.)

*   Knight, G. P., Nelson, W., Kagan, S., & Gumbiner, J. (1982).
        Cooperative - competitive social orientation and school
        achievement among Anglo-Americans and Mexican-American
        children. *Contemporary Educational Psychology*, *7*, 97-106.
        (Cited above as Item 405.)

520.   Lambiotte, J. G., Dansereau, D. F., O'Donnell, A. M., Young, M.
        D., Skaggs, L. P., & Hall, R. H. (1988). Effects of
        cooperative script manipulations on initial learning and transfer.
        Cognition and Instruction, *5*(2), 103-121.

Four types of cooperative study scripts were used by paired undergraduate psychology student to test effects on initial recall and on transfer to individual tasks. Groups one and two used a cooperative teaching (CT) script. Partners read one passage, then taught the material to the other. Groups three and four used variations of cooperative learning (CL) during which partners read both passages and alternated summarizer and listener roles. All four groups studied an additional passage individually to allow for measurement of transfer. Results shows that CT groups outperformed CL groups on initial recall, but not on transfer to individual tasks. Playing a teacher role significantly improved recall. Not significant were frequency of summarization and expectancy manipulations. CT script users reported higher motivation and concentration, and less boredom and fatigue, both while reading the material and while teaching material to their partners.

521.   Lambiotte, J. G., Dansereau, D. F., O'Donnell, A. M., Young, M. D., Skaggs, L. P., Hall, R. H., & Rocklin, T. R. (1987). Manipulating cooperative scripts for teaching and learning. *Journal of Educational Psychology, 79*(4), 424-430.

Three different scripts for cooperative interactions were tested using same-sex pairs of undergraduate psychology students: 1. cooperative teaching--partners each read only one passage, then taught each other the information they had read; 2. cooperative learning -- both partners read both passages, stopping periodically to summarize the material to each other; 3. cooperative microteaching--each partner read alternate pages of both passages, stopping to teach each other the material they had read.
Students using the cooperative teaching script significantly outperformed students in the other groups. Students playing a teaching role recalled significantly more information for the passage they taught. There was no significant difference in recall among "learners" of all three groups.

522.   Lambiotte, J. G., Dansereau, D. F., Rocklin, T. R., Fletcher, B., Hythecker, V. I., Larson, C. O., & O'Donnell, A. M. (1987). Cooperative learning and test taking: Transfer of skills. *Contemporary Educational Psychology, 12,* 52-61.

Discusses a study designed to test effects of cooperative learning upon studying and test taking. Four treatments were used: Cooperative learning/cooperative testing, cooperative learning/individual testing, individual learning/cooperative testing, and individual learning/individual testing. After receiving instruction on learning and test-taking strategies, students in cooperative groups worked together, while students in individual groups worked alone. Results indicate that cooperative learning positively affects recall performance and accuracy.

*   Lang, N. A. (1983). The effects of a cooperative learning technique, Teams-Games-Tournament, on the academic achievement and attitude toward economics of college students enrolled in a Principles of Microeconomics course. University of Georgia. *Dissertation Abstracts International, 44,* 1517A. (Cited above as Item 080.)

523.   Larsen, C. O., Dansereau, D. F., O'Donnell, A. M., Hythecker, V. I., Lambiotte, J. G., & Rocklin, T. R. (1985). Effects of metacognitive and elaborative activity on cooperative learning and transfer. *Contemporary Educational Psychology, 10,* 342-348.

Examined two basic questions regarding the role of metacognition and elaboration in cooperative learning: 1. "What is the relative contribution of metacognitive vs. elaborative activity to text processing performance during cooperative learning?" 2. "What impact does the activity of the listener during cooperative learning have on subsequent transfer to individual learning?" Findings reveal that "metacognitive activities facilitate cooperative learning and elaborative activities facilitate transfer to individual learning." Concludes that cooperative learning strategies should be tailored to instructional goals.

524.   Laughlin, P. R. (1978). Ability and group problem solving. *Journal of Research and Development in Education, 12,* 114-120.

Explores the success of cooperative groups in problem solving. The subjects in the study were 528 college students who were ranked according to a test on synonyms. Laughlin also compares homogeneous and heterogeneous grouping, size of grouping, and the way a group comes to a consensus. He found that homogeneous groupings of high ability students had more sources of knowledge to pool together than homogeneous grouping of low ability students. Group performance was proportional to the number of high ability students in the group.

525. Laughlin, P. R., & Johnson, H. H. (1966). Group and individual performance on a complementary task as a function of initial ability level. *Journal of Experimental Social Psychology, 2,* 407-414.

Reports the results of a study designed to test the effects of group and individual performance upon test results. Results indicated that students working in groups experienced greater achievements gains that did students working alone. Concludes that cooperative group structures have a significant positive effect upon improvement scores of subjects.

526. Laughlin, P. R., & Sveeney, J. D. (1977). Individual-to-group and group-to-individual transfer in problem solving. *Journal of Experimental Psychology, Human Learning, and Memory, 3* (2), 246-254.

The authors investigated whether the order in which people participated in groups had some bearing on the transfer of learning from individuals to group or group to individuals. In two experiments done, the results were the same. Groups outperformed individuals but there was no carry over from group to individual performance. Groups performed better if the individuals had already attempted the problem on their own.

527. Lazarowitz, R., Baird, H., Bowlden, V., & Hertz-Lazarowitz, R. (l982). *Academic Achievements, Learning Environment, and Self-Esteem of High School Students in Biology Taught in Cooperative-Investigative Small Groups.* Unpublished manuscript, The Technion, Haifa, Israel.

*   Leming, J. S. (1985). Cooperative learning processes - some advantages. *NASSP Bulletin, 69,* 63. (Cited below as Item 629.)

*   Lew, M., Mesch, D., Johnson, D. W., & Johnson, R. (1986). Components of cooperative learning: Effects of collaborative

skills and academic group contingencies on achievement and mainstreaming. *Contemporary Educational Psychology, 11*, 229-239. (Cited above as Item 238.)

* Lyons, V. M. (1982). A study of elaborative cognitive processing as a variable mediating achievement in cooperative learning groups. University of Minnesota. *Dissertation Abstracts International, 43*, 1090A. (Cited above as Item 033.)

* MacGregor, S. K. (1988). Structured walk-through. *The Computing Teacher, 15*(9), 7-10. (Cited above as Item 100.)

528. Mahoney, J. V., Jr. (1988). Effectiveness and efficiency of individual and small group cooperative learning in CPR instruction. Texas A & M University. *Dissertation Abstracts International, 49*, 3237A.

"The purpose of the study was to evaluate the effectiveness and efficiency of individual and small group cooperative learning with a technology-based instructional delivery system to teach CPR. To accomplish this purpose, six research questions were examined. These questions were designed to determine if there were significant differences in cognitive achievement scores, attainment of psychomotor performance skills, learning time, confidence to perform CPR, types of cognitive errors committed, and types of psychomotor performance errors among subjects who undergo CPR training in an individually structured learning mode and those who undergo training in a cooperatively structured learning mode as dyads and triads." Findings indicate that individual learners and cooperative group learner had no significant difference in achievement scores and psychomotor skill performance evaluations. Cooperative group learners did require less time to learn and did express a higher degree of self-confidence than individual learners.

529. McClintock, E., & Sonquist, J. A. (1976). Cooperative task-oriented groups in a college classroom: A field application. *Journal of Educational Psychology, 69*(5), 588-596.

The study was an "attempt to conceptualize, explore, and evaluate the viability and impact of alternative social structures appropriate for college settings." A class of 89 college students (five chose not to participate) was divided into small task-oriented groups either randomly or by sociometric choice. Results showed that under individual reward conditions, sociometric groups were more likely to function outside the classroom. Under shared reward conditions both random and sociometric groups were equally viable. Working in groups did not affect grades on individual tests, but did result in better performance on team projects. Authors found that the overall ability of students to cope with the course was not affected by group participation. A small group of students, however, who did poorly on the first individual task then worked in groups, were found to perform significantly better on a second individual task than comparable students who did not participate in groups during the course.

530.   McDonald, B. A., Larson, C. O., Dansereau, D. F., & Spurlin, J. E. (1985). Cooperative dyads: Impact on test learning and transfer. *Contemporary Educational Psychology, 10*, 369-377.

Investigated the "effectiveness of a systematic cooperative learning strategy on (A) the initial acquisition of college-level textbook materials and (B) on the transfer of skills learned in a cooperative situation to individual learning." Findings indicate that "cooperative strategy facilitates initial learning and leads to a positive transfer on a subsequent individual learning task." Concludes that variations in cooperative learning activities facilitate transfer from cooperative to individual learning.

531.   McGlynn, R. P. (1972). Four-person group concept attainment as a function of interaction format. *The Journal of Social Psychology, 86*, 89-94.

Discusses the findings of a study involving high school students who solved "four concept-attainment problems in one of three randomly assigned conditions of interaction format: cooperation, competitive pairs, or competitive individuals." Results indicate that "on the basic measure of problem solving product (number of card choices to solution) performance decreased linearly with degree of cooperation, but only the difference between total cooperation and total competition was significant. For one measure of problem solving process (untenable hypothesis ratio) the cooperative formal resulted in a lower tenable hypothesis ratio than competitive-pair or competitive-individual formats which did not differ significantly.

On the other measure of problem solving process (focusing strategy) competing individuals employed significantly less focusing then either competitive pairs or four competitive individuals which did not differ significantly." Results support the hypothesis that achievement is greater when students work cooperatively instead of competitively.

532.   Mesch, D., Johnson, D. W., & Johnson, R. T. (1988). Impact of positive interdependence and academic group contingencies on achievement. *The Journal of Social Psychology, 128*, 345-352.

"The effects of positive goal interdependence and positive goal and positive reward interdependence on achievement were investigated. The control group (n=26) consisted of American students in a 10th-grade social studies class, and the experimental group (n=28) consisted of American students in a 10th-grade social studies class that included four academically disabled and isolated 10th-grade students (3 male and 1 female). The results indicated that cooperation promotes higher achievement than competition does, and that both positive goal and reward interdependence are needed to maximize student achievement."

*   Mesch, D., Lew, M., Johnson, D. W., & Johnson, R. T. (1986, July). Isolated teenagers, cooperative learning, and the training of social skills. *The Journal of Psychology, 120*(4), 323-334. (Cited above as Item 322.)

533.   Michaelson, L. K., Cragin, J. P., & Watson, W. E. (1981). Grading and anxiety: A strategy for coping. *Exchange: The Organizational Behavior Teaching Journal, 6*, 32-36.

Outlines cooperative structures that are effective in reducing both students' and teachers' anxieties about grades. Presents a step-by-step lesson plan for classroom implementation.

*   Morgan, B. M. (1987). Cooperative learning: Teacher use, classroom life, social integration, and student achievement. *Dissertation Abstracts International, 48*, 3043A. (Copies available exclusively from Micrographics Department, Doheny Library, USC, Los Angeles, CA 90089-0182) (Cited below as Item 417.)

534.   Nattiv, A. (1986). The effects of cooperative learning instructional
        strategies on academic achievement among sixth grade social
        studies students. *Dissertation Abstracts International, 47,* 3651A.
        (University Microfilms Order Number ADG86-29488 8704)

            Researched the effects of three types of cooperative learning
        strategies (combinations of Jigsaw II and Co-op Co-op) and a
        traditional comparison group on student achievement. "Results
        of the curriculum-specific tests indicated significantly greater
        performance in two of the three cooperative learning methods
        compared to the control group."

535.   Nederhood, B. (1986). The effects of student team learning on
        academic achievement, attitudes toward self and school, and
        expansion of friendship bonds among middle school students.
        Dissertation Abstracts International, 47, 1175A. (University
        Microfilms Order Number ADG86 13193 8610)

            Analyzed the effects of 34 teachers' use of Student Team
        Learning. "Found significant, positive results linking a teacher's
        use of Student Team Learning with positive classroom
        involvement, increased numbers of friends, higher academic
        expectations, and increased self-confidence. No significant
        differences were found for academic achievement measures or for
        a measure of improved race relations."

536.   O'Donnell, A. M., Dansereau, D. F., Hall, R. H., Skaggs, L. P.,
        Lambiotte, J. G., Hythecker, V. I., and Young, M. D. (1988).
        Cooperative procedural learning: Effects of prompting and pre-
        versus distributed planning activities. *Journal of Educational
        Psychology, 80*(2), 167-171.

            Cooperating dyads made up of 98 undergraduate psychology
        students completed a two-session experiment involving the
        effects of cooperative learning strategies on the enactment and
        recall of a medical procedure (i.e. how to set up and start an
        intravenous infusion). Four experimental conditions were used:
        1. no-strategy individuals; 2. prompting-only dyads, who did not
        plan prior to practice; 3. distributed-planning-with-prompting
        dyads, who intermittently planned how to perform prior to
        practice; and 4. preplanning-with-prompting dyads, who planned
        the entire procedure prior to practice. Distributed planners
        performed best on a variety of measures, including performance

and oral communication of the procedure and attitude towards their partners. No between-groups differences were found for written recall. The preplanning strategy, similar to typical technical training, with the study of target material separated from actual hands-on experience, did not result in good performance, communication of the procedure, or attitude toward a co-worker.

537.   O'Donnell, A. M., Dansereau, D. F., Rocklin, T. R., Hythecker, V. I., Lambiotte, J. G., Larson, C. O., & Young, M. D. (1985). Effects of elaboration frequency on cooperative learning. *Journal of Educational Psychology, 77*(5), 572-580.

Cooperative interaction and multiple elaboration activity were found to lead to better performance when descriptive information was being learned but not when procedural information was being learned. Ninety introductory psychology students were assigned to one of four groups: multiple elaboration dyads, single elaboration dyads, multiple elaboration individuals, and single elaboration individuals. A technical text passage was studied according to the experimental condition and a second passage was then studied alone. When students were allowed to incorporate elements of the learning strategy (MURDER, an expansion of the SQ3R study strategy) into their own study plans, they did slightly better than when they were required to use the entire strategy. This was possibly due to the previously established study habits and techniques used by the college students.

538.   O'Donnell, A. M., Rocklin, T. R., Dansereau, D. F., Hythecker, V. I., Young, M. D., & Lambiotte, J. G. (1987). Amount and accuracy of information recalled by cooperative dyads: The effects of summary type and alternation of roles. *Contemporary Educational Psychology, 4*, 386-394.

"The present experiment examined the effects of summary type and the alternation of roles within a cooperative scenario on the amount and accuracy of information recalled." Eight participants were randomly assigned to one of three groups: (1) Cumulative Alternating Summary Group, (2) Noncumulative alternating Summary Group, and (3) Cumulative Fixed Role Group. . . There were no differences in the amount and accuracy of information recalled as a result of summary type. Students who played the fixed role of recaller recalled more information than students in other groups but recalled it less accurately. Alternating between the roles of recaller and listener seems to improve the accuracy with which information is recalled." The study was based upon the point that the potential of cooperative leaning has not been completely revealed and that important parameters and boundaries have not been outlined.

* Oh, H. A. (1988). The effects of individualistic, cooperative task and cooperative incentive structures on college student achievement in computer programming in BASIC. Illinois State University. *Dissertation Abstracts International, 49*, 1688A. (Cited above as Item 104.)

* Parker, R. E. (1985). Small-group cooperative learning - improving academic learning, social gains in the classroom. *NASSP Bulletin, 69*, 48-57. (Cited below as Item 645.)

539. Petersen, R. P. (1985). The effects of cooperative interdependence in equalizing female and male differences in achievement, verbal interactions, and change in perceived status. *Dissertation Abstracts International, 46*, 2975A. (University Microfilms Order Number ADG85-26500. 8604)

Investigated "three factors -- goal structure, gender, and group gender composition -- within four dependent variables: achievement, verbal interaction, perceived leadership, and perceived status."

540. Peterson, P. L., & Swing, S. R. (1985). Students' cognitions as mediators of the effectiveness of small-group learning. *Journal of Educational Psychology, 77*(3), 299-312.

Forty-three second and third grade students were video-taped engaging in small group work while completing a mathematics seatwork task. Students were then shown segments of these videotapes and asked to explain their conceptions of student explanations during the group work. Results indicated a significant positive relation among cognitions about explaining, small-group behavior, and seatwork achievement. Students' conceptions of a good explanation as one that provides specific content were significantly positively related to achievement as well as to effective explaining behavior in the small group.

541.   Raffini, J. P. (1988). *Student Apathy: the Protection of Self-Worth.*
        What Research Says to the Teachers. Washington, D.C.:
        National Education Association. 26 pp. (ERIC Document
        Reproduction Service No. ED 297198).

> Educational practices contributing to the apathy of students
> include a perceptual view of behavior, the view that self-worth
> equals achievement, norm-referenced evaluation, and success as
> ability and effort. Discusses four strategies that will allow
> students to succeed with reasonable levels of effort: 1. Individual
> goal-setting that allows students to define their own criteria for
> success; 2. Outcome-based instruction and evaluation which take
> away the element of competition between faster and slower
> students; 3. Attribution retraining which can help students view
> failure as a lack of effort rather than a lack of ability; and 4.
> Cooperative learning activities which help students learn to
> contribute to group as well as individual goals.

*   Reynolds, M. C. (1989). Students with special needs. In M. C.
        Reynolds (Ed.) *Knowledge base for the beginning teacher*, (pp.
        129-142). New York: Pergamon Press. (Cited above as Item
        258.)

542.   Rolheiser, C. N. B. (1986). Four models of teaching: A meta-
        analysis of student outcomes (strategies, memory, cooperative
        learning, synectics). *Dissertation Abstracts International, 48,*
        39B. (University Microfilms Order Number ADG87-05887
        8705)

> Compared the effects of "four theory-driven models of
> teaching" (including Group Investigation) on student learning.
> Meta-analysis was used to analyze and synthesize experimental
> research on the strategies.

543.   Ross, D. D. (1983). Ten tarnished truths reconsidered. *Educational
        Forum, 48,* 35, 42-46.

> Offers a rebuttal to "Instruction: Ten Tarnished Truths" by
> Paul S. George by arguing that students, including low
> achievers, should learn more than basic skills. They should be
> taught independence, responsibility, and persistence. Points out
> that teacher-centered classrooms do not provide opportunities for

learning these concepts and that cooperative grouping is a successful alternative.

*   Ross, J. A., & Raphael, D. (1990). Communication and problem solving achievement in cooperative learning groups. *Journal of Curriculum Studies*, 22(2), 149-164. (Cited above as Item 057.)

*   Schaps, E., Solomon, D., & Watson, M. (1985/1986). A program that combines character development and academic achievement. *Educational Leadership*, 43(4), 32-35. (Cited below as Item 651.)

*   Sharan, S., Kuffell, P., Hertz-Lazarowitz, R., Bejarano, Y., Raviv, S., & Sharan, Y. (1985). Cooperative learning effects on ethnic relations and achievement in Israel: Junior-high-school classrooms. In R. Slavin, S. Sharan, S. Kagan, R. Hertz-Lazarowitz, C. Webb, & R. Schmuck (Eds.), *Learning to Cooperate, Cooperating to Learn*, (pp. 313-344). New York: Plenum Press. (Cited above as Item 427.)

*   Sharan, S., & Shachar, H. (1988). *Language and Learning in the Cooperative Classroom*. New York: Springer-Verlag. 176 pp. (Cited above as Item 044.)

*   Sharan, Y., & Sharan, S. (1989/1990). How effective is group investigation? *Educational Leadership*, 47(4), 18. (Cited below as Item 657.)

*   Sherman, L. (1986, November). *Cooperative learning strategies in secondary mathematics and science classes: Three comparative studies*. Papers presented at the Annual Meeting of the School Science and Mathematics Association, Lexington, KY. (Cited above as Item 173.)

*   Shirley, O. L. B. (1988). The impact of multicultural education on the self-concept, racial attitude, and student achievement of black and white fifth and sixth graders. University of Mississippi. *Dissertation Abstracts International*, 49, 1364A. (Cited above as Item 428.)

*   Slavin, R. E. (1977). How student learning teams can integrate the desegregated classroom. *Integrated Education*, 15, 56-58. (Cited above as Item 430.)

*   Slavin, R. E. (1978). Student teams and comparison among equals: Effects on academic performance and student attitudes. *Journal of Educational Psychology, 70*(4), 532-538. (Cited above as Item 331.)

*   Slavin, R. E. (1980). Effects of student teams and peer tutoring on academic achievement and time-on-task. *Journal of Experimental Education, 48,* 252-257. (Cited above as Item 058.)

*   Slavin, R. E. (1981). Cooperative learning and desegregation. *Journal of Educational Equity and Leadership, 1,* 145-161. (Cited above as Item 434.)

*   Slavin, R. E. (1982). *Cooperative learning: Student Teams.* Washington, D.C.: National Education Association. 32 pp. (Cited above as Item 017.)

*   Slavin, R. E. (1983). *Cooperative Learning.* NY: Longman. 147 pp. (Cited below as Item 659.)

544.   Slavin, R. E. (1983). When does cooperative learning increase student achievement? *Psychological Bulletin, 94*(3), 429-445.

         Reviews 46 research studies investigating the effects of the cooperative learning method on students' achievement in regular elementary and secondary schools. Results suggest that group rewards and individual accountability are major factors in the effectiveness of cooperative learning methods.

545.   Slavin, R. E. (1988). Cooperative learning and student achievement. *Educational Leadership, 46*(2), 31-33.

         A highly significant article. Slavin notes that over the years numerous and impressive claims have been made about the effectiveness of cooperative learning. While many of these are true, the research shows that to produce achievement gains, cooperative learning methods must include both group goals and individual accountability. He also provides a succinct, but informative discussion about the achievements gained when using various cooperative learning methods.

*   Slavin, R.E., & Oickle, E. (1981). Effects of cooperative learning teams on student achievement and race relations: Treatment by

race interactions. *Sociology of Education*, *54*(3), 174-180.
(Cited above as Item 437.)

*   Tateyama-Sniezek, K. M. (1990). Cooperative learning: Does it
improve the academic achievement of students with handicaps?
Exceptional Children, *56*, 426-437.   (Cited above as Item
270.)

546.   Thomas, A. (1989). Ability and achievement expectations:
Implications of research for classroom practice. *Childhood
Education*, *65*, 235-241.

Summarizes research that addresses the problem of reluctant
learners by summarizing "some research-based perspectives on
children's thinking about their own achievement" and discussing
"effective tactics for classroom intervention and teacher
influence." Provides research findings about reattribution
training that promotes cooperative learning, especially in special
education classes. Also summarizes research that supports
cooperative learning strategies. "Noncompetitively organized
classes use strategies that incorporate individual contracts, self-
recording of progress, cooperative group learning and task choice
to help students develop individual goal-setting skills associated
with task involvement and a mastery focus."

547.   Valiant, G., Glachan, M., & Emler, N. (1982). The stimulation of
cognitive development through co-operative task performance.
The British Journal of Educational Psychology, *52*, 282-288.

"Seventy-eight children, identified as pre-operational with
respect to multiple classification skills and understanding of left-
right relations, were provided with one of three forms of training.
Two of these involved children working in pairs on classification
problems (collective conditions), the difference between the two
conditions being where each child stood in relation to the other
and to the task. In the third form of training, children attempted
the same problems but worked alone (individual condition).
During post-tests, children trained in collective conditions
progressed significantly more than those trained in the Individual
condition with respect to both multiple classification skills and
conceptions of left-right relations. Results are discussed in terms
of the role of social interaction in cognitive development."

548.   Watson, S. B. (1988). *Cooperative learning and group educational modules: Effects on cognitive achievement of high school biology students.* University Microfilms Order Number ADG89-07658. 8907.

         Implication is that there is an "additive effect" in using cooperative learning and that heterogeneous grouping and group incentives seem necessary to maximize achievement.

*   Webb, N. M. (1982). Peer interaction and learning in cooperative small groups. *Journal of Educational Psychology, 74*(5), 642-655. (Cited above as Item 182.)

549.   Webb, N. M. (1984). Sex differences in interaction and achievement in cooperative small groups. *Journal of Educational Psychology, 76*(1), 33-44.

         Seventy-seven students in two junior high school mathematics classes worked for two weeks in majority-female, majority-male, or groups with equal numbers of males and females. Results showed that achievement and interaction results related to the ratio of females to males in a group. Females and males showed equal achievement and similar interaction patterns in groups with equal numbers of females and males. In majority-female groups, females directed most of their interaction to males and showed lower achievement than males. In majority-male groups, males tended to ignore females and showed somewhat higher achievement than did females. The author finds these results to be consistent with other research and offers possible explanations for her findings.

550.   Webb, N. M. (1984). Stability of small group interaction and achievement over time. *Journal of Educational Psychology, 76*(2), 211-224.

         One hundred and ten students in three average-ability junior high school mathematics classrooms worked for one semester in small groups. Group interaction and achievement were measured in two 3-week instructional units, 3 months apart. Results indicated in both units that giving explanations was positively related to achievement and receiving no explanation in response to a question or error was negatively related to achievement. Group interaction partially mediated the effects of relative ability within the group and intellectual achievement responsibility on achievement. In contrast to the stability of relationships among variables over time, student and group behavior tended to be unstable over time.

*   Williams, M. S. (1988). The effects of cooperative team learning on student achievement and student attitude in the algebra classroom. University of Alabama. *Dissertation Abstracts International, 49,* 3611A. (Cited above as Item 184.)

*   Wilcox, R. E. (1988). Using CASE software to teach undergraduates systems analysis and design. *Technological Horizons in Education, 15,* 71-73. (Cited above as Item 111.)

551.   Yager, S. O. (1985). The effects of structural oral discussion during a set of cooperative learning lessons on achievement and attitude. *Dissertation Abstracts International, 46,* 1588A. (University Microfilms Number ADG85-1887. 8512)

"The results indicate that structuring student discussion with cooperative learning groups contributes to the efficacy of cooperative learning. The results show a significantly positive increase on all measures [academic self-esteem, class cohesion, cooperative learning, positive goal interdependence, resource interdependence, and alienation] for both [structured and non-structured student discussions] and superior achievement scores on both measures for the structured discussion condition."

552.   Yager, S., Johnson, D. W., & Johnson, R. T. (1985). Oral discussion, group-to-individual transfer, and achievement in cooperative learning groups. *Journal of Educational Psychology, 77*(1), 60-66.

The effects of cooperative learning on daily achievement, postinstructional achievement, and retention were compared in three ways: 1. groups in which oral discussion was structured; 2. groups in which oral discussion was unstructured, and; 3. individualistic learning. Seventy-five second graders were randomly assigned to the conditions stratified for sex and ability level. Results indicated that students in cooperative groups performed significantly higher on the accuracy of daily work. All ability levels in the structured oral discussion cooperative condition scored higher on the postinstructional and retentions test (taken individually) than student did in the other conditions. Students in the unstructured oral discussion condition scored higher on the tests than students did who learned individually. "The results indicate that group-to-individual transfer does take place within cooperative learning groups and that orally summarizing the material being learned and the monitoring of others' summaries contributes to the efficacy of cooperative learning."

553.   Yager, S. O., Johnson, R.T., Johnson, D. W., & Snider, B.   (1986). The impact of group processing on achievement in cooperative learning groups. *The Journal of Social Psychology, 126*, 389-397.

"The impact on achievement of (A) cooperative learning, in which members discussed how well their group was functioning and how they could improve its effectiveness, (B) cooperative learning without any group processing, and (C) individualistic learning were compared on daily achievement, post-instructional achievement, and retention. Third-grade American students (N=84) were randomly assigned to the three conditions, stratifying for sex and ability level. The results indicate that the high-, medium-, and low-achieving students in the cooperation with group processing condition achieved higher on all three measures than did the students in the other two conditions. Students in the cooperation without group processing condition achieved higher on all three measures than did the students in the individualistic condition."

F. COOPERATION AND COOPERATIVE LEARNING: GENERAL INFORMATION

554. Adcock, D., & Segal, M. (1983). *Play Together Grow Together: A Cooperative Curriculum for Teachers of Young Children*. White Plains, NY: Mailman Family Press. 142 pp.

A guide for teachers of children 3-6 years old. It takes a different approach to cooperative learning in that it should be developed naturally instead of learned. Areas of concentration are social skills, sharing, group work, and consideration of others.

555. Ambrose, E., & Miel, A. (1958). *Children's Social Learning: Implications of Research and Expert Study*. Washington, D.C.: Association for Supervision and Curriculum Development. 120 pp.

Provides an analysis of the process by which children acquire social learnings. The four chapters address the following: 1. A Perspective on Social Learning; 2. Interrelationships of Environment and Social Learnings; 3. A School Which Facilitates Selection of Democratic Social Learnings; and 4. Social Learning and Needed Research. Particularly instructive is a section entitled "An Environment Structured for Selected Interaction" (pp. 92-102) in Chapter 3.

556. Archer, J. A. (1988). Feedback effects on achievement, attitude, and group dynamics of adolescents in interdependent cooperative groups for beginning second language and culture study. University of Minnesota. *Dissertation Abstracts International, 49*, 3658A.

Discusses the findings of a study comparing the effects of individual with group feedback to group feedback alone. Dependent variables were individual student achievement, positive attitude development, and group dynamics. Results indicate that "feedback about individuals and their groups is more effective than feedback about group performance alone" in all these areas.

557.   Augustine, D. K., Gruber, K. D., & Hanson, L. R. (1989/1990). Cooperation Works! *Educational Leadership, 47*(4), 3.

A testimonial to the effects of cooperative learning by three teachers (grades 6, 3, 4, respectively). Discusses effects on achievement, use with gifted students, and dramatic changes they have witnessed regarding perspectives on both teaching and learning.

558.   Bar-Tal, D., & Geser, D. (1980). Observing cooperation in the classroom group. In S. Sharan, P. Hare, C. D. Webb, & R. Hertz-Lazarowitz (Eds.), *Cooperation in Education* (pp. 212-225). Provo, UT: Brigham Young University Press.

"Reports on the development of a conceptualization and operationalization of cooperation, allowing for a qualitative and quantitative examination in various groups under natural situations, including the classroom content. [In doing so, it] includes a report on a small-scale study to demonstrate the application of the conceptual model and the use of the research instrument designed to measure cooperative behavior."

559.   Bashey, J. V. (1988). The cooperative learning model: An assessment of current practices and implications for use within the Bellevue School District (Washington). Seattle University. *Dissertation Abstracts International, 49*, 2085A.

Discusses the findings of an exploratory study that reviews current literature and explores the use of cooperative learning in the Bellevue School District in Bellevue, Washington. Responses from teachers, principals, and students indicate that they "viewed cooperative learning as having more strengths than weaknesses," even though they "have not discovered that special education and gifted students also benefit from the use of cooperative learning methods."

560.   Bell, M. L., Roubinek, D. L., & Southard, R. M. (1989). Parental perceptions of cooperative learning. *Clearing House, 63*, 114-116.

Discusses the findings of a study designed to determine the opinion of parents concerning the use of cooperative learning in elementary classrooms. Results indicate that most parents have positive perceptions of cooperative learning and want their child[ren] to be in classrooms where it occurs. They were also positive in their views concerning the necessity of teaching social skills. One area of concern seemed to be the use of group grades. Even though they did express a need to become more familiar with relevant research, the parents felt that cooperative learning is a useful strategy.

561.   Bouton, C., & Grath, R. Y. (1983). Students in learning groups. *New Directions for Teaching and Learning, 4,* 37-82.

Questions the effectiveness of many traditional teaching strategies. Offers three components of successfully structured cooperative groups: the construction of knowledge and learning, the active involvement of students, and the development of skills and abilities. "In addition to affecting cognitive learning, the group experience affects attitudes and behavior." Concludes with a brief discussion of limitations and difficulties of group learning.

562.   Brandt, R. (Ed.). (1989/1990). Educational Leadership: Cooperative Learning [Special Issue]. *Educational Leadership, 47* (4), 3-66.

Contains informative articles by researchers (e.g., Roger and David Johnson, Spencer Kagan, Shlomo and Yael Sharan, Robert Slavin, etc.) as well as elementary and secondary teachers on such topics as group investigation, successful methods for incorporating social skills into cooperative learning lessons, the latest research on various facets of cooperative learning, a model staff development program for implementing cooperative learning into a district's schools, etc. Each of the articles is separately annotated in this bibliography.

563.   Brandt, R. (1987). Is cooperation un-American? *Educational Leadership, 45*(3), 3.

Discusses the current popularity of cooperative learning in classrooms across the U.S., cites research by Johnson and Johnson, Slavin, and Joyce in regard to the benefits of using cooperative learning, and concludes that while Americans "have always prized individuality" we also need teamwork.

564.   Brandt, R. (1987). On cooperation in schools: A conversation with David and Roger Johnson. *Educational Leadership, 45*(3), 14-19.

An informative interview with two of the main researchers and proponents of cooperative learning. The following issues/points are discussed: just how widespread cooperative learning is at the classroom level, the empirical support for cooperative learning, various outcomes that result when cooperative learning is used correctly, the five elements (positive interdependence, face-to-face interaction, individual accountability, group process, and social skills) it takes to make cooperative learning work, and the type of support system teachers need in order to successfully implement this strategy.

565.   Bregman, G. (1989, October). Cooperative learning: A new strategy for the artroom. *School Arts*, pp. 32-33.

Discusses how art teachers can combine a traditional ceramics project with cooperative learning to bring about a more powerful learning experience. Briefly describes components of cooperative learning, and explains how to set up the ceramics/cooperative learning project and how to evaluate the learning exercise.

566.   Brokenberg, S. B. (1979). The effects of cooperative learning environments and interdependent goals. *Merrill Palmer Quarterly, 25*, 121-132.

Reports the results of a study designed to test the effect that cooperative learning environments have upon conformity in school-age children. Three sub-issues are discussed: 1. the effect that performing a task with interdependent goals without interpersonal interaction has upon conformity, 2. the effect that group interaction has upon subsequent conformity, and 3. the extent to which cooperative environment influences subsequent, non-interdependent experiences within the same groups. Results indicate that "the more positive the experience, the more likely children are to conform" and that "children whose cooperative groups are cooperative in process conform more than children whose groups are not cooperative in process."

567.   Brubacher, M., Payne, R., and Pickett, K. (Eds.). (1990).
        Perspectives on Small Group Learning. Oakville, Ontario:
        Rubicon Publishing Co.

        Includes the following chapters on cooperative learning:
        Shlomo Sharan's "The Group Investigation Approach to
        Cooperative Learning: Theoretical Foundations"; David and
        Roger Johnson's "What is Cooperative Learning?"; David and
        Roger Johnson's "Cooperative Classrooms"; Yael Sharan's
        "Group Investigation: Expanding Cooperative Learning"; Laurel
        Robertson's "Cooperative Learning AlaCLIP"; Spencer Kagan's
        "Cooperative Learning for Students Limited in Language
        Proficiency"; and Ioane Coucian's "Cooperative Learning and
        Second Language Teaching." Many of the other articles (e.g.,
        "The Role of the Teacher in Small Group Learning," "A Climate
        for Small Group Learning," "Using Group Process to transform
        the Educational Experience," etc.) should also be of interest to
        educators working with cooperative learning.

568.   Bruning, J. L., Sommer, D. K., & Jones, B. R. (1966). The
        motivational effects of cooperation and competition in the
        means-independent situation. *The Journal of Social Psychology*,
        68, 269-274.

        Reports the findings of a study based upon Deutsch's
        hypothesis that the cooperative situation motivates individuals
        more highly than a competitive one. Knowing that the results
        of several studies implied that competition may be more highly
        motivating than cooperation, this study hypothesized that "if the
        nature of the experimental task is such that no interaction or
        pooling of information is necessary (means independent),
        motivation will probably be higher in the competitive than in
        the cooperative situation." Two experiments, each involving
        different tasks, were conducted. One group was instructed to
        function as a cooperative group, and the other was instructed to
        compete against one another. Findings of the first experiment
        support the hypothesis that competition results in increased
        performance. Findings of the second experiment reveal that
        competition does not result in statistically significant increase in
        achievement. Concludes that "task variables do interact with
        motivation level, thus determining whether competition inhibits
        or facilitates performance in the means-independent situation."

569.   Buckholdt, D., & Wodarski, J. (1978). Effects of different
         reinforcement systems on cooperative behaviors exhibited by
         children in classroom contexts. *Journal of Research and
         Development in Education, 12*(1), 50-68.

         The authors conducted a study comparing cooperative groups
         in which both the tutor and tutee received tokens if they made
         progress, groups that were rewarded regardless of whether
         progress was made, and groups that were not rewarded at all. The
         first group gained more. The authors' second study found that
         pre-schoolers need constant praise in order to do well. They also
         concluded that their study has raised further questions about
         cooperative groups.

570.   Cohen, E. G. (1986). *Designing Group-Work: Strategies for the
         Heterogeneous Classroom.* NY: Teachers College Press. 208
         pp. [Foreword by John I. Goodlad]

         Discusses and illustrates how students can more actively
         contribute, share, and learn when group-work is integrated into
         the classroom. Acknowledges the problems and successes of
         group-work and provides numerous useful suggestions for
         remedying such problems. Intended for use by elementary and
         secondary school teachers, this volume combines easy to
         understand theory and teaching suggestions. Individual chapters
         address the following: why it's worthwhile to use groups, the
         problems one faces when using groups, planning strategies, etc.
         Chapter 4 is entitled "Preparing Students for Cooperation," and
         focuses on training for cooperation, and cooperation and
         prosocial behavior.

571.   Cole, C. C., Jr. (1982). *Improving Instruction: Issues and
         Alternatives for Higher Education.* (AAHE-ERIC/ Higher
         Education Research Report No. 4). Washington, D. C.:
         American Association for Higher Education.

         Discusses several issues involved when educators attempt to
         improve classroom instruction. Among the topics discussed are
         the imperatives for improved instruction, implications of recent
         learning theories, issues and concepts related to improving
         instruction, relevancy of faculty attitudes, data on methods of
         instruction, and research on improving instruction. Included in

the section that presents data on methods of instruction is a brief review of cooperative learning.

572. Collier, G., & Clark, R. (1986). Syndicate methods: Two styles compared. *Higher Education, 15*, 609-618.

A descriptive analysis of two types of cooperative groups, unstructured and formal, used at the University of Newcastle, New South Wales. Areas addressed include size and composition of groups, roles of group members, development of higher order skills, and management of related research.

573. Crary, E. (1984). *Kids Can Cooperate*. P.O. Box 2002, Santa Barbara, CA 93120: Animal Town Game Co. 112 pp.

A guide for parents and teachers which shows them how to resolve quarrelling among children. Emphasizes showing them how to develop problem solving skills. Not specifically cooperative learning, but could prove useful when implementing cooperative learning activities.

574. Department of Cooperation and Cooperative Development -- Education Unit. (1983). *Working Together, Learning Together*. Saskatoon, Saskatchewan: The Saskatchewan Teachers' Federation.

A guide for elementary and secondary teachers who plan to or are already implementing cooperative learning in the classroom. Includes chapters on definitions, critical elements of cooperative learning groups, teacher's role in cooperative learning, lesson plans, how to deal with problems, and research.

575. DePaulo, B. M., Tang, J., Webb, W., Hoover, C., Marsh, K., & Litowitz, C. (1989). Age differences in reactions to help in a peer tutoring context. *Child Development, 60*, 423-439.

Reports the findings of several hypotheses concerning peer tutoring, including a hypothesis that tested the effects of cooperative learning principles applied to a peer tutoring situation. Findings reveal that cooperative structures resulted in "more supportive helping conditions" and that "those dyads were characterized by positive socioemotional outcomes," but poor academic performance by the tutees.

576.   Deutsch, M. (1949). A theory of co-operation and competition.
        Human Relations, 2, 129-152.

        A landmark article on the subject of cooperation. "The
        purpose of this article is to sketch out a theory of the effect of
        co-operation and competition upon small (face-to-face) group
        functioning." Deutsch addresses the following issues and
        concepts: definitions of "co-operation" and "competition," basic
        concepts in the theory of co-operation and competition,
        implications resulting from a study of the basic concepts,
        psychological implications inherent in various types of social
        situations, hypotheses that test the effects of co-operation and
        competition upon group processes, and relationships of group
        concepts. He also states 34 hypotheses designed to test the
        effects of co-operation upon self-esteem, substitutability,
        cathexis, individuality, helpfulness, organization motivation,
        communication, group productivity, and interpersonal behavior.

577.   Deutsch, M. (1949). An experimental study of the effects of co-
        operation and competition upon group process. *Human
        Relations*, 2, 199-231.

        "In the present article an experimental study of the effects of
        co-operation and competition upon group process will be
        reported. The study has two purposes: (i) to provide evidence
        directly relevant to the hypotheses about group functioning that
        were developed in the preceding article ["A Theory of Co-
        operation and Competition"] and thus indirectly to provide the
        basis for evaluation of the theory of co-operation and
        competition from which these hypotheses were developed; (ii) to
        stimulate the use of experimental methods in group research by
        demonstrating once again. . . that experimental methods are both
        feasible and rewarding in the investigation of group problems."
        Results of the five basic hypotheses tested by Deutsch
        include the following: (1) Students involved in cooperative
        situations are more positively interdependent than students in
        competitive situations. (2) Greater substitutability exists for
        actions among individuals in the cooperative situation than
        among individuals in competitive situations. (3)A larger
        percentage of actions of others will be positively cathected"
        among individuals in co-operative activities than among
        individuals in competitive activities. (4) Positive individuality
        exists among individuals in cooperative, not competitive

situations. (5) Individuals in co-operative activities exhibit helpful behavior, whereas individuals involved in competitive activities exhibit obstructiveness.

Concludes that educators should question whether traditional competitive grading systems produce "the kind of interrelationship among students, the task-directedness, and personal security that are in keeping with sound educational objectives."

578. Deutsch, M. (1962). Cooperation and trust: Some theoretical notes. In M. R. Jones (Ed.), *Nebraska Symposium on Motivation*, (pp. 275-319). Nebraska: University of Nebraska Press.

An important document on cooperation, the paper is divided into three sections: 1. the psychological consequences of cooperation and competition; 2. the conditions necessary to establish cooperative situations; and 3. the relationships between trust and cooperation. A key finding is that "a cooperative orientation primarily leads the individual to make a cooperative choice and results in mutual gain, while a competitive orientation primarily leads the individual to make a non-cooperative choice and results in mutual loss." The article is necessary reading for anyone interested in the concepts of cooperation and competition.

579. Deutsch, M. (1979). Education and distributive justice: Some reflections on grading systems. *American Psychologist, 34*, 391-401.

Focuses on the grading procedures of teachers and offers alternatives to many of the competitive methods currently used to allocate grades. Presents the effects of both cooperative and competitive distribution of grades. Concludes by asking the thought-provoking question, "If our schools were to foster a cooperative system of education where each student stood to gain rather than lose by achievements of other students, would the competitive, meritocratic ideology that helps to legitimate socioeconomic inequality in our society be undermined?"

580. Dewey, J. (1981). The Dewey School. *John Dewey: The Later Works, 11*, Carbondale, IL: Southern Illinois University Press, 193-201.

Dewey discusses the basic principles of the experimental school. Basic skills were to be taught through activities. Discipline was to come from "shared community life." The school had failures, but they were failures to meet a perfect ideal. He gives basic guidelines for the organization of the school. Cooperation was expected among teachers as well as children.

581.   Dewey, J. (1977). The relation of the school to the community. *John Dewey: The Middle Works*, *8*(7), Carbondale, IL: Southern Illinois University Press, 314-338.

Dewey discusses the development of the idea of school from the pioneers through industrial times. To the pioneers, school was a way to get ahead of others around you. With the Industrial Revolution, the need for popular schools increased. Dewey asserts that three things must be changed in modern schools to make them effective: Subject-matter, the way teachers teach, and what the pupils do. Dewey talks about the public schools in Indiana which emphasize cooperation between students and between the school and community. The grades are mixed in labs and the older children help the younger children.

582.   Dewey, J. (1976). The school and social process. *John Dewey: The Middle Words, 1*, Carbondale, IL: Southern Illinois University Press, 15-20.

Dewey argues in favor of the "New Education." He discusses the need for children to be active, and gives examples of children learning science, geography, and history by discerning for themselves how to turn cotton and wool into cloth. He discusses the paradox that it is wrong for children to help each other in schoolwork, but good to help each other in other activities. He also discusses the need for learning social order in school.

583.   Digby, A. (1988). An overview of cooperative team learning. *Focus*, *8*, 17-20.

Presents an overview of the basic concepts involved in making cooperative team learning effective in classroom situations. Discusses the structure of cooperative groups, including the teacher's role and the students' roles. Summarizes both the advantages and the disadvantages of the cooperative learning situation.

584.   Dishon, D., & O'Leary, P. W. (1984). *A Guidebook for
        Cooperative Learning: A Technique for Creating More Effective
        Schools.* Holmes Beach, FL: Learning Publications.
        [Foreword by David W. Johnson and Roger T. Johnson]

        Presents a rather general overview of certain cooperative
        learning strategies (basically Learning Together and Jigsaw), and
        specific steps for assisting teachers in acquiring the skills needed
        to implement such strategies. Includes chapters on planning
        lessons, lesson plan implementation, the teacher's role during
        group work, social skills processing, etc. Also includes lesson
        plan worksheets, observation forms, examples of processing
        statements, sample processing sheets, suggestions for rewards,
        and sample lesson plans. The text is weakened by its lack of
        attention to the strategies developed by Slavin, Sharan, Kagan,
        and their colleagues as well as some of the most effective forms
        of cooperative learning strategies. Many of the suggested lesson
        plans are perfunctory and may not be of real value in the
        classroom.

585.   Epstein, S. (1962). Comments on Dr. Deutsch's paper. In M. R.
        Jones (Ed.), *Nebraska symposium on motivation,* (pp. 319-320).
        Nebraska: University of Nebraska Press.

        A commentary on "Cooperation and Trust: Some
        Theoretical Notes" by Morton Deutsch published in Nebraska
        Symposium on Motivation, 1962. Concludes that Deutsch has
        produced "psychological research with a social conscience."
        Comments that Deutsch's experiments illustrate the use of the
        decision-making task, a strategy that might prove useful in other
        investigations. Agrees that in competitive situations, "even the
        winner loses."

586.   Faber, A., & Mazlish, C. (1982). *How to talk so kids will listen
        and listen so kids will talk.* P.O. Box 2002, Santa Barbara, CA
        93120: Animal Town Game Co. 256 pp.

        A valuable guide for parents and teachers on the art of
        communicating and negotiating with children in order to solve
        problems. Useful suggestions may help teachers successfully
        implement cooperative learning groups.

587.   Friesen, J. W., & Wieler, E. E. (1988). New robes for an old order:
        Multicultural education, peace education, cooperative learning,
        and progressive education. *The Journal of Educational
        Thought/Revue de la Pensee Educative*, 22, 46-56.

        Briefly describes the origins and basic features of
        multicultural education, peace education and cooperative learning,
        and examines common goals and objectives of the three. Asserts
        that the underlying philosophical bases of these movements is
        not readily discernible and blames the proponents of these
        "movements" for not making them clear. Also argues that each
        of these "movements" are strikingly similar in focus to that of
        the earlier Progressive movement. A key concern of the authors
        is that before educators totally embrace any of these concerns,
        they need to critically examine each vis-a-vis their own
        philosophy, practicality, etc. Overall, the authors' critique of
        cooperative learning is incomplete and weak.

588.   Gardner, A., Kohler, M. C., & Riessman, F. (1971). *Children
        Teach Children: Learning by Teaching*. New York: Harper &
        Row, Publisher, 180 pp.

        While this book is not about cooperative learning per se, its
        insights into the various methods and value of having young
        students teach other students is both fascinating and instructive.
        The six chapters in this volume are: 1. Introduction: Every
        Child a Teacher; 2. A Survey of Learning Through Teaching
        Programs; 3. How It Works: The Mechanisms; 4. Youth
        Tutoring Youth: From demonstration to Implementation; 5.
        How to Do It; and, 6. Conclusion: A Strategy for Change.

589.   Gibbs, J. (1987). *Tribes: A Process for Social Development and
        Cooperative Learning*. Santa Rosa, CA: Center Source
        Publications.

        This volume, which describes a process/program for
        developing supportive leaning environments in schools through
        the use of various concepts inherent in cooperative learning,
        contains a chapter entitled "Cooperative Learning Groups." It
        discusses how teachers can personalize the curriculum, integrate
        cooperative group methods with the Tribes Process, and how to
        develop a Jigsaw cooperative learning lesson.

590.   Glassman, E. (1980). The teacher as leader. In K. E. Eble (Ed.),
        Improving Teaching Styles. *New Directions for Teaching and
        Learning, No. 1*, (pp. 31-40). San Francisco: Jossey-Bass.

        Discusses leadership theories as they apply to classroom
        teachers and to three teaching strategies: Lecturing, discussion
        groups, and cooperative learning. With regard to cooperative
        learning, the author states that "the teaching method that has
        excited me most in enabling me to achieve the sometimes
        conflicting goals I had set for myself and my students is the use
        of the Cooperative Learning Group." Discusses the roles of
        teachers who use cooperative groups.

591.   Glatthorn, A. A. (1987). *Curriculum Renewal*. Alexandria, VA:
        Association for Supervision and Curriculum Development. 126
        pp.

        Chapter seven in this volume on curriculum planning and
        development discusses individual differences of students and
        describes mastery learning, cooperative learning, and computer-
        assisted instruction.

592.   Gose, M. D. (1989). A teacher's exceptional use of classroom time:
        A caveat. *Kappa Delta Pi Record, 25*, 9-11.

        A case study that describes one teacher's use of time. A
        proponent of cooperative learning, the observed teacher "taught
        much differently than the way in which most teachers teach - in
        an activity-based, student-centered mode." Concludes that
        cooperative learning structures benefit both students and teachers.

593.   Graves, N. B., and Graves, T. D. (Eds.). (1987). *Cooperative
        Learning--A Resource Guide*. 28 pp. (Available from the
        International Association for the Study of Cooperation in
        Education, 136 Liberty Street, Santa Cruz, CA 95060.)

        This bibliography is comprised of 120 titles and references
        on various aspects of cooperative learning. The major sections
        of the bibliography are as follows: Specific Cooperative
        Learning Strategies, Creating a Cooperative Classroom Climate,
        Cooperative Outdoor Education, Cooperative Learning & Science
        Education, Cooperative Learning & Mathematics, Cooperative
        Learning & Computers, Cooperative Learning & Social Studies,

Cooperative Learning & Language Arts, and Second Language Learning.

594.   Graves, T. D. (1988). Response to Myers. *The International Association for the Study of Cooperation in Education*, *9*(3, 4), 22-23.

Myers comments that the research to date on cooperative learning has had "little positive impact on teaching practice" because researchers take too isolated a view or research a method without a theory for the sake of completing a thesis, rather than building on previous work. He also writes that research reports are written for other researchers, not for teachers. Myers notes that the teacher's sacrifice of power in the classroom is a major obstacle to cooperative learning, as well as students' expectation that they will be taught. Myers lists specific questions about "practical classroom issues" that should be addressed by cooperative learning. Graves, in his response, comments that IASCE research is cumulative and theory based. In regard to Myers' questions, Graves encourages all teachers to become researchers, and vice-versa.

595.   Gunter, M. A., Estes, T. H., & Schwab, J. H. (1990). *Instruction: A Models Approach*. Needham Heights, Mass: Allyn and Bacon. 269p.

Text for teacher education methods classes. Chapter 11 provides a solid introduction to specific cooperative learning strategies, including: Jigsaw II, Teams-Games-Tournaments (TGT), and Student Teams-Achievement Division (STAD). Lists specific steps for implementation, including "Pointers for Using Cooperative Learning Teams Effectively."

596.   Gurney, R. (1989). The classroom that is a "Playground of the mind." *Vocational Education Journal*, *61*, 23-24.

Describes an exemplary film animation program in a California high school. Three features of the program are close relationships with industry and community resources, interdisciplinary approaches, and cooperative learning activities. Gives helpful suggestions for developing similar programs; only a limited number of comments deal with the incorporation of cooperative learning techniques.

597.   Hanshaw, L. G. (1982). Test anxiety, self-concept, and the test
        performance of students paired for testing and the same students
        working alone. *Science Education*, *66*(1), 15-24.

        Matched pairs of nonscience majors in college fundamentals
        of science classes were tested for levels of test anxiety and
        academic self-concept. Students working alone and in pairs were
        given part one of a test; they reversed conditions for part two of
        the test.
        Results showed that the self-concept score and the test
        anxiety-debilitating score were among significant predictors of
        paired-test performance, though not all classes showed significant
        differences for all correlations. Cooperative groups received
        higher mean scores than students who worked alone.
        Recommendations for further research are included: 1. more
        extensive research in paired testing and relationship to test
        anxiety and academic self-concept; 2. to develop more and better
        test anxiety and self-concept instruments specific to college-level
        students; 3. students be given more opportunities to work in
        cooperative pairs; and 4. how students will perform individually
        on a retest of questions previously studied under cooperative
        conditions.

598.   Harvard Educational Letter Staff. (1986). Cooperative learning. *The
        Harvard Educational Letter*, *2*(5), 1-3.

        Addresses the following: "What Is Cooperative Learning?"
        "What Do Students Learn?" "Current Practice," and "In Practice:
        Cooperation in Colorado." Cites the work and research of Robert
        Slavin, Roger and David Johnson, and Nel Noddings.

599.   Johnson, D. W. (1975). Affective perspective taking and
        cooperative predisposition. *Developmental Psychology*, *11*(6),
        869-870.

        Tests the hypothesis that cooperativeness and affective
        perspective-taking are positively correlated by interviewing three
        samples of elementary school children. The findings show that a
        correlation is present, but there is no evidence to indicate where
        the relationship is directed.

600.   Johnson, D. W. (1979). Maintaining classroom control and
         discipline. In D. W. Johnson, *Educational Psychology* (pp. 384-
         411). Englewood Cliffs, New Jersey: Prentice-Hall, Inc.

         Discusses types of discipline strategies. Explains three
         types of organizational influence strategies: communicating role
         expectations, involving students in setting rules, referring
         students to the school's social services. Contains a specific
         section on using peer influence strategies in a cooperative
         learning goal structure to control behavior. Teacher-influence
         strategies for discipline included competent instruction, behavior
         modification, negotiating, conflicts of interest, and managing
         one's own emotions. Physiological and psychological reasons
         for misbehavior are briefly mentioned.

601.   Johnson, D. W. (1979). Specifying learning goals and goal
         structures. In D. W. Johnson, *Educational Psychology* (pp. 130-
         163). Englewood Cliffs, New Jersey: Prentice-Hall, Inc.

         Provides a rationale for instructional goals and objectives
         and discusses Gagne's taxonomy of learning outcomes. Explains
         how to write instructional objectives considering interaction
         patterns, learning outcomes, and three main goal structures:
         cooperative, competitive, and individualistic. Johnson compares
         the three and emphasizes the importance of cooperative goal
         structures on achievement and affective outcomes of instruction.

602.   Johnson, D. W. (1987). *Human Relations and Your Career: A
         Guide to Interpersonal Skills* (2nd ed.). Englewood Cliffs, New
         Jersey: Prentice-Hall, Inc. 330 pp.

         Designed to teach students in career training programs the
         interpersonal and group skills they need to be successful.
         Experiential learning procedures are used to help students learn
         practical interpersonal skills. Each chapter begins with a
         questionnaire introducing the terms, concepts, and skills to be
         learned. Exercises are followed by relevant theory in social
         psychology to help students reach conclusions about their
         experiences.
         The role of the teacher is explained and instruction and
         suggestions given for organizing students into cooperative
         groups. Students use learning contracts and participate in
         competitive tournaments. Evaluation and grading are explained.

An informative, readable, practical book. If not used as a class text, should be included in a career education teacher's professional library.

603. Johnson, D. W., & Ahlgren, A. (1976). Relationship between student attitudes about cooperation and competition and attitudes toward schooling. *Journal of Educational Psychology, 68*(1), 92-102.

Over 2,400 students in grades two to twelve of a midwestern school district responded to items on the Minnesota School Affect Assessment. Correlations were sought of relationships between scales measuring attitudes toward cooperation and competition and scales measuring attitudes toward school personnel, motivation to learn, involvement in learning, self-worth as student, other students, and restraints on student behavior. Results showed attitudes towards toward cooperation and competition were almost completely independent across grades two to twelve. The authors found that cooperativeness was consistently related to a broad range of positive attitudes toward schooling experience at all grade levels. They found that competitiveness changed its pattern of correlates, showing relationships to several positive attitudes only in high school.

604. Johnson, D. W., Falk, D., Martino, L., & Purdie, S. (1976). The evaluation of persons seeking and volunteering information under cooperative and competitive conditions. *The Journal of Psychology, 92*, 161-165.

Sixty-three black and white, male and female, high school and college students were assigned to heterogeneous groups of four, then asked to rank the value of fifteen items. A member of each group had been trained to model appropriate information seeking or information volunteering conditions. Results of the study confirmed the hypotheses that under cooperative conditions, the seeking of information would be evaluated more positively than would the volunteering of information, while under competitive conditions, the reverse would be true.

605. Johnson, D. W., & Johnson, F. P. (1982). *Joining Together: Group Theory and Group Skills* (2nd ed.). Englewood Cliffs, New Jersey: Prentice-Hall, Inc., 510 pp.

Theory and exercises are integrated into an inquiry aproach to learning about small-group dynamics. Twelve chapters cover a variety of group-related subjects: "Group Dynamics," "Leadership," "Decision-Making," "Group Goals," "Communication within Groups," "Controversy and Creativity," "Conflicts of Interest," "The Use of Power," "Cohesion, Member Needs, Trust, and Group Norms," "Problem Solving," "Leading Learning and Discussion Groups," and "Leading Growth Groups." Classroom teachers will appreciate the readibility and organization of the book and will want to use many of the carefully explained exercises and check-lists with their own students as they train them to work in groups.

606.   Johnson, D. W., & Johnson, R. T. (1976). Students' perceptions of and preferences for cooperative and competitive learning experiences. *Perceptual and Motor Skills*, *42*, 989-990.

Students were surveyed to see if they viewed the structure of their school as being cooperative or competitive. Sixth graders from both traditional and open schools and eleventh graders from a traditional school reported that their schools were predominately competitive. Only 36% of 110 students questioned viewed learning in their schools as being taught cooperatively. Sixty-five percent of all students reported preferring cooperative learning structures. Little difference was found between sixth graders in the traditional and open-school settings.

607.   Johnson, D. W., & Johnson, R. T. (1984). *Cooperation in the classroom*. Edina, Minnesota: Interaction Book Company. 297pp.

The manual used by the Johnsons in their cooperative learning workshops. Contains practical suggestions for teaching collaborative skills to students. The seven chapters: "What Is Cooperative Learning," "The Teacher's Role in Cooperation," "Research Evidence on Cooperative Learning," "Creating Positive Interdependence," "Teaching Students Collaborative Skills," "Processing for Effective Cooperative Learning groups," "Building a Climate for Acceptance of Differences," provide an excellent overview in the use of cooperative learning methods. Practical suggestions and clear explanations of activities will

allow teachers to immediately implement introductory
cooperative learning activities into their classes.

608.   Johnson, D. W., & Johnson, R. T. (1985). Cooperative learning
        and adaptive education. In M. C. Wang & H. J. Walberg (Eds.),
        Adapting Instruction to Individual Differences, (pp. 105-134).
        Berkeley, CA: McCutchan Publishing Corporation.

At the outset of the chapter the Johnsons define adaptive
instruction and discuss how cooperative learning is an excellent
adaptive learning strategy. Under the discussion of cooperative
learning they discuss the following: critical components of
cooperative learning, achievement paradox, social
interdependency and achievement, internal dynamics of
cooperative learning groups, other achievement-related outcomes,
structuring adaptiveness into cooperative learning groups, and
socialization paradox.

609.   Johnson, D. W., & Johnson, R. T. (1985). The internal dynamics
        of cooperative learning groups. In R. Slavin, S. Sharan, S.
        Kagan, R. Hertz-Lazarowitz, C. Webb, & R. Schmuck (Eds.),
        Learning to Cooperate, Cooperating to Learn, (pp. 103-124).
        New York: Plenum Press.

In their discussion of "the internal processes within
cooperative learning groups that mediate or moderate the
relationship between cooperation and productivity as well as
interpersonal attraction among students," the Johnsons address
the following: Theory of social interdependence, their research
efforts and procedures, social interdependence and achievement,
social interdependence and relationships among students, and
various variables that illustrate internal dynamics of cooperative
learning groups (e.g., type of task, quality of learning strategy,
controversy versus concurrence seeking, time on task, cognitive
processing, peer support, active mutual involvement in
learning, ability levels of group members, psychological support
and acceptance, attitudes toward subject areas, fairness of grading,
etc.).

610.   Johnson, D. W., & Johnson, R. T. (1987). *Learning Together &
        Alone: Cooperative, Competitive, & Individualistic Learning*.
        Englewood Cliffs, NJ: Prentice-Hall. 193 pp.

Discusses methods for systematically using cooperative, competitive, and individualistic learning in the classroom. Chapter one compares the use of the three types of instruction with an emphasis on developing interdependence among students. Chapter two discusses the importance of peer relationships, student interaction patterns, and instructional outcomes of cooperative, competitive, and individualistic learning. Chapters three, four, and five explain the structuring of each of the three types of learning. Additional chapters discuss "student acquisition of collaborative skills," how to create positive interdependence, and explain group processing. Chapter nine is devoted exclusively to teacher concerns such as classroom management, high and low achievers, and cooperation among teachers. An epilogue stresses the importance of cooperative learning to the future of education.

611.   Johnson, D. W., & Johnson, R. T. (1988, January). *Cooperative Classrooms, Cooperative Schools*. Minneapolis, MN: University of Minnesota's Cooperative Learning Center. 10 pp.

Provides a brief, general overview of cooperative learning. Includes sections entitled "What is Cooperative Learning?" "What Do We Know About Cooperative Learning?" "How Does Cooperation Work?" "Can We Expand Our Understanding to Cooperative Learning?" "What Procedures Can a Teacher or Administrator Use?" and "Who Is Implementing Cooperative Learning?"

612.   Johnson, D. W., & Johnson, R. T. (1988). Cooperative learning. *Focus* [a publication of the Teacher Education Division of the School of Education & Psychology, Missouri Southern State College], 2(1) 1-3.

Includes sections entitled: "What is Cooperative Learning?" "How Is Cooperative Learning Different From Traditional Grouping?" "Types of Cooperative Learning" and "What Do We Know About Cooperative Learning?"

613.   Johnson, D. W., & Johnson, R. T. (1989). Basic elements of cooperation. In D. W. Johnson & R. T. Johnson (Eds.), *Cooperation and Competition: Theory and Research* (pp. 57-76). Edina, MN: Interaction Book Company.

Outlines the basic criteria which insure cooperative learning
will be effective. Proves that there is more to effective group
work than just placing people with one another and expecting
them to produce. Instead, the cooperative situation must
promote interaction, frequent use of group skills, and positive
interdependence.

614.   Johnson, D. W., & Johnson, R. T. (1989). *Leading the
Cooperative School*. Edina, Minnesota: Interaction Book
Company. 273 pp.

Focuses on using cooperative learning strategies to enable
teachers and administrators to work together to achieve shared
goals. "What is good for students, is even better for faculty."
While recognizing that most teachers work independently or even
competitively and are often reluctant to interrupt the status quo,
the Johnsons have written a book encouraging and outlining a
systematic change of attitudes toward and adoption of cooperative
working environments in the schools. A research-based rationale
supporting cooperating learning is included along with practical
strategies for structuring cooperative faculty teams. The book is
a valuable aid for administrators interested in restructuring their
schools to a cooperative learning and teaching format. The
Johnsons have included an excellent summary of their recent
meta-analysis of the research on cooperative, competitive, and
individualistic research.

615.   Johnson, D. W., Johnson, R. T., & Anderson, D. (1978). Student
cooperative, competitive, and individualistic attitudes, and
attitudes toward schooling. *The Journal of Psychology, 100,*
183-199.

Responses of over 8,100 fourth to twelfth grade students to
the Minnesota School Affect Assessment were analyzed to
identify correlations between student attitudes toward
cooperation, competition, and individualism and student attitudes
toward school personnel, motivation to learn, involvement in
learning, self-esteem, other students, and restrictions on student
behavior.   Researchers found that cooperativeness was related
to a broad range of positive attitudes toward schooling experience
at all grade levels. Competitiveness showed relationships to
positive attitudes only in junior and senior high. Individualistic
attitudes generally showed no correlations to school related

attitudes. Contrary to the findings of Piaget and Kohlberg, little evidence was found that cooperativeness changes developmentally. Competitiveness does change developmentally, gaining more positive traits in junior and senior high. Individualism seems to be stable after the fourth grade. Authors warn that the desire to work alone without interruption may signal social maladjustment rather than independence.

616.   Johnson, R. T., & Johnson, D. W. (1987). Cooperative learning. In R. T. Johnson, D. W. Johnson, & E. J. Holubec (Eds.), *Structuring Cooperative Learning: Lesson Plans for Teachers 1987* (pp. 3-11). Edina, MN: Interaction Book Company.

Brief overview of cooperative learning, including history, definitions, explanations of student methods of interaction, and what research suggests about cooperative, competitive, and individualistic learning. Encourages the return to basics by emphasizing cooperative learning groups in the classroom. The Johnsons consider working cooperatively with others to be the "keystone" to building and maintaining stable marriages, families, careers, and friendships.

617.   Jones, J. J. (1955). The Nature of the Co-operative Assignment. *Progressive Education, 32,* 17-18.

"In this article the co-operative assignment is treated as more in keeping with the implications of democracy than is the traditional daily-lesson assignment. So viewed, it is held to be a part of the teaching process rather than a preparation for teaching. On this account it lends itself naturally to the aim of securing self-dependency in learning." States that cooperative learning fosters self-discipline, as well as increased achievement and satisfaction with school.

618.   Joyner, R. (1988). Cooperative learning: Just another pretty fad? *Focus* [a publication of the Teacher Education Division of the School of Education & Psychology, Missouri Southern State College], *2* (1), 1, 3.

Discusses essential components needed in a cooperative learning lesson if it is to be successful (e.g., a group goal that is important to all members and both individual and group accountability), and briefly discusses research findings vis-a-vis which grade levels the use of cooperative learning is most likely to be met with success.

619.   Kagan, D. M. (1987). Cognitive style and instructional preferences: Some inferences. *Educational Forum, 51*, 393-403.

Discusses the results of four cognitive style studies. Using the Myers-Briggs and the Inquiry Mode inventories, Kagan found that a correlation existed between cognitive styles of the participants (kindergarten teachers, graduate students, elementary teachers, and undergraduate students) and instructional methods used in the classroom. Infers that "a clear dichotomy appears to be drawn between effective vs. analytic instruction" and that "the most cognitively capable teachers may eschew student-centered teaching methods, because they perceive them to be soft on cognitive content." Concludes that Dewey's child-centered approach to education and Bagley's analytical approach should be complementary instructional styles and that educators should assist students in developing cognitive skills in ways that enhance their independence.

620.   Kindred, L. (1988). Using cooperative learning strategies in the classroom. *Focus* [a publication of the Teachers Education Division of the School of Education and Psychology, Missouri Southern State College], *2*, 3-4.

Provides an advocate's (a fourth grade teacher) views regarding the use of cooperative learning strategies. Talks about resounding success as well as instances of failure when there was a lack of attention to implementing key components.

621.   Kobus, D. K. (1983, May). *A conceptualization of educational theory relevant to a community-based global education approach.* Paper presented at the Working Conference on Using the Local Community in Global Education, Columbus, OH. (ERIC Document Reproduction Service No. ED 243 736).

Contains a brief history of cooperative learning and discusses the benefits of cooperative learning to global education.

622.   Kohn, A. (1987). It's hard to get left out of a pair. *Psychology Today, 21*, 53-57.

An interesting and informative profile of David and Roger Johnson, two of the leading researchers, teacher trainers, and advocates of cooperative learning. They discuss why they are such keen advocates of cooperative learning, explain what cooperative learning is, and talk about their research on cooperative learning, and the practical aspects of that research.

623.   Kuehnle, D. S. (1988). Problem approach effects on student oral behavior. University of Maryland. *Dissertation Abstracts International, 49,* 1686A.

"This study investigated the effects of a cooperative small group instructional approach on four categories of students' oral behaviors: operational, competitive, substantive, and cooperative." Findings revealed that substantive and cooperative oral behaviors increased, that no significant change in competitive oral behaviors occurred, and that operational behaviors decreased. Concludes that cooperative learning is effective and that teachers should be trained to use various strategies with an emphasis on leadership skills.

624.   Lapp, D., Flood, J., & Thrope, L. (1989). Cooperative problem solving. *The American Biology Teacher, 51,* 112-115.

Stresses that secondary school teachers should consider cooperative learning activities as an alternative to large-group lectures. Narrowing their discussion to cooperative problem solving, the authors discuss the basic procedures involved in implementing the program in the classroom: identifying objectives, orienting students, designing teams, explaining team tasks, monitoring and facilitating group interaction, preparing students for learning from their textbooks, and evaluating group and individual success.

625.   Larson, C. O. (1984). Technical training: An application of a strategy for learning structured and functional information. Texas Christian University. *Dissertation Abstracts International, 45,* 3359B.

Examined the effectiveness of cooperative learning as a technique for acquiring and implementing technical information. Outlined a practical strategy, which is based upon general text

processing principles, for learning structural and functional
material.

626.   Larson, C. O., Dansereau, D., Hythecker, V. I., O'Donnell, A. M.,
        Young, M. D., Lambiotte, J. G., & Rocklin, T. R. (1986).
        Technical training: An application of a strategy for learning
        structural and functional information. *Contemporary Educational
        Psychology, 11*(3), 217-228.

        Acknowledges that research concerning the "development of
        learning strategies for acquiring technical information" is limited.
        "The present experiment tested a strategy, developed from
        principles on general text processing, for learning technical
        material, specifically, structural and functional information. In
        addition, the effectiveness of cooperative learning was examined
        as a technique for learning technical information and as a vehicle
        for implementing the strategy. The results demonstrated that
        cooperative learning was effective for acquiring structural and
        functional information and the technical learning strategy was
        effective for acquiring structural information."

627.   Lawler, J. (1980). Collective and individual in Soviet Education
        Theory. *Contemporary Educational Psychology, 5*, 163-174.

        A theoretical article that describes the "main line of
        development of collective methods of education during the past
        years in Soviet theory and innovative educational practice" and
        attempts to "draw some general conclusions about the nature of
        the relation between concepts of collective and individuality."
        Believes that Soviet education "has been moving simultaneously
        in the direction of developing individual initiative and interests in
        the part of students and in the direction of developing collective
        or cooperative methods of education." Reports that
        psychological literature favors the superiority of cooperative
        orientations on both the social and cognitive development of
        students. Summarizes that a "reorientation of classroom goal
        structures from a competitive to a more cooperative orientation
        does not imply the abandonment of traditional commitment to
        the individual." Concludes that the American educator can learn
        a great deal about effective educational practice, including
        cooperative learning activities, from the Soviet Union.

628.   Lee, W. B. (1983). Freinet, the unknown reformer. *Educational Forum, 48*, 97-113.

> Discusses the educational doctrines of Freinet, a French educator whose progressive beliefs parallel those of Dewey. Freinet proposed the replacement of instruction with innovative techniques developed by teachers. Having the opportunity to visit a classroom based upon the principles of Freinet, Lee observes that "the desks were scattered in small clusters around the room and the teacher was moving informally among the children aiding and encouraging them while they were working individually or cooperatively with classmates on a variety of subject matter assignments."

629.   Leming, J. S. (1985). Cooperative learning processes - some advantages. *NASSP Bulletin, 69*, 63.

> Briefly summarizes the benefits of using cooperative learning. Stresses that students in cooperative learning groups show improvement not only in academic achievement but also in social skills.

630.   Lemlech, J. K. (1990). *Classroom Management: Methods and Techniques for Elementary and Secondary Teachers*, 2nd ed. White Plains, NY: Longman, Inc. 339 pp.

> Text for use in teacher education methods courses. Chapter 3 "Managing Group Behavior: Grouping for Better Teaching" includes an interesting discussion on the problems of classroom management and the implementation of cooperative learning. The rest of the chapter discusses variations in group work and offers workable solutions to common management problems.

631.   Lifton, W. M. (1953). Group classroom techniques. *Progressive Education, 30*, 210-214.

> Describes cooperative group techniques used in a college-level counseling course to "promote cooperative evaluation. Participants in the small groups improved in interpersonal skills, recognized the teacher as a resource person, and defined their areas of skill development." Observes that each group member saw "the group as devoted to helping them to improve themselves" and to attain mutual goals.

632.   Lockheed, M. E. (1977). Cognitive style effects on sex status in
       student work groups. *Journal of Educational Psychology, 69*(2),
       158-165.

           Twenty-seven groups, each composed of two males and two
       females, were used to study the mediating effect of field
       independence on sex difference in activity and influence. Ninth,
       tenth, and eleventh grade students were matched for verbal ability
       and field independence within groups and video-taped discussing a
       decision-making task. Tapes were coded for individual verbal
       activity and influence. Results indicate Sex X Cognitive Style
       interaction effects with males more active and influential than
       females in field-dependent groups, males more active but not
       more influential than females in middle-range groups, and males
       and females equally active and influential in field-independent
       groups. (Field-dependent persons were more likely than field-
       independent persons to conform to authority, report lower self
       expectations, to be more sensitive to social cues, to favor more
       stereotyped roles for themselves, and to hold more stereotyped
       beliefs about sex roles.

633.   Lyons, V. M. (Ed.). (1980). *Structuring Cooperative Learning
       Experiences in the Classroom: The 1980 Handbook.* University
       of Minn. A Cooperation Network Publication.

           A useful resource for teachers of all disciplines and at all
       grade levels. Section I, written by Roger and David Johnson,
       reviews the definitions and rationale for implementing
       cooperative learning, Section II deals with the establishment of a
       cooperative learning environment. Section III concentrates on
       the development of social skills. Sections IV, V & VI contain
       lesson plans used by teachers who are experienced in using
       cooperative techniques. Section VII discusses evaluation
       procedures.

634.   Michaelson, L. K. (1983). Team learning in large classes. *New
       Directions for Teaching and Learning, 14,* 13-22.

           Based upon the premise that cooperative groups actively
       involve students in the learning process and produce high levels
       of attendance, performance and satisfaction. Targeting college
       students, the author offers suggestions for forming groups,
       building and maintaining group cohesiveness, sequencing

instructional activities, organizing the material, developing and managing group-oriented classroom activities, organizing the class schedules, developing an effective grading system, providing feedback, and handling student challenges. Concludes the article by providing evidence that cooperative teams do facilitate academic learning, development of social skills, and positive attitudes toward the educational process.

635.   Miel, A. (1952). *Cooperative Procedures in Learning*. New York: Bureau of Publications, Teachers College, Columbia University.

An early and significant volume on the value and place of cooperation in the classroom as well as a discussion of procedures teachers can use to implement cooperation in the class. It reports the findings of classroom teachers and other school people who worked with the staff of the Horace Mann-Lincoln Institute of School of Experimentation (at Teachers College, Columbia University) in an effort to learn more about cooperative procedures in schools. It is comprised of the following: Introduction: The Story of a Cooperative Study; Part One: Opportunities for Cooperative Procedures in Schools; and Part II: Trouble Points Met by Teachers in Using Cooperative Procedures. Chapters that are particularly fascinating and instructive are: "Getting Started With Cooperative Procedures in Schools," "Teacher Preparation for Use of Cooperative Procedures," "Developing Group Membership Skills," "Making Effective Use of Small Groups," "Meeting Needs of Individuals Within the Group," and "Gathering Evidence of Pupil Growth in and Through Cooperative Procedures."

636.   Minnesota State Department of Education (1985). *School Effectiveness: Cooperative Learning Groups*. St. Paul, MN.

Describes the key concepts and main benefits of cooperative learning, examines latest research, and provides suggestions for implementation Includes instruments for classroom visitations designed to assist teachers to increase their use of cooperative learning, and school-level assessment of the use of cooperative learning. Also includes sample cooperative learning lessons, and three papers by David and Roger Johnson on cooperative goal interdependence, cooperative, competition and individualistic goal interdependence, and cooperative, competitive, and individualistic learning.

interdependence, and cooperative, competitive, and individualistic learning.

637.   Moorman, C., & Dishon, D. (1983). *Our Classroom: We Can Learn Together*. Englewood Cliffs, NJ: Prentice-Hall. 214 pp.

Includes a chapter entitled "Managing the Classroom for Cooperation" (pp. 125-147), which provides a brief overview of the philosophy and methods found in certain cooperative learning strategies.

638.   Myers, C. B., & Myers, L. K. (1990). *An Introduction to Teaching and Schools*. Orlando, FL: Holt, Rinehart and Winston, Inc. 629 pp.

Comprehensive text designed for prospective teachers. Cooperative learning is one of five models of instruction explained in chapter ten. Briefly discusses the theory behind the models, summarizes STAD, TGT, TAI, and Jigsaw II strategies, then assesses the models' effectiveness. Discussion is research-based and concludes that cooperative learning "seems to produce a variety of positive results much of the time, including improvement in academic achievement, social relationships, cooperative work skills, and self-esteem."

639.   Nicholls, J. G. (1983). Conceptions of ability and achievement motivation: A theory and its implications for educators. In S. G. Paris, G. M. Olson, & H. W. Stevenson (Eds.), *Learning and Motivation in the Classroom*, (pp. 211-237). N. J. : Lawrence Erlbaum.

Presents cooperative learning as one instructional strategy that minimizes competition and gives students more responsibility for their own learning. Concludes that "cooperative methods may both reduce ego-involvement and foster task-involvement -- a concern to learn and understand without an emphasis on whether one has thereby demonstrated higher or lower capacity than that of others."

640.   Nickolai-Mays, S. & Goetsch, K. (1986). Cooperative learning in the middle school. *Middle School Journal, 18*, 28-29.

Argues that the middle level classroom is the ideal
environment to use group tasks and cooperative learning.
Addresses philosophical considerations, the planning needed to
implement group learning, and the evaluation of the students'
work.

641.   Office of Educational Research and Improvement (Ed.). (1987).
        What Works. Research about Teaching and Learning. Second
        Edition. Washington, DC.: Department of Education, Office of
        Education Research and Improvement. (ERIC Document
        Reproduction Service No. ED 280 940).

Fifty-nine significant findings from education research are
included in this easy-to-read, practical guide for parents and
teachers. Each finding is limited to one page and organized into
three parts: 1. The research finding; 2. Comment, comprised of
several paragraphs explaining the research; and 3. references, a
listing of several major studies to support the finding.
Cooperative learning is discussed on page twenty-one. It is
reported that "students in cooperative learning teams learn to
work toward a common goal, help one another learn, gain self-
esteem, take more responsibility for their own learning, and
come to respect and like their classmates."

642.   O'Leary, P. W., & Dishon, D. (1985). Cooperative learning. In A.
        Costa (Ed.) *Developing Minds: A Resource Book for Teaching
        Thinking,* (pp. 179-180). Alexandria, VA: Association for
        supervision and curriculum Development.

Briefly discusses five principles of cooperative learning
(e.g., distributed leadership, heterogeneous grouping, positive
interdependence, social skills acquisition, and group autonomy),
along with seventeen teacher behaviors the authors suggest are
needed for implementing cooperative learning in an effective
manner.

643.   Orlick, T. (1978). *Winning Through Cooperation: Competitive
        Insanity -- Cooperative Alternatives.* Washington, D. C.:
        Acropolis. 278 pp.

Based upon the premise that cooperation is more beneficial
than competition, the author reviews relevant literature on
competition and cooperation, including works by Deutsch. After

comparing the outcomes of cooperation and competition, he offers viable alternatives to competition, stating that "it is so important to create games and learning environments where no one feels like a loser." He then devotes several chapters to in-depth discussions of various cooperative learning activities, including the Jigsaw, that classroom teachers will find most useful. An excellent resource for teachers who are interested in the effects of cooperation as compared to those of competition and who are searching for cooperative learning techniques adaptable to a variety of classroom settings.

644.   Parker, R. E. (1984). Small-group cooperative learning in the classroom. *OSSC Bulletin, 27* (7). (ERIC Document Reproduction Service No. ED 242 065).

Discusses a "groups of four" technique in which students work together in groups of four for two weeks observing the following rules: 1. each group member is responsible for his or her own behavior; 2. each group member must be willing to help any other group member who asks for help; and 3. the teacher can be asked for help only when all four group members have the same question. The roles of teacher and student are further discussed.   One section, "Implementation of Cooperative Learning," discusses factors to be considered when incorporating cooperative learning strategies into the curriculum. Appendices describe cooperative learning models and discuss them under two major headings: peer tutoring methods and group investigation methods. Some of the methods discussed are not truly cooperative learning.

645.   Parker, R. E. (1985). Small-group cooperative learning - improving academic learning, social gains in the classroom. *NASSP Bulletin, 69,* 48-57.

Presents a brief overview of the research on cooperative learning and asserts that "in view of the benefits of cooperative learning for enhancing both academic achievement and social goals, schools must take a serious look at restructuring classrooms to provide for cooperation among students." Describes both the physical arrangement and the types of learning activities that are observed in a cooperatively structured classroom. Acknowledges that the implementation of cooperative learning involves changes. Parker discusses the role of both principals and teachers in the change process. Concludes that if the issues are addressed carefully, cooperative learning can be beneficial to the academic and social development of students at all grade levels.

646.   Pepitone, E. A. (Ed.). (1980). *Children in Cooperation and Competition.* Lexington, MA: Lexington Books.

Part I, which was written by Pepitone, covers the following: Major Trends in Research on Competition and Cooperation, 1897-1980; theoretical orientation on competition and cooperation; and the research methodology used in a majority of the studies presented in Part II. Part II is comprised of a series of research reports on competitive, cooperative, and collaborative interactions among students. Concludes with a lengthy list of useful references (pp. 413-439).

647.   Poirier, G. A. (1970). *Students as Partners in Team Learning Through Diagnostic and Individualized Teaching.* Berkeley, CA: Center of Team Teaching. 240 pp.

Poirier's team learning approach was a predecessor of the cooperative learning strategies later developed by Slavin, et al. Of this method Poirier states that "underlying the concept of team learning is the assumption that through diversification of teaching and learning, ways may be devised to reach and teach all of the students most of the time even within the heterogeneous class...The micro-societies in team learning reflect the make-up of the society in the classroom because they include both bright and weak students....Team learning involves a cooperative-competitive approach to learning and provides both an avenue for individualized teaching by redetermining the role of the teacher and a method for individualizing learning by more active participation of the students." Various chapters describe the team learning concept, team learning activities, and methods for rating, scoring, and rewarding.

648.   Rath, J. (1987). Enhancing understanding through debriefing. *Educational Leadership, 45*(2), 24-27.

In this general overview on the value of debriefing, Rath notes that "the recent work in cognitive psychology and cooperative learning supports the claim that debriefing enhances

learning. Yeager, Johnson and Johnson (1985) assert that recent
meta-analysis demonstrate that intermittent summarizing or
recalling increase students' ability to remember what they
learned. They further claim that 'cognitive rehearsal' -- the
process that occurs when students talk about what they have
learned -- is one of the most promising of the mediating
variables examined to account for the success of cooperative
learning."

649. Rhodes, J., & McCabe, M. (1985). *Simple Cooperation in the
Classroom. Beginner's Guide to Establishing Cooperative
Groups.* Willits, CA: ITA Publication.

A guide for teachers who wish to try cooperative learning
groups. Text shows teachers how to view the class and each
group within the class.

650. Roy, P. A. (1982). *Structuring Cooperative Learning Experiences in
the Classroom: The 1982 Handbook.* Minneapolis, MN:
University of Minnesota. 464 pp.

Sections I-IV ("Introduction to Cooperative Learning,"
Cooperative Learning and Mainstreaming," "Positive Peer
Relationships," and "Teaching Social Skills") provides an
overview of cooperative learning: Sections V-X ("Primary,"
"Intermediate," "Junior High," "Senior High," "College/Adult,"
and "Activities") are comprised of cooperatively structured
lessons which teach both an academic skill and a social skill; and
Section XI ("Resources") presents recommended readings, sample
cooperative learning posters, and a suggested lesson plan format.
While focus of the lessons is rather eclectic (e.g., "First Grade
Computer Math," "Conservation Controversy," "A Comparison
of One-Way and Two-Way Communications," "Basic Vocabulary
Lesson in Economics," and "Writing a Chapter Analysis") the
breadth of cooperative strategies used is extremely limited and
does not reflect the great diversity available to teachers today.

651. Schaps, E., Solomon, D., & Watson, M. (1985/1986). A program
that combines character development and academic achievement.
Educational Leadership, 43(4), 32-35.

Discusses the Child Development Project of San Ramon,
California, which claims to produce intellectual gains while also

influencing students' prosocial behavior. The purpose of the project is to "refine, increase, and coordinate five types of activities that most teachers or parents already do to some degree," including engaging children in cooperative activities and promoting social understanding. Presents an overview of the program, discusses research that has examined how the projects works, and discusses the effects that the program has had. Also includes a sidebar entitled "Cooperative Learning in Action" (p. 34) which presents a scenario of children in a second grade class using cooperative learning.

652.   Schmuck, R, & Schmuck, P. A. (1983). *Group Processing in the Classroom*. Dubuque, IA: William C. Brown Co. 384 pp.

A guide for teachers who wish to implement a cooperative classroom curriculum. Topics include cohesion, communication, and conflict.

653.   Schniedewind, N., & Davidson, E. (1987). *Cooperative Learning, Cooperative Lives: A Sourcebook of Learning Activities for Building a Peaceful World*. Dubuque, Iowa: Wm. C. Brown Company Publishers. 538 pp.

Among the chapters in this volume are the following: "Why Cooperative Learning and Living"; "The Nuts and Bolts of Implementing Cooperative Learning" (which is divided into the following sections: "Cooperative Learning in a Nutshell," "Models of Cooperative Learning," "Teaching Formats for Cooperative Lessons," "Structuring Cooperative Learning in the Classroom," "Potential Problems and Solutions," and "Evaluation"); "Joining Together at School"; and "Working Together for Worldwide Interdependence and Peace." It also includes a a section of resources (e.g., "Teaching formats for Cooperative Learning," "Evaluation Formats for Cooperative Learning," "What Would You do if . . .?" and "Teacher and Students Say . . .?"), and a detailed bibliography.

654.   Seels, B., & Glasgow, Z. (1990). *Exercises in Instructional Design*. Columbus, OH: Merrill Publishing Company. 236 p.

Chapter 11, "The Team Approach" covers conditions and requirements for cooperative group work.

655. Sharan, S., Hare, P., Webb, C. D., & Hertz-Lazarowitz, R. (Eds.).
      (1980). *Cooperation in Education.* Provo, Utah: Brigham
      Young University Press. 420 pp.

      Based on the proceedings of the first International
      Conference on Cooperation in Education, this highly informative
      volume is comprised of 25 essays on various aspects of
      cooperative learning. Section 1 ("Life in Schools and
      "Classrooms") includes essays of small group methods, school
      programs, and research. Section 2 is entitled "Professional
      Training," and Section 3 is entitled "School-Community
      Relations." It includes pieces by such noted cooperative learning
      specialists as Elliot Aronson, Spencer Kagan, Shlomo Sharan,
      and Robert E. Slavin. Pertinent essays in this volume are
      separately annotated in this bibliography.

656. Sharan, S., & Sharan, Y. (1976). *Small-Group Teaching.*
      Englewood Cliffs, NJ: Prentice Hall. 236 pp.

      A comprehensive overview of small-group teaching.
      Includes chapters on a rationale for using small groups and
      describes how small groups work, types of small groups, and
      organizing small-group learning.

657. Sharan, Y., & Sharan, S. (1989/1990). How effective is group
      investigation? *Educational Leadership, 47*(4), 18.

      Discusses research findings on the group investigation
      method vis-a-vis academic achievement, social interaction, and
      teacher reaction to implementation of a new teaching strategy.

658. Shepperd, J. A., and Wright, R. A. (1989). Individual contributions
      to a collective effort: An incentive analysis. *Personality and
      Social Psychology Bulletin, 15*(2), 141-149.

      "Social Loafing" often occurs during group work when
      students feel their contribution is unnecessary to the good of the
      group. Students work harder in groups when desirable incentives
      are applied. In this study, students were asked to generate uses
      for an object either alone or in a group. Half were offered an
      incentive for a good performance (either group or individual) and
      half were not. Social loafing was found when students worked as
      part of a group when the incentive was not provided.

659.   Slavin, R. E. (1983). *Cooperative Learning*. NY: Longman. 147 pp.

An outstanding text that thoroughly integrates research findings with the author's analysis of cooperative learning. Addresses the following: definition of key concepts, discussion of various cooperative learning strategies, a review and analysis of the literature regarding cooperative learning and its impact on student achievement and intergroup relations, a section on mainstreaming academically handicapped students, and a presentation of evidence of the effects of cooperative learning on non-cognitive outcomes such as self-esteem and classroom behavior. One of the most interesting and provocative conclusions is "that the effects of cooperative learning...are primarily *motivational* effects, not *process* effects; cooperative incentive structures explain the effects of cooperative learning on achievement."

660.   Slavin, R. E. (1986). *Educational Psychology: Theory into Practice*. Englewood Cliffs, NJ: Prentice-Hall. 672 pp.

Includes a section on cooperative and competitive goal structures (pp. 378-379), and cooperative learning methods (pp. 379-385). Briefly discusses research on cooperative learning; and under a section entitled "theory into practice," there is an overview of the Student-Teams-Achievement Divisions (STAD) strategy.

661.   Slavin, R. E. (1987). A visit to a cooperative school. *Educational Leadership*, 45(2), 11.

Provides a scenario of what a "cooperative school" (one in which cooperative learning is used in the 3 R's and across every grade level, and where teachers are working cooperatively to help students to learn) would look like if such a program were implemented.

662.   Slavin, R. E. (1987). Cooperative learning and the cooperative school. *Educational Leadership*, 45(2), 7-13.

Slavin claims that with "cooperative learning programs capable of being used all year in the 3 Rs, it is now possible to design an elementary school program based upon a radical principle: students, teachers, and administrators can work cooperatively to make the school a better place for working and learning." Among the issues he discusses are: "What is cooperative learning and why does it work?" "Under what conditions is cooperative learning effective?" "Comprehensive cooperative learning models," and "The cooperative school today."

663. Slavin, R. E. (1987). Developmental and motivational perspectives on cooperative learning: A reconciliation. *Child Development*, *58*, 1161-1167.

Slavin describes a classroom in which each individual and group is treated differently, and in which there is constructive feedback. First, the child browses through books and decides what to do. The teachers gives initial help. The student soon is able to focus on material he needs. Slavin asserts that important information isn't always learned in regular courses. If the student finds no meaning in what he learns he will forget it. Slavin says a critical look must be taken at what is usually considered "important."

664. Slavin, R. E. (1988). Research on cooperative learning: Why does it matter? *Newsletter. The International Association for the Study of Cooperation in Education*, *9*(3,4), 3.

Slavin's statements emphasize the importance of continuing research into cooperative learning. His first reason for continuing research is to ensure that cooperative learning achieve the status of a practical, effective method so that it cannot simply go out of style with the next "back-to-basics" movement. Secondly, Slavin wishes to establish a clear set of elements "essential" to cooperative learning, so that teachers may add their own modifications while understanding what is essential, to use cooperative learning for greatest effectiveness (for example, team scores are cited as an essential part of Student Team Learning, and it is noted that many cooperative strategies are equal in effectiveness to whole-class methods). Finally, the ethical aspect is noted.

665. Slavin, R. E. (1988). The cooperative revolution in education. *The School Administrator*, *45*, 9-13.

Speaks about the popularity and pervasiveness of
cooperative learning in U.S. schools, describes cooperative
learning, and briefly discusses key research findings. Also talks
about how it is possible to design a school based "on the radical
principle that students, teachers, and administrators can work
cooperatively to make the school a better place for learning in
the classroom, integration of special education and remedial
services, peer coaching, cooperative planning, building-level
steering committee, and cooperation with parents and community
members."

666.   Slavin, R. E. (Ed.). (1989). *School and Classroom Organization.*
        Hilldale, New Jersey: Lawrence Erlbaum Associates, Publishers.
        274 pp.

        Contains an entire chapter on cooperative learning (Slavin's
        "Cooperative Learning and Student Achievement") and brief
        discussions of Team Assisted Individualization in two other
        chapters (Slavin's "A Theory of School and Classroom
        Organization" and Leinhardt's and Bickel's "Instruction's the
        Thing Wherein to Catch the Mind that Falls Behind"). Contains
        Items 061 and 063.

667.   Slavin, R. E. (1989/1990). Here to stay - or gone tomorrow?
        Educational Leadership, 47(4), 3.

        A powerful and insightful article on the dangers of
        widespread adoption of cooperation learning by large numbers of
        teachers who only have "half-knowledge" about the strategies.

668.   Slavin, R. E. (1990). *Cooperative Learning: Theory, Research, and
        Practice.* Englewood Cliffs, NJ: Prentice Hall. 173 pp.

        An outstanding handbook for elementary and secondary
        school teachers, it includes up-to-date research findings, a host of
        practical ideas (including step-by-step advice for implementing
        various cooperative learning strategies), and resources (including
        sample worksheets, quizzes, and award certificates). One of the
        most unique and valuable components of the volume are the
        section entitled "Teachers on Teaching," where practicing
        teachers comment on their experiences concerning various
        aspects of cooperative learning. The seven chapters are entitled
        as follows: An Introduction to Cooperative Learning,

Cooperative Learning and Student Achievement, Cooperative Learning and Outcomes Other Than Achievement, STAD and TGT, TAI and CIRC, Task Specialization Methods, and Other Cooperative Learning Methods and Resources. Also includes a lengthy bibliography.

669.   Slavin, R. E., Karweit, N. L., & Madden, N. A. (1989). *Effective Programs for Students at Risk*. Boston: Allyn and Bacon. 450 pp.

Three chapters (Chapter 2, Slavin, et al.'s "Effective Classroom Programs for Students at Risk"; Chapter 10 Larrivee's "Effective Strategies for Academically Handicapped Students in the Regular Classroom"; and Chapter 12, Slavin, et al.'s "Effective Programs for Students at Risk: Conclusion for Practice and Policy") in this volume briefly discuss Cooperative Integrated Reading and Composition (CIRC) and Team Assisted Individualization (TAI), and the role they have and can play in addressing the needs of students at risk. (Each of the aforementioned chapters is separately annotated in this bibliography.)

670.   Smith, K. A. (1986). Cooperative learning groups. In S. F. Schomberg (Ed.), *Strategies for Active Teaching and Learning in University Classrooms* (pp. 18-26). Minneapolis, MN: Communication Services, Continuing Education and Extension, University of Minnesota.

Provides a brief overview of cooperative learning. Includes sections entitled "How to Get Started," "Sample Applications," "Challenges and How to Deal With Them," "The Rewards," and "Where to Get Help."

671.   Smith, S. A. (1966). Toward a theory of cooperation-experiments using nonzero-sum games. *The Journal of Social Psychology*, *69*, 277-289.

An article "directed toward utilizing a formulation derived from experimentation on risk-taking behavior -- Atkinson's model of motivation -- to help explain the results of several studies of cooperation and noncooperation in nonzero-sum games." Reports that incentive, expectancy, and motive are three

major variables that determine strength and probability of a
cooperative response.

672.   Spurlin, J. E., Dansereau, D. F., Larson, C. O., & Brooks, L. W.
        (1984). Cooperative learning strategies in processing descriptive
        text: Effects of role and activity level of the learner. *Cognition
        and Instruction, 1*, 451-463.

        Details the results of a study designed to: 1. provide more
        information on the importance of recall and listening during
        cooperative learning; 2. to determine the effectiveness of
        metacognition and elaboration; 3. to test the effects of
        cooperative learning when compared to those of individualized
        instructional strategies; and 4. to gather subjective evaluations of
        cooperative learning groups. Results indicated that listening
        activities and role assignments and important to the success of
        cooperative learning. Subjective evaluations indicate that
        students with alternating roles were more enthusiastic about
        cooperative learning than students who were assigned fixed roles.
        Results also indicated that students in cooperative groups
        outperformed students studying alone.

673.   Taylor, D. M., & Tyler, J. K. (1986). Group members' responses
        to group-serving attributions for success failure. *The Journal of
        Social Psychology, 126*, 775-781.

        "The present study attempted to assess the extent to which
        group members are sensitive to attributional styles for group
        performance. Self-serving and group-serving response patterns
        were prepared by the experimenter, in the form of answers given
        by hockey players to a questionnaire, and these were presented to
        members of different hockey teams. Respondents reacted
        consistently more favorably when the player exhibited the group-
        serving pattern, especially in terms of the contribution such a
        person could make to group cohesiveness." Concludes that the
        use of basic elements of cooperative learning is appropriate for a
        variety of situations, both academic and non-academic.

674.   Totten, S. & Sills, T. M. (1989-1990). Selected resources for using
        cooperative learning. *Educational Leadership, 47*(4), 66.

        A brief selection of readings for classroom teachers.

675.   Ward, B. A. (1987). *Instructional Grouping in the Classroom.*
        Portland, OR: Northwest Regional Educational Laboratory.
        (ERIC Document Reproduction Service ED 291 145).

        Synthesis of research on instructional grouping practices in
        the classroom for use by teachers, school principals, and others
        interested in improving educational opportunities for students.
        Answers the questions "What types of instructional groups are
        used by teachers?" and "Why is motivational grouping used?"
        Lists and discusses cautions regarding use of instructional groups
        and ends with implications for school policy on use of
        instructional groups and teacher training.

676.   Wasserman, S. (1989). Children working in groups? It doesn't
        work! *Childhood Education, 65,* 201-205.

        Offers a rebuttal to teachers who exclaim, "Children working
        in groups? It doesn't work!" Reminiscing about her days as a
        classroom teacher, the author admits that "children cannot move
        from highly directed, teacher-controlled classroom experiences
        into mature, wise, thoughtful, and responsible interpersonal
        behaviors in a single day" but that they can "learn to work
        cooperatively in groups over time, gaining sufficient cognitive
        power to undertake and carry out tasks that require higher-order
        functioning." A personal narrative, the article offers insight into
        both the initial frustration and the resulting joys of cooperative
        learning.

677.   Watson, E. R. (1980). Small-group instruction. In A. B. Knox
        (Ed.), *Teaching adults effectively,* (pp. 55-63). *New Directions
        for Continuing Education, No. 6.* San Francisco: Jossey-Bass.

        Points out that small-group, cooperative learning activities
        in learner-centered formats have a significant positive effect upon
        the level of achievement of adult learning. Also discusses roles
        of learners and teachers, group composition, and describes out
        comes. Concludes that "group cohesion can enable peers to
        provide assistance that can increase achievement and reduce
        attrition."

678.   Weaver, R. L., II. (1983). The small group in large classes.
        Educational Forum, 48, 65-73.

Presents a format for successfully using small-group instruction with large classes (fifty or more students). Suggests that cooperative groups can be used effectively to illustrate assigned reading material, to develop new ideas, to discuss lecture materials, to solve problems, and to test students. The author presents sample questions and activities for achieving these five objectives. Concludes the article by summarizing the benefits of cooperative groups instruction: a dynamic classroom setting, opportunities for social developments, and involved students.

679.   Williams, M. H. (1972). Does Grouping Affect Motivation? *The Elementary School Journal, 73*(3), 130-137.

The author found that groups formed homogeneously by ability tended to have lower academic motivation than heterogeneous groups. The study also found that, overall, girls tended to be more motivated than boys. She suggests further research to validate or expand the findings. She concludes that motivation is the result of combined environmental influences and hereditary influences, and that more research is needed to develop methods of positively manipulating the environmental influences (within the classroom) to maximize motivation.

680.   Wood, K. D. (1989). Using cooperative learning strategies. *Middle School Journal, 20*, 24-25.

Discusses benefits of cooperative learning as revealed in research, and offers eight very broad suggestions for successful implementation of cooperative learning in the classroom. Includes a sample of a weekly schedule for a seventh grade class. Wood's eight suggestions would have been much more useful if they had been more specific.

681.   Wood, K. D. (1987). Fostering cooperative learning in middle and secondary level classrooms. *Journal of Reading, 31*, 10-19.

Discusses research on cooperative learning, achievement and attitudes, methods of grouping (e.g., associational dialogue, dyadic learning, needs grouping, the buddy system, cybernetic sessions, research grouping, interest grouping, ability grouping, tutorial grouping, random grouping, social grouping, team or competitive grouping), and benefits of social interaction.

682. Workie, A. (1974). The relative productivity of cooperation and competition. *The Journal of Social Psychology, 92,* 225-230.

Reports the findings of a study that tested the hypothesis that "group productivity decreases in the following order: Intragroup cooperation with intergroup cooperation, intragroup cooperation without reference to another group, intragroup cooperation with intergroup competition, intragroup competition with intergroup cooperation, intragroup competition without reference to another group, and intragroup competition with intergroup competition." High school students participated in groups receiving differential instructions in a card game with an appropriate reward structure. As hypothesized, cooperation was found to be significantly more productive than competition." The findings also supported the order of productivity as stated in the original hypothesis.

IV. RESEARCH ON COOPERATION

683.   Altenhein, M. R. (1955). The activity program on the college level. *Progressive Education, 32*, 12-13, 16.

Admits that cooperatively structured activities are not common in teacher education programs. Details an experiment involving students in an introductory elementary education course. Lists qualities and skills that emerged as necessary for a group to function properly: 1. cooperation; 2. sense of responsibility and reliability; 3. loyalty and mutual interest; 4. sharing; 5. development of critical thinking; 6. good use of judgment; 7. organization before presentation; 8. evaluation; and 9. good listening habits. "For a group to function, each member must do his part to co-ordinate his efforts with those of others in the group and discharge the responsibilities delegated to him by the group."

684.   Charlesworth, W. R., & Dzur, C. (1987). Gender comparison of preschoolers' behavior and resources utilization in group problem solving. *Child Development, 58*, 101-200.

A study based upon the theory that girls function better in cooperative groups than boys, this article reports findings that tested the hypothesis that four- and five-year-old girls and boys in the same-sex problem solving groups would perform equally well when the group task required various cooperative and self-serving behaviors to reach a mutual goal. Reports that girls and boys perform equally well in both competitive and cooperative groups.

685.   Druian, G., & Butler, J. A. (1987). *School Improvement Research Series. Research You Can Use.* Portland, OR: Northwest Regional Educational Laboratory. (ERIC Document Reproduction Service No. ED 291 145).

Includes three types of research summaries: "topical synthesis," "close-ups," and "snapshots." "Effective Schooling Practices and At-Risk Youth: What the research shows." by Greg

Druian and Jocelyn Butler is the single topical synthesis.
"Close-ups" include short definitions and essential research
findings. Snapshots give quick looks at programs in operation
in school districts around the country, including "Cooperative
Learning: Independence High School" by Jocelyn A. Butler.
Also included is a booklet, "Effective School Practices: A
Research Synthesis." Findings cover the classroom, the school
building, and the district.

686.   Gottheil, E. (1955). Changes in social perception contingent upon
       competing and cooperating. *Sociometry*, *18*, 132-137.

       Describes a study designed to investigate the effects of group
       cooperation and competition upon an individual's perception of
       the group with regard to acceptance, rejection, and indifference.
       Involved three groups of eighth-grade students. One group
       participated in a competitive assignment, another participated in
       a cooperative assignment, and the third participated in neither. A
       sociometric test was administered both before and after the group
       work. A comparison revealed that students in both the control
       group and the competitively structured group experienced no
       change in perception. A significant increase in the positive
       perception of the cooperative group members was reported.

687.   Grossack, M. M. (1954). Some effects of cooperation and
       competition upon small group behavior. *Journal of Abnormal
       and Social Psychology*, *49*, 341-348.

       An important study on cooperation and competition that
       tested two basic hypothesis: 1. the relationship between
       cohesiveness and cooperation and 2. the relationships between
       communication and cooperation. Findings indicated that students
       in cooperative groups exhibited more group cohesiveness and
       acceptance than did students in competitive groups and that
       students in cooperative groups experienced better and more
       frequent communications than did students in competitive
       groups.

688.   Harper, G., Sacca, K., & Mahedy, L. (1988). Classwide peer
       tutoring in a secondary resource room program for the mildly
       handicapped. *Journal of Research and Development in
       Education*, *21*(3), 76-83.

The subjects in this study were 205 students in a racially mixed school. At first the teachers lectured for two days, then handed out study guides for the students to complete on their own. After four weeks, CWPT (classwide peer tutoring) was introduced. The class was divided into two teams, and each team was divided into partners. The partners quizzed each other and obtained points for their team by giving correct answers. More students earned scores of over 90% during CWPT than during regular lectures. The students and teacher seemed to like CWPT better.

*   Hernandez, N. G., & Descamps, J. A. (1986). *Review of factors affecting learning of Mexican-Americans.* Paper presented at the National Association for Chicano Studies, El Paso, TX. (ERIC Document Reproduction Service No. ED 267 946). (Cited above as Item 393.)

689.   Johnson, D. W. (1970). *The Social Psychology of Education.* New York: Holt, Rinehart and Winston, Inc. 314 pp.

One of the earliest works by David Johnson. The book is an introduction to the social psychology of education. Johnson provides insights in how social psychologists think and work in addition to providing applications of social psychological research and theory to education. The emphasis is on the classroom and how social psychological concepts affect student performance and interaction.

690.   Johnson, D. W. (1989). *Cooperation and Competition: Theory and Research.* Edina, Minn: Interaction Book Company. 257 pp.

Over 500 studies were included in this meta-analysis. Studies were analyzed and coded for: sample size, group size, length of study, subject area, control condition, random assignment, teacher rotation, curriculum same, conditions checked, study's methodological quality. Chapters individually abstracted. Contains items 031, 308, 309, 310, 311, 312, 356, 357, and 613.

*   Johnson, D. W., & Johnson, R. T. (1989). *Cooperation and Competition: Theory and Research.* Hillsdale, NJ: Lawrence Erlbaum. 258 pp. (Cited above as Item 513.)

691.   Loomis, J. L. (1959). Communication, the development of trust, and cooperative behavior. *Human Relations, 12,* 305-316.

Reports the findings of a study with a two-fold purpose: (1) to describe conditions suitable for cooperation and (2) to determine the effects of communication upon a cooperative relationship. To meet the first objective, the author listed four basic conditions of cooperation, including interdependent goal setting. An experiment involving various levels of communication revealed that communication did have a positive effect upon levels of cooperation.

692.   May, M., & Doob, L. W. (1937). Competition and cooperation. *Social Science Research Council Bulletin.* New York: Social Science Research Council.

Addresses the following: Theory of competition and cooperation, experimental approaches to problems of competition and cooperation, sociological approaches to the study of competition and cooperation, anthropological approach to competition and cooperation, and the life history approach to the study of competition and cooperation.

693.   Miller, R. S., Goldman, H. J., & Schlenker, B. R. (1978). The effects of task importance and group performance on group members' attributions. *The Journal of Psychology, 99,* 53-58.

Ninety-six male introductory psychology students participating in groups of four were asked to complete a twelve-item social sensitivity test represented as either important or unimportant. Feedback was then given to groups indicating that they had done very well or very poorly.
Results showed that task importance did not affect students attributions of personal responsibility for the group outcome or their perceived personal worth to the group. Students felt, however, that the average and best group member were worth more to the group after a success than a failure.

694.   Nelson, L., & Madsen, M.C. (1969). Cooperation and competition in four-year-olds as a function of reward contingency and subculture. *Developmental Psychology, 1*(4), 340-344.

Thirty-six pairs of four-year-olds (black Head Start, white Head Start, and white middle-class) played an adaptation of Madsen's Cooperation Board game which requires cooperative interaction in order to earn prizes.

Results found that the children were sensitive to the cues for cooperation and competition. When cooperative cues were present, children quickly helped each other move the pointer of the game to a target spot, allowing both to earn a prize. When only one prize was offered, students resisted each other and in 25% of the trials, no one was able to win a prize. Some children were able to "take turns" winning the prize, thereby setting up a cooperative interaction. Usually, however, a dominance-submission relationship occurred in which, after a brief struggle, one child gave up and helped the other win. There was no significant different between ethnic pairs.

*   Pairs, B. R. (1985). Effects of cooperative learning on race/human relations: Study of a district program. *Spectrum, 3*, 37-43. (Cited above as Item 419.)

695.   Pepitone, E. A. (1977). Patterns on interdependency in cooperative work of elementary children. *Contemporary Educational Psychology, 2*, 10-24.

"Following a theoretical analysis of factors which foster interpersonal cooperation, this study explored conditions conducive to school children's working together harmoniously and productively." Findings indicate that "while goal interdependence was sufficient to bring about friendly interactions, it did not maximize occurrence of group-oriented behavior. Children worked together most, and performance was significantly better, under conditions where task requirements, task roles, and group roles were present together. A strong consistent pattern of sex differences was found, with boys showing greater independence from experimental role inductions than did the girls, whose cooperative work patterns and performance increased systematically as their interdependence was strengthened in the five conditions."

696.   Pepitone, E. A. (1980). Facilitation of interdependencies in role-related cooperative conditions. In E.A. Pepitone (Ed.), *Children in Cooperation and Competition*, (pp. 187-208). Lexington, MA: D. C. Heath.

Discusses the results of a study "intended to demonstrate precisely how perceptions of interdependencies can be raised in the cooperative work of children and what accompanying consequences may be expected of performance." Results indicated that group members accepted common goals, worked in non-threatening environment, and displayed positive social skills. The article concludes with in-depth analysis of the following: school climate and cooperation, interrelationships of task requirements and roles, sex differences in behavior and performance, and implications for educational theory and practice.

697.   Pepitone, E. A. (1980). Major trends in research on competition and cooperation, 1897-1980. In E. A. Pepitone (Ed.), *Children in Cooperation and Competition*, (pp. 3-65). Lexington, MA: D. C. Heath.

Focusing on research involving children, the opening chapter of a collection of studies on cooperation and competition describes the research within the context of social psychology, notes relationships between sociopolitical events and trends in behavioral science, and provides a framework for present and future studies. Arranged by decades, the comprehensive review of research presents the results of many landmark studies and theoretical papers.

698.   Pepitone, E. A. (1980). Theoretical orientation. In E. A. Pepitone (Ed.), *Children in Cooperation and Competition*, (pp. 67-104). Lexington, MA: D. C. Heath.

A follow-up to "Major Trends in Research on Competition and Cooperation," this chapter "provides a more detailed consideration of the implications of these conceptualizations." Among the topics discussed are characteristics and requirements of competitive conditions and characteristics and requirements of cooperative conditions. Concludes with ten major propositions with regard to competition and cooperation.

699.   Pepitone, E. A., & Vanderbilt, C. E. (1980). Sharing in kindergarten children. In E.A. Pepitone (Ed.), *Children in Cooperation and Competition*, (pp. 175-186). Lexington, MA: D. C. Heath.

Discusses a study based upon the assumption "that complex cooperative conditions demand the exercise of required task and group roles, which in turn rest in fundamental orientations toward the requirements...of others in a given task environment." The study was designed to test the effects of a child's need for specific resources and a partner's need for specific resources upon a child's giving behavior. Results indicated that sharing occurs in cooperative social situations and is a "response to needs and action and/or the nature of the presence of another person in the context of one's own state."

700. Pepitone, E. A., Loeb, H. W., & Murdock, E. M. (1980). Age and socioeconomic status in children's behavior and performance in competition and cooperative working conditions. In E.A. Pepitone (Ed.), *Children in Cooperation and Competition*, (pp. 209-250). Mass: D. C. Heath.

Details two simultaneous studies designed to test the effects upon the social skills and self-esteem of various socioeconomic status. Results indicated that students in cooperative groups exhibited more positive interpersonal behaviors than did students involved in competitive structures and that more complex products were produced from cooperative groups than from competitive groups. Overall, the level of performance was greater for cooperative groups than for competitive groups.

701. Polloway, E. A., Cronin, M. E., and Patton, J. R. (1986). The Efficacy of Group versus One-to-One Instruction: A Review. *Remedial and Special Education*, 7(1), 22-30.

The article summarizes the results of several studies of group vs. one-to-one instruction in terms of effectiveness, efficiency, and social benefits. The two methods were found to be equally effective, though group instruction was found to be more time efficient (the same skills were acquired in less time in groups). Groups were also more economically efficient. The group situation also provided more of the social interaction necessary for integration into regular schools. The authors also note that the student spends more time with the teacher in a group situation than in one-to-one learning.

702. Rekosh, J. H., & Feigenbaum, K. D. (1966). The necessity of mutual trust for cooperative behavior in a two-person game. *The Journal of Social Psychology*, 69, 149-154.

Discusses a study that attempted to demonstrate that trust is a crucial factor in cooperative groups. Reports findings similar to those of Deutsch, that trust of other people does play an important role in the actions and responses of each group member. Concludes that "mutual trust is a necessary ingredient for cooperative behavior."

703.   Rosenberg, S. (1960). Cooperative behavior in dyads as a function of reinforcement parameters. *Journal of Abnormal and Social Psychology, 60*, 318-333.

Discusses a study designed "to describe a number of reinforcement parameters in terms appropriate to dyadic cooperation and to study these parameters experimentally." Findings indicated that the type and frequency of reinforcement and/or reward given has a definite influence upon cooperative behavior.

704.   Saigh, P. A. (1980). The effects of positive group reinforcement on the behavior of Lebanese school children. *The Journal of Social Psychology, 110*, 287-288.

Consisting of twenty-two students enrolled in a private Lebanese school, the study focused on the effect of positive group reinforcement. Rewards were contingent upon collective "good behavior." Findings revealed that students worked cooperatively to achieve set goals and to receive corresponding rewards.

705.   Schick, C., & McGlynn, R. P. (1976). Cooperation versus competition in group concept attainment under conditions of information exchange. *The Journal of Social Psychology, 100*, 311-312.

Discusses the findings of an experiment that studied cooperation vs. competition under conditions where all subjects had an opportunity for discussion. "This was accomplished by using pairs of dyads where discussion was permitted within each dyad but not between the two dyads which were either cooperating or competing with each other." The hypothesis that was tested was that "if competition itself has an inhibiting effect, both overhearing and nonoverhearing competitive groups would perform more poorly than cooperative groups. All groups showed increased achievement. The findings suggest that all groups in the present study were performing at a level previously attained only by discussing cooperative pairs, and a comparison between the mean scores obtained in this study and the equivalent means for discussing cooperative pairs in previous studies provided further support for this notion."

706.   Seitchik, M. (1982). The relationship of student involvement to group-relevant personality traits. *Education, 102*, 289-294.

Discusses a two-week study that examined how "group-relevant personality traits relate to student perceptions of their own involvement." One unit of instruction during the two-week period focused on cooperatively structured groups. Findings indicate that the need for approval, the desire to work hard, and the desire to work in groups were significantly related to student involvement at the beginning of a semester. At the end of the treatment period only the relationship between the desire to work hard and student involvement remained significant.

707.   Sharan, S. (Ed.). (1990). *Cooperative Learning: Theory and Research*. New York: Praeger. 314 pp.

Contains the following essays: George Knight and Elaine Bohlmeyer's "Cooperative Learning and Achievement: Methods for Assessing Causal Mechanisms"; David and Roger Johnson's "Cooperative Learning and Achievement"; Norman Miller and Hugh Harrington's "A Situational Identity Perspective on Cultural Diversity and Teamwork in the Classroom"; Rachel Hertz-Lazarowitz and Hana Shachar's "Teachers' verbal Behavior in Cooperative and Whole-Class Instruction"; Gordon Wells, Gen Ling M. Chang and Ann Maher's "Creating Classroom Communities of Literate Thinkers"; Reuven Lazarowitz and Gabby Karsenty's "Cooperative Learning and Students' Academic Achievement, Process Skills, Learning Environment, and Self-Esteem in Tenth-Grade Biology Classrooms"; Gunter Huber and Renate Eppler's "Team Learning in German Classrooms: Processes and Outcomes"; Shlomo Sharan and Ada Shaulov's "Cooperative Learning, Motivation to Learn, and Academic Achievement"; Elizabeth Cohen, Rachel Lotan, and Lisa Catanzarite's "Treating Status Problems in the Cooperative Classroom"; Daniel Solomon, et al.'s "Cooperative Learning as Part of a Comprehensive Classroom Designed to Promote

Prosocial Development'; Robert Slavin's "Comprehensive
Cooperative Learning Model: Embedding Cooperative Learning
in the Curriculum and the School"; and Shlomo Sharan's
"Cooperative Learning: A Perspective on Research and
Practice."

*   Sharan, S., & Kuffell, P. (with collaboration of Brosh, T. & Pelleg,
R.). (1984). *Cooperative Learning in the Classroom: Research
in Desegregated Schools.* Hillsdale, NJ: Lawrence Erlbaum
Associates, Publishers. 176 pp. [Foreword by Seymour
Sarason.] (Cited above as Item 426.)

708.   Simmons, C. H., King, C. S., Tucker, S. S., & Wehner, E. A.
(1986). Success strategies: Winning through cooperation or
competition. *The Journal of Social Psychology, 126,* 437-444.

Reports the findings of a study designed to test the
hypothesis that "cooperative and competitive behavior strategies
affect attitudes toward success." Ranging in ages from 16 to 51,
147 male and female adults wrote stories in response to a
modified version of Horner's (1972) success cue and completed a
personality trait list for their cue figures. "Subjects were given
one of four cues that varied sex of cue figure (Anne vs. John) and
behavioral strategy (cooperative vs. competitive). Both measures
yielded differences as a function of the strategy variable, with
significantly more positive stories written in response to the
cooperative strategy cue than to the competitive strategy cue."

709.   Simmons, C. H., Wehner, E. A., Tucker, S. S., & King, C. S.
(1988). The cooperative/competitive strategy scale: A measure
of motivation to use cooperative or competitive strategies for
success. *The Journal of Social Psychology, 128,* 199-205.

Details a study based upon previous research that
"demonstrated that the use of either a cooperative or a
competitive strategy to achieve success has a strong influence on
attitudes of North Americans toward the successful outcome. In
the present study, a scale was constructed to measure positive and
negative attitudes toward success and toward competitive and
cooperative success strategies. The Cooperative/Competitive
Strategy Scale yielded three subscale factors: 1. motivation to
use competitive strategies to achieve success; 2. motivation to
use cooperative strategies to achieve success; and 3. motivation

to avoid competitive strategies and their successful outcomes. There were no sex or age differences in subscale responses. Significant correlations were obtained between total scores on the Fear of Success Scale (Zuckerman & Allison, 1976) and both competitive subscales of the Cooperative/Competitive Strategy Scale. The cooperative strategy subscale was independent of scores on the Fear of Success Scale, suggesting that further research on the fear of success concept would include cooperative as well as competitive strategies and should separate strategy from outcome in measuring motivation to achieve or avoid success."

710.   Skaggs, L. P., Rocklin, T. R., Dansereau, D. F., Hall, R. H., O'Donnell, A. M., Lambiotte, J. G., & Young, M. D. (1990). Dyadic learning of technical material: Individual differences, social interaction and recall. *Contemporary Educational Psychology*, *15*, 47-63.

Discusses a study that examined "the relationships among specific individual characteristics, interaction patterns exhibited by dyads in a cooperative learning situation, and recall of the studied information." Findings indicated that a strong relationship between individual differences and recall existed but that the relationship between interaction variables and recall was weak. Concludes that the study "revealed general relationships among individual differences, dyadic interactions., and recall which are descriptive of the processes occurring within the cooperative learning scenario."

*   Slavin, R. E. (1983). When does cooperative learning increase student achievement? *Psychological Bulletin*, *94*(3), 429-445. (Cited above as Item 544.)

*   Slavin, R. E. (1988). Cooperative learning and student achievement. *Educational Leadership*, *46*(2), 31-33. (Cited above as Item 545.)

*   Slavin, R. E. (1988). Research on cooperative learning: Why does it matter? *Newsletter. The International Association for the Study of Cooperation in Education*, *9*(3,4), 3. (Cited above as Item 664.)

711.   Solomon, D., Watson, M., Battistich, V., Schaps, E., Tuck, P.,
        Solomon, J., Cooper, C., & Ritchey, W. (1985). A program
        to promote interpersonal consideration and cooperation in
        children. In R. Slavin, S. Sharan, S. Kagan, R. Hertz-
        Lazarowitz, C. Webb, & R. Schmuck (Eds.), *Learning to
        Cooperate, Cooperating to Learn*, (pp. 371-401) New York:
        Plenum Press.

        Describes a project whose purpose was to develop and
        evaluate the effectiveness of a comprehensive school- and home-
        based program (Child Development Program) to enhance pro-
        social tendencies in young children. Discusses the theoretical
        model used, the program, evaluation of the program, significance
        of the program, and future directions.

712.   Taylor, D. M., Doria, J., & Tyler, J. K. (1983). Group performance
        and cohesiveness: An attribution analysis. *The Journal of
        Social Psychology, 119*, 187-198.

        "The study addressed the issue of how cohesiveness can be
        maintained in the face of group failure as well as success. It was
        hypothesized that two group-serving patterns of attributions for
        success and failure enhance cohesion: (a) diffusing responsibility
        for performance to the entire group rather than focusing on
        specific subgroups or individual group members and (b)
        attributing more responsibility for failure to self and less to other
        group members, and not attributing a more than equal share of
        success to self." Results indicate that a group-serving attribution
        style also enhances good interpersonal relationships among team
        members.

713.   Thomas, E. J. (1957). Effects of facilitative role interdependence on
        group functioning. *Human Relations, 10*, 347-366.

        Discusses a study designed to test the effects of facilitation
        among subjects in interdependent roles upon responsibility,
        efficiencies of goal attainment, emotional tension, and group
        cohesiveness. Results indicated that interdependence has a
        significant positive effect upon all of the variables.

714.   Tjosvold, D., Johnson, D.W., & Johnson, R. T. (1984). Influence
        strategy, perspective-taking, and relationships between high- and

low-power individuals in cooperative and competitive contexts. *The Journal of Psychology, 116,* 187-202.

While many researchers view unequal power relationships to be negative, these authors take a positive stance. They state that power differences pervade all human relationships and the exertion of power is a constantly changing entity as individuals adapt to each other's behavior. They hypothesize that a positive view of unequal power relationships will be confirmed under cooperative conditions.

Sixty-four college students were randomly assigned to four conditions, high or low power and cooperative or competitive context. Students negotiated an exchange of resources in dyads. Results showed that within competitive unequal-power dyads, the higher-power person used coercion and the low-power person tried to negotiate. Both high- and low- power students focused on individual goals and tried to control the other. Cooperative dyads, however, found that both high- and low-power students influenced each other, helped and trusted each other, and were better able to understand the other's perspectives. Unequal power did not seem to detract from effective working relationships in cooperative contexts.

*   Wood, K. D. (1987). Fostering cooperative learning in middle and secondary level classrooms. *Journal of Reading, 31,* 10-19. (Cited above as Item 681.)

V. BOOK REVIEWS

715.   Deutsch, M. (1986). [Review of *Learning to Cooperate,*
        Cooperating to Learn by R. Slavin, S. Sharan, S. Kagan, R.
        Hertz-Lazarowitz, C. Webb, & R. Schmuck (Eds.)] *Teachers*
        College Record, 87, 630-633.

        Deutsch, one of the pioneer researchers on the effects of
        cooperation and competition, praises the volume under review for
        presenting "an excellent overview of the work currently being
        done on cooperative learning." He does, though, criticize the
        volume for being repetitive and suffering from a lack of
        integration despite the "helpful introductions" to the various
        chapters in the book.

716.   Fenton, C. J. (1990). [Review of *Cooperative learning in*
        mathematics: A handbook for teachers by Neil Davidson].
        Arithmetic Teacher, 37, 57.

        Reviews the anthology of twelve articles by authors
        representing all levels of mathematics instruction. Points out
        that both the appendix and the introduction contain useful
        information. Concludes that the "blend of research, theory, and
        practical suggestions makes this book helpful both to teachers
        who are just beginning to use cooperative learning in
        mathematics and to those who have had much experience."

717.   Graves, N. B., and Graves, T. D. (1988). [Review of CLIP &
        TIME: Two Complementary, Site-Based Educational Change
        Projects]. *Newsletter. The International Association for the*
        Study of Cooperation in Education, 9(3,4), 17.

        The goal of the Cooperative Learning Implementation
        Project (CLIP) is to implement CL throughout the Redwood
        City (CA) School District. The program is based on the
        Johnsons' Learning Together model. Emphasized are the
        teaching of cooperative skills, "peer coaching," and "teacher
        support groups." TIME, part of the UCSB Tri-County
        Mathematics Project, emphasizes "dissemination of a specific

philosophy of mathematics education, with CL serving as a major instructional strategy. TIME works through series of workshops and seminars for teachers, who then teach what they have learned to other educators. The program focuses on "feelings, but those of the students and of their teachers;" this is cited as a possible reason for its success.

718. Johnson, D. W. (1984). [Review of *Learning in Groups* by C. Bouton & R.Y. Garth (Eds.)]. *Educational Leadership, 41*(8), 46.

Johnson, a strong advocate of cooperative learning, states that "any educator interested in college teaching, adult education, or small group learning will find this book interesting and useful."

719. McDougall, D. (1986). [Review of *Cooperative learning* by R. E. Slavin]. *The Journal of Educational Thought/Revue de la Pensee Educative, 20,* 161-163.

Basically a positive review; however, McDougall asserts that for those teachers who are new to cooperative learning, the book does not provide enough detail vis-a-vis various cooperative learning strategies. Suggests that such individuals should first read introductory texts by Aronson and Johnson and Johnson, then go on to this volume which they should find provocative and interesting.

720. Quina, J. H., Jr. (1972). [Review of *Individualizing Educational Systems: The Elementary and Secondary School*]. *Educational Forum, 37,* 111-112.

Believes that the book is a useful educational resource, mainly because it presents the strengths and weaknesses of popular curriculum trends. Presenting a limited summary of the sections on team teaching, flexible scheduling, and individualizing instruction, Quina stresses that a variety of trends are discussed in the book, including cooperative learning, independent study, and nongraded instruction. Quina also recommends the book because it describes the trends in relation to content areas and offers suggestions to administrators for successful implementation of the techniques.

721.   Roberts, C., & Roberts, A. (1988). [Review of *Curriculum
        Renewal* by Allan Glatthorn]. *National Forum, 68*, 42-43.

        "Written with remarkable clarity, this little book (intended
        as an 'operator's manual' for educators) is such a useful blueprint
        that any intelligent reader interested in reform could use it as s/he
        participates in curriculum revision." Includes a helpful research
        review on various instructional approaches, including cooperative
        learning. Points out that the least useful information deals with
        Gatthorn's Cooperative Education Model, a model that merges
        the principles of mastery learning, cooperative learning, and
        computerized instruction and that needs more research before it is
        implemented.

722.   Sharan, S. (1988). [Review of Cooperative Strategies by D.
        Dansereau, in C. Weinstein, E. Goetz, and P. Alexander (eds.),
        Learning and Study Strategies, NY: Academic Press, 1988.]
        Newsletter. *The International Association for the Study of
        Cooperation in Education, 9*(3,4), 13.

        Sharan found Dansereau's research to be noteworthy for
        pioneering work on the potential value of combining research on
        cooperative learning with cognitive information processing.

723.   Sharan, S. and Graves, T. D. (1988). [Review of *Cooperative
        Integrated Reading and Composition: Two Field Experiments* by
        R. Stevens, N. Madden, R. Slavin, and A. M. Farnish, (1987).
        Reading Research Quarterly, 22, (4), 433-454]. *Newsletter.
        The International Association for the Study of Cooperation in
        Education, 9*(3,4), 7-8.

        The article summarizes two studies of CIRC, dealing with
        Slavin's theory of a "multiplicative relationship" in classroom
        organization, "that various parts of the program complement
        each other in such a way that their overall effect is greater than
        the sum of their parts." Recommended are "homogeneous
        reading groups" for instruction, and "heterogeneous cooperative
        learning groups" for practice of skills. Emphasized activities are
        "oral reading," "reading comprehension skills," (identifying story
        elements and plot), and "practice in writing, using a process
        model with its cycle of planning, drafting, revising, editing, and
        publishing." In both studies the plan is implemented; the second
        experiment lasted twice as long and students attended a "writer's

workshop" once a week. Both studies showed improvement, with organization most improved in the first study, and ideas in the second.

724.   Slater, J. M. (1955). [Review of *Teaching with Groups*].
       Progressive Education, 32, 95-96.

States that the publication is a timely one that addresses many fears and problems associated with small-group learning. Concentrates on the role of the teacher in cooperatively structured classrooms. "The relationships which these teachers seek to promote are to be achieved through multi-directional interaction so conducted as to promote and facilitate classroom learning." Stresses that if students are properly motivated, they will assume responsibility for planning, conducting, and evaluating the group activities. The teacher's role is as a resource person and facilitator. Points out that the book emphasizes small-group problem solving and contains relevant bibliographical entries for research reports on increased achievement through group activities.

725.   Slavin, R. E. (1988). [Review of *Language and Learning in the Cooperative Classroom* by Sharan, S., and Shachar, H. (1988). New York, Springer Verlag.] Newsletter. *The International Association for the Study of Cooperation in Education, 9*(3,4), 4-6.

Slavin reviews a book which summarizes a study on the "Group Investigation" method, where students decide on an aspect of a broad topic that they would like to research in depth, and in small groups research the aspect and develop a project or report to deliver to the class. In this way all students "learn more about a topic, and in greater depth, than any one of them could on their own." The study was carefully set up to equalize socioeconomic differences, teachers were trained in Group Investigation methods and allowed to practice before the study began. "In contrast to the situation in most studies of CL [cooperative learning], then, teachers and students were quite experienced in using the cooperative methods."
Results were higher achievement, more speaking turns taken, and more words spoken per turn than in a whole class group. There was more "symmetry between Middle-Eastern and European students in verbal interaction." "Finally, the Group

Investigation method, when well implemented, taps into intrinsic motivations to learn, promotes complex thinking and discussion skills, and maximizes student initiative and responsibility.

VI.   FILM/VIDEOS

726.   *CIRC* [Videotape] Available from Dissemination Office, Center for
        Research on Elementary and Middle Schools, Johns Hopkins
        University, 3503 N. Charles St., Baltimore, MD 21228.

        Describes the CIRC (Cooperative Integrated Reading and
        Composition Program) while showing it being implemented in a
        classroom. The video is useful for providing awareness of CIRC
        to staff members.

727.   *Cooperative Learning* [1/2" VHS. Videotape] Available from
        Teaching Inc., P.O. Box 788, Edmonds, WA 98020.

        This video is "filled with both practical ideas and many
        elementary classroom clips highlight the following: the
        importance of cooperative learning, the type of classroom
        routines that need to be taught; and the necessary social skills
        that need to be taught. Also includes one complete lesson with a
        master teacher demonstrating how to set up a cooperative lesson
        for a writing assignment, with emphasis on giving 'put-ups' and
        listening skills."

728.   Johnson, D. W., & Johnson, R.T. (Writers and producers). (1979).
        Controversy in the Classroom [16mm. film or VHS Videotape].
        Available from Interaction Book Company, 7208 Cornelia
        Drive, Edina, MN 55435.

        Written and produced by Roger and David Johnson in 1979,
        this film presents fifth and sixth grade students reenacting a
        "structured cooperative controversy." The film is intended for use
        in courses on conflict.

729.   Johnson D. W., & Johnson, R. T. (Writers and producers). (1981).
        Belonging [16 mm film or VHS Videotape]. Available from
        Interaction Book Company, 7208 Cornelia Drive, Edina, MN
        55435.

This film presents the experiences of a special education student who is mainstreamed into a classroom via cooperative learning.

730. Johnson, D. W., & Johnson, R. T. (Writers and producers). (1983). *Circles of Learning* [l6mm. film or VHS Videotape]. Available from Interaction Book Company, 7208 Cornelia Drive, Edina, MN 55435.

The primary focus of this film is on the teaching and learning of social skills needed in cooperative learning settings.

731. Slavin, R. E., Johnson, R. T., & Johnson, D. W. (1990). *Cooperative Learning* (Video Tape Program). Alexandria, VA: ASCD.

A five-tape set of video tapes designed to communicate to staff, school board members, and parents how cooperative learning increases student achievement and enhances the development of social skills. Step-by-step procedures are demonstrated for turning existing lessons into cooperative learning lessons. Tape 1 explains the value of cooperative learning by showing institutions and businesses where cooperation and teamwork have become vital for success. Explains why teamwork must be structured and planned, why individual accountability increases in small-group work, why social skills must be taught, and why cooperative learning improves students' abilities to become better learners.

Tape 2 shows teachers implementing cooperative learning in the classroom. Demonstrates the basic elements of any cooperative learning lesson and a five-step lesson planning process which includes adaptation of existing lessons to cooperative learning lessons and how to make decisions about group size and composition.

Tape 3 demonstrates the steps involved in teaching students the social skills they need for effective small-group work.

Tape 4 illustrates three proven cooperative learning strategies: Student Teams Achievement Divisions (STAD), Teams Games Tournaments (TGT), and Jigsaw II.

Tape 5 shows a teacher modeling the cooperative learning process in a full-length lesson.

A comprehensive Facilitator's Manual comes with the tape set. Viewing time is over three hours. Priced at $980 (ASCD members) and $1,180 (nonmembers). Individual tapes can be purchased. The set may also be rented and an overview of the program is available for previewing.

VII. GAMES

732. *Animal Town Game Co. Catalog.* (Published yearly). P.O. Box 2002, Santa Barbara, CA 93120: Animal Town Game Co.

A catalog of games for the family or classroom which seeks to minimize or eliminate competition from everyday play. The games were specially designed to promote cooperation.

733. Brown, G. (1987). *Que Tal Si Jugamos.* (What happens if we play.) Santa Cruz, CA: IASCE.

A collection of cooperative games that are workable with participants of all ages.

734. Cornell, J. B. (1979). *Sharing Nature with Children.* Nevada City, CA: Ananda Publications. 143 pp.

A wonderful collection of 42 games and activities which are noncompetitive and each categorized by type, suggested age, goals, setting and number of players. The games and activities are carefully designed so nature is the teacher.

735. Deacove, J. (1987). *Co-op Marble Games.* R.R. 4, Perth, Ontario, Canada K7H 306: Family Pastimes.

Booklet contains original ideas for cooperative games. Adaptable for teenagers and adults.

736. Deacove, J. (1987). *Co-op Parlor Games.* R.R. 4, Perth, Ontario, Canada K7H 306: Family Pastimes.

Booklet contains original ideas for cooperative games. Adaptable for teenagers and adults.

737. Deacove, J. (1980). *Games Manual of Noncompetitive Games.* R.R. 4, Perth, Ontario, Canada K7H 306: Family Pastimes.

The games manual contains a collection of over 170 games for cooperative groups which cover various situations. The games are compatible for all ages.

738. Deacove, J. (1982). *Sports Manual of Noncompetitive Games.* R.R. 4, Perth, Ontario, Canada K7H 306: Family Pastimes.

The sports manual is designed for coaches and sports teachers of junior and senior high students. Demonstrates ways to change the rules of many competitive sports, making them cooperative.

739. DeVries, D. L., & Edwards, K. J. (1973). Learning games and student teams: Their effects on classroom process. *American Educational Research Journal, 10*, 307-318.

"This study examines the effects of using a learning game (EQUATIONS), student teams, and the games-teams combination on classroom process variables in seventh grade mathematics classes for a four-week period. Using the game created greater student peer tutoring, less perceived difficulty, and greater satisfaction with the class. Using student teams positively altered classroom process by creating greater student peer tutoring, and greater perceived mutual concern and competitiveness in the classroom. The games-teams combination resulted in greater peer tutoring than either games or teams alone. The results are interpreted using a structural theory of games and of teams." This research was later used, in part, by researchers to develop the cooperative learning strategies known as Teams/Games Tournaments and Students Teams-Achievement Divisions.

740. Edwards, K. J., DeVries, D. L., & Snyder, J. P. (1972). Games and teams: A winning combination. *Simulation and Games, 3*, 247-269.

Discusses the results of a study designed to test the effects of the combined use of nonsimulation games and student teams upon student achievement. Concludes that combining nonsimulation games with cooperative team competition had a significant positive effect upon mathematical achievement when compared to traditionally taught classes.

741.   *Family Pastimes Catalog.* (Published yearly). R.R. 4, Perth,
        Ontario, Canada K7H 306: Family Pastimes.

        A catalog of noncompetitive games which can be used in the
        home or in the classroom. The games are suitable for children of
        all ages and are a valuable cooperative learning tool.

742.   Fluegelman, A. (1976). *The New Games Book.* P.O. Box 2002,
        Santa Barbara, CA 93120: Doubleday/Animal Town Game Co.

        A collection of non-competitive games developed by people
        in the New Games Movement of the 1960's. The best of these
        games were collected by the New Games Foundation and
        presented here.

743.   Fluegelman, A. (1981). *More New Games.* P.O. Box 2002, Santa
        Barbara, CA 93120: Doubleday/Animal Town Game Co. 192
        pp.

        Second book by Fluegelman with presents non-competitive
        games created by people in the New Games movement of the
        1960's.

744.   Foster, W. K. (1984). Cooperation in the game and sport structure
        of children: One dimension of psychosocial development.
        Education, 105, 201-205.

        Points out that cooperative behavior in sports and game
        activities is a positive component of psychological development
        in young children. Stresses that cooperative groups should be
        used not only in athletic events, but also in academic settings.
        Lists seven basic components of cooperatively structured
        activities. Concludes that implementation of cooperative
        principles should have a positive influence upon psychosocial
        development of students.

*   Graves, T. (1988). Review: Armendi, R.A. The Effects of
        Cooperative Games on Preschool Children's Prosocial Behavior.
        Quezon City, Philippines: St, Joseph's College Graduate
        School. *The International Association for the Study of
        Cooperation in Education, 9*(3 and 4), 18. (Cited above as Item
        299.)

745.   Jacovino, J. A. (1980). The use of cooperatively structured games as
        a teaching strategy in a secondary school class to increase the
        group cooperative behaviors of its students. *Dissertation
        Abstracts International, 41*, 3403A. (University Microfilms
        Order Number ADG81-04506. 0000)

        "The problems of concern addressed by this study were (1) to
        investigate whether cooperatively structured games will help
        students achieve more positive group cooperation behaviors in
        the classroom, and (2) to investigate whether the cooperative
        behaviors learned through the game experience will transfer to
        other learning activities which require the students to work in
        groups without teacher intervention."

746.   Jorgensen, E, Trout, B., & Hallesy, M. (1986). *Manure, Meadows,
        and Milkshakes*. Los Altos Hills, CA: Hidden Villa
        Environmental Program. 132 pp.

        Contains a collection of games and activities for second
        through sixth graders which offers environmental education.
        Although many of these activities are for use in large groups,
        they are easily compatible for smaller cooperative groups.

747.   Knapp, C. (1985). *People Skills Primer: Blending Nature and
        Human Nature Activities*. Oregon, IL: Clifford Knapp &
        Goodman Publisher.

        A collection of over 50 activities which are to be done
        outdoors. Not only do they promote development of mutual,
        personal, and people skills, but they are also meant to promote
        awareness of nature.

748.   McLeroy, J. (1988). *Project ES-Team Handbook, Volumes 1 and 2*.
        Encino, CA.

        These two volumes include games and activities which teach
        social skills and human relations in cooperative learning groups,
        helping the teacher insure a democratic classroom environment.

749.   Orlick, T. (1975). *The Cooperative Sports and Games Book*. New
        York: Pantheon Books. 129 pp.

A collection of various cooperative games and sports. The games can be used with preschoolers on up. A majority of these games are non-competitive and come from various cultures around the world.

750.   Orlick, T. (1982). *The Second Cooperative Sports and Games Book*. New York: Pantheon Books. 255 pp.

More cooperative games and sports suitable for preschoolers to adult.

751.   Orlick, T. (1981). Positive socialization via cooperative games. *Developmental Psychology, 17*(4), 426-429.

Using activities drawn from The Cooperative Sports and Games Book by Terry Orlick (1978, New York: Pantheon Books), the study assessed the effects of a cooperative games program on the willingness of five-year-olds to share with others and to be happy when playing games outside of school.
Students in the cooperative games groups significantly increased their willingness to share over that of students in traditional games groups. Both cooperative games and traditional games groups showed increases in game-playing happiness outside of school. In school one, the cooperative groups gained significantly. In school two, however, only the traditional group gained significantly. Orlick recommended further, long-term studies to identify differences between students who increase sharing responses and those who do not.

*   Orlick, T. (1978). *Winning Through Cooperation: Competitive Insanity -- Cooperative Alternatives*. Washington, D. C.: Acropolis. 278 pp. (Cited above as Item 643.)

752.   Paulson, W. (1980). *Coaching Cooperative Youth Sports: A Values Education Approach*. La Grange, IL: Youth Sports Press.

A guide for coaches and sports teachers which shows how to include values education while participating in sports or games. Cooperative values are taught through competitive means.

753.   Project Adventure Staff. (1976). *Teaching Though Adventure, A Practical Approach*. Hamilton, MA: Project Adventure, Inc. 97 pp.

An advisory on teaching kids such skills as problem solving, cooperation, and giving them experience with adventure. Gives examples of adventure curriculums that were implemented in public middle and high schools where outdoor activities were used to spice up academic subjects.

754.   Prutzman, P., Burger, H. L., Bodenhamer, G. & Stern, L. (1978). *The Friendly Classroom for a Small Planet* . Nyack, NY: Children's Creative Responses to Conflict. 100 pp.

A collection of exercises and games which reduce conflict in cooperative groups. The book also shows teachers how to effectively create cooperative groups and solve problems.

755.   Rees, R. D. (1990). Station break: A mathematical game using cooperative learning and role playing. *Arithmetic Teacher, 37*(8), 8-12.

Outlines role-playing cooperative learning games and situations which can be implemented to help in the solving of mathematical problems. Intended for elementary and junior high school students.

*   Rekosh, J. H., & Feigenbaum, K. D. (1966). The necessity of mutual trust for cooperative behavior in a two-person game. *The Journal of Social Psychology, 69*, 149-154. (Cited above as Item 702.)

756.   Rohnke, K. (1977). *Cows Tails and Cobras*. Hamilton, MA: Project Adventure, Inc.

Designed to help children develop greater skills and a greater desire for communication, risk taking, cooperation, and learning to trust. A collection of games are presented which are meant to challenge the child.

757.   Rohnke, K. (1984). *Silver Bullets: A Guide to Initiative Problems, Adventure Games, Students and Trust Activities*. Hamilton, MA: Project Adventure, Inc.

A collection of 165 games and activities which can be played in or out of doors, with large or small groups, with little equipment, and with great or little physical activity. The games are meant to help children solve problems, cooperate, and learn to trust. All of the games were designed to increase peer support, physical coordination, confidence in oneself and togetherness.

758. Sermat, V. (1964). Cooperative behavior in mixed-motive game. *The Journal of Social Psychology, 62,* 217-239.

"Three experiments were conducted with male high-school and college students, to determine the conditions and kind of information about the other person's behavior which would affect the development of cooperative behavior in a mixed-motive game." Findings of the first two experiments reveal no significant difference in the degree of cooperative behavior. The third experiment "demonstrated that subjects made significantly fewer cooperative choices when treated with a 100 per cent cooperative program than when treated with a 100 per cent competitive program. Furthermore, this tendency to respond competitively to a cooperative treatment, and vice versa became more marked when the subjects were led to believe that 'the other person' was not aware of the outcomes."

* Shevin-Shapon, M. (1978). Cooperative instructional games: Alternatives to the spelling bee. *The Elementary School Journal, 79*(2), 81-87. (Cited above as Item 141.)

* Smith, S. A. (1966). Toward a theory of cooperation-experiments using nonzero-sum games. *The Journal of Social Psychology, 69,* 277-289. (Cited above as Item 671.)

759. Sobel, J. (1983). *Everybody Wins.* P.O. Box 2002, Santa Barbara, CA 93120: Walker and Company/Animal Town Game Co.

A collection of 393 simple games for preschool through sixth grade children. The games are able to be played on a playground, in a gym, or indoors.

760. Stanford, G., & Stanford, B. (1969). *Learning Discussion Skills through Games.* Newbury Park, CA: Sage Publications.

A guide for teachers which shows them how to help students learn the basic skills for working in groups.

761.   Villeneuve, M. J. (1980). *Jouons Ensemble.* Montreal, Canada: Les Editions de L'Homme.

Contains non-competitive activities for people of all ages. Also included is a discussion of equipment which can be used in the games which help promote cooperation.

762.   Villeneuve, M. J. (1983). *Viens Jouer.* Montreal, Canada: Les Editions de L'Homme.

Contains non-competitive activities for people of all ages. Includes a discussion of equipment which can be used in the games which help promote cooperation.

763.   Weinstein, M., & Goodman, J. (1980) *Playfair: Everybody's Guide to Noncompetitive Play.* San Luis Obispo, CA: Impact Publishers. 256 pp.

Contains a variety of over 60 cooperative games which are compatible to people of all ages. These games can be played in or out of doors, quietly or actively, and all come with clear illustrations and instructions. The games are also important in promoting teamwork.

VIII. NEWSLETTERS

764. *Cooperation Unlimited Newsletter.* (Available from Educational
Excellence, P.O. Box 68, Portage, MI 49081).

Issued six times a year, it includes information by experts,
practical tips by classroom teachers, lists of resources, and
sample lesson plans.

765. *Cooperative Learning: The Magazine for Cooperation in Education.*
(Available from the International Association for the Study of
Cooperation in Education (IASCE), 136 Liberty St., Santa Cruz,
CA 95060).

A practitioner-oriented magazine. Each issue features: tips
by and for teachers on how to implement cooperative learning; a
feature cover story on an experienced cooperative learning
teacher; cooperative learning lesson plans in a variety of content
areas; a column by leaders in the field on major controversies
within cooperative learning; regular columns on staff
development, computer applications, and research; networking on
cooperative learning programs around the world; reviews of new
cooperative learning resources; and thematic articles by leaders in
the field.

766. *Our Link: Cooperative Learning Newsletter.* (Available from the
Cooperative Learning Center, University of Minnesota, 202
Patee Hall, 150 Pillsbury Drive, Minneapolis, MN 55455).

Addresses all aspects of cooperative learning. Often includes
short lesson plans, handy hints, and listings of resources.

IX. ORGANIZATIONS

767. Center for Social Organization of Schools, The Johns Hopkins University, Department L88, 3005 N. Charles St., Baltimore, MD 21218.

Key research center headed up by Robert Slavin that keys in on cooperative learning. Also publishes research findings, teachers' guides, and classroom materials on cooperative learning.

768. Cooperation Unlimited, P.O. Box 68, Portage, MI 49081.

Provides various workshops on cooperative learning (e. g., a 1/2 day awareness session on cooperative learning strategies, a 4-day "in-depth training workshop," etc.).

769. Cooperative Learning Center, 202 Pattee Hall, University of Minnesota, Minneapolis, MN 55455.

Directed by David and Roger Johnson, it conducts research into various aspects of cooperative learning, conducts inservice programs on cooperative learning, and publishes research findings, texts, and classroom materials.

770. International Association for the Study of Cooperation in Education (IASCE), 136 Liberty St., Santa Cruz, CA 95060.

Initiated in 1979, this organization's mission is "to study all aspects of educational cooperation, including teachers working together to support and coach each other, and to develop and share curriculum materials." It sponsors international conferences on cooperative learning, and publishes *Cooperative Learning: The Magazine for Cooperation in Education.*

X. Additional Listings

A. *Academic Achievement*

771.   Slavin, R. (1990). *Ability Grouping and Student Achievement in Secondary Schools: A Best- Evidence Synthesis.* Baltimore, MD: Johns Hopkins University, Center for Research on Elementary and Middle Schools.

772.   Slavin, R. E. (Fall 1990). Achievement effects of ability grouping in secondary schools: A best-evidence synthesis. *Review of Educational Research, 60* (3): 471-499.

   Under a section entitled "Alternatives to Ability Grouping" (pp. 492-493), Slavin discusses various types of cooperative learning methods (e.g., he cites Cooperative Integrated Reading and Composition or CIRC and Team Assisted Individualization or TAI as particularly effective for use in middle schools) that have been found to be effective alternatives to ability grouping.

B. *Classroom Climate and Social Needs of Students.*

773.   Jones, M. G. (September 1990). Cooperative learning: Developmentally appropriate for middle level students. *Middle School Journal, 22* (1): 12-16.

   Includes the following sections: What is cooperative learning?; Goals of middle education and cooperative learning; A winning combination: social and emotional development; physical development; cognitive development, and achievement.

774.   McCafferty, W. D. (1990). Prosocial influences in the classroom. *The Clearing House, 63* (8), 367-370.

   Reviews research that supports the premise that the "focus of curriculum, therefore, becomes the academic, personal, and

351

social needs of the teacher, individual students, and the classroom
group as a whole." Presents cognitive, affective, and disciplinary
models that positively influence social behavior.

C. Cooperation and Cooperative Learning
(General Information)

775.   Adams, D. M., and Hamm, M. E. (1990). *Cooperative Learning:*
        Critical Thinking and Collaboration Across the Curriculum.
        186 pp.

        Unavailable for review.

776.   Carnegie Council on Adolescent Development. (1989). *Turning*
        Points: Preparing Youth for the 21st Century. New York:
        Author. 106 pp.

        A major report on the educational needs of young adolescents and
        a clarion call vis-a-vis the need for special organization of
        schools and programs for this age (10-14 year olds).
        Among the many recommendations posited herein is the need
        "to focus once again on the goal that ranking sought to achieve
        in the first place: effectively teaching students of diverse ability
        and differing rates of learning." (p. 50). One such method, the
        authors report, for reaching such a goal is cooperative learning.
        On page 51, a section entitled "Mathematics Students Cooperate
        to Accelerate" includes a discussion of Team Accelerated
        Instruction (TAI).

777.   Cohen, E. G. (October 1990). Continuing to cooperate:
        Prerequisites for persistence. *Phi Delta Kappan*, 72 (2): 134-
        138.

        An engaging article by a proponent of cooperative learning
        who initially states: "I greatly fear that -- unless developers,
        disseminators, and practitioners realize that establishing a
        cooperative learning program requires more than attending a few
        workshops and attempting to assist one another in developing
        materials and managing classrooms -- we will quickly see both
        teachers and students burn out on these new techniques (p. 135)."
        She then cogently examines the following issues: "The Need for
        New Materials," "Treatment of Status Problems" (e.g., "the

problem of unequal participation in groups"), and "Changes in the Organization of Teaching."

778. Graves, N., and Graves, T., (Eds.) (1987). *Cooperative Learning -- A Resource Guide*. 28 pp. (Available from the International Association for the Study of Cooperation in Education, 136 Liberty Street, Santa Cruz, CA 95060).

This bibliography is comprised of 120 titles and references on various aspects of cooperative learning. The major sections for the bibliography are as follows: Specific Cooperative Learning Strategies, Create a Cooperative Classroom Climate, Cooperative Outdoor Education, Cooperative Learning & Science Education, Cooperative Learning & Mathematics, Cooperative Learning & Computers, Cooperative Learning & Social Studies, Cooperative Learning & Language Arts, and Second Language Learning.

779. Harget , J. (1990). Cooperative Learning. *Illinois Teacher of Home Economics, 33* (3), 94-95, 99.

Provides an overview of cooperative learning by addressing the following topics: need for cooperation, cooperative learning theory, basic elements of cooperative learning, grouping of students, structure of groups, advantages for teachers, and the teacher's role.

780. Kagan, S. (1990). *Same Different (Holidays Edition)*. San Juan Capistrano, CA: Resources for Teachers.

Activity book for kindergarten through third grade. Students work in pairs to find differences between two similar pictures. Pictures have a holiday theme.

781. Pigford, A. B. (1990). Instructional grouping: Purposes and consequences. *The Clearing House, 63* (6), 261-263.

Discusses questions that teachers ask before using instructional grouping: 1. What is the purpose of grouping? 2. What is the task to be completed? 3. What are the instructional and management skills of the teacher? 4. What are the results of grouping?

782.   Strother, D. B. (October 1990). Cooperative learning: Fad or
         foundation for learning. *Phi Delta Kappan, 72* (2): 158-162.

         A thought-provoking and outstanding article that all teachers
         who use or plan to use cooperative learning need to read. Using
         the insights of such luminaries as Deutsch, Slavin, Sharan, and
         others, she addresses the following factors: "What makes it
         work," "Factors that lead to failure," the usefulness of specific
         cooperative learning models, and the issue as to how much
         training is needed before one can be proficient in the use of a
         model.

D.   Cultural and Ethnic Differences

783.   Jules, V. (Winter 1990). Cooperative learning and work-mate
         preferences in classrooms in secondary schools. *Contemporary
         Education, 61* (2): 65-70.

         In a heterogeneous classroom situation, where social
         interaction plays an important role in the facilitation of
         classroom learning, as a teaching strategy may be a potent device
         for creating conditions that could promote academic and social
         learning in schools.

784.   Nakagawa, M., & Pang, V. O. (1990). Cooperative pluralism:
         Moving from "me" to "we." *Social Studies and the Young
         Learning: A Quarterly for Creative Teaching in Grades K-6, 2*
         (4), 9-11.

         Discusses Cooperative Pluralism as a "synthesis of
         multicultural education, democratic education, and cooperative
         learning," and provides guidelines for developing instructional
         activities for elementary students.

E.   General Strategies (Overviews)

785.   Guskey, T. R. (September 1990). Cooperative mastery learning
         strategies. *The Elementary School Journal, 91* (1): 33-42.

         Describes the basics of cooperative learning and mastery
         learning, and then explains how these strategies are "naturally
         complementary to one another."

786. Slavin, R. E. (1990). *Student Team Learning: An Overview and Practical Guide* (Second Edition). Washington, D. C.: National Education Association.

Second edition of a popular and useful guide to cooperative learning. Especially useful for teachers working with diverse groups of students. Contains games, scoring sheets, and lesson plans. See citation 019 for first edition information.

F. Language Arts

787. Cooperative Learning in English. (October 1990). *English Journal*, *79* (6): 74-77.

The editors solicited a response from public school English teachers in regard to this question: "How are you using collaborative or cooperative learning in your classroom?" Eight short responses are included herein.

788. Curran, L. (1990). *Cooperative Learning & Literature; Lessons for Little Ones*. San Juan Capistrano, CA: Resources for Teachers.

Provides field-tested, step-by-step multi-structural lessons for kindergarten through second grade students.

789. Smith, C. F., Jr., & Hintz, J. L. (1990). Read a book in an hour: Adolescent literature through cooperative learning. *The Clearing House, 63* (5), 235-237.

Discusses a cooperatively structured lesson that allows students to read and discuss a book during a one-class session. Includes a brief overview of cooperative learning and provides practical suggestions for discussing a book " in a relaxed yet structured way."

790. Stone, J. (1990). *Cooperative Learning and Language Arts: A Multi-Structural Approach*. San Juan Capistrano, CA: Resources for Teachers.

Provides field-tested, step-by-step multi-structural lessons for kindergarten through eighth grade students.

G. *Mathematics*

791.   Ajose, S. A., and Joyner, V. G. (Summer 1990). Cooperative
        learning: The rebirth of an effective teaching strategy. *Education
        Horizons, 68* (4): 197-201.

        Two mathematics professors briefly review the literature and
        research on cooperative learning as it pertains to mathematics and
        discuss how to implement it.

792.   Andrini, B. (1990). *Cooperative Learning and Mathematics: A
        Multi-Structural Approach.* San Juan Capistrano, CA:
        Resources for Teachers.

        Provides field-tested, step-by-step multi-structural lessons
        for kindergarten through eighth grade students.

793.   Artzt, A. F., and Newman, C. M. (1990). *How to Use
        Cooperative Learning in the Mathematics Class.* Peston, VA:
        National Council of Teachers of Mathematics.

        A manual, which was developed under the auspice of the
        National Council of Teachers of Mathematics, on how to
        incorporate various cooperative learning strategies in
        mathematics classrooms across the grade levels.

794.   Artzt, A. F., and Newman, C. M. (September 1990). Cooperative
        learning. *Mathematics Teacher, 83* (6): 448-452.

        This article is comprised of the following sections: What is
        cooperative learning?; Why use cooperative learning?; How are
        Groups Formed?; How can cooperative learning be incorporated
        in the mathematics class?; and Why do students like cooperative
        learning?

795.   Burns, M. (1990). The math solution: Using groups of four. In N.
        Davidson (Ed.), *Cooperative Learning in Mathematics: A
        Handbook for Teachers,* (pp. 21-46). New York: Addison-
        Wesley Publishing Company.

        Provides practical ideas on problem solving and exploration
        with manipulative materials in groups of four with elementary
        students.

796. Crabill, C. D. (1990). Small group learning in the secondary mathematics classroom. In N. Davidson'(Ed.), *Cooperative Learning in Mathematics: A Handbook for Teachers*, (pp. 201-227). New York: Addison-Wesley Publishing Company.

Discusses procedures for group problem solving and inquiry in algebra, geometry, and algebra II/trigonometry. Applicable to the secondary classroom.

797. Davidson, N. (1990). Introduction and overview. In N. Davidson (Ed.), *Cooperative Learning in Mathematics: A Handbook for Teachers*, (pp. 1-20). New York: Addison-Wesley Publishing Company.

In his introduction, Davidson provides a detailed discussion about the place and use of cooperative learning in math courses from elementary through introductory college courses.

798. Davidson, N. (Ed.) (1990). *Cooperative Learning in Mathematics: A Handbook for Teachers*. New York: Addison-Wesley Publishing Co. 400 pp.

An outstanding and valuable resource for teachers of mathematics in elementary school through college. It includes essays which all have a practical focus (e.g., "The Math Solution: Using Groups of Four"; "Student Team Learning in Mathematics"; "Cooperative Learning and Computers in the Elementary and Middle School Math Classroom"; "Cooperation in the Mathematics Classroom: A User's Manual"; "Implementing Group Work: Issues for Teachers and Administrators.") It includes essays by some of the most noted educational researchers and developers on cooperative learning (e.g., Neil Davidson, David and Roger Johnson, Robert Slavin) and numerous educators at various grade levels.
Contains items 795, 796, 797, 799, 800, 801, 802, 803, 804, 805, 806, 807, 808.

799. Davidson, N. (1990). The small-group discovery method in secondary- and college- level mathematics. In N. Davidson (Ed.), *Cooperative Learning in Mathematics: A Handbook for Teachers*, (pp. 335-361). New York: Addison-Wesley Publishing Company.

Discusses how to use guided discovery methods in
cooperative groups with high school and college students, by
focusing on the subject of calculus.

800.   Dees, R. L. (1990). Cooperation in the mathematics classroom: A
        user's manual. In N. Davidson (Ed.) *Cooperative Learning in
        Mathematics: A Handbook for Teachers*, (pp. 160-200). New
        York: Addison-Wesley Publishing Company.

        Provides an overview as to how teachers can incorporate
        cooperative activities in the classroom in order to bring about
        classroom cooperation.

801.   Johnson, D. W., and Johnson, R. T. (1990). Using cooperative
        leaning in math. In N. Davidson (Ed.) *Cooperative Learning in
        Mathematics: A Handbook for Teachers*, (pp. 103-125). New
        York: Addison-Wesley Publishing Company.

        "A general conceptual model of cooperative learning with a
        detailed discussion of its basic elements."

802.   Lotan, R. A., and Benton, J. (1990). Finding out about complex
        instruction: Teaching Math and science in heterogeneous
        classrooms. In N. Davidson (Ed.) *Cooperative Learning in
        Mathematics: A Handbook for Teachers*, (pp. 47-68). New
        York: Addison-Wesley Publishing Company.

        Discusses a bilingual integrated math and science program
        for elementary schools with a particular emphasis on classroom
        status problems.

803.   Male, M. (1990). Cooperative learning and computers in the
        elementary and middle school math classrooms. In N.
        Davidson (Ed.) *Cooperative Learning in Mathematics: A
        Handbook for Teachers*, (pp. 126-159). New York: Addison-
        Wesley Publishing Company.

        Examines three cooperative learning strategies as applied to
        the use of computers in elementary and middle school math
        classrooms.

804.   Robertson, L., Graves, N., and Tuck, P. (1990). Implementing
        group work: Issues for teachers and administrators. In N.

Davidson (Ed.) *Cooperative Learning in Mathematics: A Handbook for Teachers*, (pp. 362-379). New York: Addison-Wesley Publishing Company.

Discusses "issues affecting the use of cooperative learning in mathematics with an emphasis on teachers' decision making and factors affecting implementation."

805.   Sheets, C., and Heid, M. K. (1990). Integrating computers as tools in mathematics curricula (Grades 9-13): Portraits of group interactions. In N. Davidson (Ed.) *Cooperative Learning in Mathematics: A Handbook for Teachers*, (pp. 265-294). New York: Addison-Wesley Publishing Company.

Discusses "group interactions in algebra and calculus using computers as tools for mathematical explorations and problem solving."

806.   Slavin, R. E. (1990). Student team learning in mathematics. In N. Davidson (Ed.) *Cooperative Learning in Mathematics: A Handbook for Teachers*, (pp. 69-102). New York: Addison-Wesley Publishing Company.

Discusses various team learning methods for mastery of facts and skills.

807.   Terwel, J. (1990). Real math in cooperative groups in secondary education. In N. Davidson (Ed.) *Cooperative Learning in Mathematics: A Handbook for Teachers*, (pp. 228-264). New York: Addison-Wesley Publishing Company.

"Cooperation in small groups in heterogeneous classes in the Netherlands using math in real-life situations."

808.   Weissglass, J. (1990). Cooperative learning using a small-group laboratory approach. In N. Davidson (Ed.) *Cooperative Learning in Mathematics: A Handbook for Teachers*, (pp. 295-334). New York: Addison-Wesley Publishing Company.

"Free exploration and guided discovery in cooperative groups using a variety of concrete models."

H. Science

809.   Trowbridge, L. W., and Bybee, R. W. (1990). *Becoming a
          Secondary School Science Teacher.* Columbus, OH: Merrill
          Publishing Co. 504 pp.

          This science methods textbook includes a section entitled
          "Cooperative Learning" (pp. 306-310) which includes an
          overview of cooperative learning, a component entitled "Steps
          for Designing Lessons -- Applying the Cooperative Learning
          Model," and a guest editorial by David and Roger Johnson
          entitled "A Message to Teachers" on structuring student
          interactions in the classroom (pp. 96-97).

I. Social Studies

810.   Bower, B. (1990). *The Effect of a Multiple Ability Treatment on
          Status and Learning in the Cooperative Social Studies
          Classroom.* (Doctoral Dissertation, Stanford University).

          Bower compared the achievement gains for two groups of
          high school history students and found that "multi-ability tasks
          were more effective in a cooperative learning setting than tasks
          that primarily focus on linguistic abilities."

811.   Steinbrink, J. E., and Jones, R. M. (January/February 1990).
          Team learning in social studies. *Social Studies and the Young
          Learner, 2* (3): 3-5.

          An overview of how to use cooperative learning in the
          elementary social studies classroom. Includes the following
          sections: Preparing materials for cooperative group work,
          implementing two-level cooperative small groups, and hints and
          suggestions.

J. Students with Special Needs

812.   Robinson, A. (1990). Cooperation or exploitation? The argument
          against cooperative learning for talented students. *Journal for the
          Education of the Gifted, 14* (1), 9-27.

          Reviews the following disadvantages of using cooperative
          learning with academically talented students: 1. limiting

instruction to grade level materials, 2. presenting information to meet the needs of grade-level students, and 3. using basic skills measures to evaluate student achievement. Also points out problems with the existing research base and its applicability to talented students. Among the problems discussed are sampling, treatment comparisons, contradictory results for higher level outcomes, and overgeneralization. Concludes that cooperative learning does produce positive outcomes, but that the strategy should be used cautiously to avoid exploiting gifted students for the benefit of the other students.

813. Robinson, A. (1990). Cooperation, consistency, and challenge for academically talented youth. *Journal for the Education of the Gifted, 14* (1), 31-36.

In her response to Robert Slavin's article "Ability Grouping, Cooperative Learning and the Gifted," the author discusses areas of agreement with Slavin and offers suggestions for understanding and using cooperative learning with talented students.

814. Sicola, P. K. (1990). Where do gifted students fit? An examination of middle school philosophy as it relates to ability grouping and the gifted learner. *Journal for the Education of the Gifted, 14* (1), 37-49.

Examines the middle school philosophy as it relates to ability grouping and the gifted learner. "A review of the literature indicates that the reasoning used to support heterogeneity at the middle level is based on developmental needs of young adolescents, the concern over social discrimination associated with grouping practices, and the need for positive role models." States that even though cooperative learning may be an excellent strategy for some students, its effectiveness in meeting the academic and affective needs of gifted students in a heterogeneous classroom has not been sufficiently demonstrated by research.

815. Slavin, R. E. (1990). Ability grouping, cooperative learning and the gifted. *Journal for the Education of the Gifted, 14* (1), 3-8.

Points out that "it is possible to reduce the use of tracking and of separate enrichment programs for the gifted, increase the use of cooperative learning, and meet the learning needs of gifted students better than in traditionally organized classes." Reviews research findings that support the effectiveness of cooperative learning with accelerated groups. Concludes by emphasizing that the best way to meet the needs of all learners, including the gifted, is to modify the structure of traditional classrooms.

816.   Slavin, R. E. (1990). Cooperative learning and the gifted: Who benefits? *Journal for the Education of the Gifted, 14* (1), 28-30.

A response to Ann Robinson's article "Cooperation or Exploitation? The Argument against Cooperative Learning for Talented Students." Agrees that the research base for application of cooperative learning to gifted classes is "virtually nonexistent." Points out that many studies have reported the benefit of using cooperative learning for high achievers and that the "extrapolation to accelerated programs seems straightforward."

K.   *Teacher Education/Staff Development*

817.   Kagan, S. (1990). *Cooperative Learning Workshops for Teachers.* San Juan Capistrano, CA: Resources for Teachers.

For teachers who want to put together workshops on cooperative learning. Over 100 pages of background material and suggestions.

818.   Lyman, L. & Foyle, H. C. (1990). *Cooperative Grouping for Interactive Learning: Students, Teachers, and Administrators.* Washington, D.C.: National Education Association.

This volume in the NEA School Restructuring Series presents a plan for extending cooperative learning throughout a school, from students to administrators. Includes specific strategies and plans for implementation with useful examples and activities.

Indexes

AUTHOR INDEX

SUBJECT INDEX

Soviet education theory, 627
STAD, 595, 638, 660
support system for teachers,
    564
technical training, 625, 626
test anxiety, 597
TGT, 595, 638
theory of, 576, 577, 578, 585,
    594, 647, 668, 671
time, use of, 592
Tribes, 589

**Cooperative Integrated
Reading and Composition
(CIRC), 025-027**

basal-related activities, 027
CIRC, 026, 027
evaluation procedures, 027
group composition, 027
heterogeneous groups, 025,
    027
language arts, 025, 027
reading, 025, 027
at-risk students, 026
"Success for All," 026
teacher's manual, 025
writing, 025, 027

**Cultural and Ethnic
Differences,   377-445**

acceptance rates, 419
achievement, 405, 417, 419,
    427, 428, 437
activities, 420
African (East), 418
Afro-American, 402, 428, 429,
    438
at-risk students, 411
biracial learning teams, 385
birth order, 404
Chinese-Americans, 381

classroom perceptions, 419
conflict resolution, 421
contact theory (Allport), 435
cooperative pluralism, 784
cross-ethnic, 384, 394, 395
cross-gender, 384, 415, 416,
    443
cross-race, 415, 424, 431, 432
cross-socioeconomic 415
Cuban-American, 377
culture, 397
desegregation, 387, 391, 392,
    403, 406, 413, 414, 423,
    426, 430, 433, 434, 435,
    442
ethnic relationships, 416, 427,
    441, 443, 444, 445
family size, 404
friendships, 389, 390
GI, 426
global village, 421
Hispanic, 416, 439
interdependence 386
intergroup bias, 388
interpersonal attraction, 378
Israeli, 425, 426
Jigsaw, 397, 434
leadership behaviors, 416
Learning games, 384
locus of control, 381
low achievers, 396
low-income, 397
magnet schools, 412
MENTOR, 407
Mexican, 409
Mexican-American, 383, 393,
    398, 399, 400, 402, 404,
    405, 410
migrant students, 407
minority teachers, 411
Native American, 408
New Zealand, 440
overview, 426

"Success for All," 245, 246,
   267
TAI, 246, 259, 264, 265, 266,
   267
TGT, 263
Title I, 237
trainable retarded, 235
Translation Writing, 250
urban, 245, 258
visually handicapped, 222

Student Teams Achievement Division (STAD), 055-059

academically handicapped, 056
achievement, 058
communication, 057
discussion groups, 055
English as a second language,
   055
evaluation of, 055
implementation of, 059
problem solving, 057
social acceptance, 056
time on task, 058

Teacher Education/Staff Development, 446-499

achievement, 468
Atlas complex, 462
attitude, 467
benefits of, 450
classroom management, 489
Co-op Co-op, 451
coaching, 487, 488, 490
collaborative learning, 454
college, 480
collegiality, 449
continuing education, 491
cooperation, teaching of, 482
cooperative skills, teaching of,
   450

debriefing, 446
ecological approach, 466
educational psychology, 469
effective teaching, 492
English as a Second Language,
   481
evaluation, 477, 486
French classes, 467
future of, 453
getting started, 457, 458, 459,
   474
GI, 451, 483
gifted and talented, teachers of,
   465
groups of four, 455
hypothesizing skills, 448
implementation of, 446, 486
inservice, 460
interpersonal relationships, 456
intervention strategies, 479
Jigsaw, 446, 451, 463, 468
Jigsaw II, 451, 478
laboratory approach, 494
Learning Together, 446, 447,
   551
management, 455
middle school teachers, 461
motivation, 456
overview, 463, 464, 470, 484,
   485
philosophy of, 478
pitfalls of, 450
quality of learning, 456
reward systems, 486
roles, teacher/student, 452,
   471, 477
scoring system management,
   450
self-esteem, 456
self-perceptions, 498
Small-Group Mathematics,
   451
sociogram, 485